The McGraw-Hill PC Programmer's Desk Reference

Other Related Canton/Sanchez Books

The McGraw-Hill PC Programmer's Desk Reference

Maria P. Canton
North Dakota State University
Fargo, North Dakota

Julio Sanchez
Montana State University, Northern
Havre, Montana

McGraw-Hill, Inc.

New York   San Francisco   Washington, D.C.   Auckland   Bogotá
Caracas   Lisbon   London   Madrid   Mexico City   Milan
Montreal   New Delhi   San Juan   Singapore
Sydney   Tokyo   Toronto

Library of Congress Cataloging-in-Publication Data

Canton, Maria P.
    The McGraw-Hill PC programmer's desk reference / Maria P. Canton,
Julio Sanchez.
       p.   cm.
    ISBN 0-07-057203-8 (hc.)—ISBN 0-07-057204-6 (pb.)
    1. Electronic digital computers—Programming. I. Sanchez, Julio.
II. Title.
QA76.6.C36   1996
005.265—dc20   96-33756
                                                  CIP

McGraw-Hill

A Division of The McGraw·Hill Companies

ISBN 0-07-057203-8 (hc)
ISBN 0-07-057204-6 (pbk)

*The sponsoring editor for this book was Jerry Papke, the editing
supervisor was Bernie Onken, and the production supervisor was
Donald Schmidt. It was set in Century Schoolbook by Skipanon
Software Company.*

Printed and bound by R. R. Donnelley & Sons Company.

McGraw-Hill books are available at special quantity discounts to use as
premiums and sales promotions, or for use in corporate training programs. For more information, please write to the Director of Special
Sales, McGraw-Hill, 11 West 19th Street, New York, NY 10011. Or contact your local bookstore.

 This book is printed on recycled, acid-free paper containing a
minimum of 50% recycled de-inked fiber.

Preface

The McGraw-Hill PC Programmer's Desk Reference is intended as a technical, illustrated dictionary for programmers, software developers and project managers, students, and other PC enthusiasts and professionals. The book is designed to include core programming information for the languages C, BASIC, Pascal, and Assembly language, as well as an extensive list of programming-related topics. The host system is the IBM Personal Computer and compatible machines from 1981 to the present.

The book is based on the notion that programmers or other professionals in the software development field often require a specific piece of technical information for the purpose at hand. For example, a developer working in BASIC may remember that one or two $ signs can be present as format elements in a PRINT USING statement, but may not exactly recall what action is associated with the use of a single or a double $ symbol, or if the adopted implementation of the BASIC language supports both options. This information is available in the reference manuals, tutorials, and textbooks, but is not always easy to find. In this case the programmer has to spend valuable time searching through the index and table of contents of half a dozen texts to find out how the BASIC $ format code is used in a specific implementation.

In addition, laptop and portable computers have made it possible for programmers to take their work on the road. However, the portability does not extend to the programmer's reference library. A typical programmer would have to carry several volumes to ensure that the required information is at hand, namely: the operation manual and reference for the implementation in use, texts or reference books on architecture and hardware, one or more books on the programming language or languages, and perhaps one or more problem solvers. The proposed programming dictionary is designed to substitute all of these books regarding the fundamental programming information of four of the most popular PC programming languages. It offers a practical option to the laptop programmer who cannot take along the entire reference library.

The subject matter included in the book can be related to the following topics:

1. keywords and syntax
2. sub-programs
3. data types
4. programming tools and characteristics of commercial compilers and interpreters
5. program environment
6. common algorithms
7. CPU and coprocessor instructions
8. number systems and digital logic
9. system hardware and programmable components
10. program development and software engineering

11. microcomputers, options, and devices
12. basic concepts and general terminology
13. brief code samples and problem solver
14. software companies and vendors
15. advanced programming
16. historical notes

The topics are listed in alphabetical order, inter-related, and cross-referenced. Words and phrases that appear in boldface letters reference other entries in the dictionary. Bold-italics typeface is used to separate consecutive words or phrases that are also individual entries. For example: **integer arithmetic** *function* indicates that the term *integer arithmetic* is a dictionary entry and that so is the term *function*. All text parts in boldface or boldface italics are the equivalent of hypertext entries.

Brackets are used following the entry text to indicate the current classification. The classification topics are:

[Assembler] 80x86 Assembly Language
[C] C and C++
[MS-Pascal] Microsoft Pascal
[BASIC] Traditional BASIC
[QuickBASIC] Microsoft QuickBASIC
[input/output]
[PC hardware and architecture]
[video systems]
[historical]

The authors would like to thank the friends and associates who provided advice, support, and assistance in this project. At McGraw-Hill Jerry Papke, D. Schmidt, Bernie Onken, and Donna Namorato have been involved in the production of this book. We owe a very special thanks to Dr. Karen LaRoe, Vice Chancellor for Academic Affairs at Montana State University, Northern, for continued support of our writing projects as well as to Dr. Richard Fisher, Academic Vice Chancellor. Our thanks also go to Virgil Hawkinson, Roger Stone, Jay Howland, Sharon Lowman, and Patsy Brady, also at MSU Northern.

This book was written while both coauthors were conducting graduate studies at North Dakota State University in Fargo. We would like to thank the faculty and staff at the NDSU Department of Computer Science and Operations Research for all the kindness and considerations that have made us feel part of this campus.

Fargo, North Dakota   Maria P. Canton
                                                             Julio Sanchez

The McGraw-Hill PC Programmer's Desk Reference

- -

(See increment and decrement operators).

$DYNAMIC (metacommand)

[QuickBASIC] Command format is:
REM $DYNAMIC
Specifies that any array dimensioned after this point in the program should have its memory allocated dynamically at run-time. An advantage of dynamic arrays is that they may be erased to free up memory or REDIMensioned to change their size. Array memory allocation is automatically dynamic if the array is local to a non-STATIC procedure, the array is DIMensioned using a variable, or the array is declared in a COMMON or REDIM statement.

+ +

(See increment and decrement operators).

#define

[C] Preprocessor directive. The program line
#define PI 3.1415927
instructs the compiler to thereafter associate the word PI with the numerical value 3.1415927. The #define *keyword* is the C language operator that associates an identifier (name) with a text string or numerical value. The pound sign (#) identifies a compiler directive, also called a *preprocessor command*. This preprocessor command must be followed by a space, which in this case serves as a *separator symbol*.

#include

[C] Preprocessor directive. The program line
#include <stdio.h>
is an include preprocessor command. When this line is encountered the C compiler searches for a file named stdio.h and inserts its contents at this point in the source. The stdio.h file, which is called a header or include file, contains

declarations and definitions that are necessary to the printf() and scanf() library functions used by the program.

The filename referenced in the #include directive is enclosed in angle brackets. This is the generally accepted C language syntax for referencing a *standard library file* located in the default directory. An alternative way of entering the filename is by enclosing it in double quotation marks; for example:

#include "myfile.h"

This format is preferred when the referenced file is one created by the programmer or when it is not located in the default path.

486

[**PC hardware and architecture**] The 486 microprocessor, of the Intel iAPX family, was introduced in 1989. The chip, which uses 32-bit architecture, includes on-chip memory management, a floating-point processor, a cache controller, and 8K of static RAM. The implementation of all these features in a single package requires over 1.2 million transistors, which made the 486 one of the most complex and powerful microprocessor at the time of its release.

To the programmer, the 486 appears similar to an 80386/80387 system with cache memory. The following list contains the differences in the programming models of the 80386 and 486 processors:

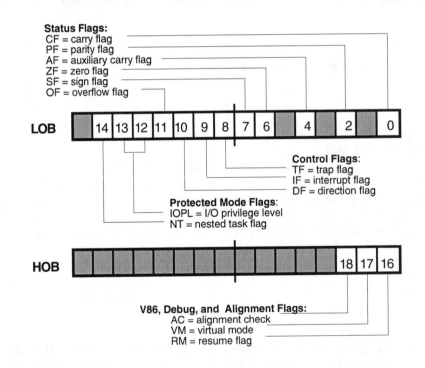

486 Flags Register

1. The AC flag (alignment check) has been added to the 80386 flag register. This flag is used in conjunction with a new AM bit in CR0.

2. Five new bits, labeled CD, NW, AM, WF, and NE, are implemented in the CR0 register. The function of these bits is related to the cache memory controller and to the on-chip floating-point processor.

3. Two new bits are implemented in the CR3 register. These bits are designated PCD and PWT. The PCD bit performs a page-level cache disable function. The PWT bit controls page-level cache write-through in an external cache, on a cycle-by-cycle basis.

4. Six new opcodes have been added to the instruction set.

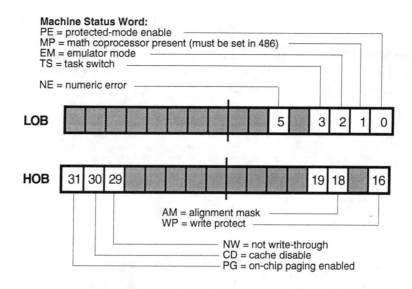

486 Machine Status Word Register

80286 architecture

[PC hardware and architecture] The 286 CPU is formed by four processing units which operate independently and in parallel. This design is called a *pipeline architecture*. The bus unit (BU) prefetches instructions from memory in a manner similar to that of the bus interface unit of the 8086 processors. In operation, the BU assumes that the instructions are located sequentially in memory. If execution continues at a nonsequential location, the instruction queue is cleared and prefetching must be reinitiated. The bus unit handles all memory and port access operations for the CPU.

The instruction unit (IU) reads the operation codes in the queue created by the bus unit, decodes the instructions, and places them, three deep, in a decoded instruction queue. The execution unit (EU) obtains the opcodes from this queue and performs the arithmetic and logical operations of each instruction. Finally, the address unit (AU) provides the memory management and protection functions of the 286 and converts protected-mode virtual addresses into physical addresses.

The 80286 CPU contains 15 internal registers, classified as follows:

1. Data registers

2. Index and pointer registers

3. Segment registers

4. Status and control registers

The data, index, and segment registers of the 80286 are identical to those of the 8086 CPU (see 8086 architecture).

One difference between the 80286 and its predecessors is in the status and control registers. The 286 flag register has two additional fields, designated as NT and IOPL, for use in protected-mode execution. In addition, the CPU is equipped with a new control register, also for protected-mode operation, called the machine status word register, or MSW.

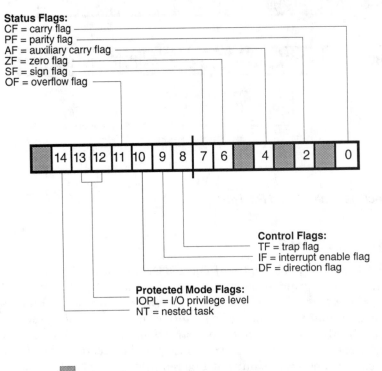

80286 Flags Register

80286 Flags

BIT	FLAG NAME	CODE	FUNCTION
14	Nested task	NT	Indicates a nested task condition during task switch operations
12–13	I/O privilege	IOPL	Controls access to input/output devices and designates the lowest task level with I/O privilege
11	Overflow	OF	Set to show arithmetic overflow
10	Direction	DF	Used to determine the direction of string moves
9	Interrupt enable	IF	Used to enable and disable maskable interrupts
8	Trap	TF	Places the CPU in the single-step mode (used mainly by debugger programs)
7	Sign	SF	Used in signed arithmetic to show whether the result is positive (SF = 0) or negative (SF = 1)
6	Zero	ZF	Set if the result of the previous operation is zero
4	Auxiliary carry	AF	Used in decimal arithmetic to show a carry out of the low nibble or a borrow from the high nibble
2	Parity	PF	Set if the result of the previous operation has an even number of 1 bits (used mainly to check for data transmission errors)
0	Carry	CF	Set if there is a carry or a borrow to the high-order bit of the result. Also used by rotate instructions

80286 Machine Status Word Register

[PC hardware and architecture] This register has no counterpart in 8086 or 8088 systems. Its purpose is to show the configuration and status of the 80286 special functions that are not available in the 8086 CPU. The register is 16 bits wide, but only the lower 4 bits are meaningful.

The MSW register bits can be considered as supplementary flags, whose functions are as follows:

1. PE (*protected-mode enable*). The PE flag places the 286 in protected mode. Since this bit cannot be cleared, real mode can be reactivated only by a system RESET.

2. MP (*math coprocessor present*). The MP flag indicates that the 80287 chip is installed in the system.

3. EM (*emulator mode*). The emulator flag indicates that no 80287 is available in the system. If the 286 encounters an ESC instruction with EM = 1 and MP = 0, the processor automatically executes interrupt 07H. A handler located at this vector can emulate the 80287 in software.

4. TS (*task switch*). The task switch flag is set with the first use of the math coprocessor within a task. This allows software protection of the coprocessor context.

The machine status word flags are modified with the LMSW (load machine status word) instruction. If the PE flag is set when LMSW executes, the 80286 enters protected mode. This instruction can be used only by operating-system software. Application programs can read the MSW flags using the SMSW (store machine status word) instruction.

80286 memory management

[**PC hardware and architecture**] The architecture of the 80286 chip increases the 1-Mbyte physical memory address space of 8086 systems to 16 Mbytes. The total memory space visible to a protected-mode program, called the virtual address space, is one gigabyte. Application programs executing in 80286 protected mode do not have access to physical memory. In protected mode, the four segment registers, CS, SS, DS, and ES, do not reference a physical memory address. Instead, they load an index value into a special table (descriptor table) that is managed by the operating system. In this manner, the segment base element in the physical address remains invisible to the application.

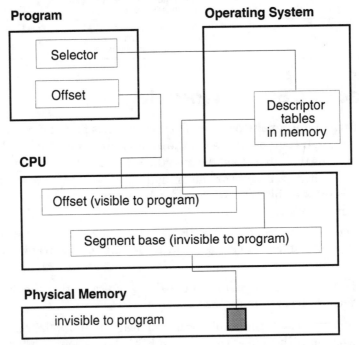

80286 Virtual Memory

In protected mode, the segment registers are designated as the segment selectors CS, SS, DS, and ES. Each selector contains a 13-bit field (index field) which represents the sequential order of one of 8192 possible segments (2^{13}) in each descriptor table. The TI (table indicator) field selects one of two possible descriptor tables, labeled global and local descriptor tables. This increases the number of possible segments to 16,384 (2^{14}). Since each segment can be as large as 64K (2^{16}), the total virtual address space in 80286 protected mode is 1 gigabyte.

The selector also has a table indicator field (TI bit) that marks either a local or a global address space. The global address space is used for system-level data and services that are shared with applications. The local address space is private to each particular task.

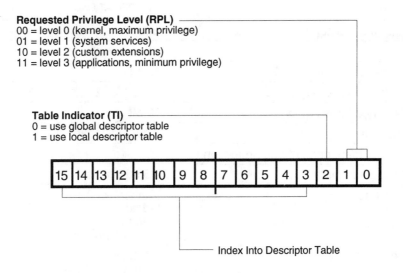

Requested Privilege Level (RPL)
00 = level 0 (kernel, maximum privilege)
01 = level 1 (system services)
10 = level 2 (custom extensions)
11 = level 3 (applications, minimum privilege)

Table Indicator (TI)
0 = use global descriptor table
1 = use local descriptor table

| 15 | 14 | 13 | 12 | 11 | 10 | 9 | 8 | 7 | 6 | 5 | 4 | 3 | 2 | 1 | 0 |

Index Into Descriptor Table

80286 Segment Selector Register

80286

[PC hardware and architecture] Introduced by Intel in 1982. The 80286 is a descendant of the 8086 and 8088. The 286 provides on-chip memory management, which makes possible the simultaneous execution of several tasks. The PC AT microcomputer was the first IBM machine equipped with the 80286 microprocessor. The chip is used in the XT 286 and the PS/2 Model 50 and Model 60, the Compaq 286, the Tandy Model 1000-TX and Model 3000-HL, the Hewlett-Packard Vectra, and others.

The most important features of the Intel 80286 are:

1. Sixteen Mbytes of physical address space

2. One gigabyte of virtual address space

3. A *real address* operating mode in which the 286 emulates and is compatible with the 8086/8088 CPU

4. A *protected virtual address* operating mode which implements the advanced features of the 286

5. On-chip memory management

6. A protection mechanism based on four privilege levels

7. Multitasking support by providing a separate logical address space for each task

80286 Microprocessor Hardware Summary

CHARACTERISTIC	SPECIFICATIONS
Mathematical coprocessor	80287
Bus interface	16 bits
Internal data path	16 bits
Available clock frequencies	6, 8, 10, 12.5, and 20 MHz
Memory addressability	16 Mbytes
Virtual memory	Yes, 1 gigabyte/task
Memory management and protection	Yes
I/O addressability	65,535 ports
Registers	Arithmetic: 8 Index: 4 Segment: 4 General purpose: 8
Intel support chips	Clock: 82284 Controller: 82288 Interrupts: 8259-A DMA: 82258 Timer: 8253/54 DRAM: 8207/8208
Number of pins	68
Power requirements	5.V

80386 — architecture

[PC hardware and architecture] Internally, the 386 chip is divided into six independent units that can execute in parallel with one another. This design, sometimes called a *pipeline architecture*, makes possible the execution of over 3 million instructions per second.

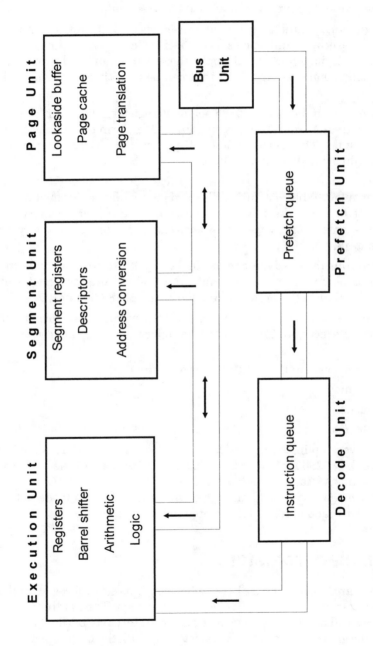

80386 Pipeline Architecture

The independent execution units of the 80386 microprocessor operate as follows:

1. The *bus unit* is the interface of the 80386 with the outside world. The unit handles the processor's interaction with coprocessor chips.

2. The *execution unit* contains all the general-purpose and control registers. Input into the execution unit comes from the decoder and from the bus unit. The arithmetic logic unit (ALU) is part of the execution unit. The execution unit is the only element of the CPU that can be directly controlled by the programmer.

3. The *segment unit* contains the 80386 segment registers. This unit receives read-write addresses from the execution unit in the form of a displacement and a scaled index. The segmentation unit performs the virtual-to-physical conversion, which yields a linear address.

4. The *page unit* takes part in virtual-to-physical address conversions when paging is enabled. When paging is disabled, the address obtained by the segment unit becomes the physical address used to access memory. Together, the segment and page units form the microprocessor's memory management unit, or MMU.

5. The *prefetch unit* takes advantage of idle bus cycles to read the next four bytes of instructions from memory into the 16-byte prefetch queue. Its operation is similar to the prefetch function of the 80286 bus unit.

6. The *decode unit* converts the instructions into an internal format that expedites their execution. These individual operations are called *microinstructions*.

The 80386 can operate in three different processing modes:

1. Real address mode

2. Protected mode

3. Virtual 8086 mode

The 80386 powers up in the *real address mode*, or real mode. This mode is very similar to the 80286 real mode (see 80286 architecture). In the real mode the 80386 appears as a fast and enhanced 8086 CPU.

The *protected mode* is the 80386 native environment. In this mode, all the features of the CPU and of its 32-bit architecture are available.

80386 — auxiliary registers

[PC hardware and architecture] The 80386 contains several registers that are not normally visible to the applications programmer. Some of these auxiliary (sometimes called ancillary) registers have counterparts in the 286 CPU. For example, the global descriptor table register (GDTR), the interrupt descriptor table register (IDTR), the local descriptor table register (LDTR), and the task register (TR) have equivalent structures in the 80286.

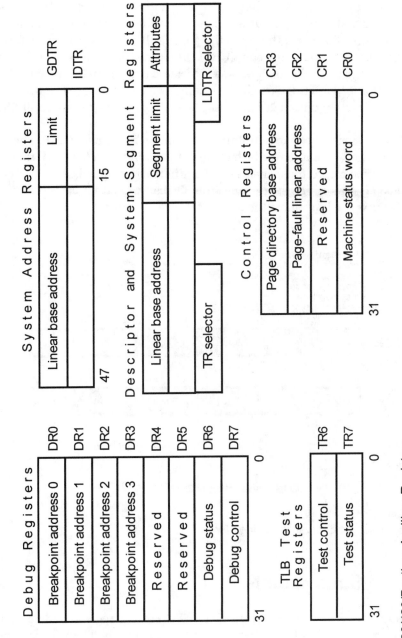

80386/486/Pentium Auxiliary Registers

Some of the 80386 auxiliary registers originated with this CPU and serve to support its unique features. For instance, the 386 contains support hardware to implement instruction and data breakpoints during debugging. This is accomplished through four debug address registers, a debug control register, and a debug status register. Other registers are used to support the memory paging feature of the 386; these are the page fault address register (CR2) and the page directory base register (CR3). For converting linear addresses to physical addresses, the 386 uses a special cache named the translation lookaside buffer, or TLB. The CPU contains two registers used in testing the TLB during system initialization. These test registers are designated TR6 and TR7.

The 80386 stores the machine status word in control register CR0. There are two bits in the 386 status word which do not exist in the 286. One of them, the extension type bit, records whether the mathematical coprocessor is an 80287 or an 80387. This is necessary, since the 386 can use either coprocessor chip. The PG bit is used to enable the paging feature.

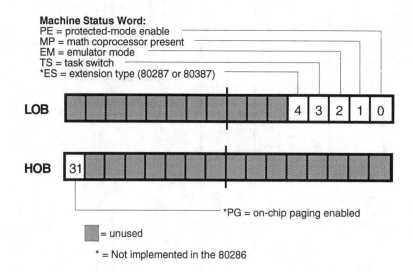

80386 Machine Status Word Register

80386 — Eflags register

[PC hardware and architecture] The 80386 flag register, named eflags, contains two significant bits that are not present in the 80286. These are the VM (virtual-mode) flag, used in enabling the 80386 virtual 8086 mode, and the RF (resume flag) bit, used in debugging with the breakpoint registers.

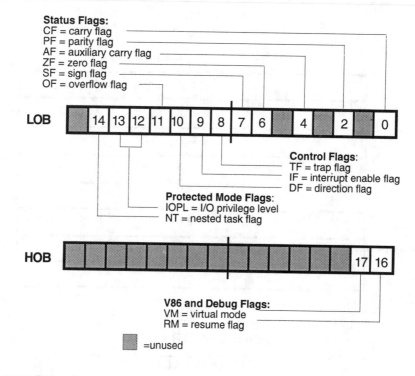

80386 Flags Register

80386 — memory organization

[PC hardware and architecture] The 32-bit registers and data paths of the 80386 allow 4 gigabytes of physical address space (2^{32} = 4,294,967,296 bytes). This is four times the virtual memory space of a 286 system. The virtual address space of the 386 protected mode consists of 16,383 linear spaces of 4 gigabytes each. The 4-gigabyte linear memory representation is called a *flat memory model*. The 64-terabyte logical address space representation of virtual memory is called the *segmented memory model*.

The unit for a contiguous address space retains the name of *segment*, but each 386 segment may be as large as 4 gigabytes, in contrast with 8086 and 80286 segments, which cannot exceed 64K. A single 80386 register (32 bits wide) can serve as a pointer into this 4-gigabyte address space.

The 386 contains the same number of data and pointer registers as its predecessors, the 8086, the 8088, and the 80286. However, in the 386 these eight registers are 32 bits wide. The four general registers, EAX, EDX, ECX, and EBX, can also be addressed as 16-bit or 8-bit registers by using the 8086 register names: AX (AH and AL), DX (DH and DL), CX (CH and CL), and BX (BH and BL). The 32-bit registers EBP, ESI, EDI, and ESP can also be addressed by their 16-bit names BP, SI, DI, and SP. This 80386 feature ensures downward compatibility with the 8086 and 80286 microprocessors.

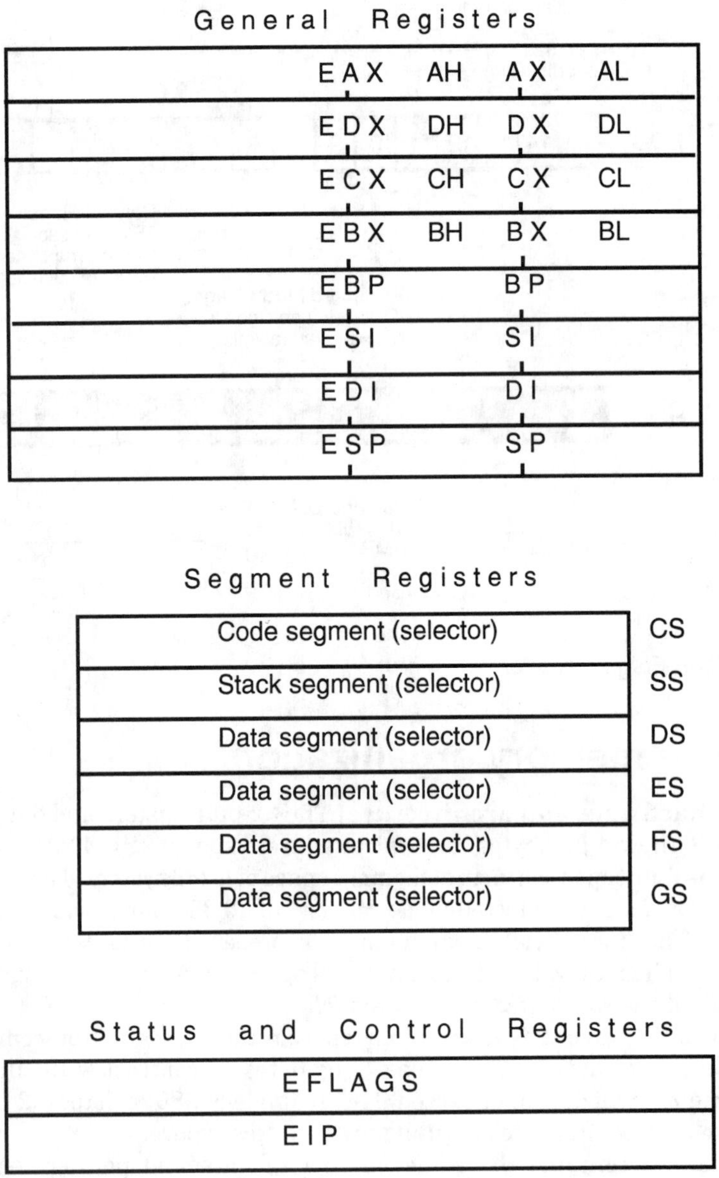

General Registers

E A X	AH	A X	AL
E D X	DH	D X	DL
E C X	CH	C X	CL
E B X	BH	B X	BL
E B P		B P	
E S I		S I	
E D I		D I	
E S P		S P	

Segment Registers

Code segment (selector)	CS
Stack segment (selector)	SS
Data segment (selector)	DS
Data segment (selector)	ES
Data segment (selector)	FS
Data segment (selector)	GS

Status and Control Registers

EFLAGS
EIP

80386 General Registers

The 80386 contains a total of six segment registers, two more than the 8086, 8088, and 80286. The segment register classification is slightly different, since the designation of ES as an extra segment is no longer used. Instead, the segment registers DS, ES, FS, and GS are all labeled data segments. The segment registers are still 16 bits wide, and operate similarly to the segment registers in the 80286. Note that the increased address space of the 80386 is the result of the expansion of the offset component of the logical address from 16 to 32 bits, while the segment base component continues to be a 16-bit register. The instruction pointer register (EIP) holds the offset of the currently executing instruction.

80386 — virtual 8086 mode

[PC hardware and architecture] This mode, characteristic of the 386, allows the execution of one or more 8086 programs in a protected mode environment. This means that programs designed and coded for the single-task 8086 environment can be multitasked in the 80386 virtual 8086 mode.

The V86 mode is based on the concept of a *virtual machine*, in which the program can execute as if it were in its native 8086 environment. To the 8086 program, the 80386 (in V86 mode) appears as an 8086 machine. But the microprocessor alone cannot create this environment. On IBM microcomputers, 8086 emulation requires software that handles interrupts, exceptions, and input/output operations in a manner consistent with the 80386 protected mode.

80386

[PC hardware and architecture] The 80386, introduced in 1985, is a 32-bit Intel microprocessor of the Intel IAPX family. The chip is used in the IBM PS/2 Model 70 and Model 80, the Compaq 386, the Tandy Model 4000 and Model 5000, and many others. The architecture of the 386 is based on a 32-bit bus, internal data path, and registers. This means that the processor can address 4 gigabytes (4294 million bytes) of physical memory. Its virtual address space is extended to 64 terabytes. The 80386 is compatible with its predecessors in the Intel IAPX family (the 8086, 8088, 80186, 80188, and 80286). MS DOS programs for the 8086 and 80286 run in the 80386. Furthermore, the 80386 is capable of multitasking programs developed for the DOS environment. The 80286 protected mode is emulated by the 80386, with very few variations. Therefore, applications and system programs developed for the 80286 protected mode execute unmodified in the 386. (See 80286 Architecture).

Like its predecessor, the 80286, the 386 chip provides memory management and protection and supports multitasking. The 386 architecture permits the simultaneous use of several operating systems.

80386 Microprocessor Hardware Summary

CHARACTERISTIC	SPECIFICATIONS
Mathematical coprocessor	80287 or 80387
Bus interface	32 bits
Internal data path	32 bits
Available clock frequencies	12.5, 16, 25, and 33 MHz
Memory addressability	4 gigabytes
Virtual memory	64 terabytes/task
Memory management and protection	Yes, with paging
I/O addressability	65,535 ports
Registers	Arithmetic: 8 Index: 8 Segment: 6 General-purpose: 8
Intel support chips	Clock: 82384 Controller: TTL or PAL Interrupts: 8259-A DMA: 82258 Timer: 8253/54 DRAM: PAL
Number of pins	132
Power requirements	5 V

8086 — architecture

[PC hardware and architecture] The 8086 CPU contains 14 internal registers. These registers can be classified as follows:

1. Data registers
2. Index and pointer registers
3. Segment registers
4. Status and control registers

Each of the four data registers can hold 16 bits of information. The upper and lower halves of each data register can be addressed independently. These 8-bit half-registers of AX, BX, CX, and DX are designated AH and AL, BH and BL, CH and CL, and DH and DL.

The data registers are used in arithmetic and logical operations and in performing data transfers. Usually the programmer can designate which data register is used in an instruction, but there are cases in which the instruction set specifically designates a data register for a certain operation. The following table shows implicit use of the 8086 registers:

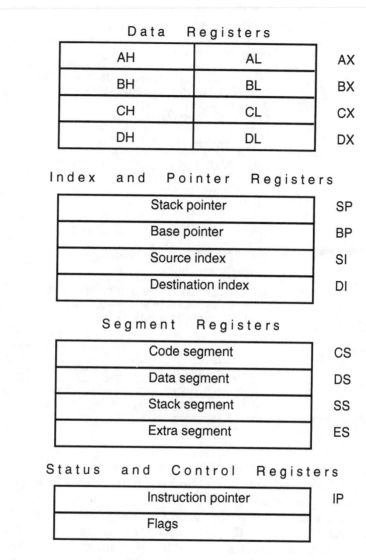

Data Registers

AH	AL	AX
BH	BL	BX
CH	CL	CX
DH	DL	DX

Index and Pointer Registers

Stack pointer	SP
Base pointer	BP
Source index	SI
Destination index	DI

Segment Registers

Code segment	CS
Data segment	DS
Stack segment	SS
Extra segment	ES

Status and Control Registers

Instruction pointer	IP
Flags	

8086 Machine Registers

The 16-bit registers called stack pointer (SP), base pointer (BP), source index (SI), and destination index (DI) usually contain offset values for addressing elements within a segment. They can also be used in arithmetic and logic operations. The two pointer registers, SP and BP, provide easy access to items located in the current stack segment. The index registers, SI and DI, are used in accessing items located in the data and extra segments. If no special provisions are contained in the instruction, the pointer registers refer to the current stack segment, and the index registers refer to the current data segment. SI and DI are used implicitly in string operations.

Implicit Use of 8086 Data Registers

REGISTER	USED IMPLICITLY IN
AX	MUL, IMUL (word-size source operand) DIV, IDIV (word-size source operand) IN (word input) OUT (word output) CWD String operations
AL	MUL, IMUL (byte-size source operand) DIV, IDIV (byte-size source operand) IN (byte input) OUT (byte output) XLAT AAA, AAD, AAM, AAS (ASCII operations) CBW (convert to word) DAA, DAS (decimal arithmetic) String operations
AH	MUL, IMUL (byte-size source operand) DIV, IDIV (byte-size source operand) CBW (convert to word)
BX	XLAT
CX	LOOP, LOOPE, LOOPNE String operations with REP prefix
CL	RCR, RCL, ROR, ROL (rotates with byte count) SHR, SAR, SAL (shifts with byte count)

The segment registers are the 16-bit registers named code (CS), data (DS), stack (SS), and extra (ES) segments. These registers are used in addressing the 1-Mbyte 8086 memory space by dividing it into 16 segments of 64K each.

All instructions must reside in the current code segment, addressed through the CS register. The offset of the instruction is determined by the IP register. Program data is usually located in the data segment, addressed through the DS register. The stack is addressed through the SS register. The extra segment register, as the name implies, can be used to address operands, data, memory, and other items outside the current data and stack segments. Many IBM programs use the ES segment register as a pointer into video display memory.

8086 — flags

[PC hardware and architecture] The 16-bit status word or flag register holds 3 control and 6 status bits, called the *flags*. The unused bits in the status register cannot be accessed directly in the 8086 CPU.

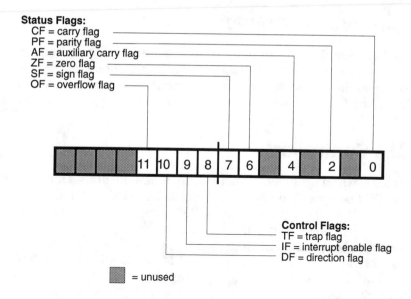

Status Flags:
CF = carry flag
PF = parity flag
AF = auxiliary carry flag
ZF = zero flag
SF = sign flag
OF = overflow flag

Control Flags:
TF = trap flag
IF = interrupt enable flag
DF = direction flag

= unused

8086 Flags Register

8086 Flags

BIT	FLAG NAME	CODE	FUNCTION
11	Overflow	OF	Set to show arithmetic overflow
10	Direction	DF	Used to determine direction of string moves
9	Interrupt enable	IF	Used to enable and disable maskable interrupts
8	Trap	TF	Places the CPU in the single-step mode (used mainly by debugger programs)
7	Sign	SF	Used in signed arithmetic to show whether the result is positive (SF = 0) or negative (SF = 1)
6	Zero	ZF	Set if the result of the previous operation is zero
4	Auxiliary carry	AF	Used in decimal arithmetic to show a carry out of the low nibble or a borrow from the high nibble
2	Parity	PF	Set if the result of the previous operation has an even number of 1 bits (used mainly to check for data transmission errors)
0	Carry	CF	Set if there is a carry or a borrow to the high-order bit of the result. Also used by rotate instructions

8086 — instruction pointer

[PC hardware and architecture] The status and control registers include the instruction pointer and the flags. The instruction pointer register (IP) holds the offset from the beginning of the code segment to the next instruction to be executed. The IP register cannot be manipulated directly by the programmer.

8237 DMA Controller

[PC hardware and architecture] This chip is used in all IBM microcomputers of the PC line (except the Pcjr), in Model 25 and Model 30 of the PS/2 line, and in many IBM-compatible machines. PS/2 computers with Micro Channel architecture use a proprietary IBM DMA controller.

The IBM Personal Computer uses the Intel 8238-2 DMA controller, the XT uses the 8237A-5, and the AT and the PS/2 Model 25 and Model 30 use two 8237A-5 chips. However, from a programming viewpoint, these versions of the Intel integrated circuit can be considered identical. Therefore, we will refer generically to the 8237 DMA controller in the following discussion.

The Intel 8237 is a dedicated microprocessor designed for transferring data from memory to memory or between memory and input/output devices. Memory-to-memory transfers are not possible in the PC and XT because of the use of the DMA channels. The maximum data transfer rate is 1.6 Mbytes/s, but in 8088 systems the 8237 is programmed to allow the CPU access to the bus after each transfer. This reduces the transfer rate to 422K/s

8237 DMA Controller Transfer Channels

CHANNEL NUMBER	PRIORITY	USE IN PC
0	1 (highest)	Memory refresh
1	2	Not assigned
2	3	Diskette drive
3	4 (lowest)	Hard disk (if installed)

Memory-to-memory transfers are not possible in PC and XT systems because the 8237 requires channel 0 for this operation. However, AT-type machines do not use the DMA controllers for memory refresh operations, which are handled through independent circuitry.

AT-class machines use the Intel 8237A-5 DMA controller, which is almost identical to the one in the PC and the XT. However, there are substantial differences in how the DMA operations are performed. In the first place, the AT machines use a separate integrated circuit for memory refresh. This frees DMA channel 0 for other operations. A second difference is the use of two 8237 chips with four channels each.

8237 DMA Controller Transfer Channels (AT)

CONTROLLER NUMBER	CHANNEL NUMBER	USE
1	0	Not assigned
	1	Synchronous data link control (SDLC)
	2	Diskette drive
	3	Not assigned
2	4	Cascade for controller 1
	5	Not assigned
	6	Not assigned
	7	Not assigned

The presence of three additional channels (channel 4 is used to cascade the first four channels) requires additional page registers. Channels 0, 1, 2, and 3 of the AT, associated with DMA controller number 1, are compatible with the 8237 DMA controller used in the PC and PC XT. AT channels 5, 6, and 7, associated with DMA controller number 2, support 16-bit data transfers throughout the 16-Mbyte address space. In channels 5, 6, and 7, DMA takes place in blocks of 128K. For this reason, the base count is a word instead of a byte.

Page Register Assignments (AT)

PORT NUMBER	CHANNEL NUMBER	USE
87H	0	Unassigned
83H	1	Unassigned
81H	2	Diskette
82H	3	Hard disk
8BH	5	Unassigned
89H	6	Unassigned
8AH	7	Unassigned
8FH	NA	Memory refresh

8250 UART

(see serial communications controllers)

8253/8245 timer — programming

[PC hardware and architecture] Programming of the 8253/8254 timer takes place in two operations. The first one consists of selecting the channel to be accessed, the latching method, the mode, and the binary or BCD numerical base. The selection is performed by sending the corresponding bit pattern to the command register. (See 8253/8254 timer).

The pulse rate for each timer channel is determined by the internal clock rate of 1,193,180 beats per second and by the value stored in the latch register. For example, if the latch register of timer channel 0 is initialized with a value of 4, the 1,193,180 times per second pulse is converted to one-fourth of this value (297,500 times per second). Since the largest number that can be stored in a 16-bit latch register is 65,536, the slowest possible pulse of a timer channel can be calculated by dividing the pulse rate by this maximum:

$$\frac{1,193,180}{65,536} = 18.2 \text{ cycles per second}$$

The output of channel 0 is connected to the IRQ0 interrupt line. For this reason, interrupt 08H, which is the timekeeping routine in the IBM BIOS, receives control 18.2 times per second.

The BIOS initialization routines set timer channel 0 to approximately 18.2 cycles per second. However, the programmer can increment the frequency by entering another divisor word for this channel. Because the value 65,536 is the largest number that can be represented in 16 bits, timer channel 0 cannot be made to operate at a slower rate than 18.2 cycles per second. Nevertheless, a program can effectively reduce this frequency by skipping one or more beats.

Many mechanical and digital devices operate at rates faster than 18.2 cycles per second. For instance, dot-matrix printers can output more than 100 characters per second, and normal transmission speeds in serial communications usually exceed 1000 bits per second. To accommodate fast devices, it is possible to accelerate the rate of any timer channel to a maximum of more than one million pulses per second by adjusting the value held in the channel's latch register.

Since timer channel 1 is used in memory refresh, it should not be modified or used for any other purpose. Timer channel 2, normally routed to the speaker, can be modified and used for other functions. However, since channel 2 is not linked to a hardware interrupt line, the program has to poll the channel's counter register.

Because channel 0 is linked to the interrupt system, every time the counter register is decremented to zero, an INT 08H is automatically executed. A program can set a specific time cycle by modifying the value in the latch register, then installing an intercept routine of INT 08H in order to receive control at every beat of the new cycle. However, the programmer using timer channel 0 should consider that its beat is also used by the interrupt 08H service routine to keep the system time-of-day clock and to time diskette motor operations. If the frequency of timer channel 0 is changed, the diskette's motor shutoff time is altered, with unpredictable results, and the time-of-day counters become useless. These consequences can be avoided by designing an interrupt service routine that maintains 18.2 cycles per second to the original handler, although the interrupt may be taking place at a different rate.

The following formula calculates the divisor required to obtain a certain frequency on a timer channel:

$$\frac{1,193,180}{\text{desired frequency}} = \text{new divisor}$$

The calculations can also be based on the frequency produced by the maximum divisor value (65,536). The following code fragment shows the encoding for changing the frequency of timer channel 0 from 18.2 cycles per second to 182 cycles per second.

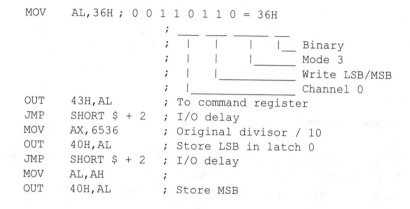

```
MOV     AL,36H ; 0 0 1 1 0 1 1 0 = 36H
               ;   ___ ___ _____ __
               ;   |   |     |    |__ Binary
               ;   |   |     |_____ Mode 3
               ;   |   |_____ Write LSB/MSB
               ;   |_____ Channel 0
OUT     43H,AL ; To command register
JMP     SHORT $ + 2  ; I/O delay
MOV     AX,6536      ; Original divisor / 10
OUT     40H,AL       ; Store LSB in latch 0
JMP     SHORT $ + 2  ; I/O delay
MOV     AL,AH        ;
OUT     40H,AL       ; Store MSB
```

To adjust the system to the increased speed of timer channel 0, it is necessary to find a way to maintain a rate of 18.2 cycles per second to the BIOS original interrupt 8 handler. This can be accomplished by establishing a secondary counter, which is primed with the factor of the frequency increase. The new intercept routine decrements this secondary counter on every cycle. When the counter reaches zero, execution is transferred to the original BIOS routine. Note that interrupt 1CH is called by INT 08H on exit from this service. For this reason it cannot be used as an intercept.

8253/8254 Programmable Interval Timer

[**PC hardware and architecture**] The Intel 8253 timer is used in IBM microcomputers that use the 8086 or the 8088 microprocessor. Microcomputers that use the 80286 or later CPUs are usually equipped with the Intel 8254-2 or with proprietary circuits that are compatible with the 8254.

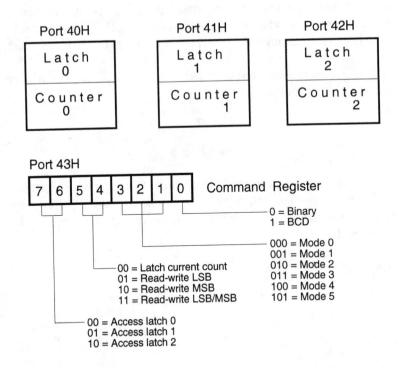

8253 Timer Diagram

The 8253 timer is driven by the system clock, but the hardware divides the clock beat so as to generate a square wave with a frequency of 1.19318 Mhz (1,193,180 times per second). The 8253/8254 timer has three internal and independent counters known as channels 0, 1, and 2.

Each channel has a 16-bit latch register and a 16-bit counter. In operation, each tick of the internal timer (1,193,180 times per second) decrements the value in the counter register for that channel. When the count reaches zero, the channel generates a signal on its output line. Channels 0, 1, and 2 are initialized so that at the end of each counting cycle, the counter register is automatically reloaded with the value stored in the latch.

In addition to the latches and counter registers, the 8253 has a 1-byte command register that is used for programming the chip's operation. The command register is shown in the lower part of the 8253 Timer diagram. Bits 6 and 7 of the command register serve to select which access latch is active. Bits 4 and 5 determine how latching takes place. Note that the latch registers hold one word of data (16 bits), while port input/output operations take place one byte at a time. Setting bits 4 and 5 of the command register to the read-write LSB then MSB option allows reading or writing to the latch registers by issuing two consecutive IN or OUT instructions. This is the latching mode enabled during the BIOS initialization of the 8253.

Bits 1, 2, and 3 of the command register are used to select one of six modes in which each channel can operate. Mode 2 is used by the BIOS for timer channel 1, which is dedicated to memory refresh operations in non-Micro Channel systems. Mode 3, which generates a symmetrical wave, is used by the BIOS for timer channels 0 and 2.

The 8253 timer has several preassigned functions in IBM systems:

1. Timer channel 0 is connected to the IRQ0 interrupt line. Each pulse of this channel generates an interrupt type 08H, which is vectored to the BIOS time-of-day clock. This channel is also used in timing diskette motor operations. The pulse rate is approximately 18.2 times per second.

2. Timer channel 1 is linked to the memory refresh mechanism (DMA controller) on IBM microcomputers that do not use Micro Channel architecture. This channel is undocumented in Micro Channel systems. In PS/2 Models 25 and 30, it is used in system diagnostics.

3. Timer channel 2 is routed to the internal speaker and used in generating sounds.

4. Timer channel 3 is a watchdog timer that can be used to determine if IRQ0 is not being serviced and also in counting operations. This channel exists only in PS/2 Micro Channel systems.

Timer-Related Interrupts

TYPE CODE	NAME	OPERATIONS
08H	System timer	Driven by timer channel 0 at a rate of 18.2 times per second. Maintains a count used to determine time of day. Decrements a counter used to turn off the diskette motor. Calls a user routine at interrupt 1CH on every timer tick.
1AH	Time of day	BIOS service to read and set the internal counters maintained by the system timer.
1CH	User timer	Allows a user-written routine which is called by INT 08H 18.2 times per second.

8259A — programming

[PC hardware and architecture] Programming the 8259A consists of initializing the chip to a certain operation mode and controlling its functions during interrupt processing. Both initialization and control take place through commands sent by the CPU to the 8259A. In IBM microcomputers, each 8259A is addressed through two ports. These ports are used for the chip's initialization and control commands.

There are four initialization commands (designated ICW1 to ICW4) and three operation commands (OCW1 to OCW3). Initialization and operation commands are output to the two access ports for each 8259A

8259A Interrupt Mapping in One-Controller Systems

LINE	TYPE	ADDRESS	EXTERNAL DEVICE
IRQ0	08H	0020H	Timer channel 0
IRQ1	09H	0024H	Keyboard (unused in PCjr)
IRQ2	0AH	0028H	Color Graphics Adapter (unused in PCjr)
IRQ3	0BH	002CH	Serial port 2 (built-in serial port in PCjr)
IRQ4	0CH	0030H	Serial port 1 (internal modem in PCjr)
IRQ5	0DH	0034H	Fixed disk in PC and XT (vertical retrace in PCjr)
IRQ6	0EH	0038H	Diskette
IRQ7	0FH	003CH	Parallel port 1

8259A Interrupt Mapping in Two-Controller Systems

Controller Number 1

LINE	TYPE	ADDRESS	EXTERNAL DEVICE
IRQ0	08H	0020H	Timer channel 0
IRQ1	09H	0024H	Keyboard
IRQ2	0AH	0028H	Cascade for controller 2
IRQ3	0BH	002CH	Serial port 2
IRQ4	0CH	0030H	Serial port 1
IRQ5	0DH	0034H	Parallel port 2 in AT Reserved in PS/2 systems
IRQ6	0EH	0038H	Diskette
IRQ7	0FH	003CH	Parallel port 1

Controller Number 2

LINE	TYPE	ADDRESS	EXTERNAL DEVICE
IRQ8	70H	01C0H	Real-time clock
IRQ9	71H	01C4H	Redirected to IRQ2
IRQ10	72H	01C8H	Reserved
IRQ11	73H	01CCH	Reserved
IRQ12	74H	01D0H	Reserved in AT Auxiliary device interrupt in PS/2 systems
IRQ13	75H	01D4H	Math coprocessor
IRQ14	76H	01D8H	Hard disk controller
IRQ15	77H	01DCH	Reserved

8259A Access Ports in the PC

CONTROLLER	ADDRESS	DESIGNATION
Controller number 1	20H	First access port
	21H	Second access port
Controller number 2	A0H	First access port
	A1H	Second access port

The 8259A can differentiate between an initialization sequence and an operation command because an initialization sequence begins with an OUT instruction to the first control port (even-numbered port), in which bit 4 of the command byte is set, while operation commands to the first control port must have bit 4 clear.

Once initialized the 8259A is ready to accept interrupt requests on its eight lines. The interrupt mask register of the 8259A permits enabling and disabling of the individual interrupt lines. The *first operation command* (OCW1) is used to read or write to the interrupt mask register. This command is output through the second control port, which is mapped to port 21H in one-controller systems and to port A1H in two-controller systems.

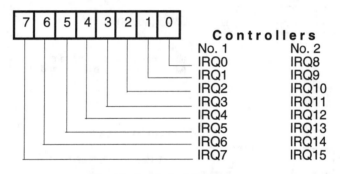

Bit = 1 to disable the interrupt line
Bit = 0 to enable the interrupt line

8259A Interrupt Mask Register Bitmap

As the 8259A sends an interrupt signal to the processor through the INTR line, it automatically suspends all other interrupts. This explains why the interrupt service routine must signal the 8259A that processing of the interrupt has concluded, so that other interrupts can be allowed. The end-of-interrupt signal constitutes the *second operation command* (OCW2). This command is output through the first control port, which is mapped to port 20H in one-controller systems and to port A0H in two-controller systems. In the PC, the command code is the value 20H. The following code fragment demonstrates the end-of-interrupt command to the 8259A:

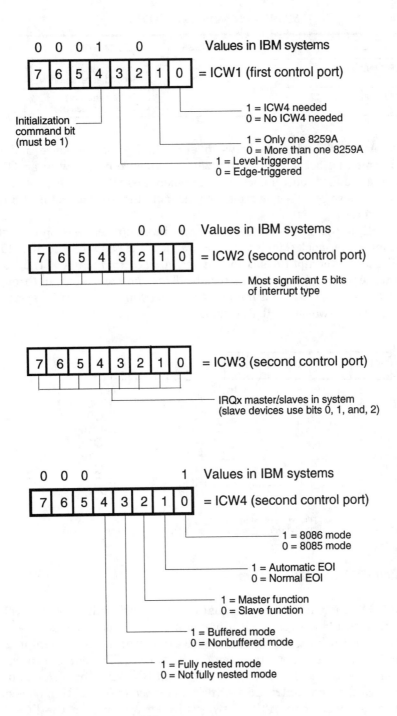

8259A Initialization Command Words

```
; Signal end-of-interrupt to controller number 1
      MOV    AL,20H        ; "End-of-interrupt" code
      OUT    20H,AL        ; To first control port
```

The *third operation command* (OCW3) allows reading of the interrupt request register (IRR) and the in-service register (ISR) in the 8259A. It also contains a polling control bit used in operating additional 8259A controllers that access the CPU through the input/output channel.

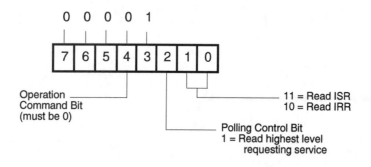

8259A Third Operation Command (OCW3) Bitmap

8514/A Display Adapter

[historical] [video systems] In 1987 IBM introduced a high-end video graphics system intended for applications that demand high-quality graphics, such as CAD, desktop publishing, graphical user interfaces to operating systems, image editing, and graphics art software. The video system, which was named the 8514/A Display Adapter, was capable of displaying 1024-by-768 pixels in 256 colors. Compared to VGA mode number 18 (640 by 480 pixels in 16 colors) this 8514/A graphics mode offers 2.5 times the number of screen pixels and 16 times as many colors. The 8514/A system was superseded by the XGA standard, with which it is compatible.
(See also: XGA).

A

A2DRQQ

[MS-Pascal] Heading: (A, B: REALS): REALS;
Arithmetic function. Return the arc tangent of (A/B). Both A and B, as well as the return value, are of type REAL8. This function is from the MS-FORTRAN runtime library and must be declared EXTERN.

A2SRQQ

[MS-Pascal] Heading: (A, B: REAL4): REAL4;
Arithmetic function. Return the arc tangent of (A/B). Both A and B, as well as the return value, are of type REAL4. This function is from the MS-FORTRAN runtime library and must be declared EXTERN.

AAA

[Assembler] 8086 machine instruction. Mnemonic for ASCII Adjust after Addition. AAA is executed following an ADD instruction to change the contents of the AL register to valid, unpacked BCD digits in the range 0H to 9H. The high-order nibble is zeroed. The CF and AF are updated. OF, PF, SF, and ZF are undefined.
Sample code:

```
        ; Addition of two unpacked BCD digits
            MOV     AH,0        ; Clear AH
            MOV     AL,7H       ; AL = unpacked BCD 7
            MOV     CL,3H       ; CL = unpacked BCD 3
            ADD     AL,CL       ; AL = AL + CL = 0AH
            AAA                 ; Adjust result
        ; AH = 01H and AL = 00H. CF is set to indicate overflow
```

AAD

[Assembler] 8086 machine instruction. Mnemonic for ASCII Adjust before Division. Notice that unpacked BCD digits are called ASCII numbers in Intel literature. AAD is executed before dividing two unpacked BCD digits so that the quotient will be an unpacked BCD digit in the range 0H to 9H. The DIV instruction returns the quotient in AL and the reminder in AH. The high-order nibbles of AL and AH are zeroed. PF, SF, and ZF are updated. AF, CF, and OF are undefined.

Sample code:

```
        ; Action of AAD on the division of two unpacked BCD digits
                MOV     AH,0          ; Clear AH
                MOV     AL,9H         ; AL = unpacked BCD 9
                MOV     CL,4H         ; CL = unpacked BCD 4
                AAD                   ; Adjust dividend
                DIV     CL            ; Perform 9/4
        ; At this point AL = 02H (quotient), and AL = 01H
        ; (reminder)
```

(See also: DIV).

AAM

[Assembler] 8086 machine instruction. Mnemonic for ASCII Adjust after Multiplication. AAM is executed after multiplying two unpacked BCD digits so that the product will be one or two unpacked BCD digits in the range 0H to 9H. After multiplication the high-order digit is found in AH and the low-order one in AL. Overflow is not possible since the product of two unpacked BCD digits cannot exceed one word (i.e. 9H times 9H equals 08H 01H).

Sample code:

```
        ; Action of AAM on the multiplication of two unpacked BCD
        ; digits
                MOV     AH,0          ; Clear AH
                MOV     AL,9H         ; AL = unpacked BCD 9
                MOV     CL,8H         ; CL = unpacked BCD 8
                MUL     CL            ; Binary multiplication
                AAM                   ; Adjust product to BCD
        ; At this point AH = 07H and AL = 02H
```

AAS

[Assembler] 8086 machine instruction. Mnemonic for ASCII Adjust after Subtraction. AAS is executed following a SUB instruction to change the contents of the AL register to a valid, unpacked BCD digits in the range 0H to 9H. The high-order nibble is zeroed. The CF and AF are updated. OF, PF, SF, and ZF are undefined.

Sample code:

```
        ; Subtraction of two unpacked BCD digits
                MOV     AH,0          ; Clear AH
                MOV     AL,9H         ; AL = unpacked BCD 9
                MOV     CL,5H         ; CL = unpacked BCD 5
                SUB     AL,CL         ; Binary subtraction
```

```
            AAS                      ; Adjust result to BCD
    ; AH = 00H and AL = 05H.
```

ABORT

[MS-Pascal] Heading: (CONST STRING, WORD, WORD);
An extend level intrinsic procedure. Halts program execution in the same way as an internal runtime error. The STRING (or LSTRING) is an error message. The string parameter is a CONST, not a CONSTS parameter. The first WORD is an error code. The second WORD, which can be anything, is sometimes used to return a file error status code from the operating system.

The parameters, as well as any information about the machine state (program counter, frame pointer, stack pointer) and the source position of the ABORT call are given in a termination message or are available to the debugging package. If the $runtime switch is on, then error messages report the location of the procedure or function that has called the routine in which abort was called.

ABS

[MS-Pascal] heading: (X : NUMERIC): NUMERIC;
Arithmetic function. Returns the absolute value of X. Both X and the return value are of the same numeric type: REAL4, REAL8, INTEGER, WORD, or INTEGER4. Since WORD values are unsigned, ABS (X) always returns X if X is of type WORD.

ABS (function)

[BASIC] [QuickBASIC] Returns the absolute value of the operand, which can be any numeric expression.
Example:
```
    PRINT ABS(7*(-3))
```
Result: 35

ACDRQQ

[MS-Pascal] Heading: (CONSTS A: REAL8): REAL8;
Arithmetic function which returns the are cosine of A. Both A and the return value are of type REAL8. This function is from the MS-FORTRAN runtime library and must be declared EXTERN.

ACSRQQ

[MS-Pascal] Heading: (CONSTS A: REAL4): REAL4;

Arithmetic function which returns the are cosine of A. Both A and the return value are of type REAL4. This function is from the MS-FORTRAN runtime library and must be declared EXTERN.

ADC

[Assembler] 8086 machine instruction. Mnemonic for ADd with Carry. Performs the addition of two byte- or word-size operands. If the carry flag is set at the time of ADC execution, one more is added to the sum. The instruction is typically used in multiword addition routines in order to carry the overflow from one digit stage into the next one. Updates AF, CF, OF, PF, SF, and ZF. Sample code:

```
      ; Fragment to perform multiword addition of two doubleword
      ; operands stored in the user's DATA segment
      DATA   SEGMENT
      NUM1   DW      0011H,0FFFFH ; First addend
      NUM2   DW      0011H,0FFFFH ; Second addend
      SUM    DD      0H           ; Storage for sum
      DATA   ENDS
      CODE   SEGMENT
             MOV     AX,NUM1 + 2  ; Get high-order words
             MOV     BX,NUM2 + 2
             ADD     AX,BX        ; Add. Carry need not be
                                  ; considered
             MOV     WORD PTR SUM + 2,AX ; Store high-order of sum
             MOV     AX,NUM1      ; Get low-order words
             MOV     BX,NUM2
             ADC     AX,BX        ; Add numbers plus previous carry
             MOV     WORD PTR SUM,AX    ; Store low-order of sum
      ; At this point DS:SUM = 0034FFFEH
```

ADD

[Assembler] 8086 machine instruction. Mnemonic for ADDition. Performs the addition of two byte- or word-size operands. Updates AF, CF, OF, PF, SF, and ZF. Sample code:

```
      ; Addition of two binary numbers
             MOV     AX,0 ; Clear accumulator
             ADD     AX,170       ; AX = 170
             ADD     AX,30        ; AX = 200
```

Address-of operator

[C] In C the programmer can obtain the address of a variable by means of the *address-of* operator, which is the & symbol. For example, the following statement prints the address of the variable num1:

```
printf("Address of num1 variable is: 0x%X", &num1);
```
Note that because it is usual practice to represent addresses in hexadecimal form, the %X conversion-type code is used.
Since the address of a variable is a constant assigned by the system software, it cannot be changed by the programmer. The statement

```
&num1 = 0x8600;
```

is illegal.

Addressing modes

[Assembler] The various ways in which an operand can be identified are called the *addressing modes*. For example, a memory location can be identified using its sequential number (direct addressing) or by a register that contains this value (register indirect addressing). *Addressing modes* for *register* and *immediate* operands are simple. Register operands are addressed using the register names. Some 80x86 instructions allow addressing the 8-bit portions of a machine register, for example:

```
MOV     CL,21
```

or the entire 16-bit register, for example:

```
MOV     AX,1234
```

There are no addressing options for immediate operands, although most assemblers allow representing immediate values in decimal, binary, and hexadecimal notation.
Reference to a machine register is always interpreted to mean the register's contents; for example, the instruction

```
MOV     AL,AH
```

consists of copying the contents of the AH register into AL. On the other hand, a reference to a memory location can relate to either its address or its contents. In order to access the contents of a memory operand, the CPU must know the two address elements: the segment and the offset. The segment determination is usually performed according to the type of instruction and the applicable ASSUME statement, although the programmer can override the assumption and request a specific segment register. The offset portion of the operand's address (known as the *effective address*) is determined according to the memory addressing mode used in the operand. For example, a program can read the contents of a memory location at a specific address, as follows:

```
MOV     AX,[140H]
```

This instruction loads the AX register with the contents of the memory location at offset 140H in the currently assumed data segment register. The bracket symbols enclosing the address portion of the operand are called the *indirection indicators*. These symbols signal to the assembler that it is the *contents of* location 140H that must be loaded into AX and not the immediate value 140H.

Direct addressing takes place when a offset element of a memory location is referred specifically in the operand, or if an item is represented by its variable name; for example, the instruction

```
MOV    AL,[BYTE_ITEM]
```

loads the AL register with the contents of the byte-size memory variable named BYTE_ITEM. In this case the bracket symbols are superfluous because the assembler assumes that a reference to a variable always means the contents of the variable. This instruction is more frequently coded in the form:

```
MOV    AL,BYTE_ITEM
```

In order to simplify processing of multiple data items, a program can set a processor register as a pointer to one of the items in the set and access other items by manipulating this pointer.

```
MOV    SI,OFFSET BUFFER     ; Setup pointer
MOV    AL,[SI]              ; Buffer  character to AL
```

Note the use of the indirection indicators (brackets) to specify *the contents of the memory location pointed at by SI*. Not all registers can be used as pointers to memory data. The ones that can be used as pointers are the *index registers* (SI and DI) and the *base registers* (BX and BP). Pointers can also be used to store items in memory.

The index and base registers, SI, DI, BX, and BP, also allow adding a displacement to the contents of the pointer register. These addressing modes are called *based addressing* if the base registers BX or BP are used as operands, or *indexed addressing* if the index registers SI or DI are used.

AIDRQQ

[MS-Pascal] Heading: (CONSTS A: REAL8): REAL8;
Arithmetic function. Return the integral part of A, truncated toward zero. Both A and the return value are of type REAL8. This function is from the MS-FORTRAN runtime library and must be declared EXTERN.

AISRBQ

[MS-Pascal] Heading: (CONSTS A: REAL4): REAL4;

Arithmetic function. Returns the integral part of A, truncated toward zero. Both A and the return value are of type REAL4. This function is from the MS-FORTRAN runtime library and must be declared EXTERN.

ALLHQQ

[MS-Pascal] Heading:(SIZE : WORD): WORD;
Library function (heap management). Returns 0 if the heap is full, 1 if the heap structure is in error, or MAXWORD if the allocator has been interrupted. Otherwise it returns the pointer value for an allocated variable with the size requested.

ALLMQQ

[MS-Pascal] Heading: (WANTS : WORD): ADSMEM;
A library function (segmented heap management). Returns a long segmented address of type ADSMEM. ALLMQQ takes a parameter "wants" that is a memory request in bytes.

A number "0" in the ".r" field of the segmented address returned by ALLMQQ indicates that memory of the requested "wants" size could not be allocated. A number "1" indicates that the long segmented heap is invalid.

Alphanumeric Data

[C] Alphanumeric data refer to items that serve as textual designators and that are not the subject of conventional arithmetic. By the same token the letters of the alphabet and other nonnumeric symbols are often used as designators. The programmer can designate one or more numeric symbols as alphanumeric data if these are used for nonmathematical purposes, as is often the case with telephone numbers, numbers used in street addresses, zip codes, social security numbers, and others.

In C, alphanumeric data belong to the integral data type and require the char specifier. This means that data items defined using the char specifier are considered a number or a character depending on how the item is defined in the program. For example, the variable declaration

```
char num_var = 65;
```

defines a numeric variable named num_var and initializes it to a value of 65. On the other hand, the declaration

```
char alpha_var = 'A';
```

defines an alphanumeric variable named alpha_var and initializes it to the alphanumeric character "A." Note that in this case the single quote symbols are used to enclose the alphanumeric character.

A string is a contiguous set of alphanumeric characters. In practice, the set can consist of a single character. C strings can be defined as constants or as variables.
In the line

```
printf("Enter radius: ");
```

the string constant "Enter radius: " is defined within the printf() statement. A string constant can also be created with the #define statement, for example, the line:

```
#define USA "United States of America\n\n"
```

equates the name USA with the string in quotes. Later in the program we display this constant with the line

```
printf(USA);
```

At compile time the name USA is substituted with the defined string, which includes two newline escape codes.

AND

[Assembler] 8086 machine instruction. Mnemonic for AND logical. Performs a logical AND operation of two operands. A bit in the result is set if the corresponding bits of both operands are 1, otherwise the result bit is cleared. In bit masking operations ANDing with a 0 clears the bit position while ANDing with a 1-bit preservers the original value of the position bit.
Code sample:

```
; ANDing 00100011B with 00001111B
        MOV     AL,00100011B ; First operand
        AND     AL,00001111B ; Mask
;
; At this point AL = 00000011B
; Low nibble was preserved while high nibble was cleared
```

AND

[Boolean logic] One of the fundamental operations of digital logic. The AND operation requires that both inputs (a and b) be true for the result (R) to be true. The following is the truth table for the AND operation:

```
INPUT    |  OUTPUT
---------|--------
a  &  b  |    R
---------|--------
0     0  |    0
1     0  |    0
0     1  |    0
1     1  |    1
```

The AND gate performs the AND function of two or more inputs.

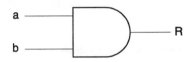

AND Gate with Two Inputs

AND — bitwise operator

[C] The AND bitwise operator (&) performs a Boolean AND of the operands. This determines that a bit in the result will be set only if the corresponding bits are set in both operands. A frequent use of the AND operator is to clear one or more bits without affecting the remaining ones. This is possible because ANDing with a 0-bit always clears the result bit, and ANDing with a 1-bit preserves the original value of the first operand. Programmers sometimes refer to one of the operands of a bitwise operation as a *mask*. The effect of an AND mask can be pictured as a filter that passes the bits that are ANDed with a 1-bit and clears the bits that are anded with a 0-bit, as in the following example:

```
                    0101 0111B
BITWISE AND         1111 0000B
                    ----------
                    0101 0000B
```

The following program tests bit number 7 of an unsigned int variable by ANDding with a binary mask:

```c
#include <stdio.h>
main()
{
    unsigned user_input;
    unsigned bit_mask = 128;
    unsigned result = 0;
```

```
        printf("\n\nEnter an integer number between 1 and 255: ");
        scanf("%u", &user_input);
            result = user_input & bit_mask;
            printf("\nInput anded with 10000000B is: %u", result);
}
```

ANDRQQ

[MS-Pascal] Heading: (CONSTS A: REALS) : REALS;
Arithmetic functions. Return the truncated integral part of A rounded away
from zero. Both A and the return value are of type REAL8. This function is from
the MS-FORTRAN runtime library and must be declared EXTERN.

ANSRQQ

[MS-Pascal] Heading: (CONSTS A : REAL4) : REAL4;
Arithmetic functions. Returns the truncated integral part of A rounded away
from zero. Both A and the return value are of type REAL4. This function is from
the MS-FORTRAN runtime library and must be declared EXTERN.

ARCTAN

[MS-Pascal] Heading: (X : REAL): REAL;
Arithmetic function. Returns the arctangent of X in radians. Both X and the
return value are of type REAL. To force a particular precision, declare ATSRQQ
(CONSTS REAL4) and/or ATDRQQ (CONSTS REAL8) and use them instead.

Arithmetic functions

[MS-Pascal] [Turbo Pascal] All functions on REAL data types check for an
invalid (uninitialized) value. They also check for particular error conditions and
generate a runtime error message if an error condition is found.
The following arithmetic functions are available in MS Pascal:

```
Turbo Pascal        MS Pascal        Operation
Abs                 ABS              Absolute value
ArcTan              ARCTAN           Arctangent
Cos                 COS              Cosine
Exp                 EXP              Exponential
Frac                ----             Fractional part
Ln                  LN               Natural log
Pi                  ----             Value of Pi
Sin                 SIN              Sine
Sqr                 SQR              Square
Sqrt                SQRT             Square root
```

The MS-FORTRAN runtime library in MS-Pascal provides several additional arithmetic functions, including arc and hyperbolic functions, decimal logarithms, tangent, minimum and maximum, and powers. These must be declared with the EXTERN directive.

Arithmetic operators

[C] Some C language operators are the familiar mathematical symbols, such as the + and minus signs, while other operators are computer equivalents. For instance, because the conventional symbol for division is not available in most computer keyboards, C and other programming languages use the slash (/) to represent division operations. By the same token, the letter x is replaced by the asterisk (*) in representing multiplication.

C Arithmetic Operators

OPERATOR	DESCRIPTION
+	Addition
-	Subtraction
*	Multiplication
/	Division
%	Remainder

The *remainder* (%) operator, sometimes called the *modulo* or *modulus*, gives the remainder of a division. For example, in a program in which the variable rem is an unsigned integer, the expression

```
rem = 14 % 3;
```

assigns the value 2 to the variable rem, because 14 divided by 3 equals 4, with a remainder of 2.

ARPL

[Assembler] 80386 machine instruction. Mnemonic for Adjust Requested Privilege Level of the selector field. The instruction is used in operating systems code to ensure that the selector parameter does not request more privilege than the caller is allowed. The encoding requires two operands: the first one is a selector value stored in a 16-bit memory variable, the second operand is a word register. If the two low-order bits of the first operand (requested privilege level bits) is less than that of the second operand, ZF is set and the RPL field of the first operand is increased to match the second one.

Arrays

[QuickBASIC] There are two methods of storing arrays, dynamic and static. The memory locations for a static array are set aside at compile time and this portion of memory may not be used for any other purpose. The memory locations for a dynamic array are assigned at runtime and can be freed for other purposes. Although dynamic arrays are more flexible, static arrays can be accessed faster. QuickBASIC uses the dynamic allocation of arrays if either the range in a DIM statement is specified by a variable or the programmer insists on dynamic allocation with a $DYNAMIC metacommand.

Arrays

[C] Most programming languages, C included, allow the grouping of several data items of the same type into an individualized data structure called an *array*. In C a string is defined as an array of char-type elements, and a string variable (array) is not considered an independent data type but a collection of char-type characters.

The most important characteristic that distinguishes an array from other data structures is that in an array all the elements must belong to the same data type. Other C data structures can contain elements of different data types. In the line:

```
char college_addr[] = {"1211 N.W. Bypass\n"};
```

the string variable named college_addr is defined as being of char-type. Note that because the declaration takes place outside a function (before main) the variable is external and therefore visible to all functions in the module as well as to other modules.

The bracket symbols are used to identify an array. For example:

```
static char usa_name[14] = {"United States"};
```

In this case the number 14, enclosed in the brackets, is a count of the number of letters in the initialization string ("United States") plus one NULL terminator that is automatically added by the compiler at the end of the array. When the array is initialized in the declaration, the programmer can omit this character count, which is then calculated at compile time. Also optional in string arrays are the brace symbols enclosing the initialization string.

An array can also contain numeric data. For example, the array

```
int nums_array1[] = { 50, 60, 700 };
```

contains the following numeric values:

```
nums_array[0] =   50
nums_array[1] =   60
nums_array[2] =  700
```

Note that the index number used in addressing the first array element is [0].

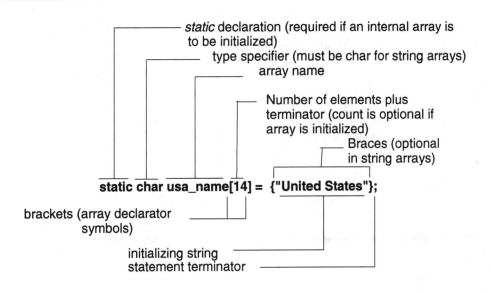

String Array

ASC (function)

[BASIC] [QuickBASIC] Returns the ASCII code for the first character of a string or string expression.
Example:

```
S$ = "Test"
PRINT ASC(S$)
```

Result: 84

ASDRQQ

[MS-Pascal] Heading: (CONSTS A: REALS): REALS;
Arithmetic function. Returns the arcsine of A. Both A and the return value are of type REAL8. This function is from the MS-FORTRAN runtime library and must be declared EXTERN.

Assembler Directives

[Assembler] The operation field of an assembly language statement can contain a microprocessor instruction or an assembler directive. Assembler directives serve as orders to the assembler program. An instruction is an operational command to a hardware element of the system, whereas an assembler directive is a command to a software element. Instructions are determined by the characteristics of the microprocessor, while directives depend on the particular assembler programs. The following statement contains the DB (define bytes) assembler directive:

```
GREETING        DB        'Hello, I am your IBM computer$'
```

The word GREETING in this assembly language statement is a variable name. Variable names are made up by the programmer, usually so that the name represents the contents of the variable.

ASSIGN

[MS-Pascal] Heading: (VAR F; CONSTS N: STRING);
File system procedure (extend level I/O). Assigns an operating system filename in a STRING (or LSTRING) to a file F.

ASSRQQ

[MS-Pascal] Heading: (CONSTS A: REAL4): REAL4;
Arithmetic function. Returns the arcsine of A. Both A and the return value are of type REAL4. This function is from the MS-FORTRAN runtime library and must be declared EXTERN.

ATN (function)

[BASIC] [QuickBASIC] Returns the arctangent of a numeric argument. The result is in radians. The range depends on the implementation. Multiply by 180 to convert radians to degrees. Range is PI/2 to -PI/2 radians.
Example:

```
PRINT ATN(3)
```

Result: 1.249046

Attributes and directives

[MS-Pascal] An attribute gives additional information about a procedure or function. Attributes are available at the extend level of Microsoft Pascal. They are placed after the heading, enclosed in brackets, and separated by commas. Available attributes include ORIGIN, PUBLIC, FORTRAN, PURE, and IN-TERRUPT.

A directive gives information about a procedure or function, but it also indicates that only the heading of the procedure or function occurs, by replacing the block (declarations and body) normally included after the heading. Directives are available in standard Pascal. EXTERN and FORWARD are the only directives available. EXTERN can only be used with procedures or functions directly nested in a program, module, implementation, or interface. This restriction prevents access to nonlocal stack variables.

The following table displays the attributes and directives that apply to procedures and functions:

Attributes and Directives for Procedures and Functions

NAME	TYPE	PURPOSE
FORWARD	directive	Lets you call a procedure or function before you give its block in the sourcefile
EXTERN	directive	Indicates that a procedure or function resides in another loaded module
PUBLIC	attribute	Indicates that a procedure or function may be accessed by other loaded modules
ORIGIN	attribute	Tells the compiler where the code for an EXTERN procedure or function resides
FORTRAN	attribute	Specifies a calling sequence for compatibility with Microsoft FORTRAN
INTERRUPT	attribute	Gives a procedure a special calling sequence that saves program status on the stack
PURE	attribute	Signifies that the function does not modify any global variables

The following rules apply when you combine attributes in the declaration of procedures and functions:

1. Any function may be given the PURE attribute.

2. Except for the PURE attribute, procedures and functions with attributes must be nested directly within a program, module, or unit.

3. A given procedure or function may have only one calling sequence attribute, that is, either FORTRAN or INTERRUPT, but not both.

4. PUBLIC and EXTERN are mutually exclusive, as are PUBLIC and ORIGIN.

The EXTERN directive may be used in an implementation by declaring all EXTERN procedures and functions first, but not ORIGIN.

Except for the ORIGIN attribute, a module heading may contain a group of attributes that apply to all directly nested procedures and functions. The ORIGIN attribute applies to a single procedure or function.

If the PUBLIC attribute is one of a group of attributes in the heading of a module, an EXTERN attribute given to a procedure or function within the module explicitly overrides the global PUBLIC attribute. If the module heading has no attribute clause, the PUBLIC attribute is assumed for all directly nested procedures and functions.

The PUBLIC attribute allows a procedure or function to be called by other loaded code. It cannot be used with the EXTERN directive. The EXTERN directive permits a call to some other loaded code, using either the ORIGIN address or the linker. PUBLIC, EXTERN, and ORIGIN provide a low level way to link MS-Pascal routines with other routines in MS-Pascal or other languages. A procedure or function declaration with the EXTERN or FORWARD directive consists only of the heading, without an enclosed block. EXTERN routines have an implied block outside of the program. FORWARD routines are fully declared (have a block) later in the same compiland. Both directives are available at the standard level of MS-Pascal. The keyword EXTERNAL, is a synonym for EXTERN.

The PURE attribute applies only to functions, not to procedures. Conversely, INTERRUPT applies only to procedures, not to functions. PURE is the only attribute that can be used in nested functions .

AUTO (command)

[BASIC] Automatically generates a line number when the Enter key is pressed. The command format is:

```
AUTO[number][,[increment]]
```

where number is the start value for the first line and increment is the increase of each subsequent line number.
Example:

```
AUTO 20,5
```

Result: produces line numbers 20, 25, 30,...

Auxiliary device port

[input/output] [PC hardware and architecture] All models of the PS/2 line and most PC-compatible machines, include an auxiliary device port. This port is usually accessed via a 6-pin miniature DIN connector identical to the one used for the keyboard. In PS/2 systems the signals and voltage are the same in both connectors.
Like the keyboard, the auxiliary device port is coupled to the 8042 keyboard controller described. The auxiliary device port can be used with any serial input device compatible with the Intel 8042. IBM and other vendors manufacture a serial mouse for PS/2 systems that connects to the auxiliary device port. In operation, the PS/2 serial mouse is compatible with application software written for the Microsoft mouse.

B

BCD

[Assembler] Acronym for Binary Coded Decimal. Computer storage format for integers whereby each decimal digit is converted to binary and stored separately. In unpacked BCD format each decimal digit is coded into one byte of storage (i.e. twenty-seven decimal equals 02H 07H). In packed BCD format each decimal digit is coded into one nibble of storage (i.e. twenty-seven decimal equals 27H).

BEEP (statement)

[BASIC] [QuickBASIC] Produces a beeping sound on the PC speaker. In BASIC the frequency is 800Hz and the duration is of 0.25 s. The statement PRINT CHR$(7) is equivalent to BEEP.
Example:
BEEP

BEGOQQ

[MS-Pascal] A library procedure (initialization). BEGOQQ is called during initialization, and the default version does nothing. However, you may write your own version of BEGOQQ to invoke a debugger or to write customized messages, such as the time of execution, to a terminal screen.

BEGXQQ

[MS-Pascal] Library procedure (initialization). BEGXQQ is the defined entry point for the load module after the program is linked and loaded. As the overall initialization routine, BEGXQQ performs the following actions:

1. Resets the stack and the heap
2. Initializes the file system
3. Calls BEGOQQ
4. Calls the program body

BEGXQQ may be useful for restarting after a catastrophic error in a ROM-based system. However, invoking this procedure to restart a program does not take care of closing any open files. Similarly, it does not reinitialize variables originally set in a VALUE section or with the initialization switch on.

Binary Coded Decimal (See BCD).

Binary file

[BASIC] [QuickBASIC] A file that has been opened with a statement of the form OPEN filespec FOR BINARY AS #n is regarded simply as a sequence of characters occupying positions 1, 2, 3,.... At any time, a specific location in the file is designated as the "current position." The SEEK statement is used to set the current position. Collections of consecutive characters are written to and read from the file beginning at the current position with PUT and GET statements, respectively. After a PUT or GET statement is executed, the position following the last position accessed becomes the new current position.

Binary numbers

[PC hardware and architecture] The computers built in the United States during the early 1940s used decimal numbers and analog electrical circuits. In 1946 John Von Neumann and others decided that the computing machinery was easier to build and performed more reliably if the electronic circuits were based on two states, using cells that were either on or off. The binary system of numbers is the simplest possible set of symbols with which we can count and perform arithmetic. Most of the difficulties in understanding the binary system result from this simplicity.

Note that the binary numbers match the physical state of the electronic cell. If we think of each cell as a miniature light bulb, then the binary number 1 can be used to represent the state of a charged cell (light bulb on) and the binary number 0 to represent the state of an uncharged cell (light bulb off). In this sense we often say that a *bit is set* if its binary value is 1 and that a *bit is reset*, or clear, if its binary value is 0.

bit fields

[C] The bitwise operators can be used to manipulate the individual bits within an integral data type. These operations can be further simplified by using the #define directive to isolate individual bits or fields. For example, since each binary digit corresponds to a power of two, we can mask the individual bits as follows:

```
#define  BIT0_MASK  01
#define  BIT1_MASK  02
```

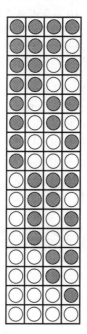

0	0	0	0
0	0	0	1
0	0	1	0
0	0	1	1
0	1	0	0
0	1	0	1
0	1	1	0
0	1	1	1
1	0	0	0
1	0	0	1
1	0	1	0
1	0	1	1
1	1	0	0
1	1	0	1
1	1	1	0
1	1	1	1

Electronic Cells and Binary Numbers

```
#define   BIT2_MASK   04
#define   BIT3_MASK   08
#define   BIT4_MASK   16
#define   BIT5_MASK   32
#define   BIT6_MASK   64
#define   BIT7_MASK   128
```

Thereafter a program can use these bit masks in conjunction with the bitwise operators AND, OR, XOR, and NOT, to test and change the individual bits in an integral variable.

In addition to the bitwise operators, C allows the definition of individual bits within a structure composed of one or more members of an integral data type. This specialized type of structure is called a *bit field*. The following is a bit field structure declaration:

```
struct low_bits {
        unsigned int bit0    : 1;
        unsigned int bit1    : 1;
        unsigned int bit2    : 1;
        unsigned int bit3    : 1;
        unsigned int bits4_7 : 4;
        unsigned int padding : 8;
} mask_1;
```

Note that the colon is used in the type declaration of a bit field structure to assign a dimension to each field. In the declaration for the tag low_bits, the first four fields, named bit0, bit1, bit2, and bit3, are declared to be one bit wide, while the field named bits4_7 is declared to be four bits wide, and the field named padding is declared to be eight bits wide.

We have seen that a structure variable can be created at the time of the type declaration. In the previous bit field we have created a variable named mask_1. The fields in this variable can now be accessed by means of the membership operator (.). For example, we can initialize bits 0 to 3 to a value of one and the remaining bits to zero with the statements

```
mask_1.bit0 = mask_1.bit1 = mask_1.bit2 = mask_1.bit3 = 1;
mask_1.bits4_7 = mask_1.padding = 0;
```

However, C does not allow direct access to a bit field variable. In other words, a C statement cannot reference the variable mask_1 as it would a conventional variable. For example, the program fragment

```
unsigned int value, result;
value = 127;
result = value & mask_1;
```

is illegal since the & operator cannot be applied to a structure variable. According to Kernighan and Ritchie the only operations that can be performed on structures are obtaining the structure's address by means of the & operator and accessing the structure members. Therefore, a structure variable, such as mask_1 cannot be accessed as a unit. However, since there are no restrictions regarding pointers to structures we can use the address-of and the indirection operators to gain access to a bit field variable.

Bits

(See memory organization).

Bitwise operators

[C] Allow manipulating the individual bits of an integral data type.

C Bitwise Operators

OPERATOR	DESCRIPTION
&	Bitwise AND
|	Bitwise OR
^	Bitwise XOR
~	Bitwise NOT (complement)
<<	Bitwise shift left
>>	Bitwise shift right

The first four operators perform logical functions on the individual bits of the operands. By adopting the convention that associates a binary 1 with the concept of logical true and a binary 0 with false, we can use binary numbers to show the results of a logical operation. In this manner we can state

```
1 OR 0 = 1
1 AND 1 = 1
1 AND 0 = 0
NOT 1 = 0
```

It is sometimes useful to think of the binary numbers to the left of the equal sign as meaning presence or absence of an element and the binary to the right of the equal sign as representing true or false. A *truth table* is a listing of all possibilities that result from a logical operation. The truth tables for the bitwise-logical operators AND, OR, XOR, and NOT are as follows:

Truth Tables For Bitwise Operations

AND		OR		XOR		NOT	
0 0	0	0 0	0	0 0	0	0	1
0 1	0	0 1	1	0 1	1	1	0
1 0	0	1 0	1	1 0	1		
1 1	1	1 1	1	1 1	0		

Although the bitwise operators AND, OR, and NOT perform similar functions as their logical counterparts, the logical operators return the value of 1 if the statement is true and 0 if false but do not change the actual contents of the variables. The bitwise operators, on the other hand, manipulate variable data, and the result can be different from the previous value.
(See also: AND, OR, XOR, and NOT bitwise operators).

BLOAD (command)

[BASIC] [QuickBASIC] Purpose: Loads a memory image file into memory. The command format is:

```
BLOAD filespec [,offset]
```

where filespec is a string expression for the file specification. In BASIC 2.0 and later the filespec can contain a path. Offset is an integer expression in the range 0 to 65535. This is an offset at which the file will be loaded into the current segment specified by the latest DEF SEG statement. If offset is omitted, the one specified at BSAVE is assumed. That is, the file is loaded into the same location from which it was BSAVED.

When a BLOAD command is executed, the named file is loaded into memory starting at the specified location. BLOAD is intended for use with a file that has been previously saved with BSAVE. These commands are useful for loading and saving machine language programs, but they are not restricted to assembly language. Any segment can be specified as the target or source for these statements through the DEF SEG statement. This is a useful way of saving and displaying screen images.

The following example loads the screen buffer for the VGA color text modes, which is at segment address HB800. Line 50 loads PICTURE at offset 0, segment &HB800:

```
10 'load the screen buffer
20 'point SEG at screen buffer
30 DEF SEG= &HB800
40 'load PICTURE into screen buffer, at offset 0
50 BLOAD "PICTURE", 0
```

The example for the BSAVE command illustrates how PICTURE was saved.

BOUND

[Assembler] 80286 machine instruction. Mnemonics for check array index against BOUNDs. The code checks if an array index is within the limits of the addressed array. The first operand is a general purpose register containing the array index. The second operand is the address of two consecutive memory locations that hold the upper and lower limits of the array. The BOUND instruction compares the index register with the limits stored in memory variables and executes an interrupt 5H if the index is less than the first location or greater than the second one. Since in the PC environment interrupt 5H is normally vectored to the Print Screen function, the BOUND instruction has been seldom used.

Code sample:

```
DATA    SEGMENT
ARRAY_LIM      DW     0,100          ; Limits
ARRAY_DATA     DW     100 (DUP '?') ; Storage for array
DATA    ENDS
;
CODE    SEGMENT
        INC    SI     ; Bump array pointer to next item
        BOUND  SI,ARRAY_LIM ; Check for limits
; Error trap is at interrupt 5H
; Execution continues if array is within bound
```

break statement

[C] The *break* statement provides a way for exiting a switch construct or the currently executing level of a loop. The *break* statement cannot be used outside a *switch* or *loop* structure. Note that, in the case of a nested loop, the *break* statement exits the innermost loop level. This action is shown by the following trivial program:

```
#include <stdio.h>
main()
{
    unsigned int number = 1;
    unsigned char letter;
    while (number < 10 ) {
        printf("number is: %i\n", number);
        number ++;
            for (letter = 'A'; letter  'G'; letter ++) {
                printf("  letter is: %c\n", letter);
                    if (letter == 'C')
                        break;
            }
        }
    }
```

The listed program contains two loops. The first one, a *while* loop, displays a count of the numbers from 1 to 9. The second, or inner loop, displays the capital letters A to F, but the *if* test and associated *break* statement interrupt execution of this nested loop as soon as the letter C is reached. In this example, because the *break* statement acts on the current loop level only, the outer loop resumes counting numbers until the value 10 is reached.

BSAVE (command)

[BASIC] [QuickBASIC] Saves portions of the computer's memory on the specified device. Command format:

```
BSAVE filespec, offset, length
```

where filespec is a string expression for the file specification. In BASIC 2.0 and later filespec can contain a path. Offset is an integer expression in the range 0 to 65535. This is the offset into the segment declared by the last DEF SEG. Saving starts from this location. Length is an integer expression in the range 1 to 65535 which represents the length of the memory image to be saved. If offset or length is omitted, a syntax error occurs and the operation is canceled. Using the DEF SEG statement the programmer can specify any segment as the source segment for the BSAVE data. For example, you can save an image of the screen by doing a BSAVE of the screen buffer. (See BLOAD command). Example:

A DEF SEG statement must be used to set up the segment address to the start of the screen buffer. The offset of 0 and length &H4000 specify that the entire 16K screen buffer is to be saved.

```
10 'Save the color screen buffer
20 'first point segment at screen buffer
30 DEF SEG= &HB800
40 'save buffer in file PICTURE   (offset = 0, length = 4000H)
50 BSAVE "PICTURE", 0, &H4000
```

BSF

[Assembler] 80386 machine instruction. Mnemonic for Bit Scan Forward. One of the 80386 CPU instructions for bit scanning and testing. BSF opcode scans the source operand low-to-high and stores in the destination operand the bit position of the first 1-bit found. If all bits of the source operand are 0 then the ZF is set, otherwise the ZF is cleared. BSF requires word or doubleword operands; byte operands are not allowed.

Code Sample:

```
; Use BSF to determine the number of the first bit set
; (low-to-high order) in the source operand
      MOV   AX,10001000B ; Right-to-left first bit
                         ; set is number 3
      BSF   BX,AX        ; AX bit number into BX
; At this point BX = 03 since the first bit set is in bit
; position number 3 when read low-to-high. ZF is clear
```

(See also: BSR).

BSR

[Assembler] 80386 machine instruction. Mnemonic for Bit Scan Reverse. One of the 80386 CPU instructions for bit scanning and testing. BSR opcode scans the source operand high-to-low and stores in the destination operand the bit position of the first 1-bit found. If all bits of the source operand are 0 then the ZF is set, otherwise the ZF is cleared. BSR requires word or doubleword operands; byte operands are not allowed.

Code Sample:

```
; Use BSR to determine the number of the first bit set
; (high-to-low order) in the source operand.
      MOV   AX,10001000B ; Bits 7 and 3 are set
      BSR   CX,AX        ; AX bit number into CX
                         ; read high-to-low
; At this point CX = 7 since bit number 7 of AX is the first
; bit set when read high-to-low. ZF is clear
```

(See also: BSF).

BSWAP

[Assembler] 486 machine instruction. Mnemonic for Byte SWAP. Reverses the byte order in a 32-bit machine register.

BSWAP operation

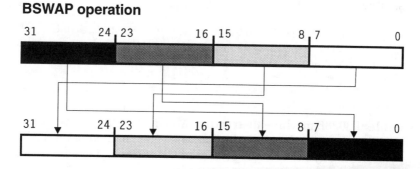

BSWAP Instruction

One use of BSWAP is converting data between the little endian and the big endian formats by reversing the order of unpacked decimal digits loaded from a memory operand into a 32-bit machine register.

For example, assume that the four unpacked decimal digits are stored in a memory operand with the least significant digit in the lowest order location, as would be the case in a conventional BCD format. However, when these digits are loaded into a machine register by means of a MOV instruction their order is reversed. The following code simulates this situation:

```
; Using BSWAP to reverse digit order
DATA    SEGMENT
FOUR_DIGS    DB     01H,02H,03H,04H
.

.
CODE    SEGMENT
.

.
; Load memory digits into 32-bit machine register
       LEA    SI,FOUR_DIGITS        ; Pointer to unpacked BCD
       MOV    EAX,DWORD PTR [SI]; Load digits into EAX
; EAX = 04030201H             ; Swap bytes in EAX
       BSWAP  EAX
; EAX = 01020304H
```

BT

[Assembler] 80386 machine instruction. Mnemonic for Bit Test. The bit testing instructions BT (bit test), BTS (bit test and set), BTR (bit test and reset), and BTC (bit test and complement) were introduced with the 80386 CPU processor. BT stores the value of the bit indicated by the first operand and the bit number indicated by the second operand, in CF. The BT instruction can be followed by JC or JNC instruction to direct execution according to the state of the tested bit.

Code sample:

```
        MOV    AX,10001000B ; Set value in operand
        BT     AX,3         ; Test AX bit 3
    ; Carry flag is set since AX bit 3 is set
```

BTC

[Assembler] 80386 machine instruction. Mnemonic for Bit Test and Complement. BTC stores the value of the bit indicated by the first operand and the bit number indicated by the second operand in CF and complements (toggles) the bit.

Code sample:

```
        MOV    AX,10001000B ; Set value in operand
        BTC    AX,1         ; Test AX bit 1
    ; Carry flag is clear since bit 1 is cleared
    ; AX = 10001010B since bit 1 is toggled (complemented)
    ; by BTC
```

BTR

[Assembler] 80386 machine instruction. Mnemonic for Bit Test and Reset. BTR stores the value of the bit indicated by the first operand and the bit number indicated by the second operand in CF and clears the corresponding bit.

Code sample:

```
        MOV    AX,10001000B ; Set value in operand
        BTR    AX,3         ; Test AX bit 3
    ; Carry flag is set since bit 3 was set in the destination
    ; AX = 10000000B since bit 3 is reset by BTR
```

BTS

[Assembler] 80386 machine instruction. Mnemonic for Bit Test and Set. BTR stores the value of the bit indicated by the first operand and the bit number indicated by the second operand in CF and sets the corresponding bit.

Code sample:

```
        MOV    AX,10000000B ; Set value in operand
        BTS    AX,3         ; Test AX bit 3
```

```
; Carry flag is clear since bit 3 was clear in the
; destination
; AX = 10001000B since bit 3 is set by BTS
```

(See also: LOCK).

BYLONG

[MS-Pascal] Heading: (INTEGER-WORD, INTEGERWORD): INTEGER4; Extend level intrinsic function. Converts WORDs or INTEGERs (or the LOWORDs of INTEGER4s) to an INTEGER4 value. BYLONG concatenates its operands:

```
DYLONG (A, B) = ORD (LOWORD (A)) + 65535 + WRD (HIWORD (B))
```

If the first value is of type WORD, its most significant bit becomes the sign of the result.

Byte (See memory organization).

BYWORD

[MS-Pascal] Heading: (ONE-BYTE, ONE-BYTE): WORD; An extend level intrinsic function. Converts bytes (or the LOBYTEs of INTEGERs or WORDs) to a WORD value. Takes two parameters of any ordinal type. BYWORD returns a WORD with the first byte in the most significant part and the second byte in the least significant part:

```
BYWORD (A, B) = LOBYTE(A) * 256 + LOBYTE(B)
```

If the first value is of type WORD, its most significant bit becomes the sign of the result.

C

C language — ANSI C

[C] In 1982 a technical committee of the American National Standards Institute (ANSI) proposed a standard for C language. This standard, referred to as ANSI C, was approved in 1989. In this manner ANSI C became the industry-level authority for the language and its implementations. In some respects ANSI C maintained the original design and essence of the C language, but in certain fields the standard tried to overcome limitations of K & R C. One of the consequences of these efforts on the part of the ANSI C developers has been a considerable expansion of the language, sometimes estimated at twice its original size, and also more complex.

C language — authorities

[C] The traditional authority on C is a book titled *The C Programming Language*, by Brian W. Kernighan and Dennis M. Ritchie (Prentice-Hall, 1978). This book, sometimes known as the white book due to its cover color, contained the original definition of C and became a de facto standard for the language which is referred to as "K & R C."

C language — characteristics

[C] The following are the most often-cited advantages of C:

1. C is not a specialized programming language; therefore, it is suitable for developing a wide range of applications, from major system programs to minor utilities.
2. Although C is a small language, it contains all the necessary operators, data types, and control structures to make it generally useful.
3. C includes an abundant collection of library functions for dealing with input/output, data and storage manipulations, system interface, and other functions not directly implemented in the language.
4. C data types and operators closely match the characteristics of the computer hardware. This makes C programs efficient as well as easy to interface with assembly language programs.

5. C is not tied to any particular environment or operating system. The language is available on machines that range from microcomputers to mainframes. For this reason, C programs are portable; that is, they are relatively easy to adapt to other computer systems.

The following are the most often noted disadvantages of C:

1. C is not the easiest language to learn. Beginners find that some constructions in C are complicated and difficult to grasp.

2. The rules of C are not very strict, and the compiler often permits considerable variations in the coding. This allows some laxity in style, which often leads to incorrect or inelegant programming habits.

3. Although the language itself is small and portable, most of the C library functions are devised to operate on a specific machine. This sometimes complicates the conversion of C language software to other implementations or systems.

C language — coding style

[C] C language is flexible in the use of *white space* (tabs, spaces, and other inactive characters) and in the positioning of separators and delimiters so that the programmer can format the code according to personal preference. For example, we can place the left brace delimiter on a separate line and used tab to indent program lines, as follows:

```
main()
{
    float radius = 0;

    printf("Enter radius: ");
    scanf("%f", &radius);
    printf("\nArea is: %f", PI *(radius * radius));
}
```

Alternatively, the left brace delimiter can be placed on the same line as the main function and maintain the program lines flush with the left margin, in this manner:

```
main() {
float radius = 0;

printf("Enter radius: ");
scanf("%f", &radius);
printf("\nArea is: %f", PI *(radius * radius));
}
```

Most personal coding styles are acceptable, as long as they do not compromise the readability of the code or the basic principles of structured programming.

C language — input and output facilities

[C] C does not deal directly with input or output devices. There are no C language keywords equivalent to the PRINT or the INPUT statements of BASIC. This does not mean that a C language program cannot perform input or output operations, but rather that these operations are performed by means of library functions and macros that are not an intrinsic part of the language. Input and output library facilities in C can be classified into four groups:

1. Character I/O facilities, such as getchar() and putchar()
2. String I/O facilities, such as gets() and puts()
3. Formatted I/O facilities, such as scanf() and printf()
4. Stream I/O facilities, such as fscanf and fprintf()

C language — PC implementations

[C] Several software companies have developed C compilers for the IBM microcomputers. Some of these products have gained and lost popular favor as other versions or implementations of C were introduced to the market. Some of the better-known implementations of C for the IBM microcomputers are the Microsoft C++ and Quick C compilers, IBM C-2 compiler (which is a version of Microsoft C licensed to IBM), Intel iC-86 and iC-286 compilers, Borland Turbo C, Turbo C Professional, and C++, Lattice C, Aztec C, Zortech C, and Metaware High C.

C language — program elements

[C] A C language source file consists of a series of symbolic and explicit program elements, sometimes called *expressions*, that can be interpreted by the compiler. Some of these program elements would be undecipherable to a person unfamiliar with C. Other elements of the program are quite understandable even to someone totally unfamiliar with C. For example, the following C source is compiled into a program that requests from the user the radius of a circle and proceeds to calculate and display its area:

```
/* C program to calculate the area of a circle */
/*           Program name: AREA.C              */
#include >
#define PI 3.1415927

main()
{
   float radius = 0;

   printf("Enter radius: ");
```

```
        scanf("%f", &radius);
        printf("\nArea is: %f", PI * (radius * radius));
    }
```

(See also: comment, preprocessor directive, identifiers, reserved words, variables, and functions).

C programming language

[C] C is a computer programming language originally designed and implemented by Dennis Ritchie in 1972 while working at the Bell Laboratories. The first version of C ran under the UNIX operating system on a DEC PDP-11 machine. The predecessor of C is a language called BCPL (Basic Combined Programming Language) developed in 1969 by Martin Richards of Cambridge University. The name C language originated in the fact that Bell Laboratories' version of BCPL, which was developed by Ken Thompson, is named B.

C is often described as a relatively small, compact, and simple high-level programming language suitable for general use. During the 1970s C was generally associated with the UNIX operating system. In fact, the newer versions of UNIX are written in C. The language became more popular in the 1980s, mainly due to its use in microcomputers. During this period several major software and hardware companies adopted C as their preferred programming medium. Today C is available in most microcomputers and in many mainframe and mini computers.

It is generally accepted that C is a member of the ALGOL family of programming languages. Therefore, it is closely related to the algebraic languages, such as ALGOL and Pascal, and not as similar to BASIC or FORTRAN.

CALL

[Assembler] 8086 machine instruction. Mnemonic for CALL procedure. The CALL instruction is the fundamental means for accessing a subroutine in 80x86 assembler. When executing a CALL instruction the CPU stores the instruction pointer (IP register) of the next instruction to be executed in the stack and transfers control to the destination operand, which can be a label, a procedure name defined with the PROC directive, a memory variable, or a machine register. RET is coded in the subroutine to return execution to the instruction following the CALL. Calls to a procedure located in the same code segment are designated as NEAR calls, while calls to procedures in a different code segment are designated as FAR. In the FAR call the return address stored in the stack includes both the segment and the offset elements. NEAR calls store only the offset element of the address.

Procedures created with the PROC directive are defined as type NEAR or FAR. If the CALL instruction and the target procedure appear in the same module, then the assembler automatically selects a NEAR or FAR call according to the procedure's segment address. If the target procedure is located in a different module, the assembler uses the EXTRN declaration to determine if the call is to be of NEAR or FAR type. By the same token, if the RET instruction is in a procedure declared to be of type FAR then the return is to a segment:offset address. If the procedure is declared to be of NEAR type, then the return is to an offset in the same segment. The programmer can override the assembler's assumption by using the NEAR PTR or FAR PTR operators in the CALL instruction's operand, for example:

```
CALL    FAR PTR ROUTINE_1
```

or

```
CALL    NEAR PTR ROUTINE_2
```

Starting with MASM version 5.0, the return instruction can also specify a near or far destination: RETF (return far) is used to return to a segment:offset address, and RETN (return near) to return to an address in the same segment. The destination of a CALL instruction can be a memory variable, an element of an array, a machine register, or a combination thereof. For example, if RTN_TABLE holds the address of several routines and BX is the offset of a particular routine within the table, then it is possible to code:

```
CALL    FAR PTR RTN_TABLE[BX]
```

Code sample:

```
CODE    SEGMENT
        CALL    MULTIPLY_RTN ; Call near procedure
; Execution return to the line following the CALL
        .
        .
        .
MULTIPLY_RNT PROC   NEAR
; Procedure to multiply the contents of the AL, BL, and
; CL registers
        XOR     AH,AH           ; Clear AH
        MUL     BL              ; AL times BL
        MUL     CL              ; AL times CL
        RET
MULTIPLY_RTN ENDP
```

CALL (statement)

[BASIC] Calls an assembly language subroutine. Instruction format:

```
CALL numvar [(variable [,variable]....)]
```

where numvar is the name of a numeric variable. The value of the variable indicates the offset of the subroutine into the current segment as defined by the last DEF SEG statement. Variable is the name of a variable to be passed as an argument to the assembly language subroutine.

The CALL statement is a way of interfacing assembly language programs with BASIC.

CALL (statement)

[QuickBASIC] Transfers control to a QuickBASIC subroutine. The CALL keyword can be omitted. CALL (or the alternative form CALLS) can also be used to transfer execution to a procedure coded in another language. In this case the instruction format is:

```
CALL name [call-argument_list]
```

or

```
CALLS name [call-argument_list]
```

CALL ABSOLUTE (statement)

[QuickBASIC] Transfers control to a machine language routine. The instruction format is:

```
CALL ABSOLUTE ([argument_list,] integer_variable)
```

CALL INTERRUPT (statement)

[QuickBASIC] Allows programs to perform calls to DOS and BIOS software interrupts. Instruction format:

```
CALL INTERRUPT (int_num, inregs, outregs)
```

where int_num is the number of the software interrupt, inregs

Cassette recorder

(See storage devices -- sequential access).

CBW

[Assembler] 8086 machine instruction. Mnemonic for Convert Byte to Word. Extends the sign bit (bit 7) of the AL register to all bits of the AH register, thus

converting a signed byte into a signed word. CBW can produce unexpected results with unsigned operands.
Code sample:

```
        MOV     AL,10001111B ; Bit 7 is set
        CBW                  ; Extend bit 7 to AH
; AH now is 11111111B
        MOV     AL,00001111B ; Bit 7 is clear
        CBW                  ; Extend bit 7 to AH
; AH now is 00000000B
```

CDBL (function)

[BASIC] [QuickBASIC] Converts integer, long integer, and single-precision numbers to double-precision. If x is any number, then the value of CDBL(x) is the double-precision number determined by x.
Example:

```
A = 345.67
PRINT A; CDBL(A)
```

Result: 345.67   345.6700134277344

Note: in this example the conversion accuracy is limited to the accuracy of the source operand.

CDQ

[Assembler] 80386 machine instruction. Mnemonic for Convert Word to Quadword. Extends the sign bit (bit 31) of the EAX register to all bits in the EDX register, thus converting a signed doubleword into a signed quadword. CDQ can produce unexpected results with unsigned operands.
(See also: CWD).

Centronics Printer Interface

[PC hardware and architecture] While serial communications have been regulated by several generally adopted standards, parallel communications are not well standardized. The *Centronics Printer Interface*, which was developed by a printer manufacturer, is the convention most frequently associated with parallel communications.

The Centronics convention establishes the use of 36-pin connectors, but most PC implementations use the 25-pin D-shell. In this respect, the printer ports in the IBM microcomputers are nonstandard.

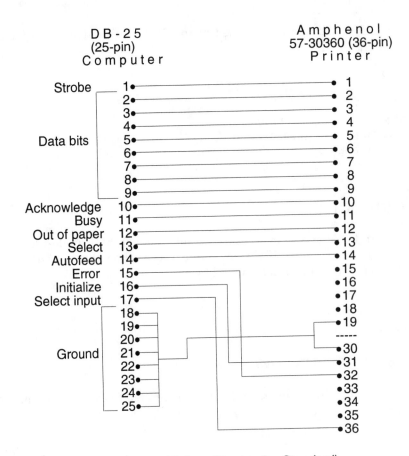

Wiring Diagram from Parallel Printer (Centronics Standard)

The Centronics convention establishes lines and signals for data transmission and handshaking.

The lines on adapter pins 2 to 9 contain the eight bits that form the transmitted character. The *strobe* line is used to pulse the character to the printer. Several lines are used by the printer to report its status. By holding high the *busy* line, the printer informs the computer that it cannot receive a new character. When it has finished receiving a character and is ready for the next one, the printer pulses the *acknowledge* line. The *select* line informs the sender that the printer is selected (active), and the *out-of-paper* line informs the sender that the printer is not available due to this condition.

The control lines to activate printer functions are designated *autofeed*, *initialize*, and *select input*. When the autofeed function is set, the printer automatically executes a line feed after each line is printed. The initialize line activates internal printer initialization routines. The select input line is used to select and unselect individual printers. The *error* line reports that the printer has encountered an error condition.

Centronics Printer Interface Lines in IBM Systems

	DB-25 PIN NUMBER	DIRECTION		VOLTAGE	SIGNAL NAME	
		PC*	PS/2			
	1	⇒	⇔	-	Strobe	
C	2	⇒	⇔	+	Data bit number 0	
	3	⇒	⇔	+	Data bit number 1	P
O	4	⇒	⇔	+	Data bit number 2	
	5	⇒	⇔	+	Data bit number 3	R
M	6	⇒	⇔	+	Data bit number 4	
	7	⇒	⇔	+	Data bit number 5	I
P	8	⇒	⇔	+	Data bit number 6	
	9	⇒	⇔	+	Data bit number 7	N
U	10	⇐	⇐	-	Acknowledge (ACK)	
	11	⇐	⇐	-	Busy	T
T	12	⇐	⇐	+	Out of paper (PE)	
	13	⇐	⇐	+	Select (SLCT)	E
E	14	⇒	⇒	-	Autofeed (XT)	
	15	⇐	⇐	-	Error	R
R	16	⇒	⇒	-	Initialize printer (INIT)	
	17	⇒	⇒	-	Select input (SLCT IN)	
	18–25				Ground	

Note:
* PC systems include the non-Micro Channel models of the PS/2 line (Models 25 and 30).

CGA

(See color graphics adapter).

CHAIN (statement)

[BASIC] [QuickBASIC] Passes control to another program. A statement in the format:

```
CHAIN filespec
```

loads and executes the source code program contained in filespec. If an extension is not specified .BAS is appended. It is possible to pass variables to the called program by placing COMMON statements in the two programs. Example:

```
CHAIN "A:TEST1"
```

Character set

[video systems]
The character set used in the Personal Computer includes the ASCII character codes (range 20H to 7FH), as well as two areas of graphics characters, one in the range 01H to 1FH, and another one in the range 80H to FFH (see figure). The characters and symbols can be classified as follows:

1. The ASCII characters. These include the letters of the alphabet, the Arabic numerals, and conventional symbols (20H to 7FH)
2. Four playing card suits (03H to 06H)
3. Two genetic symbols (0BH and 0CH)
4. Two musical notes (0DH and 0EH)
5. Two proofreader's marks (14H and 15H)
6. An assortment of drawing symbols, including circles, arrows, and faces
7. Letters and symbols for the Spanish, French, and German alphabets
8. Special characters for drawing boxes and lines (B3H to DFH)
9. Shading symbols (B0H to B2H)
10. Mathematical and engineering symbols (F0H to FDH)
11. An assortment of Greek letters (E1H to EDH)
12. Symbols for yen, pounds, cents, fractions, and others

Note that the graphic characters in the range B0H to DFH were designed for constructing screen boxes and for shading areas. Although the character generator does not include bitmaps for the entire rectangle of dots in these graphic characters, the hardware fills in the empty spaces so that uninterrupted shades and lines are shown on the screen.

CHDIR (command)

[BASIC] [QuickBASIC] Changes the current directory on the specified disk drive to the subdirectory specified by path. Command format:

```
CHDIR path
```

where path is a valid MS-DOS pathname.
Example:

```
CHDIR "C \"
```

changes the current path to the root directory of the C drive. If the drive letter is omitted the default drive is used.

CHDRQQ

[MS-Pascal] Heading: (CONSTS A: REAL8): REAL8;
Arithmetic function that returns the hyperbolic cosine of A. Both A and the return value are of type REAL8. This function is from the MS-FORTRAN runtime library and must be declared EXTERN.

characters 0H to 7FH							
HEX	0	1	2	3	4	5	6	7
0		►		0	@	P	`	p
1	☺	◄	!	1	A	Q	a	q
2	☻	↕	"	2	B	R	b	r
3	♥	‼	#	3	C	S	c	s
4	♦	¶	$	4	D	T	d	t
5	♣	§	%	5	E	U	e	u
6	♠	▬	&	6	F	V	f	v
7	●	↨	'	7	G	W	g	w
8	◘	↑	(	8	H	X	h	x
9	○	↓	)	9	I	Y	i	y
A	◙	→	*	:	J	Z	j	z
B	♂	←	+	;	K	[	k	{
C	♀	∟	,	<	L	\	l	|
D	♪	↔	-	=	M	]	m	}
E	♫	▲	.	>	N	^	n	~
F	☼	▼	/	?	O	_	o	Δ

PC Character Set

	characters 7FH to FFH							
HEX	8	9	A	B	C	D	E	F
0	Ç	É	á	▒	└	╨	α	≡
1	ü	æ	í	▓	┴	╤	β	±
2	é	Æ	ó	█	┬	π	Γ	≥
3	â	ô	ú	│	├	╙	π	≤
4	ä	ö	ñ	┤	─	╘	Σ	⌠
5	à	ò	Ñ	╡	┼	╒	σ	⌡
6	å	û	ª	╢	╞	╓	μ	÷
7	ç	ù	º	╖	╟	╫	τ	≈
8	ê	ÿ	¿	╕	╚	╪	Φ	°
9	ë	Ö	⌐	╣	╔	┘	θ	∙
A	è	Ü	¬	║	╩	┌	Ω	·
B	ï	¢	½	╗	╦	█	δ	√
C	î	£	¼	╝	╠	▄	∞	n
D	ì	¥	¡	╜	═	▌	φ	2
E	Ä	₧	«	╛	╬	▐	∈	■
F	Å	ƒ	»	┐	⊥	▄	∩	

CHR

[MS-Pascal] Heading: (X : ORDINAL): CHAR;
Data conversion function. Converts any ordinal type to CHAR. The ASCII code for the result is ORD (X). This is an extension to the ISO standard, which requires X to be of type INTEGER. An error occurs if ORD (X) > 255 or ORD (X) < 0. The error is caught only if the range checking switch is on.

CHR$ (function)

[BASIC] [QuickBASIC] Converts an ASCII code to its equivalent character. Instruction format:

```
S$ = CHR$(n)
```

where *n* must be an unsigned integer in the range 0 to 255.
Example:

```
PRINT CHR$(66)
```
Result: B

CHSRQQ

[MS-Pascal] Heading: (CONSTS A: REAL4): REAL4;
Arithmetic function that returns the hyperbolic cosine of A. Both A and the return value are of type REAL4. This function is from the MS-FORTRAN runtime library and must be declared EXTERN.

CINT (function)

[BASIC] [QuickBASIC] Convert long integer, single-precision, and double-precision numbers to integer. *x* must be in the range -32768 to 32767 otherwise an overflow error occurs. The fractional part is rounded up.
Example:

```
PRINT CINT(88.99);
PRINT CINT(88.11);
PRINT CINT(-3.88)
```

Result: 89   88   -4

CIRCLE (statement)

[BASIC] [QuickBASIC] Draws an ellipse on the screen if a graphics mode is enabled. The statement format is:

```
CIRCLE (x,y),r[,color[,start,end[,aspect]]]
```

where the (x,y) are the coordinates of the center of the ellipse, r is the radius. Color is an integer representing the color attribute according to the current video mode. In medium resolution modes the color attribute is defined by the COLOR statement (range 0 to 3). In the high resolution mode the range is 0 and 1. In either case 0 is the background color attribute. The foreground attributes are 3 and 1, respectively. Start and end are angles in radians in the range 2*PI to -2*PI. Aspect is a numeric expression that determines whether the figure is a circle or an ellipse.

   The angles are positioned in the conventional manner, that is counterclockwise, with 0 on the x-axis.

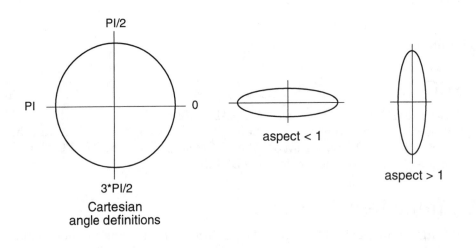

PI/2

PI   0

3*PI/2

Cartesian
angle definitions

aspect < 1

aspect > 1

CIRCLE Statement on the Cartesian Plane

   If the start of the end angle is negative, the ellipse is connected to the center point with a line. This is useful in drawing pie-shaped figures.
The aspect parameter serves a double purpose: to compensate for non-symmetrical screen modes and to draw elliptical figures. An example of the first use of the aspect parameter is when the video display is set in BASIC's SCREEN 1 mode, with a resolution of 320 by 200 pixels. In this case the relation between the vertical and horizontal pixel density is the ratio between the pixels, which is 5/6. Therefore to draw a circle while in the SCREEN 1 mode the aspect ratio must be 5/6. Other VGA modes (such as mode 18) have the same pixel density

vertically as horizontally. BASIC's SCREEN 12 command selects VGA mode number 18. In this case an aspect value of 1 produces a circle.
Example:

```
' Draw a circle with the following dimensions:
' origin: x = 160, y = 100
' radius: 80
' aspect: 1
CLS
SCREEN 12
CIRCLE (160, 100), 80, , , , , 1
```

Since the aspect parameter introduces an intentional deformation on the circle geometry, it can also be used to draw an ellipse. In a symmetrical video mode, such as the one enabled with the SCREEN 12 statement, a value other than 1 produces an ellipse, as shown in the preceding figure.

Circular and elliptical arcs are drawn by means of a CIRCLE statement in which the start, end parameters correspond to less than 360 degrees (2*PI radians).
Example:

```
' Draw a circular arc with the following dimensions:
' origin: x = 160, y = 100
' radius: 80
' start: 0
' end: PI/2 radians
' aspect: 1
CLS
SCREEN 12
  PI = 3.141593
CIRCLE (160, 100), 80, , 0, PI / 2, 1
```

CLC

[Assembler] 8086 machine instruction. Mnemonic for CLear Carry flag. CLC clears CF without affecting any other flag or register. CLC (as well as CMC and STC) is used in conjunction with the RCL and RCR instructions.
(See also: CMC, STC, RCL, and RCR).

CLD

[Assembler] 8086 machine instruction. Mnemonic for CLear Direction flag. CLD clears DF without affecting any other flag or register. CLD is preceding a string instruction forces incrementing of the SI or DI registers.
(See also: STD, MOVS, CMPS, INS, OUTS, SCAS, LODS, and STOS).

CLEAR (command)

[BASIC] [QuickBASIC] Sets all numeric variables to zero and all string variables to NULL. Also resets all elements of static arrays to their default values, closes all files, deletes all dynamic arrays from memory, and reinitializes the stack. The statement format is:

```
CLEAR [,[n][,m]]
```

where n is a byte count that sets the size of the BASIC data segment and m defines the size of the stack.
Example:

```
CLEAR ,32768, 2048
```

Result: Clear variables and arrays, set data segment to 32K, and stack to 2K.

CLI

[Assembler] 8086 machine instruction. Mnemonic for CLear Interrupt flag. CLI clears IF without affecting any other flag or register. After the execution of CLI internal interrupts are not recognized by the CPU. The STI instruction performs the reverse action, that is, it sets the interrupt flag. In protected mode IF is cleared if the current privilege level is as privileged as IOPL.

CLNG (function)

[QuickBASIC] Converts integer, single-precision, and double-precision numbers to long integer numbers. x must be in the range -2,147,483,648 to 2,147,483,647, otherwise an overflow error occurs. Fractional values are rounded up.

Clock — system

[PC hardware and architecture] Every computer system must contain a means of producing the pulse that runs the digital circuits. This clock signal serves to synchronize the different electronic components in the system. In the PC the system clock is external to the microprocessor and its type and speed are determined by the system's CPU. Nevertheless, some Intel microprocessors used in IBM-compatible microcomputers use an on-chip clock generator.

Clock Generators for Intel Microprocessors

	8086	8088	80186	80188	80286	80386
Clock	8284A	8284A	On-chip	On-chip	82284	82384
Speed, MHz	4, 7, 8, 10	4, 7, 8	8, 10, 12.5	8, 10	6, 8, 10 12.5	12.5, 16, 25

CLOSE

[MS-Pascal] Heading: (VAR F);
File system procedure (extend level I/O). Closes a file ensuring that the file access is terminated correctly.

CLOSE (statement)

[BASIC] [QuickBASIC] Closes the file or device and terminates the association between the file and its number. Statement format:

```
CLOSE [[#]file [,[#]file]...]
```

where file is the BASIC filenumber assigned to the file to be closed. CLOSE with no operand closes all open files or devices.
Example:

```
CLOSE #1, #2, #3
```

CLS (statement)

[BASIC] [QuickBASIC] Clears the screen and positions the cursor at the upper-left corner. In QuickBASIC the CLS statement can include an optional viewport, in the format:
```
CLS v
```
where v designates the viewport to be cleared. The statement CLS 0 clears the entire screen. The statement CLS 1 clears the active graphics viewport if one exists; otherwise, it clears the entire screen. The statement CLS 2 clears only the text viewport.

CLTS

[Assembler] 80386 machine instruction. Mnemonic for CLear Task-Switched flag in CR0. CLTS is used in operating system software to clear TS (task switch flag) in register CR0. TS is set every time a task switch takes place. The application of the TS flag is related to managing processor extensions, such as the math coprocessor chip. If TS is set then the execution of an ESC instruction is trapped. If MP and TS are both set, then the execution of a WAIT instruction is trapped.

CMC

[Assembler] 8086 machine instruction. Mnemonic for CoMplement Carry flag. Toggles CF to its opposite value without affecting any other flag or register.

CMP

[Assembler] 8086 machine instruction. Mnemonic for CoMPare. Sets AF, CF, OF, PF, SF, and ZF as if a subtraction had been performed but does not change the operand values. The compare instruction is usually followed by a relative jump instruction which directs execution according to the results of the comparison. For example, if CMP is followed by JG (jump if greater) the jump will be taken if the destination operand is greater than the source operand. Code sample:

```
; Perform a jump according to a compare operation
      CMP    AL,20H         ; Compare with 20H
      JG     AL_BIGGER      ; Go if AL > 20H
      JL     AL_SMALLER     ; Go if AL < 20H
; At this point AL = 20H
          .
          .
          .
AL_BIGGER:
          .
          .
AL_SMALLER:
```

CMPS/CMPSB/CMPSW/CMPSD

[Assembler] 8086 machine instruction. Mnemonic for CoMPare String. Compares the byte (CMPSB), word (CMPSW), or doubleword (CMPSD) addressed by the destination operand (DI register) to the one addressed by the source operand (SI register) and sets AF, CF, OF, PF, SF, and ZF accordingly. Also updates DI and SI to point to the next element in the string. If CMPS is followed by JG (jump if greater) the jump will be taken if the destination operand is greater than the source operand. If CMPS is prefixed with REPE or REPZ the comparison continues while CX is not zero and the string elements are equal. This format is usually designated as "compare while not end-of-string and equal." If CMPS is prefixed with REPNE or REPNZ the comparison continues while CX is not zero and the string elements are not equal. This format is usually designated as "compare while not end-of-string and not equal." If the address size is 16 bits, then SI, DI, and CX registers are used. If the address size is 32 bits, then ESI, EDI, and ECX registers are used. After execution of CMPS, SI and DI (optionally ESI and EDI) are bumped to point to the next string element. If DF is cleared, the pointer registers are incremented. If DF is set, the pointer registers are decremented.

The CMPS instruction deviates from Intel practice of designating the left operand as a destination and the right one as the source. In the case of CMPS the first operand is SI or ESI (source) and the second operand is DI or EDI (destination).

CMPS is assembled assuming that the segment for the source operand (SI or ESI) is DS and the segment for the destination operand (DI or EDI) is ES. A segment override can be used with the source but not with the destination. Code sample:

```
; String comparison with CMPS
DATA    SEGMENT
STRING1      DB      '12345ABCDE'
STRING2      DB      '1234567890'
DATA    ENDS
;
CODE    SEGMENT
        PUSH    DS      ; DS to stack
        POP     ES      ; Now ES = DS
        LEA     SI,STRING1   ; Source pointer
        LEA     DI,STRING2   ; Destination pointer
        MOV     CX,10        ; Character counter
        CLD                  ; Compare forward
REPE    CMPSB           ; Compare strings, byte-by-byte
                        ; until CX = 0
; In this case CX not zero and ZF clear since the strings
; are different at the sixth character
```

CMPXCHG

[Assembler] 486 machine instruction. Mnemonic for CoMPare and eX-CHanGe. CMPXCHG requires three operands. The source must be a machine register. The destination can be either a machine register or a memory variable. The third operand is the accumulator, which can be either AL, AX, or EAX. If the value in the destination and the accumulator are equal then CMPXCHG replaces the destination operand with the source. In this case ZF is set. Otherwise, the destination operand is loaded into the accumulator. In either case the flags are set as if the destination operand had been subtracted from the accumulator. CMPXCHG is primarily intended for manipulating semaphores at the operating system level.
(See also: CMPXCHG8B).

CMPXCHG8B

[Assembler] Pentium machine instruction. Mnemonic for CoMPare and eX-CHanGe eight Bytes. CMPXCHG8B requires three operands. The source must be a 64-bit value in ECX:EBX. The destination must be a memory variable. The third operand is the accumulator pair EDX:EAX. If the values in the destination and the accumulator are equal then CMPXCHG8B replaces the destination operand with the source. In this case ZF is set. Otherwise, the destination operand is loaded into the accumulator. In either case the flags are set as if the destination operand had been subtracted from the accumulator. CMPXCHG8b

is primarily intended for manipulating semaphores at the operating system level.
(See also: CMPXCHG).

COLOR (statement)

[BASIC] [QuickBASIC] Sets the colors for the foreground, background, and screen border. The syntax of the COLOR statement depends on whether the active video mode is text or, as set by the SCREEN statement.
When BASIC is first started, the color is initially set to white on black. In text mode set the following color attributes are possible:

```
Foreground      1 of 16 color attributes
                character blink is optional
Background      1 of 8 color attributes
Border          1 of 16 color attributes
```

TEXT MODES:
Statement format:

```
COLOR [foreground] [,[background] [,border]]
```

where foreground is a numeric expression in the range 0 to 31, representing the character color. Background is a numeric expression in the range 0 to 7 determining the background color. Border is a numeric expression in the range 0 to 15 determining the screen border.
In 16-color modes the following colors are available as foreground:

```
0 Black      8 Gray
1 Blue       9 Light Blue
2 Green      10 Light Green
3 Cyan       11 Light Cyan
4 Red        12 Light Red
5 Magenta    13 Light Magenta
6 Brown      14 Yellow
7 White      15 High-intensity White
```

Colors 8 to 15 can be considered as "light" or "high-intensity" values of colors 0 to 7.
Characters can be made to blink by setting foreground equal to 16 plus the number of the desired color. That is, a value range from of 16 to 31 causes blinking characters. Only colors 0 through 7 are available for the background attribute in text mode.
In the monochrome modes the following foreground attributes are available:

```
0            Black
1            Underlined character with standard
```

```
                        foreground color
          2 to 7 Standard foreground color
```

The following background attributes are available in the monochrome text modes:

```
     0-6          Black
     7            Standard foreground color
```

Note: Attribute 7 as a background attribute appears as the standard color only when it is used with a foreground attribute of 0, 8, 16, or 24 (black). By the same token, black (attributes 0, 8, 16, or 24) as a foreground attribute shows up as black only when used with a background attribute that creates reverse image characters. Black used with a background attribute of 0 makes the characters invisible.

In either the monochrome or color modes the following should be noted:

1. The foreground attribute can equal background attribute. This makes any character displayed invisible. Changing the foreground or the background attribute makes subsequent characters visible again.

2. Any parameter can be omitted. Omitted parameters assume the previously installed value.

3. A Missing Operand Error is produced if the COLOR statement ends in a comma (,), but the color change takes place.

4. Any values entered outside the range 0 to 255 result in an illegal function call error. Previous values are retained.

Example:

```
     ' Set foreground to yellow, background to blue, and border
     ' color to black in a color text mode
     COLOR 14,1,0
```

GRAPHICS MODE:
Statement format:

```
     COLOR [background] [, [palette]]
```

where background is an integer in the range 0 to 15 which specifies the background attribute. Palette is either 0 or 1 and selects a palette color. Color attribute 0 is always the current background. COLOR can select one of three color attributes for the foreground color to be used with PSET, PRESET, LINE, CIRCLE, PAINT, VIEW, and DRAW.

In BASIC the COLOR statement in graphics mode has meaning only for medium resolution. Using COLOR in high resolution results in an Illegal function call error. The colors selected with each palette are as follows:

Color	Palette 0	Palette 1
1	Green	Cyan
2	Red	Magenta
3	Brown	White

In QuickBASIC text-only mode (SCREEN 0) COLOR produces either special effects (such as underlined text) or colors, depending on the type of monitor. In screen mode 1, two palettes of four colors each are available. The statement format is:

```
COLOR background, palette
```

Text appears in color 3 of the selected palette and graphics may be displayed in any color of that palette.

In VGA modes 7, 8, and 9, a palette of 16 colors is available for text and graphics. In this case the statement format is:

```
COLOR foreground, background
```

where the foreground color and background colors are assigned to the respective palette entries, range 0 to 15.

In VGA and MCGA modes 1, 2, and 13, the statement format is:

```
COLOR foreground
```

where foreground is the number of a palette entry. In this case the background is set with the statement:

```
PALETTE 0, color
```

Color Graphics Adapter (CGA)

[historical] [video systems] The CGA was the first color and graphics card developed and distributed by IBM for the Personal Computer. The card displays in the following modes:

1. *Mode 0.* 40 by 25 black-and-white alphanumeric mode. The text characters are displayed in 16 shades of grey. Characters are double width, and only 40 can be fitted on a screen line. This mode is not compatible with the Monochrome Display Adapter.

2. *Mode 1.* 40 by 25 color alphanumeric mode. Double-width characters in the same format as mode 0, but in color. This mode is not compatible with the Monochrome Display Adapter.

3. *Mode 2.* 80 by 25 black-and-white alphanumeric mode. The text characters are displayed in 16 shades of grey. 80 characters are displayed per screen line. The screen structure in this mode is compatible with that of the Monochrome Display Adapter.

4. *Mode 3*. 80 by 25 color alphanumeric mode. The text characters are displayed with 16 possible foreground colors and 8 possible background colors. The screen structure in this mode is compatible with that of the Monochrome Display Adapter.

5. *Modes 4, 5, and 6*. These are the graphics modes. In these modes the programmer can control the state of each individual screen dot, also called a picture element or pixel. Mode 4 is in color, and modes 5 and 6 are in monochrome.

COM(n) (statement)

[QuickBASIC] Enables, disables, or defers trapping of the nth communications port. The statement format is:

```
COM n
```

where *n* is ON, OFF, or STOP.

Comma operator

[C] The comma (,) is used in C both as a separator and as an operator. In this last context it is usually called the sequential evaluation operator. In practice, the action of the comma operator is primarily limited to identifying compound elements in a *for* loop.

Comments

[C] The lines

```
/* C program to calculate the area of a circle */
/*          Program name: AREA.C              */
```

are program comments. The symbols /* are used in C to mark the start of a text area that is ignored by the compiler. The symbols */ indicate the end of the *comment*. Comments are used to document or explain program operation. The actual contents of a comment are ignored by the program. In this example a separate comment for each line is used, but the two text lines can be included in a single program comment.

COMMON (statement)

[BASIC] [QuickBASIC] Passes a variable to a chained program. Statement format is:

```
COMMON variable [,variable]]
```

where variable is the name of the variable passed to the chained program. Arrays can be specified by appending "()" to the variable name. COMMON statement is used with the CHAIN statement. It is recommended that COMMON appear at the beginning of the program.

Although the names of corresponding COMMON variables need not be the same, corresponding variables must be of the same type. The type of each variable is either determined by a type-declaration tag or by inserting words of the form AS type. When the statement in the form:

```
COMMON SHARED var1, var2,...
```

appears in a program, the specified variables are shared with all procedures in the program. COMMON statements must appear before any executable statements in a program. COMMON statements may not appear inside a procedure.

Communications

[**PC hardware and architecture**] Computer communications refer to the exchange of data between computers and terminals and to the transmission of data to processing devices. The definition includes data transmission to any type of peripheral equipment and through any type of internal or external, wired or wireless data path. In this sense it is correct to refer to communications between a computer and devices such as the keyboard, the video display, the diskette, the hard disk drive, or even a satellite in space, as data communications.

However, in the context of PC hardware, communication facilities usually refer to the serial port, the parallel port, the various modems, and networking.

Communications hardware

[**PC hardware and architecture**] Independent vendors furnish additional cards or devices that serve as PC communications ports. Some of these cards provide either a parallel or a serial port, or both. These devices are more popular for machines of the PC line, since serial and parallel ports are part of the standard hardware in the models of the PS/2 line and the PC compatible machines. Modems are not a standard component in most PC microcomputer, and are usually purchased separately as internal or external add-ons.

In the PC line the parallel port is output-only and is used almost exclusively as a printer interface. In the PS/2 line, and many PC compatibles, the parallel port is bidirectional. Normally, the serial port follows the RS-232-C communications protocol, but serial cards for newer standards are available.

Communications — parallel

[PC hardware and architecture] Serial communication methods transmit data consecutively, in the form of electrical pulses over the same physical line. In parallel communications the data bits are transmitted simultaneously, over different lines. The most obvious advantage of parallel data transmission is a higher speed. The disadvantages are that more connecting elements are required in the physical interface and that parallel transmission is more sensitive to noise and interference. In spite of this high-speed capability, microcomputer systems have traditionally used the parallel port primarily as a printer output.

Communications — serial

[PC hardware and architecture] Serial communications take place by transmitting and receiving data in a stream of consecutive electrical pulses that represent bits. The Electronic Industries Association (EIA) has sponsored the development of several standards for serial communications, such as RS-232-C, RS-422, RS-423, and RS-449. In this designation the characters RS stand for the words Recommended Standard. The simplest to implement and most used serial communications standard is the RS-232-C voltage level convention.

Compound assignment operators

[C] A set of convenience operators that provides a way for writing more compact code by allowing the combination of the simple assignment operator (=) with an arithmetic or bitwise operator. For example, to add 4 to the variable x we can code

```
x = x + 4;
```

or we can combine the addition operator (+) with the simple assignment operator (=) and code

```
x += 4;
```

In both cases the final value of x is the initial value plus 4, but the latter form reduces the size of the program. This combination of the simple assignment operator with any other binary operator is often called a compound assignment.

Note that the simple assignment operator always comes last in the compound assignment and that the compound assignment form cannot be used with the NOT (~) bitwise unary operator or with the unary increment (+ +) or decrement (- -) operator. This is because a unary (one element) statement does not require a simple assignment; therefore the compound assignment form is meaningless.

C Compound Assignment Operators

OPERATOR	DESCRIPTION
+=	Compound assignment addition
-=	Compound assignment subtraction
*=	Compound assignment multiplication
/=	Compound assignment division
%=	Compound assignment remainder
&=	Compound assignment bitwise AND
|=	Compound assignmemt bitwise OR
^=	Compound assignment bitwise XOR
<<=	Compound assignment left shift
>>=	Compound assignment right shift

Compound statement

(See statement blocks).

CONCAT

[MS-Pascal] Heading: (VARS D: LSTRING; CONSTS S: STRING);
String intrinsic procedure that concatenates S to the end of D. The length of D increases by the length of S. An error occurs if D is too small, i.e., if UPPER (D) < D.LEN + UPPER (S).

conditional expressions

[C] A special construct that allows operating on three different variables. This construct, which is the only ternary structure in C, uses the two conditional operators ? and : in the following manner:

```
exp1 ? exp2 : exp3
```

This conditional expression performs a similar function as the *if-else* construct. For example, to assign to the variable min_val the smaller of two integer variables, *a* and *b*, we could code

```
if (a < b) {
        min_val = a;
    else
        min_val = b;
}
```

Using the conditional construct we can code

```
min_val = (a < b) ? a : b;
```

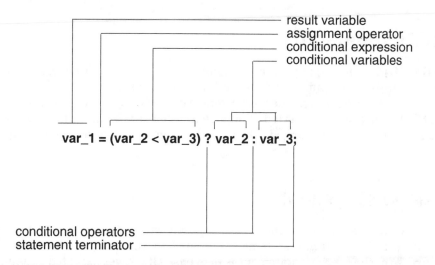

Structure of the C Conditional Construct

Observe, in this statement, that the conditional expression is formed by the elements to the right of the assignment operator (=). In a conditional expression we can distinguish three operands: The first operand [in this case (a < b)] evaluates either to logical true (1) or to false (0). If it evaluates to true, then the value of the expression is the second operand (in this case the variable a). On the other hand, if $(a < b)$ evaluates to false, then the value of the conditional expression is the third operand (in this case the variable b).

conditional statements

[C] Some simple computer programs consist of operations that are performed in sequence, however, most practical applications require decision-making operations in order to choose among two or more possible processing options available at a certain time. C provides several decision-making structures that make it possible for a program to select between two or more processing options. The major decision-making mechanisms in C are the *if* and the *switch* constructs. The conditional operator (?:) can be used in decision making.

CONST (statement)

[QuickBASIC] Replace every occurrence of the named constant with the value of the expression. The statement format is:

```
CONST name = expression
```

The replacement takes place before any lines of the program are executed. Unlike LET, CONST does not set up a location in the program's memory for a variable. The assigned value is called a "symbolic" or "named" constant.

CONT (command)

[BASIC] Resumes program execution (continues). The statement is used to resume execution after Ctrl-Break has been pressed or a STOP or END statement has executed. The most common use of CONT is in debugging, where a STOP statement is inserted to break execution so that the value of variables can be examined or changed. The CONT statement is not available in Quick-BASIC.

continue statement

[C] While the *break* statement can be used with either a switch or a loop construct, the *continue* statement operates in relation only to loops. The purpose of the *continue* statement is to bypass all not-yet-executed statements in the loop and return to the beginning of the loop construct. Continue can be used with *for*, *while*, and *do* loops. For example, the following program contains a *for* loop to display the letters A to D; however, the *continue* statement serves to bypass the letter C, which is not displayed:

```
#include <stdio.h>
main()
{
    unsigned char letter;
        for (letter = 'A'; letter < 'E'; letter ++) {
            if (letter == 'C')
                continue;
            printf("  letter is: %c\n", letter);
        }
}
```

Like the *goto* statement, the abuse of the *continue* statement often leads to code that is difficult to follow and decipher.

convenience operators

[C] A group of operators that performs functions designed to make the language easier to use, to improve performance, or to make the code more compact or readable. These operators can typically be substituted by other expressions. The convenience operators include increment (++) and decrement (--), and the compound assignment operators.

COPYLST

[MS-Pascal] Heading: (CONSTS S: STRING; VARS D: LSTRING);

String intrinsic procedure that copies S to LSTRING D. The length of D is set to UPPER (S). An error occurs if the length of S is greater than the maximum length of D, i.e., if UPPER (S)> UPPER (D).

COPYSTR

[MS-Pascal] Heading: (CONSTS S: STRING; VARS D: STRING);
String intrinsic procedure that copies S to STRING D. The remainder of D is set to blanks if UPPER (S) < UPPER (D). An error occurs if the length of S is greater than the maximum length of D, i.e., if UPPER (S) > UPPER (D).

COS

[MS-Pascal] Heading: (X: NUMERIC): REAL;
Arithmetic function which returns the cosine of X in radians. Both X and the return value are of type REAL. To force a particular precision, declare CNSRQQ (CONSTS REAL4) and/or CNDRQ& (CONSTS REAL8) and use them instead.

COS (function)

[BASIC] [QuickBASIC] Calculates the trigonometric cosine function of the angle in radians.

CPU architecture

(See microprocessor).

CPUID

[Assembler] Pentium machine instruction. Mnemonic for CPU Identification. Provides information to software about the vendor, family, model, and stepping of the microprocessor on which it is executing. An input value loaded into the EAX register indicates what information should be returned by the instruction. Following execution of the CPUID instruction with a zero in EAX, the EAX register holds the highest input value understood by the CPUID instruction. For the Pentium processor, the value in EAX is a one. In this case the instruction also provides a vendor identification string contained in the EBX, EDX, and ECX. Four characters are stored in each register. For Intel processors, the vendor identification string "GenuineIntel" is stored as follows:

```
EBX = "Genu", with G in the low nibble of BL
EDX = "ineI", with i in the low nibble of DL
ECX = "ntel", with n in the low nibble of CL
```

If the CPUID instruction is executed with a value of 1 in EAX the returned information is bitmapped as follows:

```
REGISTER    BITS      DATA
   EAX      0-3       Microprocessor stepping id.
            4-7       Model code (first modes is 0001B)
            8-11      Family (5 = Pentium)
            12-31     RESERVED
   EBC      0-31      RESERVED
   ECX      0-31      RESERVED
   EDX      0         1 = FPU on chip
            1-6       Confidential Intel information
            7         1 = Machine Check Exception supported
            8         1 = CMPXCHG8B instruction supported
            9-31      RESERVED
```

CSNG (function)

[BASIC] [QuickBASIC] Converts integer, long integer, and double-precision numbers to single-precision numbers.

CSRLIN (variable)

[BASIC] [QuickBASIC] Returns the screen line at which the cursor is located.

CVI, CVL, CVS, CVD (functions)

[BASIC] [QuickBASIC] Convert string variables to numeric variables, as follows:

```
CVI              converts a 2-byte string
CVL/CVS          convert a 4-byte string
CVD              converts an 8-byte string
```

These statements provide a way for converting string values read from random-access files into numeric values.
(See also: MKI$, MKS$, and MKD$).

CVSMBF/CVDMBF (functions)

[QuickBASIC] Convert single- and double-precision numbers that have been converted to strings by earlier versions of BASIC (GWBASIC, BASICA, and early versions of QuickBASIC) and entered into random-access files, back into numeric formats. CVSNBF is used for single-precision and CVDMBF for double-precision.

CWD

[Assembler] 8086 machine instruction. Mnemonic for Convert Word to Doubleword. Extends the sign bit (bit 15) of the AX register to all bits of the DX register, thus converting a signed word into a signed doubleword. CWD can produce unexpected results with unsigned operands.
Code sample:

```
        MOV     AX,0F0F0H      ; Bit 15 is set
        CWD                    ; Extend bit 15 to DX
; DX now is FFFFH
        MOV     AX,0F0FH       ; Bit 15 is clear
        CWD                    ; Extend bit 15 to DX
; DX now is 0000H
```

CWDE

[Assembler] 80386 machine instruction. Mnemonic for Convert Word to Doubleword Extended. Extends the sign bit (bit 15) of the AX register to all bits of the EAX register, thus converting a signed word into a signed doubleword. CWDE is different from CWD since CWD uses the DX:AX register pair while CWDE uses the EAX register as a destination. CWDE can produce unexpected results with unsigned operands.
Code sample:

```
        MOV     AX,0F0F0H      ; AX bit 15 is set
        CWDE                   ; Extend bit 15 to EAX
; EAX most significant word now is FFFFH
        MOV     AX,0F0FH       ; Bit 15 is clear
        CWDE                   ; Extend bit 15 to DX
; EAX most significant word now is 0000H
```

D

DAA

[Assembler] 8086 machine instruction. Mnemonic for Decimal Adjust after Addition. Intel terminology refers to packed BCD numbers as decimal numbers. For this reason, the word *decimal*, as used in the opcode DAA, refers to packed BCD digits. DAA adjusts the result after adding two valid packed BCD digits in the AL register. CF is set if there is a carry out of the high digit, that is, if the sum is larger than the value 99H. DAA updates AF, CF, PF, SF, and ZF. OF is undefined.

Code sample:

```
; Packed BCD adjustment performed by the DAA instruction
        MOV     AL,27H      ; AL now holds BCD digits 27
        MOV     AH,35H      ; AL holds the BCD digits 35
        ADD     AL,AH       ; AL = AL + AH
; At this point the sum in AL is the value 5CH
        DAA
; After adjustment AL = 62H
```

(See also: BCD and DAS).

DAS

[Assembler] 8086 machine instruction. Mnemonic for Decimal Adjust after Subtraction. Intel terminology refers to packed BCD numbers as decimal numbers. For this reason, the word *decimal*, as used in the opcode DAS, refers to packed BCD digits. DAS adjusts the contents of AL to two packed BCD digits after a subtraction operation. CF is set if a borrow was needed during the subtract. DAS updates AF, CF, PF, SF, and ZF. OF is undefined.

Code sample:

```
; Packed BCD adjustment performed by the DAS instruction
        MOV     AL,40H      ; AL now holds BCD digits 40
        MOV     AH,12H      ; AL holds the BCD digits 12
        SUB     AL,AH       ; AL = AL - AH
```

```
; At this point the sum in AL is the value 2EH
      DAS
; After adjustment AL = 28H
```

(See also: BCD and DAS).

Data conversion procedures and functions

[MS-Pascal] [Turbo Pascal] Procedures and functions to convert data from one type to another. The following are available in MS-Pascal:

```
*CHR        PACK        *TRUNC
FLOAT       PRED        TRUNC4
FLOAT4      *ROUND      UNPACK
ODD         ROUND4      WRD
*ORD        SUCC
```

The procedures marked with * are available in Turbo Pascal.

Data registers

(See machine registers).

DATA (statement)

[BASIC] [QuickBASIC] Stores numeric and string constant that are to be accessed by a READ statement. The statement format is:

```
DATA constant[,constant]...
```

where constant can be a numeric or string constant. Numeric data can be of any valid type or format. String constants need not be enclosed in quotation marks unless the string contains commas, colons, or blanks.
(See also: READ).

DATE

[MS-Pascal] Heading: (VAR S : STRING);
Clock procedure which assigns the current date to its STRING (or LSTRING) variable. If an LSTRING is passed as the parameter, the length must be set before calling the procedure. The format depends on the target operating system.

DATE$ (variable and statement)

[BASIC] [QuickBASIC] Obtains or sets the system date. The statement format is:

```
x$ = DATE$ 'obtain date (variable mode),
DATE$ = d$ 'set new date (statement mode)
```

where the current date is returns as a string in mm-dd-yyyy format.

DEC

[Assembler] 8086 machine instruction. Mnemonic for DECrement. Subtract one from the destination operand, which can be an 8-, 16-, or 32-bit register or the contents of a memory location. The operand is treated as an unsigned binary number. DEC updates AF, OF, PF, SF, and ZF. CF is not affected. Code sample:

```
; Subtract one using the DEC opcode
    MOV     AL,25       ; AL = 25
    DEC     AL          ; AL = 24
```

DECLARE SUB / DECLARE FUNCTION

[QuickBASIC] Indicates that the specified procedure is called by the program. The statement format:

```
DECLARE SUB name [param1, param2,...], or
DECLARE FUNCTION name [param1, param2.,,,]
```

where name is the subroutine or function name and param1, param2 are one or more optional parameters. DECLARE statements for each procedure are automatically inserted at the top of the program when it is saved. DECLARE statements may not appear inside procedures. The type of each parameter is either determined by a type-declaration tag or by the AS keyword. The parameters must match the corresponding parameter types in the procedure definition.

An empty pair of parentheses indicates a procedure without parameters. QuickBASIC uses the DECLARE statements to check that subprogram calls use the proper number and types of arguments.

DECODE

[MS-Pascal] Heading: (CONST LSTR : LSTRING, X: M: N): BOOLEAN;
Extend level intrinsic function that converts the character string in the LSTRING to its internal representation and assigns this to X. If the character string is not a valid external ASCII representation of a value whose type is

assignment compatible with X, DECODE returns FALSE and the value of X is undefined.

DECODE works exactly the same as the READ procedure, including the use of M and N parameters. When X is a subrange, DECODE returns FALSE if the value is out of range (regardless of the setting of the range checking switch.) Leading and trailing spaces and tabs in the LSTRING are ignored. All other characters in the LSTRING must be part of the representation.

X must be one of the types INTEGER, WORD, enumerated, one of their subranges, BOOLEAN, REAL4, REAL8, INTEGER4, or a pointer (address types need the .R or .S suffix).

In a segmented memory environment, the LSTR parameter must reside in the default data segment.

(See also: ENCODE).

DEF FN/END DEF (statements)

[BASIC] [QuickBASIC] Defines a user-created function. The format is:

```
DEF FN name [(arg [,arg]...)] = expression
```

where name is the function name, arg is one or more optional arguments, and expression defines the returned value. The type of expression (string or numeric) must match the type declared by the name field. The function definition ends with the END DEF statement. The items appearing in the argument list constitute the input for the function. If a statement is in the form: name = expression, then the output of the function is an expression.

User-created functions must be defined before they are used, otherwise an Undefined user function error takes place. This means that the function must physically appear earlier in the source text than its call. Variables inside a multiline block are global, unless they are declared early in the block to be static by a statement of the form:

```
STATIC var1, var2,...
```

Static variables are not accessible outside of the block, but they retain their values between subsequent calls to the function. An alternative, perhaps better, method for creating user-defined functions is by means of the FUNCTION statement which supports recursion and may take arrays and records as arguments.

DEF SEG (statement)

[BASIC] [QuickBASIC] Defines the current segment for a subsequent BLOAD, BSAVE, CALL, PEEK, POKE, or DEF USR statement. The statement format is:

```
DEF SEG = n
```

where n specifies that the current segment of memory in the range 0 to 65535. Segment addresses are located at 16-byte boundaries therefore the value entered in the DEF SEG statement is shifted left four bits to form the actual segment address. This means that the statement:

```
DEF SEG = &HB800
```

corresponds to physical address &HB8000. A statement DEF SEG with no operands restores the current segment to BASIC's data segment. Note that DEF and SEG must be separated by a space.

DEF USR (statement)

[BASIC] Specifies the location in memory of an assembly language program which is later accessed by the USR function. The statement format is:

```
DEF USR[n] = offset
```

where n is a digit in the range 0 to 9, which optionally identifies one of ten possible routines whose location is being defined. Offset is an integer in the range 0 to 65535. This value is added to the segment value, as determined by the DEF SEG statement, to actually locate the subroutine within the segment.

DEFtype (statements)

Forms: DEFINT, DEFLNG, DEFSNG, DEFDBL, and DEFSTR
[BASIC] [QuickBASIC] Declares a variable type and letter range as integer (DEFINT), single-precision (DEFLNG and DEFSNG), double-precision (DEFDBL), and string (DEFSTR). The statement format is:

```
DEFtype letter[-letter][,letter[-letter]]...
```

where type is INT, LNG, SNG, DBL, or STR, and letter is one of the letters of the alphabet. For example, a statement in the form:

```
DEFINT A-C
```

specifies that any "untyped" variable whose name begins with the letter range A to C is of integer type. A DEFtype statement is automatically displayed before procedures created after the DEFtype statement is placed in the main body of the program. Specific type declarations with the symbols %, !, #, or $ take precedence over a DEFtype statement.

DELETE

[MS-Pascal] Heading: (VARS D: LSTRING; I, N: INTEGER) ;
String intrinsic procedure which deletes N characters from D, starting with
D[I]. An error occurs if an attempt is made to delete more characters, starting
at I, than exist.

DELETE (command)

[BASIC] Delete program lines. Command format:

```
DELETE [line1][-line2]
```

where line1 is the number of the first program line to be deleted and line2 is
that last program line.
Example:

```
DELETE 20-100   'deletes program lines 20 through 100
DELETE 120-     'deletes from line 100 to end of program
DELETE 10       'deletes line 10
DELETE -40      'deletes all lines up to and including line 40
```

DIM (statement)

[BASIC] [QuickBASIC] Allocates storage and dimensions an array variable.
Statement format is:

```
DIM name(subs)[,var(subs)]...
```

where name is the name of the array and subs is a list of numeric expressions,
separated by commas, which define the array dimensions. The range of subs is
-32768 to 32767. In QuickBASIC the statement format:

```
DIM name(m TO n)
```

declares an array with subscripts ranging from m to n, inclusive. A statement
of the form:

```
DIM name(m TO n, o TO p)
```

declares a two-dimensional array. Three- and higher- dimensional arrays are
declared similarly. The term SHARED after the word DIM in the main body of
a program allows all procedures to access the array or variable.

Direct Memory Access (DMA)

[PC hardware and architecture] The CPU has many chores to perform in a microcomputer system. Some of these chores can be temporarily delayed while the processor handles another task, but others require immediate attention. For example, honoring an interrupt request that originated in the system timer, removing data read by a disk controller, and refreshing a memory cell about to lose its contents are operations that cannot be postponed without consequence. One way of preventing this possibility of conflict is to have an alternative mechanism for the direct control of memory access (DMA). An added advantage of this scheme is a substantial improvement in the system's memory read-write performance.

All IBM and compatible microcomputers (except for the PCjr) use direct memory access hardware. The computers of the PC line and those of the PS/2 line that do not have Micro Channel architecture (the Model 25 and Model 30) use the Intel 8237A-5 DMA controller chip. The computers of the PS/2 line with Micro Channel use a proprietary IBM VLSI component for direct memory access. This IBM chip is compatible with the 8237 but has additional capabilities that are not available in the Intel DMA component.

The DMA controllers used in IBM microcomputers are programmable and managed by the CPU. Usually, the processor loads the DMA chip with a start address where the transfer is to take place and a count for the number of bytes to be transferred. A command to start the transfer is then issued, and the DMA device takes over the system's address and data busses. At this point the processor is free to perform other operations while the transfer of data between the input/output device and memory is handled by the DMA component.

DISBIN

[MS-Pascal] Library routine. DISBIN disables interrupts; ENABIN enables interrupts; VECTTN sets an interrupt vector. The effect of these procedures varies with the target machine.

DISCARD

[MS-Pascal] Heading: (VAR P);
File system procedure (extend level I/O). Closes and deletes an open file.

Diskette and microdisk

[PC hardware and architecture] [historical] A popular medium for microcomputer data storage which consists of a thin, polyester disk coated with a metal oxide similar to that used in magnetic tapes. These magnetic disks are known as diskettes, floppy disks, floppies, and microdisks. Diskettes are manufactured in 8, 5 1/4-in, and 3 1/2-in diameters. The 8-in diskette size is not used in IBM microcomputers. The 5 1/4-in diskettes are used in all IBM microcomputers of the PC line except the PC convertible, which uses 3 1/2-in diskettes. All models of the PS/2 line use the 3 1/2-in diskette size. The 3 1/2-in diskettes come in a rigid plastic case and are sometimes called microdisks, microdiskettes, and micro floppy disks.

Information is stored on the magnetic surface of a diskette in a pattern of concentric circles called *tracks*. Each track is divided into areas called *sectors*. The read-write mechanism, similar to the ones used in tape recorders, can be moved from track to track by a stepper motor while the diskette spins on its axis.

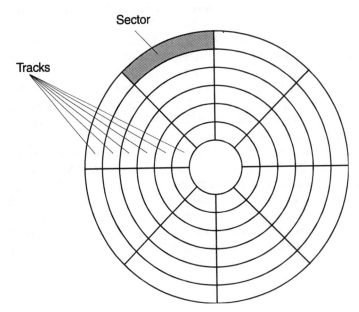

Diskette Tracks and Sectors

Diskette sectoring can be based on physical or magnetic divisions of the diskette's surface. The physical type of division is called *hard-sectoring*, and the magnetic division is called *soft-sectoring*. All IBM microcomputer diskette systems use soft-sectoring. IBM soft-sector technology uses one small hole near the center of the diskette, which is sensed by a photodiode as the start of the first sector. Thereafter, a special bit pattern identifies the start and end of the remaining sectors in each track.

Diskette and microdisk data in BIOS

[PC hardware and architecture] Many FDC commands require technical data regarding the setup and parameters of the diskette system. During the initialization routines of the POST, the IBM BIOS determines and stores the basic parameters of the diskette or microdisk system. These data, sometimes called the diskette table, are stored in an 11-byte area whose address is located by the vector for interrupt 1EH.

IBM Diskette Drive Parameter Table

OFFSET	BYTES	DESCRIPTION
0	2	Drive specification bytes
2	1	Count of timer ticks to wait before turning diskette motor OFF
3	1	Code for bytes per sector: 00 = 128 bytes 01 = 256 bytes 02 = 512 bytes (IBM standard format) 03 = 1024 bytes
4	1	Number of sectors per track
5	1	Gap length parameter
6	1	Data length parameter
7	1	Gap length for format
8	1	Fill byte to use during format
9	1	Head settle time (in milliseconds)
10	1	Motor start-up time (in 1/8 s)

Diskette and microdisk drive controller

[PC hardware and architecture] The operation and command of a diskette or microdisk drive is done through the electronic circuitry and the programmable chips contained in the drive controller. In some PC implementations the controller is furnished as an adapter card that fits in a standard or a special-purpose slot, while in others the drive controller is part of the motherboard. In most systems the diskette drive controller is a dedicated device, but in the PC AT the diskette drive controller is part of the Fixed Disk and Diskette Adapter.

The following are the fundamental functions of the drive controller:

1. To select the disk drive that will be enabled for the particular operation

2. To select the desired recording head. This function is active in double-sided systems only

3. To issue the sequence of commands necessary for moving the recording head to any desired track

4. To monitor the data on a track until a specific sector is located under the recording head

5. To issue commands to load and unload the recording head

6. To read data stored on the diskette's surface and write data onto the media surface

7. To detect errors caused by defective media, by electromagnetic noise, or by mechanical defects in the system

Diskette and microdisk drives

[PC hardware and architecture] The diskette and microdisk drive is an electromechanical device for recording data on the media's surface and for reading the recorded data. The various diskette and microdisk drives used in the IBM microcomputers vary according to media type, number of read-write heads, drive size, recording technology, and performance.

Diskette Drives in the IBM PC

MEDIA SIZE	DESIGNATION	SYSTEM	COMPATIBLE CONTROLLER
5¼-inch	5¼-in Diskette Drive (single-side)	PC	5¼-in Diskette Drive Adapter
	5¼-in Diskette Drive (double-side)	PC, XT	5¼-in Diskette Drive Adapter
	5¼-in Slimline Diskette Drive	PC, XT, Portable	5¼-in Diskette Drive Adapter
	5¼-in PCjr Diskette Drive	PCjr	PCjr Diskette Drive Adapter
	Double-Sided Diskette Drive	AT	Fixed Disk and Diskette Drive Adapter
	High Capacity Diskette Drive	AT	Fixed Disk and Diskette Drive Adapter
	PS/2 External Diskette Drive	Model 25 Model 30	5¼-in External Diskette Drive Adapter
		Micro Channel	5¼-in External Diskette Drive Adapter/A
3½-inch	720K Diskette Drive	PC Convertible	Diskette Drive Controller (on system board)
		Model 25 Model 30	Diskette Drive Interface (on system board)
	1.4/2.8-Mbyte Diskette Drive	PS/2 Micro Channel	Diskette Drive Controller (on system board)
	External Diskette Drive Model 001	PC, XT, Portable	Diskette Drive Adapter
	External Diskette Drive Model 002	AT XT 286	Model 002 Adapter Card
	Internal Diskette Drive	Specific models of the PC line	3½-in Internal Diskette Drive Adapter Card

All PC diskette and microdisk drives are capable of performing the following fundamental operations:

1. Spin the media on its axis at a fixed number of revolutions per minute.

2. Move the recording head in the direction of the media's center in discrete intervals or steps.

3. Move the recording head into contact with the media surface (load) at read-write time and away from the surface (unload) during positioning operations. This maneuver is designed to prevent excessive friction and disk wear.

4. Provide signals to the controller regarding the status of the drive and the installed media, for example:

   a   A track zero sensor informs the controller when the recording head is positioned over track number zero.

   b. An index sensor generates a signal every time the diskette's sector hole passes over a phototransistor.

   c. A write-protect sensor detects if the media has been mechanically protected from write operations.

All PC systems allow more than one physical diskette drive to be connected to the controller. This is achieved by means of a jumper or selector, located on the drive, which is set to a specific drive number. The drive is enabled when the controller emits the corresponding command containing the drive's number. When a drive is not selected, it ignores all signals on the interface.

Diskette and microdisk hardware

[PC hardware and architecture] The hardware required for the operation of a diskette storage system consists of the following elements:
1. A removable magnetic medium (the diskette or microdisk itself).
2. A diskette or microdisk drive mechanism furnished with rotational and stepper motors, and with other gadgetry required to hold and spin the diskette and to move the recording head or heads along the diskette tracks.
3. A drive controller containing the programmable and nonprogrammable electronic components necessary to operate the device.

Diskette and microdisk storage media

[PC hardware and architecture] There are several types of diskettes used in the IBM microcomputers. The most obvious difference is between the 5 1/4-in diskettes and the 3 1/2-in microdisks; however, there are other variations in diskettes of the same size.

PC Removable Magnetic Media

DISKETTE SIZE	TYPE	SYSTEMS	FORMATTED CAPACITY	MEDIA SPECIFICATIONS
5¼-in	1	PC	160K or 180K	Single side, double density, soft sectors
	2	PC, PC XT, PCjr	320K or 360K	Double side, double density, soft sectors
	3	PC AT	1.2 Mbytes	High-capacity double side, quad density, soft sectors
3½-in	4	PS/2 Model 25 Model 30	720K	Double side, double density, 1.0-Mbyte capacity
	5	PS/2 Micro Channnel	1.4 Mbytes	Double side, high-density 2.0-Mbyte capacity
	6		2.8 Mbytes	Double side, high-capacity 4.0-Mbyte capacity

Diskette and microdisk storage structures

[PC hardware and architecture] In the PC the structuring and programming of diskette and disk devices is left almost entirely to operating system software. To ensure compatibility with DOS, Windows and OS/2 have maintained the same disk and diskette storage structures and formats. For this reason, magnetic media formatted in either system can be read and written by the other one. References to DOS data structures can be considered applicable to OS/2, unless noted otherwise.

PC Diskette Storage Formats

STORAGE MEDIUM	SIDES	TRACKS	SECTORS	BYTES PER SECTOR	CAPACITY	DOS
5¼-in floppy disk SS/DD/48 TPI	1	40	8	512	160K	1.1
	1	40	9	512	180K	1.2+
5¼-in floppy disk DS/DD/48 TPI	2	40	8	512	320K	2.0
	2	40	9	512	360K	2.0+
5¼-in floppy disk DS/QD/96 TPI	2	80	15	512	1.2 Mbytes	3.0+
3½-in microdisk DS/DD/135 TPI	2	80	9	512	720K	3.0+
3½-in microdisk DS/HD/135 TPI	2	80	18	512	1.4 Mbytes	3.0+
3½-in microdisk DS/HD/170 TPI	2	80	36	512	2.8 Mbytes	3.0+

The patterns and densities used for storing magnetic data on the diskette's surface have changed in the different PCs. The original diskette drives, operating under DOS versions 1.1 and 1.2, were equipped with a single read-write head; therefore only one side of the diskette contained data. With the introduction of DOS 2.0, the single-sided drives were replaced by double-sided diskettes and drives. These drives are equipped with a recording head for each diskette surface. The magnetic track density on the diskette's surface has gone from 48 tracks per inch in the drives of the PC line (double density), to 96 tracks per inch in the PC AT (quad density), and to 135 and 170 tracks per inch in the 3 1/2-in microdisks of the PC convertible and the PS/2 line. The amount of data recorded in each sector has remained at 512 bytes for all IBM disk and diskette systems.

DISMQQ

[MS-Pascal] Heading: (BLOCK: ADSMEM);
Library routine (segmented heap management function) which takes an ADSMEM generated by ALLMQQ or GETMQQ and invokes FREMQQ to return the space described by the ADSMEM to the long heap memory pool. If errors occur, runtime messages are generated.

DISPOSE

[MS-Pascal] Heading: (VARS P: POINTER);
Dynamic allocation procedure (short form) that releases the memory used for the variable pointed to by P. P must be a valid pointer; it may not be NIL, uninitialized, or pointing at a heap item that already has been DISPOSEd. These are checked if the NIL check switch is on.

P should not be a reference parameter or a WITH statement record pointer. A DISPOSE of a WITH statement record can be done at the end of the WITH statement without problem.

If the variable is a super array type or a record with variants, the short form of DISPOSE is used to release it, regardless of whether it was allocated with the long or short form of NEW. Using the short form of DISPOSE on a heap variable allocated with the long form of NEW is an ISO-defined error not detected in MS-Pascal.

DISPOSE

[MS-Pascal] Heading: (VARS P: POINTER;T1, T2,... TN:TAGS);
Dynamic allocation procedure (long form). The long form of DISPOSE works the same as the short form. However, the long form checks the size of the variable against the size implied by the tag field or array upper bound values T1, T2,... Tn. These tag values should be the same as defined in the corresponding NEW procedure.

(See also: SIZEOF function).

DIV

[Assembler] 8086 machine instruction. Mnemonic for DIVide. DIV performs the unsigned division of an implicit dividend, located in the accumulator register, by the explicit source operand. The three possibilities are shown in the following table:

SOURCE SIZE	DIVIDEND	QUOTIENT	REMAINDER
byte	AX	AL	AH
word	DX:AX	AX	DX
doubleword	EDX:EAX	EAX	EDX

If the quotient exceeds the capacity of the destination register, as is the case in a division by zero, an interrupt 0 is generated. In the PC environment an interrupt 0 handler is provided by the BIOS. AF, CF, OF, PF, SF, and ZF are undefined.

Code sample:

```
; Word division of 123456H by 600H
        MOV    BX,600H      ; Divisor to BX
        MOV    AX,3456H     ; High of dividend
        MOV    DX,12        ; Low of dividend
        DIV    BX           ; Word division
; At this point AX = 308H (quotient), DX = 456H (reminder)
```

(See also: AAD, IDIV).

DO/LOOP (statement)

[QuickBASIC] Mark the beginning of a block of program statements to be repeated in a loop. The statement formats are:

```
DO WHILE cond
DO UNTIL cond
LOOP WHILE cond
LOOP UNTIL cond
```

where cond is the condition that is used to mark the beginning of a block in the DO form, and the end of the block in the LOOP form. Each time a statement containing WHILE or UNTIL followed by a condition is encountered, the truth value of the condition determines whether the block should be repeated or whether the program should jump to the statement immediately following the block. A DO loop may be exited at any point with an EXIT DO statement.

Do while loop

[C] In the *do while* loop the *do* keyword allows changing the operation of a *while* loop so that the terminating condition is evaluated after the loop executes. This mode of operation ensures that the loop executes at least once. For example, the following *while* loop will not execute the statement body because the variable x evaluates to 0 before the first iteration:

```
#include <stdio.h>
main()
{
    int x;
    x = 0;                          /* initialization step   */
    while (x != 0)
        printf("%i", x);            /* processing step       */
}
```

However, the program can be modified to a *do while* loop as follows:

```
#include <stdio.h>
main()
{
    int x;
    x = 0;                          /* initialization step   */
    do
        printf("%i", x);            /* processing step       */
    while (x != 0);
}
```

In this case the loop's first iteration takes place because the test is not performed until the loop body executes.

Note that the processing performed by the *while* loop is identical to the one performed by the *do while*. The *while* expression in a *do while* loop terminates in a semicolon.

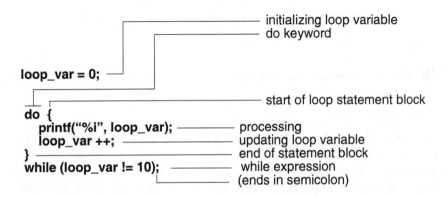

Structure of the C do while Loop

DRAW (statement)

[BASIC] [QuickBASIC] Draw a specified object defined in a string. The statement format is:

```
DRAW string
```

where string is a set of directions and parameters used to draw figures on the screen in much the same way figures are drawn with pencil and paper. The command strings constitute a small graphics language. The DRAW statement can be used to produce straight lines beginning at the last point referenced and extending in several directions. After each line is drawn, the end point of that line becomes the "last point referenced" for the next DRAW statement. The following movement commands are possible:

```
U n                      move up
D n                      move down
L n                      move left
R n                      move right
E n                      move up and right
F n                      move down and right
G n                      move down and left
H n                      move up and left
M x,y                    move absolute or relative. A + or - sign
                         in front of x indicate a relative move.
B (prefix)               move but do not plot
N (prefix)               move and return to original position
A n (command)            Set rotation angle to n * 90 degrees
TA n (command)           Turn angle by n degrees. Range of n
                         is -360 to +360. n positive indicates
                         clockwise rotation.
C n (command)            Set color n of current palette
S n (command)            Set scale to n/4 of original size.
                         Range of n is 1 to 255.
P c,b (command)          Fill closed region using border color b
                         and paint color c defined by the
                         current palette
```

If X is one of the directions and n is a number, then the statement format:

```
DRAW "Xn"
```

draws a line of *n* units in the specified direction. If a direction is preceded by the N command then the last point referenced does not change after the line is drawn. If direction is preceded by the B command, then an invisible line is drawn and the last point referenced changes to the endpoint of the invisible line. Several statements may be combined into a statement in the format:

```
DRAW "Xn Ym ..."
```

The DRAW statement does not account for nonsymmetrical screen modes, which must be compensated for in the data. The initial position of the drawing point is the screen center. In a symmetrical screen mode (such as VGA mode 18) a square is drawn by means of four equal moves.
Example:

```
'Program to draw a screen square in a symmetrical mode
 'and fill with color
CLS
SCREEN 12              'enable VGA mode 18 (640 by 480 pixels)
DRAW "BL320 BU240"  'move point to top-left screen corner
DRAW "R100 D100 L100 U100" 'draw 100 pixel square
```

Dynamic allocation procedures

[MS-Pascal] [Turbo Pascal] Procedures to allocate and deallocate data structures at runtime. MS Pascal dynamic allocation procedures are NEW, to allocate a variable in the heap, and DISPOSE, to release it. Turbo Pascal also provides FreeMem, GetMem, Mark, and Release.

E

EDIT (command)

[BASIC] Dipslays a line for editing. Command format is:

```
EDIT line
```

where line is the desired line number.

ENABIN

[MS-Pascal] Library routine (interrupt handling). Along with DISBIN and VECTIN, ENABIN handles interrupt processing. ENABIN enables interrupts; DISBIN disables interrupts; VECTIN sets an interrupt vector. The effect of these procedures may vary with the target machine.

ENCODE

[MS-Pascal] Heading: (VAR LSTR : LSTRING, X: M: N): BOOLEAN;
Extend level intrinsic function. Converts the expression X to its external ASCII representation and puts this character string into LSTR. Returns TRUE, unless the LSTRING is too small to hold the string generated. In this case, ENCODE returns FALSE: and the value of the LSTR is undefined. ENCODE works exactly the same as the WRITE procedure, including the use of M and N parameters.

   X must be of type INTEGER, WORD, enumerated, one of their subranges, BOOLEAN, REAL4, REAL8, INTEGER4, or a pointer (address types need the .R or .S suffix).

   In a segmented memory environment, the LSTR parameter must reside in the default data segment.
(See also: DECODE).

END (statement)

[BASIC] [QuickBASIC] Terminates the execution of the program, closes all files, and returns to the command level. The statements END DEF, END

FUNCTION, END IF, END SELECT, END SUB, and END TYPE are used to denote the conclusion of the respective functions, blocks, sub-programs, and user-defined record type declarations.

ENDOQQ

[MS-Pascal] Library procedure (termination). ENDOQQ is called during termination and the default version does nothing. However, you may write your own version of ENDOQQ, if you want, to invoke a debugger or to write customized messages, such as the time of execution, to a terminal screen. Since ENDOQQ is called after errors are processed, if ENDOQQ itself invokes an error, the result is an infinite termination loop. (See also: BEGOQQ).

ENDXQQ

[MS-Pascal] Termination procedure. ENDXQQ is the overall termination routine and performs the following actions:

1. Calls ENDOQQ

2. Closes any open files

3. Returns to the target operating system

ENDXQQ may be useful for ending program execution from inside a procedure or function, without calling ABORT. ENDXQQ corresponds to the HALT procedure in other versions of Pascal.

ENTER

[Assembler] 80286 machine instruction. Mnemonic for ENTER procedure. The ENTER instruction is used mostly in the coding of high-level language compilers in order to create a stack frame that allows the creation and access to local variables. The first operand determines the number of bytes allocated on the stack for local variables used by the called procedure. The second operand defines the nesting level, within the high-level language, of the procedure being called. If the operands are 16-bit elements then the processor uses the SP and BP registers. If the operands are 32-bit elements, then ESP and EBP are used. The format of the operands for the ENTER instructions is as follows:

```
ENTER  stack allocation, nesting level
```

If nesting level is zero then ENTER pushes the frame point in the stack (this subtracts two or four bytes from the original stack pointer), sets the frame pointer to the current stack pointer, and subtracts the stack allocation operand from the stack pointer. Note that the ENTER instruction is coded after the call

to the procedure. The LEAVE instruction restores the original stack and frame pointers and is coded before each RET in the procedure.
Code sample:

```
; Use of ENTER in a high-level procedure
DEMO   PROC   NEAR
; Assume that at access time to the procedure SS = 3FEH
; and SP = 000H
       ENTER  12,0   ; Allocation is 12 bytes
                     ; nesting level = 0
; At this point the following takes place:
;      BP -> stack (SP = 3FEH - 2H = 3FCH)
 ;        BP = SP (BP = 3FCH)
;      SP = SP - 12 (SP = 3FCH - CH = 3F0H)
; After the ENTER instruction code should not change the
; value of the base pointer register
            .
            .
            .
       LEAVE
; At this point SP and BP are restored to the values
; before ENTER. Data in the local frame is destroyed.
       RET
DEMO   ENDP
```

(See also: LEAVE).

ENVIRON (statement)

[BASIC] [QuickBASIC] Modifies the environment table. In QuickBASIC the environment table consists of equations of the form: name = value that is inherited from DOS. The ENVIRON statement modifies this table. The statement format:

```
ENVIRON "name-;"
```

removes any equation whose left side is name. The statement statement format:

```
ENVIRON "name = value"
```

places the element in quotes in the systems environment table.

ENVIRON$ (function)

[BASIC] [QuickBASIC] Retrieves and displays a specified string from the environment table. The function format is:

```
v$ = ENVIRON$ (param)
```

or

```
v$ = ENVIRON$ (n)
```

where param is a string representing the parameter to be retrieved and *n* is an integer in the range 1 to 255. In the string format the returned value is the text that follows param in the environment table. In the numeric argument format ENVIRON\$ returns the nth entry in the environment table, or a null string if there is no such entry.

Example:

```
PRINT ENVIRON$ ("COMSPEC")
```

Result: C:\COMMAND.COM

EOF

[MS-Pascal] File system function. Indicates whether the current position of the file is at the end of the file F for SEQUENTIAL and TERMINAL file modes. EOF with no parameters is the same as EOF (INPUT).

EOF (function)

[BASIC] [QuickBASIC] Indicates an end-of-file condition. Statement format is:

```
v = EOF(n)
```

where *n* is the filenumber specified with the OPEN statement. EOF returns -1 (TRUE) if the end-of-file has been reached, or 0 (FALSE) if not. Conversly, the condition NOT EOF(n) is true until the end of the file is reached. When used with a communications file, EOF(n) will be true if the communications buffer is empty and false if the buffer contains data.

EOLN

[MS-Pascal] File system function. Indicates whether the current position of the file is at the end of a line in the textfile F. EOLN with no parameters is the same as EOLN (INPUT).

ERASE (statement)

[BASIC] [QuickBASIC] Eliminates an array from the program. The statement format is:

```
ERASE name [,name]...
```

where name is the name of the array or arrays to be erased. For static arrays, the ERASE statement resets each array element to its default value. For dynamic arrays it deletes the array from memory. After a dynamic array has been erased it may be redimensioned. After an array is erased the memory space can be used for other purposes.

ERDEV and ERDEV$ (variables)

[BASIC] [QuickBASIC] Read-only variables that hold the error code for a device error and the device name. After a device error occurs, the value of ERDEV is the type of error. The value of ERDEV$ is the name of the device. These functions are used in error-handlers.

ERR and ERL (variables)

[BASIC] [QuickBASIC] Return the error code and line number associated with a program error. ERR is be a number identifying the type of error, and the value of the function ERL is the line number of the program statement in which the error occurred. If the statement containing the error has no line number, then the nearest line number preceding it is returned. If no line number precedes it, a value 0 is returned. These functions are used in error-trapping routines.

ERROR (statement)

[BASIC] [QuickBASIC] Simulates the occurrence of a BASIC error. The statement format is:

```
ERROR n
```

where n is a number in the range 0 to 255 and simulates the runtime error identification code.

The ERROR statement can also be used to create user-defined error codes that are different from those in BASIC. The user error code can then be tested by an error handler routine in the conventional way.

ESC

[Assembler] 8086 machine instruction. Mnemonics for ESCape. This opcodes provides a mechanism whereby a coprocessor can receive instructions from the CPU's instruction stream and make use of the processor's memory addressing facilites. The ESC instruction is useful for generating 80x87 instructions when using an assembler program that does not recognize FPU mnemonics. By the same token, it can be used to generate FPU emulated code. For example, the following macro produces the emulated opcode for the FLD instruction to load a 4-byte real operand.

```
@FLD    MACRO DEST
;; Produce emulated opcode for a 4-byte real operand
        DB      0CDH    ;; Encoding of FLD short real
        ESC     8,DEST ;; Generate opcode
        ENDM
```

The escape opcode is identified by the bit pattern 11011xxx. In general:

```
ESC     xxxyyyB,DEST  =  11011xxx ??yyy???
```

where ??yyy??? is

```
        MOD REG r/m
        ?? yyy ???
```

In the 80386 and later processors ESC tests the EM flag to determine whether coprocessor instructions are being emulated or not, and the TS flag to determine if there has been a context change since the last ESC instruction.

EVAL

[MS-Pascal] Heading: (EXPRESSION, EXPRESSION,...);
Extend level intrinsic procedure which evaluates expression parameters only, but accepts any number of parameters of any type. EVAL is used to evaluate an expression as a statement; it is commonly used to evaluate a function for its side effects, without using the function return value.

EXIT (statement)

[QuickBASIC] The EXIT statement can be used in any of the five forms:

```
        EXIT FOR            jump from FOR/NEXT loop
        EXIT SUB            jump from subprogram
        EXIT FUNCTION       jump from function
        EXIT DEF            jump from DEF
        EXIT DO             jump from DO loop
```

The statement causes program execution to jump out of the specified structure.

EXP

[MS-Pascal] Heading: (X : NUMERIC): REAL;

Arithmetic function. Returns e to the X. Both X and the return value are of type REAL. To force a particular precision, declare EXSRQQ (CONSTS REAL4) and/or EXDRQQ (CONSTS REAL8) and use them instead. Exponentiation is an addition to Pascal since this function is not part of the original language.

EXP (function)

[BASIC] [QuickBASIC] Calculates the exponential function. The function format is:

```
v = EXP(x)
```

where x is any numeric expression. EXP(x) returns e to the power x, where e is the mathematical constant 2.718282 (the base of the natural logarithm function).

Expressions and Statements

[C] Expressions are the building blocks of high-level computer languages. An expression is a character or a sequence of characters (which can include one or more operators) that result in a unique value or program action. An expression can be composed of numeric or alphanumeric characters. The following are valid C expressions:

```
x_variable
3.1415
goto LABEL
Larray[]
"Legal Department"
printf("#")
-4
z = (x * y)/2
```

A variable, a number, a string of characters, a program control keyword, a function call, and several numbers or variables connected by operators are all considered expressions.

A *statement* is the fundamental organizational element of a computer language. In C a statement consists of one or more expressions. All statements must end in a semicolon (;), which is called the *statement terminator*. In fact, the semicolon converts an expression into a statement. The following valid statements were derived from the listed expressions:

```
x_variable = -4;
goto LABEL;
Larray[] = "Legal department";
printf("#");
z = (x * y)/2;
```

EXSRQQ

(See EXP).

Extend level instrinsics

[MS-Pascal] Contains the following instrinsic procedures and functions:

ABORT	EVAL	LOWORD	BYLONG
HIBYTE	RESULT	BYWORD	HIWORD
SIZEOF	DECODE	LOBYTE	UPPER ENCODE
LOWER			

Several of these are used to compose and decompose one-byte, two-byte, and four-byte items: HIBYTE, LOBYTE, BYWORD, HIWORD, LOWORD, and BYLONG.

ENCODE and DECODE convert between internal and string forms of variables. ABORT invokes a runtime error. EVAL, LOWER, UPPER, RESULT, and SIZEOF, have special uses.

Extended Graphics Array

(See XGA).

EXTERN Directive

[MS-Pascal] The EXTERN directive identifies a procedure or function that resides in another module. The declaration consists of the heading of the procedure or function, followed by the word EXTERN. The actual implementation of the procedure or function is presumed to exist in some other module.

Note that EXTERN is an attribute when used with a variable, but a directive when used with a procedure or function. As with variables, the keyword EXTERNAL is a synonym for EXTERN. The EXTERN directive for a particular procedure or function within a module overrides the PUBLIC attribute given for the entire module. It is also permitted in an implementation of a unit for a constituent procedure or function. All such external constituents must be declared at the beginning of the implementation, before all other procedures and functions.

(See also: attributes and directives).

FABS

[**Assembler**] FPU machine instruction. Calculate absolute value of ST.

Factorial calculation

[**General programming**] A simple loop structure can be illustrated by a routine that performs the calculations required in obtaining the factorial. The factorial of a number is defined as the product of all the whole numbers that are equal to or less than the number. For example, factorial 4 (written 4!) is

$$4! = 4 * 3 * 2 * 1 = 24$$

If we create the variable fac_pro to hold the accumulated product, and the variable cur_fac to hold the current factor, we can design a program loop that calculates the factorial, as follows:

1. Initialize the variables fac_pro to the number whose factorial is to be calculated and the variable cur_fac to this number minus 1.
2. Make fac_pro equal to cur_fac times fac_pro and subtract one from cur_fac.
3. If cur_fac is greater than 1, repeat step 2, if not, terminate the loop.

Note that testing for a factor greater than 1 eliminates the trivial operation of multiplying by 1. Also note that when execution of the loop concludes, the factorial is found in the variable fac_pro.

In some programming languages the factorial can also be calculated by recursion.

(See also: for loop).

FADD

[**Assembler**] FPU machine instruction. Add source to destination with results in destination.

```
; Sample encodings:
FADD    ST,ST(2)
```

```
FADD     S_REAL
FADD     L_REAL
FADD
```

FADDP

[Assembler] FPU machine instruction. Add and pop stack.

```
; Sample encoding:
FADDP   ST(2),ST
```

FBLD

[Assembler] FPU machine instruction. Load packed BCD onto stack.

FBSTP

[Assembler] FPU machine instruction. Store stack top as a packed BCD and pop stack.

FCHS

[Assembler] FPU machine instruction. Change sign of stack top element.

FCLEX/FNCLEX

[Assembler] FPU machine instruction. Clear exception flags, IR flag and busy flag in the status word.

FCOM

[Assembler] FPU machine instruction. Compare stack top with source operand (stack register or memory). If no source, ST(1) is assumed.

```
; Sample encodings:
FCOM
FCOM     ST(2)
FCOM     S_REAL
FCOM     L_REAL
```

FCOMP

[Assembler] FPU machine instruction. Compare stack top with source and pop stack (See FCOM).

```
; Sample encodings:
FCOMP
FCOMP    ST(2)
FCOMP    S_REAL
FCOMP    L_REAL
```

FCOMPP

[Assembler] FPU machine instruction. Compare stack top with ST(1) and pop stack twice. Both operands are discarded.

FCOS

[Assembler] FPU machine instruction. Calculates cosine of stack top and returns value in ST. |ST| < 2 to the 63. Input in radians.

FDECSTP

[Assembler] FPU machine instruction. Decrement stack top pointer field in the status word. If field = 0 then it changes to 7.

FDISI/FNDISI

[Assembler] FPU machine instruction. Disable interrupts by setting mask. No action in 80287 and 80387.

FDIV

[Assembler] FPU machine instruction. Divide destination by source with quotient in destination. If no destination specified, ST is assumed.

```
; Sample encodings:
FDIV    ST,ST(2)
FDIV    ST(4),ST
FDIV    S_REAL
FDIV    L_REAL
```

FDIVP

[Assembler] FPU machine instruction. Divide destination by source with quotient in destination and pop Stack (See FDIV).

FDIVR

[Assembler] FPU machine instruction. Divide source by destination with quotient in destination, If no destination is specified, ST is assumed. Reverse divide.

```
; Sample encodings:
FDIVR    ST,ST(2)
FDIVR    ST(3),ST
FDIVR    S_REAL
FDIVR    L_REAL
```

FDIVRP

[Assembler] FPU machine instruction. Divide source by destination with quotient in destination and pop stack (See FDIVR).

FENI/FNENI

[Assembler] FPU machine instruction. Enable interrupts by clearing the mask in the control register. No action in 80287 and 80387.

Fetch-execute cycle

(See microprocessor).

fflush()

[C] The PC keyboard is an interrupt-driven device. Every time a key is pressed (or released) the computer's electronic circuitry generates a signal that *interrupts* the central processor and forces it to calculate and store a special code associated with the particular key that was activated. The code that performs these operations, called the *keyboard interrupt service routine*, is part of the BIOS program. The keystroke codes are stored in a reserved memory area named the *keyboard buffer*. Therefore, high-level input functions, such as C's scanf(), gets(), getch(), and getche(), have only to look in the keyboard buffer to find the keystrokes typed by the user.

However, due to a peculiarity of some systems, occasionally scanf() does not remove all characters stored in the keyboard buffer. This unusual action of scanf() can generate quite baffling results. For example, in the following program scanf() leaves a newline code in the keyboard buffer, which is then erroneously read by the gets() function:

```
#include <stdio.h>
#include <conio.h>
```

```
main()
{
    char word[20];
    printf("Type a word: ");
    scanf("%s", word);
    printf("word typed was: %s", word);
/*
Because scanf() leaves a newline code in the keyboard
buffer, the gets() function will fail. Inserting an
fflush(stdin); line at this point would solve the problem
*/
    printf("\n\nType another word: ");
    gets(word);
    printf("second word was: %s", word);
}
```

There are several solutions to this problem, but perhaps the simplest and most reliable one is to use a special function called *fflush()*. Observe that the header for fflush() is also in the stdio.h include file. The general action of the fflush() function is to write the contents of a buffer to a file. Regarding the standard input device, this function, as its name suggests, clears the keyboard buffer of any stray characters. This use of fflush() requires the standard name for the keyboard (*stdin*) as follows:

```
fflush(stdin);
```

FFREE

[Assembler] FPU machine instruction. Change destination stack register and tag field to EMPTY.

FIADD

[Assembler] FPU machine instruction. Add integer in memory to stack top with sum in the stack top.

```
; Sample encodings:
FIADD    S_INTEGER
FIADD    W_INTEGER
```

FICOM

[Assembler] FPU machine instruction. Compare integer in memory with stack top.

FICOMP

[Assembler] FPU machine instruction. Compare integer in memory with stack top and pop stack. Stack top element is discarded.

FIDIV

[Assembler] FPU machine instruction. Divide stack top by integer memory variable. Quotient in stack top.

FIDIVR

[Assembler] FPU machine instruction. Divide integer memory variable by stack top. Quotient in stack top.

FIELD (statement)

[BASIC] [QuickBASIC] Allocates variable space in a random-access buffer. The statement format is:

```
FIELD [#]num, width AS stringvar [,width AS stringvar]...
```

where num is the number of the file used in the OPEN statement, width is a numeric expression of the number of characters allocated to stringvar, and stringvar is the string variable used for random file access. The statement is used to define the variables used to get data out of a buffer with a GET statement, or to place data in the buffer with a PUT statement.
Example:

```
FIELD 1, 10 AS A$, 5 AS B$, 30 AS NAME$
```

Result: 10 bytes are allocated to the variable A$, 5 bytes to the variable B$, and 30 bytes to the variable NAME$. No data is actually placed in the buffer or removed from the buffer with the FIELD statement.

FILD

[Assembler] FPU machine instruction. Load word, short or long integer onto stack top. Loaded number is converted to temporary real.

```
; Sample encodings:
FILD    S_INTEGER
FILD    W_INTEGER
FILD    L_INTEGER
```

File system procedures and functions

[MS-Pascal] Most PC support various file-system procedures and functions. The following are available in most systems.

Category	Procedures	Functions
Primitive	GET	EOF
	PAGE	EOLN
	PUT	
	RESET	
	REWRITE	
Textfile I,/O	READ	
	READLN	
	WRITE	
	WRITELN	
Extended Level I/O	ASSIGN	
	CLOSE	
	DISCARD	
	READSET	
	READFN	
	SEEK	

FILEATTR (function)

[QuickBASIC] Returns information regarding an open file. The function format is:

```
FILEATTR (n,1) to identify a file types
```

or

```
FILEATTR (n,2) to obtain the DOS file handle
```

The file type return codes in the first function format are as follows:

RETURN CODE	FILE TYPE
1	INPUT
2	OUTPUT
4	APPEND
8	RANDOM
32	BINARY

FILES (command)

[BASIC] [QuickBASIC] Displays the filenames in the current directory. The command format is:

```
FILES [filespec]
```

where filespec is a string expression for the file specification, which can include DOS wildcard characters * and ?.

FILLC

[MS-Pascal] Heading: (D:ADRMEM;N:WORD;C: CHAR);
System level intrinsic procedure which fills D with N copies of the CHAR C. No bounds checking is done.
(See also: FILLSC).

FILLSC

[MS-Pascal] Heading: (D:ADSMEM;N:WORD;C: CHAR) ;
System level intrinsic procedure which fills D with N copies of the CHAR C. No bounds checking is done. The MOVE and FILL procedures take value parameters of type ADRMEM and ADSMEM, but since all ADR (or ADS) types are compatible, the ADR (or ADS) of any variable or constant can be used as the actual parameter.

FIMUL

[Assembler] FPU machine instruction. Multiply integer memory variable by the stack top. Product in stack top.

FINCSTP

[Assembler] FPU machine instruction. Add one to the stack top field in the status word. If field = 7 then it changes to 0.

FINIT/FNINIT

[Assembler] FPU machine instruction. Initialize processor. Control word is set to 3FFH. Stack registers are tagged EMPTY and all exception flags are cleared.

FIST

[Assembler] FPU machine instruction. Round stack top to integer, as per RC field in the status word, and store in integer memory variable.

FISTP

[Assembler] FPU machine instruction. Round stack top to integer, as per RC field in the status word, store in variable and pop stack.

```
; Sample encodings:
FISTP   S_INTEGER
FISTP   W_INTEGER
FISTP   L_INTEGER
```

FISUB

[Assembler] FPU machine instruction. Subtract integer memory variable from stack top. Difference to the stack top.

FISUBR

[Assembler] FPU machine instruction. Subtract stack top from integer memory variable. Difference to stack top.

FIX (function)

[BASIC] [QuickBASIC] Truncate to integer. The function format is:

```
v = FIX(x)
```

where *x* is a numeric expression. The returned value is the whole number that results from discarding the decimal part of x.

Fixed disk

(See storage -- hard disk).

Fixed Disk and Diskette Drive Adapter — PC AT

[PC hardware and architecture] One of the functions of this dual-purpose adapter used in the PC AT is to serve as a diskette drive controller. The card fits into one of the expansion slots in the system unit. The diskette functions in the controller are designed for double-density drives with write precompensation and are equipped with analog circuits for driving the clock and for data recovery. This limits the hardware that is compatible with the AT's adapter to double-sided and high-capacity diskette drives.

The adapter supports storage formats of 160K, 180K, 320K, 360K, and 1.2 megabytes per diskette. No connector for external drives is provided. The adapter can manage a total of three drives: two diskettes and one hard disk or two hard disks and one diskette drive. A difficulty frequently encountered with this adapter is that diskettes which have been written by a high-capacity drive cannot be reliably read in the conventional drives used in the other systems of the PC line. This is true even if the diskette was originally formatted in a standard drive.

Flag registers

(See machine registers, flags).

FLD

[Assembler] FPU machine instruction. Load real memory variable or stack register onto stack top. Value is converted to temporary real.

```
; Sample encodings:
FLD     S_REAL
FLD     L_REAL
FLD     TEMP_REAL
FLD     ST(2)
```

FLD1

[Assembler] FPU machine instruction. Load +1.0 onto the stack top. Constant is accurate to 64 bits (19 digits).

FLDCW

[Assembler] FPU machine instruction. Load memory variable (word) onto the control register.

FLDENV

[Assembler] FPU machine instruction. Load 14-byte environment from memory storage area.

FLDL2E

[Assembler] FPU machine instruction. Load logarithm base 2 of e onto stack top. Constant is accurate to 64 bits (19 digits).

FLDL2T

[Assembler] FPU machine instruction. Load logarithm base 2 of 10 onto stack top. Constant is accurate to 64 bits (19 digits).

FLDLG2

[Assembler] FPU machine instruction. Load logarithm base 10 of 2 onto stack top. Constant is accurate to 64 bits (19 digits).

FLDLN2

[Assembler] FPU machine instruction. Load logarithm base e of 2 onto stack top. Constant is accurate to 64 bits (19 digits).

FLDPI

Load PI onto the stack top. Constant is accurate to 64 bits (19 digits).

FLDZ

[Assembler] FPU machine instruction. Load zero onto the stack top. Constant is accurate to 64 bits (19 digits).

FLOAT

[MS-Pascal] Heading: (X : INTEGER): REAL;
Data conversion function which converts an INTEGER value to a REAL value. This function is not normally needed since INTEGER-to-REAL is usually done automatically. However, because FLOAT is needed by the runtime package, it is in included at the standard level.

FLOAT4

[MS-Pascal] Heading: (X : INTEGER4): REAL;
Data conversion function. Converts an INTEGER4 value to a REAL value. This type conversion is done automatically; however, it is possible to lose precision.

FMUL

[Assembler] FPU machine instruction. Multiply reals. Destination by source with product in destination.

```
; Sample encodings:
FMUL    ST,ST(2)
FMUL    ST(1),ST
FMUL    S_REAL
FMUL    L_REAL
```

FMULP

[Assembler] FPU machine instruction. Multiply reals and pop stack. (See FMUL).

```
; Sample encoding:
```

```
FMULP    ST(2),ST
```

FNOP

[Assembler] FPU machine instruction. Floating point no operation.

for loop

[C] The simplest iterative construct of C. The for loop is used for repeating execution of a program statement or statement block a fixed number of times. The typical *for* loop consists of the following steps:

1. An initialization step that assigns a starting value to the loop variable.
2. One or more processing statements that perform the required operations and update the loop variable.
3. A test expression that determines conditions that terminate the loop.

In the case of the *for* loop these steps are somewhat hidden in the loop structure. For example, in the following program we use a *for* loop to calculate the factorial of a number:

```
#include <stdio.h>
main()
{
    unsigned int number, fac_pro, cur_fac;
    printf("FACTORIAL CALCULATION\nEnter positive integer: ");
    scanf("%u", &number);
    fac_pro = number;
    for (cur_fac = number - 1; cur_fac > 1; cur_fac --)
        fac_pro = cur_fac * fac_pro;
    printf("Factorial is: %u", fac_pro);
}
```

In this example the expression:

```
for (cur_fac = number - 1; cur_fac > 1; cur_fac --)
```

contains a loop expression that includes elements from steps 1, 2, and 3. The first statement inside parentheses (cur_fac = number - 1) sets the initial value of the factor variable, which is part of the initialization function performed in step 1. The second statement inside the parentheses (cur_fac > 1) contains the test condition that is used to terminate the loop. This test operation is part of step 3 in the generic description. Finally, the third statement in parentheses (cur_fac - -) uses the decrement operator (- -) to indicate that the loop control variable must be diminished by 1 during each iteration. This decrement operation is part of the processing performed during step number 2 in the general description.

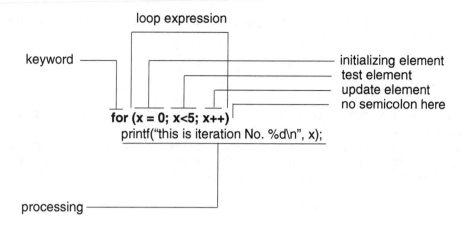

Structure of the C for Loop

Note that while the *for* loop expression does not terminate in a semicolon, it does contain embedded semicolons. In this instance the semicolon is used to separate the initialization element from the test element, and the test element from the update element, which constitute the three types of expressions in the *for* loop construct. This action of the semicolon in the *for* loop allows the use of multiple statements in each element of the loop expression. For example, the following trivial program manages the variables *x* and *y* in the same *for* loop:

```
main()
{

    unsigned int x, y;
    for (x = 0, y = 5; x < 5; x + +, y - -)
        printf("x is: %u\ny is: %u\n", x, y);

}
```

Note, in this example, that the initialization element sets the variable *x* to an initial value of 0 and the variable *y* to an initial value of 5, while the update element instructs the compiler to increment *x* and decrement *y* during each iteration. The comma operator is used to isolate the different subelements in the statement.

The second element in the *for* loop construct, labeled the *test element*, is evaluated logically during the execution of the loop. If the result is false (logical 0), the loop terminates; otherwise, loop execution continues. The programmer must remember that for the loop to execute the expression must evaluate to true. In other words, the test expression determines the condition under which the loop executes, and not its termination. For this reason the loop:

```
for (x = 0; x == 5; x++)
    printf("%u\n", x);
```

will not execute, because the test expression x == 5 initially evaluates to false. By the same token, the loop:

```
for (x = 0; x = 5; x++)
   printf("%u\n", x);
```

will execute endlessly, because x is assigned the value 5 (x = 5) during each iteration, which evaluates to logical true.

It is also possible to have a test element composed of complex logical expressions. In this case the entire expression is evaluated to determine if the condition is met. For example, the construct

```
for (x = 0, y = 5; (x < 3 || y > 1); x++, y-)
```

contains the test expression

```
(x < 3 || y > 1)
```

which evaluates to true (loop executes) if either x is less than 3 or if y is greater than 1. In this example the values that determine the end of the loop are reached when the variable $x = 4$ (the condition $x < 3$ is false) and $y = 1$ (the condition $y > 1$ is also false). Note that, in this case, the parentheses serve to improve the readability of the test expression, but that it will evaluate correctly without them.

FOR/NEXT (statements)

[BASIC] [QuickBASIC] Creates a loop structure that allows repeating a number of statements a given number of times. The statement format is:

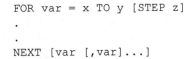

```
FOR var = x TO y [STEP z]
      .
      .
NEXT [var [,var]...]
```

where var is an integer or single-precision variable used as a counter, x is the initial value of the counter, y is the final value, and z is the increment unit. Each time the NEXT statement is reached, z is added to the value of x. This process continues until the value of x exceeds y. Although the numbers $x, y,$ and z may be of several numeric types, the lower the precision of the type, the faster the loop executes. The statement:

```
FOR count = a TO b
```

is equivalent to the statement:

```
FOR count = a TO b STEP 1
```

The index following the word NEXT is optional.

If the value of z is negative then the counter (x) is decremented during each iteration, until it is less than the final value (y). The body of the loop is skipped if the initial values are outside the loop limits. FOR/NEXT loops can be nested. Example:

```
K = 30
FOR COUNT = 1 TO 10 STEP 2
PRINT COUNT; K
  K = K + 10
NEXT COUNT
```

Result: 1 30
        3 40
        5 50
        7 60
        9 70

FORTRAN attribute

[MS-Pascal] Applies both to procedures and functions, but not to variables. Instead of the usual Pascal calling sequence, it specifies a calling sequence that is compatible with the MS-FORTRAN. This lets a program call an MS-Pascal procedure or function from MS-FORTRAN programs and vice versa.

In a 16-bit environment, MS-Pascal uses the same calling sequence as the compilers for Microsoft FORTRAN, Microsoft BASIC, and Microsoft COBOL. Thus, there is no need to give the FORTRAN attribute.

FORWARD directive

[MS-Pascal] A FORWARD declaration allows calling a procedure or function before it is declared in the source text. This permits indirect recursion, where A calls B and B calls A. A FORWARD declaration can specify a procedure or function heading, followed by the directive FORWARD. Later, the code can declare the procedure or function, without repeating the formal parameter list, attributes, or return types.

(See also: attributes and directives).

FPATAN

[Assembler] FPU machine instruction. Partial arctangent. Calculates ARCTAN = (Y/X), X is ST and Y is ST(1). X and Y must observe $0 < Y < X < +\infty$. Stack is popped. X and Y are destroyed. θ in radians.

FPREM

[Assembler] FPU machine instruction. Partial remainder. Performs modulo division of the stack top by ST(1), producing an exact result. Sign is unchanged. Formula used: Part. rem. = ST - ST(1) * quotient.

FPREM1

[Assembler] FPU machine instruction (80387). Calculates IEEE compatible partial remainder. (See FPREM).

fprintf() — library function

[C] Frequently used stream function. The difference between fprintf() and printf() is that fprintf() requires a file or stream name as a first argument. For example, the following program line uses the fprintf() function to send a text line to the standard printer device:

```
fprintf(stdprn, "This is a test line to print\n\r");
```

Note that the escape characters \n \r that follow the text string are those for the *linefeed* and *carriage return* codes. In programming printer devices both codes are necessary to start a new line, while only the \n (newline) code is necessary for the video display.

FPTAN

[Assembler] FPU machine instruction. Partial tangent. Calculates Y/X = TANθ, θ at ST, must be in the range 0 < θ pi/4. Y is returned in ST and X in ST(1). θ is destroyed. Input in radians.

FRE (function)

[BASIC] [QuickBASIC] Returns the number of bytes of unused space in BASIC's data segment. The function is implemented in three formats:

```
FRE(0)       the amount of memory available for
             new string data
FRE(-1)      the number of memory locations available
             for new numeric arrays
FRE(-2)      the smallest amount of space on the stack
             that has existed at any time during program
             execution
```

This function is useful in determining whether or not sufficient memory remains to declare a new numeric array.

FREECT

[MS-Pascal] Heading: (SIZE :WORD):WORD;
Library function which returns an estimate of the number of times NEW can be called to allocate heap variables with length SIZE bytes. FREECT takes into account DISPOSE and adjacent free blocks and is generally used with the SIZEOF function. However, it does not assume that any stack space is needed. Since stack space generally is needed, the value returned should be reduced accordingly.

FREEFILE (function)

[QuickBASIC] Returns the next available file number (in the range 1 to 255).

FREMQQ

[MS-Pascal] Heading: (BLOCK : ADSMEM) : WORD;
Library routine of the segmented heap management group. Takes an ADSMEM generated by ALLMQQ or GETMQQ and returns the space described by the ADSMEM to the long heap memory pool. The function returns a word value. If the word value is 6, FREMQQ reports no errors. If the word value is 1, the release of memory was in error.

FRNDINT

[Assembler] FPU machine instruction. Round the stack top to an integer.

FRSTOR

[Assembler] FPU machine instruction. Restore state from 94-byte memory area previously written by a FSAVE or FNSAVE.

FSAVE/FNSAVE

[Assembler] FPU machine instruction. Save state (environment and stack registers) to a 94-byte area in memory.

FSCALE

[Assembler] FPU machine instruction. Scale variable. Add scale factor, integer in ST(1), to exponent of ST. Provides fast multiplication (division if scale is negative) by powers of 2. Range of factor is -32768 ST(1) < 32768.

FSETPM

[Assembler] FPU machine instruction. Sets protected mode addressing for 80287 systems. Interpreted as FNOP in 80387.

FSIN

[Assembler] FPU machine instruction (80387). Calculates sine of stack top and returns value in ST. |ST| < 2 to the 63. Input in radians.

FSINCOS

[Assembler] FPU machine instruction (80387). Calculates sine and cosine of ST. Sine appears in ST and cosine in ST(1). |ST| < 2 to the 63. Input in radians. Tangent = sine/cosine.

FSQRT

[Assembler] FPU machine instruction. Calculate square root of stack top.

FST

[Assembler] FPU machine instruction. Store stack top in another stack register or in a real memory variable. Rounding is according to the RC field of control word.

```
; Sample encodings:
FST     ST(3)
FST     S_REAL
FST     L_REAL
```

FSTCW/FNSTCW

[Assembler] FPU machine instruction. Store control register in a memory variable (word).

FSTENV/FNSTENV

[Assembler] FPU machine instruction. Store 14-byte environment into memory storage area. (See FLDENV).

FSTP

[Assembler] FPU machine instruction. Store stack top in another stack register or in a real memory variable and pop stack. Rounding is according to the RC field in control word.

```
; Sample encodings:
FSTP    ST(2)
FSTP    S_REAL
FSTP    L_REAL
FSTP    TEMP_REAL
```

FSTSW/FNSTSW

[Assembler] FPU machine instruction. Store status register in memory variable (word).

FSUB

[Assembler] FPU machine instruction. Subtract source from destination with difference in destination.

```
; Sample encodings:
FSUB    ST,ST(3)
FSUB    ST(1),ST
FSUB    S_REAL
FSUB    L_REAL
```

FSUBP

[Assembler] FPU machine instruction. Subtract source from destination with result in destination and pop stack.

FSUBR

[Assembler] FPU machine instruction. Subtract destination from source with difference in destination.

```
; Sample encodings:
FSUBR   ST,ST(1)
FSUBR   ST(3),ST
```

```
FSUBR    S_REAL
FSUBR    L_REAL
```

FSUBRP

[Assembler] FPU machine instruction. Subtract destination from source with difference in destination and pop stack.

FTST

[Assembler] FPU machine instruction. Compare stack top with zero and set condition codes.

FUCOM

[Assembler] FPU machine instruction (80387). Unordered compare. Operates like FCOM except that no invalid operation if one operand is a NAN.

```
; Sample encodings:
FUCOM
FUCOM    ST(2)
FUCOM    S_REAL
FUCOM    L_REAL
```

FUCOMP

[Assembler] FPU machine instruction (80387). Unordered compare and pop. Like FCOMP except that no invalid operation if one operand is a NAN.

```
; Sample encodings:
FUCOMP
FUCOMP   ST(2)
FUCOMP   S_REAL
FUCOMP   L_REAL
```

FUCOMPP

[Assembler] FPU machine instruction (80387). Unordered compare and pop twice. Operates like FCOMPP except that no invalid operation if one operand is a NAN.

Function — call

[C] A programmer-defined function. It receives control when the function's name is referenced in a program statement. This reference, or *function call*, appears within main() or another programmer-defined function. C allows a function to call itself; this operation is called *recursion*.

function — matching of arguments and parameters

[C] The prototype and declaration of a function must include (in parentheses) a list of the variables whose values are passed to the function, called the formal parameter list. The function call contains, also in parentheses, the names of the variables whose values are passed to the function. Note that the term *function argument* relates to the variables referenced in the function call, while the term *function parameter* refers to the variables listed in the function declaration. In other words, a value passed to a function is an argument from the viewpoint of the caller and a parameter from the viewpoint of the called function.

Data is passed to a function in the order in which the arguments are referenced in the call and the parameters listed in the function declaration. In other words, the first argument in the function call corresponds to the first parameter in the header section of the function declaration. By the same token, the second argument referenced in the call is assigned to the second parameter in the declaration, and so on.

Function — passing array variables

[C] A pointer variable is used to gain access to the elements of an array by virtue of the fact that a function can receive the address of a variable encoded in a pointer. (See function — passing data by reference).

The following program shows access to array elements by reference:

```
#include <stdio.h>
void Show_array(char *);
main()
{
static char USA_name[] = "United States of America";
        Show_array(USA_name);
        printf("\n%s\n", USA_name);
        return(0);
}
void Show_array(char *USA_name_ptr)
{
        unsigned int counter;
        printf("\n%s\n", USA_name_ptr);
        for (counter = 0; counter << 6; counter++)
            USA_name_ptr[counter] = ' ';
        return;
}
```

Note that arrays must be passed by reference if the function is to have access to its elements. For this reason, the function declaration

```
void Show_array(char *USA_name_ptr)
```

contains a pointer variable to an array of char type. This pointer, named USA_name_ptr, allows the function to access the elements of an array declared in main(). In the preceding program the function Show_array() first displays the array and then proceeds to change its first five elements to blank spaces. This action is demonstrated by the printf statement in main().

Function — passing data by reference

[C] The mechanism of a C function allows passing to it multiple arguments, but a single one can be returned to the caller. It is possible to overcome this limitation by using external variables that are visible both to the calling and to the called functions. Another way in which a function can change the value of one or more of the caller's variables is by passing to the function the address of these variables. In this case, the default mode of operation, which consists of passing function arguments by value, is circumvented and the function arguments are passed by reference.

A C program can obtain the address of a variable by means of the address-of operator (&). On the other hand, the asterisk (indirection operator) is used to create variables that hold the address of another variable. It is by means of these operators that a calling routine can pass to a function the address of a variable and the called function can access the contents of an external variable. The process is shown in the following program:

```
#include <stdio.h>
#define PI 3.14159
void Circ_calc(float *, float *, float *);
main()
{
        float radius, diameter, circumference;
        printf("\nEnter radius of circle: ");
        scanf("%f", &radius);
        Circ_calc(&radius, &diameter, &circumference);
        printf("\nDiameter is: %f", diameter);
        printf("\nCircumference is: %f", circumference);
        return(0);
}
void Circ_calc(float *rad, float *dia, float *circ)
{
        *dia = *rad + *rad;
        *circum = *dia * PI;
        return;
}
```

In this case note that the function Circ_calc() is prototyped and declared of void return type. This is due to the fact that the function accesses the caller's variable directly, and does not return a value in the conventional way. Also note that the variables named radius, diameter, and circumference are declared inside main(), which would normally make them invisible to Circ_calc(). However, the function call statement:

```
Circ_calc(&radius, &diameter, &circumference);
```

passes to the function the address of radius, diameter, and circumference, rather than a copy of their current value. The fact that the function Circ_calc() receives pointers, rather than values, can be seen in the function prototype as well as in the declaration, which is:

```
void Circ_calc(float *rad, float *dia, float *circum)
```

In this case *rad, *dia, and *circum are pointer variables that hold the addresses of the variables named radius, diameter, and circumference.

Function — prototypes

[C] A characteristic of C is that all variables must be declared, specifying name and data type, before they can be used. However, the original version of C (defined by Kernighan and Ritchie in their 1978 book *The C Programming Language*) did not require the predeclaration of functions. Because this practice was inconsistent with the language's handling of variables and tended to obscure the code, the ANSI standard for C language (approved in 1989) introduced the predeclaration of functions. This operation is also called function prototyping.

The decision of the ANSI committee to create function declarations by means of prototypes corrected one of the most obvious weaknesses of C. But the committee also had to consider that up to that point, C language programs had been written without predeclaring functions. For this reason prototypes were introduced as a recommended, but not required, programming practice. C compilers that conform to the 1989 ANSI Standard X3.159 allow and encourage the use of function prototypes, but are also compatible with old-style code in which functions are not predeclared. However, the use of function prototypes should not be considered optional, since the Standard mentions that future versions will not allow the old-style syntax.

Some C language authors refer to function prototypes as *explicit function declarations* in contrast with the *implicit function declaration* seen in the traditional code. We prefer the term *prototype* because the term *function declaration* is used also in relation to an area of the function definition. Following the recommendations of the ANSI Standard, the use of prototypes is stressed.

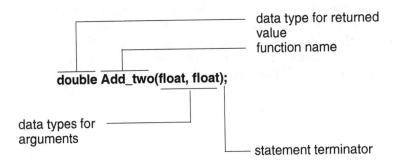

Elements of a C Function Prototype

Function — returning an MS-DOS Error Code

[C] In C compilers that run under MS-DOS the main() function can return an error code to the operating system. This error code, which must be an unsigned integer in the range 0 to 255, can be tested and interpreted by another program or by a batch file. The error code mechanism provides a convenient way of passing error data between programs and utilities; however, MS-DOS does not directly investigate error codes returned by applications. In other words, if a program is executed by typing its name on the MS-DOS command line, any returned error code is ignored. On the other hand, if the program is executed by a batch file (See the *MS-DOS User's Manual*) the batch file can investigate and act upon a returned error code.

In C programs the MS-DOS error code is returned to the operating system via a return statement at the conclusion of the main() function. The value can be represented by an unsigned integer variable or by a constant. It is usually a good programming practice to make sure that a program returns no spurious error code by concluding its execution with a return (0) statement, as follows:

```
main()
{
        .
        .
        .
    return (0);
}
```

function — structure

[C] A programmer-defined function can be described as a collection of declarations and statements, grouped under a function name, and designed to perform a specific task. Every function contains three clearly identifiable elements: the function prototype (also called the declaration), the function definition (or function itself), and the function call.

Function arguments

[C] C requires that the *function name* be followed by an open parenthesis. There cannot be a space or any other character or symbol between the last character of the function name and the open parenthesis. The parentheses following the function name are used to enclose data optionally passed to the function. The data items enclosed between the parentheses are called the *function arguments*. Some functions have no arguments. This is indicated by empty parentheses, as in main().

Function — definition

[C] The function itself usually appears in the source file after the end of the main() function. There are two sections of the function definition that can be clearly identified: the *function declaration section* (sometimes called the header) and the *function body section*. The declaration section, which is reminiscent of the prototype, contains the function name, the return type, and the data type of the parameters passed to the function. The function body section, which is enclosed in braces, contains the declarations and statements required for performing the function's processing operations.

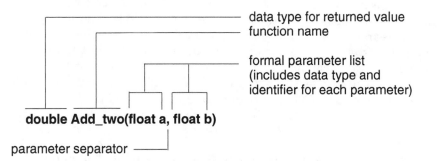

double Add_two(float a, float b)

data type for returned value
function name

formal parameter list
(includes data type and
identifier for each parameter)

parameter separator

Declaration Section of a C Function Definition

Note that, unlike the prototype, the declaration section of the function definition does not end in a semicolon. Also note that the formal parameter list includes the parameter names and the corresponding data types, while, in the prototype, the names are not referenced. This listing of parameter names and types in the function definition serves as a declaration for these variables.

The body section of the function definition is where the actual processing takes place. It can include all the program elements of C, such as variable declarations, keywords, statements, and any legal program element. There is no structural difference between the body of a programmer-defined function and the body of the main() function.

The *return* keyword ends the execution of a function. Return can include a variable, constant, expression or statement, conventionally enclosed in parentheses, that represents the value returned by the function. The only restriction is that the type of the actual returned value must conform to the one listed in the declaration and in the prototype.

FUNCTION (statement)

[**QuickBASIC**] Defines a program function. A function is a multi-statement block beginning with a statement in the format:

```
FUNCTION name(parList)
```

followed on subsequent lines by one or more statements for carrying out the task of the function, and ending with the statement:

```
END FUNCTION.
```

ParList (parameter list) is a list of variables through which values are passed to the function when it is called. Parameter types may be numeric, (variable-length) string, user-defined record type, or array. The types of the parameters may be specified with typedeclaration tags, DEFtype statements, or AS clauses. Array names appearing in the parameter list should be followed by an empty pair of parentheses. Functions are named with the same conventions as variables, except that the name may not begin with FN. The value of a variable argument used in calling a function may be altered by the function unless the variable is surrounded by parentheses. Variables are local to the function unless declared as STATIC or SHARED. A statement of the form:

```
FUNCTION name(parList) STATIC
```

specifies that all variables local to the function be treated as static by default. In this case they are invisible outside of the function but retain their values between function calls. Functions may invoke themselves recursively or they may call other procedures. However, no procedure may be defined inside of a function.

function-like macros

(See macros).

Functions

[C] A function is an element of program execution created by the programmer in order to simplify the task of designing and coding, to improve the program's readability and cohesiveness, and to make it easier to understand and maintain the code. In order to distinguish this type of functions from the main() function and from the functions available in C libraries, the former are often called programmer-declared functions, or simply functions.

Functions

[MS-Pascal] Functions are the same as procedures, except that they are invoked in an expression instead of a statement and they return a value. Function declarations define the parts of a program that compute a value. Functions are activated when the function designator, which is part of an expression, is evaluated.

A function declaration has the same format as a procedure declaration, except that the heading also gives the type of value returned by the function. Example of a function heading:

```
FUNCTION MAXIMUM (I, J: INTEGER) : INTEGER;
```

At least one assignment to the function identifier must be executed to set the return value. This must be done within the block of a function, either in the body itself, or in a procedure or function nested within the block. The compiler does not check for this assignment at runtime, unless the initialization switch is on and the returned type is INTEGER, REAL, or a pointer. However, if there is no assignment at all to the function identifier, the compiler issues an error message.

At the standard level, functions can return any simple type (ordinal, REAL, or INTEGER4) or a pointer. At the extend level, functions can return any simple, structured, or reference type.

A function identifier in an expression invokes the function recursively, rather than giving the current value. To obtain the current value, use the function RESULT, which takes the function identifier as a parameter and is available at the extend level.

The following is an example of a RESULT function used to obtain the current value of a function within an expression:

```
FUNCTION FACT (F : REAL) :REAL;
BEGIN
  FACT := 1;
  WHILE F >1 DO
    BEGIN
      FACT := RESULT (FACT) * F; F := F-1
    END
```

```
END;
```

A function identifier on the left side of an assignment refers to the function's local variable, which contains its current value, instead of invoking the function recursively. Other places where using the function identifier refers to this local variable are a reference parameter and the record of a WITH statement. All of these uses involve getting the address (not the value) of a variable.

Functions

[C] A function is a unit of program execution. Every C language program must contain one function named main. The program lines

```
main()
 {
```

indicate a main function. Program execution always begins at the main function. The programmer can create other functions and give them names following the guidelines for C identifiers. If a program has more than one function, execution always starts at the one named main, regardless of its location.

FWAIT

[Assembler] FPU machine instruction. Alternate mnemonics for WAIT. Must be used with Intel emulators.

FXAM

[Assembler] FPU machine instruction. Examine stack top and report if positive, negative, NAN, denormal, unnormal, normal, zero or empty in condition codes.

FXCH

[Assembler] FPU machine instruction. Swap contents of stack top and another stack register. If no explicit register, ST(1) is used.

FXTRACT

[Assembler] FPU machine instruction. Decompose stack top into exponent and significand. The exponent is found at ST and the significand at ST(1).

FYL2X

[Assembler] FPU machine instruction. Calculates Z = log base 2 of X. X is the value at ST and Y at ST(1). Stack is popped and Z is found in ST. Operands must be in the range $0 < X < \infty$ and $-\infty < Y < +\infty$.

FYL2XP1

[Assembler] FPU machine instruction. Calculates Z = log base 2 of (X+1). X is in ST and must be in the range $0 < |X| < (1-\sqrt{2}/2)$. Y is in ST(1) and must be in the range $-\infty < Y < \infty$. Stack is popped and Z is found in ST.

G

GET

[MS-Pascal] Heading: (VAR Fl)
File system procedure that either reads the currently pointed-to component of
F to the buffer variable F^ and advances the file pointer, or sets the buffer
variable status to empty.

GET (statement (files))

[BASIC] [QuickBASIC] Reads a record from a random access file into a buffer.
The statement format is:

```
GET [#]filenum [,number]
```

where filenum is the number used in the file's OPEN statement, and number
is the consecutive record number to be read. If number is omitted the next record
is read into the buffer.

   The GET statement is also used to retrieve data from a binary file and assign
it to a variable. If v is a variable that holds a value consisting of b bytes, then
b is 2, (for instance, if v is an integer variable). If v is an ordinary string variable,
then b equals the length of the string currently assigned to it. In this case the
statement:

```
GET #n,p,v
```

assigns to the variable v, the b consecutive bytes beginning with the byte in
position p of the binary file having reference number n. If p is omitted, then the
current file position is used as the beginning position.

GET (statement (graphics))

[BASIC] [QuickBASIC] Reads pixel points from the rectangular screen area
in the graphics mode and stores in array. The statement format is:
```
GET (x1,y1)-(x2,y2),arrayname
```

where $(x1,y1)$ are the coordinates of one corner of the rectangle, and $(x2,y2)$ are the coordinates of the opposite corner; the information is stored in arrayname. The operation performed by the graphics mode of the GET statement corresponds to read part of a graphics BitBlt (Bit Block Transfer). The write part of the BitBlt is done by a corresponding PUT statement. The size of the required array is determined by the formula:

```
s = 4+INT((x*bitsperpixel+7/8)*y
```

where x and y are the horizontal and vertical pixel dimensions of the screen rectangle, respectively. The value of bitsperpixel is 1 in high-resolution mode and 2 in medium-resolution mode. GET and PUT statements are used in image animation.

getch() and getche()

[C] The scanf() and gets() functions are convenient for entering numeric or string values from the standard input device (usually the keyboard) into variables. However, both functions require that the user press the enter key in order to terminate input. If a program needs to act on a single keystroke, both scanf() and gets() are unsatisfactory.

For these cases PC implementations of C provides two library functions, named *getch()* (pronounced get-c-h) and *getche()* (pronounced get-c-h-e), which return execution to the calling program when a single key is pressed. The headers for getch() and getche() are in the conio.h file, which must be referenced with an #include directive.

The difference between getch() and getche() is that getche() echoes the typed character on the video terminal. In contrast with scanf() and gets(), the getch() and getche() functions cannot be used to directly enter values into variables. With getch() and getche() the program recovers the keyboard character in the function itself. Therefore, the program must explicitly assign the character typed to a variable.

gets()

[C] One of the limitations of the scanf() function is that input is terminated with the first whitespace character. For this reason scanf() cannot be conveniently used to enter strings composed of several words separated by spaces or with other embedded whitespace characters.

The *gets()* function (pronounced get-es) provides a simple and convenient method of entering a character string, which can contain embedded whitespace characters such as spaces and tabs, into an array variable. The gets() function can be considered the input counterpart of puts().

gets() replaces the carriage return code that marks the end of the input string with a null character. Observe that a null character has a value of 0. Because this null is used to signal the end of the string stored in memory, it is sometimes called a *terminator code*.

The programmer must take into consideration that the null terminator code is stored with the input string and allow storage space for this additional character.

GETMQQ

[MS-Pascal] Heading: (WANTS: WORD): ADSMEM;
Library routine of the segmented heap management group. Returns a long segmented address of type ADSMEM. GETMQQ takes a parameter "wants" that is a memory request in bytes.
GETMQQ invokes ALLMQQ but in addition, issues error messages if ALLMQQ fails.

GOSUB/RETURN (statements)

[BASIC] [QuickBASIC] Branch to and return from subroutine. In traditional BASIC the GOSUB operand is a program line number. In QuickBASIC the destination is a label. When the RETURN statement is encountered execution continues at the statement following the most recent GOSUB. In QuickBASIC both the GOSUB statement and its target must be in the same part of the program, either both in the main body or both in a single procedure.

goto statement

[C] The C *goto* statement transfers execution unconditionally to a specific location in the program. The destination location, at which execution resumes, is marked by a name followed by a colon symbol. This combination of name and colon symbol is called a *label*. For example, the following code fragment tests the variable named "divisor" for a zero value, and if zero, transfers execution to a program branch labeled DIVISION_ERROR:

```
        if (divisor == 0)
                goto DIVISION_ERROR;
        .
        .
        .
DIVISION_ERROR:
      printf("\nUndefined operation\n");
```

The abuse of the *goto* statement can lead to programs in which execution jumps around the code in an inconsistent and hard-to-follow manner. Program-

mer's sometimes say that this coding style generates spaghetti code, in reference to a program logic that is as difficult to unravel as a bowl of uncut spaghetti.
Since the *goto* statement can always be substituted by other C language
structures, its use is optional and discretionary. However, most authors agree
that the *goto* statement provides a convenient way of directly exiting nested
loops, especially in case of errors or other unforeseen conditions, and that its
use is legitimate in these or similar circumstances.

GOTO (statement)

[**BASIC**] [**QuickBASIC**] Unconditional branch to the specified line (in BASIC)
or label (in QuickBASIC). This action, which corresponds to a program jump,
is often considered incompatible with the principles of structured programming. If the destination corresponds to nonexecutable data, for instance, a REM
or DATA statement, execution continues at the first executable statement
following the line or label.

GTYUQQ

[**MS-Pascal**] Heading: (LEN: WORD; LOC : ADSMEM): WORD;
Library function of the terminal I/O group. Reads a maximum of LEN characters from the keyboard and stores them in memory beginning at the address
LOC. The return value is the number of characters actually read. GTYUQQ
always reads the entire line entered. Any characters typed beyond the end of
the buffer length are lost. GTYUQQ is useful for doing terminal I/O in a
low-overhead environment. These functions are part of a collection of routines
called Unit U, which implements the MS-Pascal file system.

H

Half and full duplex modes — in serial communications

[PC hardware and architecture] If the serial communications hardware device is capable of simultaneously transmitting and receiving data, it is said to operate in full duplex mode. The term half duplex is used to describe serial communications that must take place alternatively, that is, in one direction at a time. All the serial communications controllers used in the IBM microcomputers are capable of full duplex operation.

Handshake

(See serial communications).

Hercules Graphics Card

[historical] [video systems] Hercules Computer Technologies manufactured several of the original video cards for IBM microcomputers. Their first major products was the Hercules Graphics Card, introduced in 1982. In its default mode, the HGC emulates the IBM Monochrome Display Adapter. Like the MDA, the HGC includes a parallel printer port. But, in addition to an alphanumeric mode compatible with the IBM Monochrome Display Adapter, the HGC has a bitmapped graphics mode with 720-by-348 dots definition. The Hercules Graphics Card will drive a standard IBM monochrome monitor.

In 1986, Hercules introduced a new version of the graphics card named the Hercules Graphics Card Plus. This adapter is compatible with the IBM MDA card and the Hercules Graphics Card, but also offers the possibility of displaying 3072 different characters. This company has also developed color cards that are compatible with the IBM CGA, EGA, and VGA standards as well as Windows accelerator cards and true-color cards for the high-end video market.

HEX$ (function)

[BASIC] [QuickBASIC] Returns a string representing the hexadecimal value of a decimal argument. The function format is:

```
v$ = HEX$(n)
```

where n is a whole number from -32768 to 65535. If n is negative the two's complement is computed, that is:

```
HEX$(-n) = HEX$(65536-n)
```

Hexadecimal numbers

[PC hardware and architecture] The hexadecimal number system uses the ten decimal symbols (0, 1, 2, 3, 4, 5, 6, 7, 8, and 9) as well as the first six letters of the alphabet (A, B, C, D, E, and F) to create a 16-symbol set:

decimal	hexadecimal	binary
0	0	0000
1	1	0001
2	2	0010
3	3	0011
4	4	0100
5	5	0101
6	6	0110
7	7	0111
8	8	1000
9	9	1001
10	A	1010
11	B	1011
12	C	1100
13	D	1101
14	E	1110
15	F	1111

Hexadecimal numbers are convenient because they a provide a shorthand for representing binary numbers. The hexadecimal shorthand has proved particularly useful because most modern computers use memory cells, registers, and data paths in multiples of four binary digits. Hexadecimal numbers are sometimes called hex.

HIBYTE

[MS-Pascal] Heading: (INTEGER-WORD): BYTE;

Extend level intrinsic function which returns the most significant byte of an INTEGER or WORD. Depending on the target processor, the most significant byte may be the first or the second addressed byte of the word. (See also: LOBYTE).

Hierarchy of operators

[C] All programming languages establish *rules of hierarchy* that determine the order in which each element in an expression is evaluated. For example, in the expression:

```
true_false = 5 - 4 < 3;
```

the rules of associativity determine which subtraction is performed first. In most programming languages, including C, the most common rule of associativity is left to right. Therefore the above subtraction is performed as in the expression (a minus b) minus c.

Precedence and Associativity of C Operators

PRECEDENCE	OPERATORS	DESCRIPTION	ASSOCIATIVITY
1	() [] . >	Expression	Left to right
2	- ~ ! * & ++ -- sizeof	Unary operators	Right to left
3	* / %	Multiplicative	Left to right
4	+ -	Additive	Left to rigth
5	<< >>	Bitwise shifts	Left to right
6	< <= > >=	Relational	Left to right
7	== !=	Relational	Left to right
8	&	Bitwise AND	Left to right
9	^	Bitwise XOR	Left to right
10	|	Bitwise OR	Left to right
11	&&	Logical AND	Left to right
12	||	Logical OR	Left to right
13	?:	Conditional	Right to left
14	= *= /= %= += -= <<= >>= &= |= ^=	Assignment (simple and compound)	Right to left
15	,	Sequential evaluation	Right to left

HIWORD

[MS-Pascal] Heading: (INTEGER4) : WORD;
Extend level intrinsic function that returns the high-order word of the four bytes of the INTEGER4. The sign bit of the INTEGER4 becomes the most significant bit of the WORD.

(See also: LOWORD).

HLT

[Assembler] 8086 machine instruction. Mnemonic for HaLT. Instruction designed as an alternative to an endless software loop in situations where the CPU must wait for an interrupt. HLT places the processor in its HALT state, which terminates upon the occurrence of a maskable or nonmaskable interrupt or a hardware reset. No flags are affected. In protected mode, HLT is a privileged instruction. The HLT instruction is seldom used in the PC environment.

IBM Personal Computer

[PC hardware and architecture] In 1980, IBM formed a design team for the purpose of creating a small computer. This group, based in Boca Raton, Florida, was called the Entry Systems Division. One of the team's first decisions was the selection of the Intel 8088 as the CPU for the new machines. The Intel 8086, the Motorola 68000, and the Zilog Z8000 were the other options considered by the designers. One of the factors that influenced their decision in favor of the 8088 was the economical advantages offered by the CPU's 8-bit bus.

Identifiers

[Assembler] [C] [BASIC] [Pascal] [COBOL] An identifier is a name or phase that is associated with one of the following program elements:

1. the name of a variable or constant
2. the name of a formal program parameter
3. the name of a subprogram or a location within a program
4. the name of a data type
5. the name of a program operation or function

In this context identifiers are also called simple names. The syntax requirements for identifiers change in the different languages and implementations, although it is generally accepted that identifiers must start with an alphabetical character and contain no embedded spaces.

IDIV

[Assembler] 8086 machine instruction. Mnemonic for Integer DIVide. The Intel mnemonics for signed and unsigned division opcodes is somewhat confusing since the opcode names do not precisely represent the actual operation performed by the instruction. The IDIV instruction (integer divide) refers to operations with *signed* numbers, while the DIV (divide) instruction refers to unsigned operations. The designation IDIV, in which the prefix letter "I" is associated with the word *integer*, seems to imply that *fractional* division is also available, which is not the case. The programmer must translate this use of the word *integer* to mean *signed*.

IDIV preforms the signed division of an implicit dividend, located in the accumulator register, by the explicit source operand. The three possibilities are shown in the following table:

SOURCE SIZE	DIVIDEND	QUOTIENT	REMAINDER
byte	AX	AL	AH
word	DX:AX	AX	DX
doubleword	EDX:EAX	EAX	EDX

For byte division the largest possible quotient is +127 (7FH) and the smallest negative quotient is -127 (81H). For word division the largest possible quotient is +32,767 (7FFFH) and the smallest negative quotient is -32,767 (8001H). For doubleword division the largest is 7FFFFFFFH and the smallest value is 80000001H. If the divisor is zero, a type 0 interrupt is generated. If the quotient exceeds the maximum positive value or if it is less than the minimum negative value, a type 0 interrupt is also generated. In the PC environment an interrupt 0 handler is provided by the BIOS. AF, CF, OF, PF, SF, and ZF are undefined. Code sample:

```
; Signed division of -4000 by 40
        MOV    BL,40          ; Divisor to BL
        MOV    AX,-4000       ; Signed dividend
        IDIV   BL             ; Byte division
; At this point AL = -100 (quotient), AH = 0 (reminder)
```

(See also: DIV).

IF (block)

[QuickBASIC] A block of statements beginning with a statement of the form IF condition THEN and ending with the statement END IF, indicates that the group of statements between IF and END IF are to be executed only when the condition is true. If the group of statements is separated into two parts by an ELSE statement, then the first part is executed when the condition is true and the second part when the condition is false.

IF statement

[BASIC] [QuickBASIC] Makes a decision regarding program flow based on an expression being true or false. The statement has two standard formats:

```
IF condition[,]THEN action1 [ELSE action2]
IF condition[,]GOTO line(label)[[,]ELSE action2]
```

A statement of the form IF condition THEN action1 causes the program to take the specified action if condition is true. Otherwise, execution continues at the next line. A statement of the form IF condition THEN action1 ELSE action2 causes the program to take action1 if condition is true and action2 if condition is false.

IMUL

[Assembler] 8086 machine instruction. Mnemonic for Integer MULtiply. The Intel mnemonics for signed and unsigned multiplication opcodes is somewhat confusing. The IMUL instruction (integer multiply) refers to operations with *signed* numbers, while the MUL (multiply) instruction refers to unsigned operations. The designation IMUL, in which the prefix letter "I" is associated with the word *integer*, seems to imply that *fractional* multiplication is also available, which is not the case. The programmer must translate this use of the word *integer* to mean *signed*.

IMUL preforms the signed multiplication of an implicit multiplicand, located in the accumulator register, by the explicit source operand. The three possibilities are shown in the following table:

SOURCE SIZE	MULTIPLIER	PRODUCT
byte	AL	AH:AL
word	AX	DX:AX
doubleword	EAX	EDX:EAX

IMUL clears OF and CF if the upper half of the result (AH, DX, and EDX) is not the sign extension of the lower half. When OF and CF are set, then AH, DX, or EDX contain significant digits. AF, PF, SF, and ZF are undefined.
Code sample:

```
; Multiplication of a signed word operand in BX by a
; signed byte in AL
        MOV    BX,-1234      ; Load byte multiplier
        MOV    AL,-104       ; Load multiplicand (98H)
        CBW                  ; Convert to word
; At this point AX holds FF98H
        IMUL   BX            ; -1234 * -104
; Result of -1234 * -104 is 128,336. The product is stored
; in DX:AX as 0001:F550H
```

(See also: MUL, CBW, CWD, CWDE, and IDIV).

IN

[Assembler] 8086 machine instruction. Mnemonic for INput from port. Transfers a data byte, word, or doubleword from an input port into the accumulator (AL, AX, or EAX). Access to a byte-size port number can be coded using the port number as an immediate operand, for example:

```
        IN      AL,0DAH         ; Read port DAH into AL
```

Access to a word-size port number requires loading the port into the DX register. In this case the instruction is coded as follows:

```
        MOV     DX,2122H        ; Port to DX
        IN      AL,DX           ; Input from port to AL
```

It is necessary to allow a few microseconds for the hardware to recover when coding back-to-back read and write operations to the same port. One coding scheme is based on using the $ assembler operator to represent the current value in the instruction pointer. The fact that a short jump instruction is 2-bytes long allows coding a jump to the next program line without the use of a label, as follows:

```
        OUT     21H,AL          ; Output to port 21H
        JMP     SHORT $ + 2     ; I/O delay
        IN      AL,21H          ; Read port 21H
```

The destination operand of the IN instruction can also be a word or double-word register. In this case the action of the IN instruction, although not clearly documented in Intel literature, appears to be to read the byte from port DX into the AL register, and the byte from port DX + 1 into AH, for example:

```
        MOV     DX,0AF0H        ; Base port
        IN      AX,DX           ; byte at port 0AF0H to AL
                                ; byte at port 0AF1H to AH
```

Although this instruction format is often used when accessing devices with multiple consecutive ports, its operation is hardware dependant and should be coded with caution. The doubleword format of the IN instruction:

```
        IN      EAX,DX
```

is even less reliable than the word format.

INC

[**Assembler**] 8086 machine instruction. Mnemonic for INCrement by one. Adds one to the destination operand without changing the carry flag. The destination operand, which can be a byte-, word, or doubleword-size register or memory operand, is treated as an unsigned binary. Updates AF, OF, PF, SF, and ZF. CF is not affected.
Code sample:

```
        INC     AX      ; AX = AX + 1
```

INKEY$ (variable)

[BASIC] [QuickBASIC] Reads a single character from the keyboard. Statement format is:

```
v$ = INKEY$
```

The returned value is a 0, 1, or 2 character string. A NULL string (length 0) indicates that no characters were waiting. Number, letters, and symbols are identified by a single character. Control, Alt, function, and other keys are identified by two characters, CHR$(0) followed by CHR$(n), where n is the scan code.

INKEY$ does not display the characters on the screen. It is often used in coding routines that monitor the keyboard for a key pressed without halting program execution.

Example:

```
'Retrieve character or scan code using INKEY$
K$ = INKEY$
IF LEN(K$) = 2 THEN K$=RIGHT(K$,1)
```

INP (function)

[BASIC] [QuickBASIC] Returns the byte input from a port. The function format is:

```
v = INP(n)
```

where *n* is a port number in the range 0 to 65535. INP performs a function similar to the machine instruction IN. The complementary operation is OUT.

INPUT (statement)

[BASIC] [QuickBASIC] Receives keyboard input during program execution. The statement format is:

```
INPUT[;]["prompt";] variable[,variable]...
```

where "prompt" is a string to prompt the user, and variable is the name of the variable (numeric, string, or array) that stores the input data. Upon execution of INPUT, BASIC displays a question mark and waits for the user to enter a response. This response is assigned to the variable defined in the INPUT statement. When the statement format:

```
INPUT "prompt"; variable
```

is used, the prompting message is displayed before the question mark. Statements in the format:

```
INPUT "prompt", var
```

prompt without the question mark, and statements of the format:

```
INPUT; var
```

suppress a carriage return following the entering of the response. In each of these statements, variable may be replaced by a number of variables separated by commas. After the user responds with the proper number of values (separated by commas) and presses Enter, each of the values is assigned to the corresponding variable.

Example:

```
PI = 3.1415
INPUT "ENTER RADIUS OF CIRCLE "; R
AREA = PI * R * R
PRINT "THE AREA IS "; AREA
END
```

INPUT$ (function)

[BASIC] [QuickBASIC] Returns a string of characters read from a file or from the keyboard. The function format is:

```
v$ = INPUT$(n[,[#]filenum])
```

where *n* is the number of characters to be read, and filenum is the number assigned to the file with an OPEN statement. If filenum is omitted the keyboard is read. The function action is to pause until the user types *n* characters. The string consisting of these *n* characters is then assigned to v$. A statement in the format:

```
v$ = INPUT$(n,m)
```

assigns the next *n* characters from the file number *m* to v$. If the keyboard is used no characters are echoed on the screen.

INPUT# (statement)

[BASIC] [QuickBASIC] Reads data items from a sequential file or device and assigns them to variables. The statement format is:

```
INPUT# filenum, variable[, variable]...
```

where filenum is the number assigned to the file with the OPEN statement, and variable is the name of the variable (numeric, string, or array) to which an item in the file is assigned.

INS/INSB/INSW/INSD

[Assembler] 80186/286 machine instruction. Mnemonic for INput String. Transfers a byte, word, or doubleword from an input port (in the DX register) to a memory location pointed at by ES:DI or ES:EDI, and updates DI or EDI to the next string element. The following mnemonics are used for byte, word, and doubleword operands:

```
MNEMONIC     SIZE          PORT SOURCE     DESTINATION
INSB         byte          DX              ES:DI or ES:EDI
INSW         word          DX              ES:DI or ES:EDI
INSD         doubleword    DX              ES:DI or ES:EDI
```

The destination operand must be addressable by the ES register since no segment override is possible. The port number must be in DX since no immediate port operand is allowed.

When the REP prefix is used, then the data transfer repeats as many iterations as the value stored in the CX register. In this case a block transfer takes place into the memory area originally addressed by ES:DI or ES:EDI. The direction flag determines if the move takes place towards higher- or lower-numbered memory locations.

Code sample:

```
DATA    SEGMENT
BUF_1   DB      50 DUP (0H)   ; Storage for 50 bytes
DATA    ENDS
;
CODE    SEGMENT
           .
           .
        PUSH    DS            ; DS to stack
        POP     ES            ; Now ES = DS
        LEA     DI,BUF_1      ; Pointer to memory storage
        MOV     CX,50         ; Repeat 50 time
        MOV     DX,0A21H      ; Port in DX
        CLD                   ; Direction forward
REP     INSB                  ; Input string bytes
; At this point 50 bytes have been input from port A21H and
; stored consecutively in the buffer designated with the
; name BUF_1.
```

It is documented that the INS instruction may fail with port devices that require a longer recovery time than that provided by the instruction's execution speed. See IN instruction for sample code implementing input/output delay.

Instructions

[Assembler] In the context of 80x86 assembly language, an instruction is a single operation of the microprocessor. There are over 100 instructions in the 80x86 microprocessor. A great part of the task of learning assembly language is becoming familiar with these instructions.
(See Opcode, Operand).

INT

[Assembler] 8086 machine instruction. Mnemonic for INTerrupt. Generates a software interrupt to the specified handler. The immediate operand is a value in the range 0 to 255. In the real mode the operand is indexed into a 1024-byte interrupt vector table, located at physical address 00000H. Each entry in the vector table consists of one doubleword which stores the address of the corresponding handler in segment:offset format. Therefore the location of each handler address can be calculated by multiplying the interrupt number times 4.

INT executes in real mode by decrementing SP by two, pushing the flags onto the stack as well as the far address of the following instruction, clearing TF and IF to disable single-step and maskable interrupts, and transferring execution to the handler specified in the immediate operand. Routines accessed by the INT instruction return execution by means of IRET, which pops the flags from the stack and returns execution to the instruction following INT.

In protected mode the interrupt vector is stored in the Interrupt Descriptor Table (IDT) as an array of eight-byte descriptors.
Code sample:

```
; Use if INT instruction to access BIOS keyboard service
        MOV    AX,0   ; Service request for keyboard
                      ; wait function
        INT    16H    ; BIOS keyboard service
; Execution returns with the code for the last key
; pressed
```

A special case is encoded with the instruction:

```
        INT    03H
```

In this case the assembler generates a 1-byte opcode known as the breakpoint interrupt (opcode = CCH). The programmer can use the INT 03H instruction format to force a program breakpoint when code is executed under a debugger. When the program is executed normally the INT 03H instruction has no effect.

(See also: INTO and IRET).

INTO

[Assembler] 8086 machine instruction. Mnemonic for INTerrupt on Overflow. Generates a software interrupt to vector 04H if the overflow flag is set. If OF is clear, then execution proceeds to the instruction following INTO.

INTO executes in the real mode by decrementing SP by two, pushing the flags onto the stack as well as the far address of the following instruction, clearing TF and IF to disable single-step and maskable interrupts, and transferring execution to the handler located at offset 10H in the interrupt vector table. Routines accessed by the INTO instruction return execution by means of IRET, which pops the flags from the stack and returns execution to the instruction following INTO.

INTO is designed to be used as a trap for the overflow condition in arithmetic or logical routines. Coding requires no operands, as follows:

```
INTO              ; Interrupt to vector 04H if OF = 1
```

(See also: INT).

INVD

[Assembler] 486 machine instruction. Mnemonic for INValidate Cache. The 486/Pentium internal cache memory is flushed and a special-function bus cycle to indicate that the external cache should also be flushed is issued. Data in write-back external cache is not written back.

Intel warns that INVD should be used with care since it does not write back modified cache lines, which implies that data cache may become inconsistent. Except in those cases where cache coherence with main memory is not a concern, the WBINVD instruction should be used instead.

In protected mode INVD requires privilege level 0.

(See also: WBINVD).

INVLPG

[Assembler] 486 machine instruction. Mnemonic for INVaLidate PaGe table entry or INVaLidate TLB entry. The instruction is used to ensure that there are no invalid entries in the translation lookaside buffer (TLB) which is the cache used for translating linear addresses to physical addresses.

TLB architecture consists of eight sets of data entries, labeled 0 to 7. The instruction requires one or more immediate operands in this range to indicate the entry number or numbers desired, for example:

```
INVLPF 5        ; Invalidate TLB entry 5
```

INSTR (function)

[BASIC] [QuickBASIC] Searches for the presence of a substring within a string and returns the position of the substring. An optional parameter allows setting the position for starting the search in the target string. The statement format is:

```
v = INSTR([n,]x$,y$)
```

where n is an optional numeric expression in the range 1 to 255 that designates the offset in the target string at which the search is to start, x$ is the target string, and y$ is the substring. INSTR returns 0 if the string parameters are invalid or if the substring is not found in the target string.
Example:

```
MSU$ = "MONTANA STATE UNIVERSITY"
U$ = "UNI"
PRINT  INSTR(MSU$, U$)
```

Result: 15

INT (function)

[BASIC] [QuickBASIC] Returns the largest integer that is less than or equal to the operand. The function format is:

```
v = INT(x)
```

where x is a numeric expression. The action of the INT function is to truncate positive integers and to round-down negative integers.
Example:

```
PRINT INT(66.77); INT(-33.12)
```

Result: 66   -34

IOCTL (statement)

[BASIC] [QuickBASIC] Sends a control string to an open device driver. The statement format is:

```
IOCTL [#]filenum,string
```

where filenum is the file number of the device driver, and string is an expression containing the control data.

IOCTL$ (function)

[BASIC] [QuickBASIC] Reads a control string to an open device driver. The statement format is:

```
v$ = IOCTL$([#]filenum)
```

where filenum is the file number of the device driver.

Identifier

[C] An *identifier* is a name or phrase. A C identifier consists of one or more letters, numbers, or the underscore symbol. Upper- and lower-case letters are considered different symbols by C. For example, the names ABC and aBc are considered different. An identifier cannot start with a digit. For example, the identifier 1ABC is not legal in C. The ANSI C standard requires that the compiler recognize at least the first 31 characters in an identifier. The following are legal identifiers:

```
personal_name
PI
y_121
XY_value_128
User_address_and_zipcode
```

if and if-else constructs

[C] An *if* construct consists of three elements:

1. The *if* keyword
2. A test expression, also called a *conditional clause*
3. One or more statements that execute if the test expression evaluates to a logical true (not zero)

The following program, named BEEPER, makes the PC speaker beep three times if the user presses the key labeled B. The code uses an if construct to test if the typed keystroke matches the uppercase or lowercase letter "b" as labeled in the #define statements. Note that the beeping sound is produced by using the \a control code in a printf() function.

```
#include <stdio.h>
#define BIG_B 'B'
#define LIT_B 'b'
main()
{
```

```
char typed_key;          /* variable for user keystroke /*
printf("Press the B key to beep speaker\n");
typed_key = getche();
    if (typed_key == BIG_B || typed_key == LIT_B)
        printf("\a\a\a");
}
```

The listed program is the simplest form of the if construct. In this case the compiler evaluates the expression in parentheses, following the if keyword, which is:

```
if (typed_key == BIG_B || typed_key == LIT_B)
```

If the expression evaluates to a nonzero value (true), the statement that follows is executed. If the expression evaluates to zero (false), then the statement associated with the if clause is skipped.

If statements can be nested so that the execution of a statement or statement group is conditioned to two or more conditional clauses. For example, we can modify the *if* construct in the previous program so that the uppercase keystroke for the letter b is identified, as follows:

```
if (typed_key == BIG_B || typed_key == LIT_B) {
printf("\a\a\a");
  if (typed_key == BIG_B)
  printf("\nKeystroke was B");
}
```

In the above code the *if* statement that tests for an uppercase letter b is nested inside the *if* statement that tests for upper- or lowercase characters. Therefore, the inner *if* statement is never reached if the outer one evaluates to false. The following flowchart shows a nested if construct.

if-else construct

[C] A limitation of the simple *if* construct is that it executes a statement or statement block if the conditional clause evaluates to true but that no action is taken if the expression evaluates to false. The *if-else* construct provides a way for taking separate action if a conditional clause evaluates to true or if it evaluates to false.

For instance, we could use the *if-else* so that a message indicates whether the keystroke entered by the user corresponds to the uppercase letter B. The following code fragment illustrates the coding of an *if-else* construct:

```
if (typed_key == "B")
  printf("\nKeystroke was B");
else
    printf("\nKeystroke was not B");
```

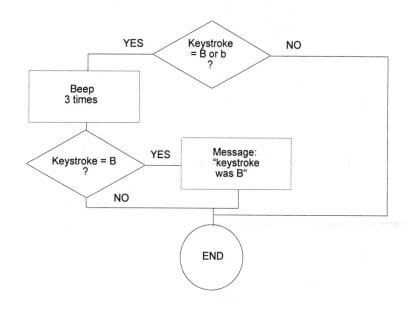

Flowchart of Nested if Construct

In typing the *if-else* construct it is customary to align the *if* and the *else* keywords, as shown in this fragment. Like the *if* clause, the *else* clause can also contain a statement block, delimited by braces if more than one statement is to execute on the *else* program branch.

Because the *else* statement is optional, it is possible to have several nested *if* constructs not all of which have a corresponding *else* clause. This situation, sometimes referred to as a *dangling else* statement, can give rise to uncertainty regarding the pairing of *if* and *else* clauses. For example, the *else* clause in the following fragment is paired with the inner if statement:

```
if (a != 0 )
        if a > 1
                printf("x is positive and non-zero);
        else
                printf("x is zero or negative);
```

In this case we have used the same indentation for the paired *if* and *else* clauses. The general rule used by the compiler in solving this ambiguity is that each *else* statement is paired with the most recent *if* that does not have an *else*. However, the programmer can use braces to force a different association between statements; for example:

```
if (a != 0 ) {
        if a > 1
```

```
        printf("x is positive and non-zero);
    }
else
    printf("x must be zero");
```

In resolving uncertainties regarding a dangling *else* statement it is important to remember that indentation is not meaningful to the compiler and that it serves only to make the code more readable.

Increment and decrement operators

[C] *Increment* (+ +) and *decrement* (- -) are unique C operators that allow adding 1 and subtracting 1 from an expression. The action of the increment and decrement operators can be seen in the following expressions:

```
x = x + 1;
y = y - 1;
```

or the equivalent increment/decrement expressions:

```
+ + x;
- - y;
```

The increment and decrement operators can be placed before or after an expression. When the operator precedes the expression it is said to be in *prefix* form. When it is placed after the expression it is said to be in *postfix* form. For example:

```
PREFIX FORM              POSTFIX FORM
z = + + x;                z = x + +;
```

The prefix and postfix forms are equivalent in unary statements. For instance, the variable x is incremented by 1 in both of these statements:

```
x + +;
+ + x;
```

However, when the increment or decrement is used in an expression that contains an assignment operator, the prefix or postfix form determines whether 1 is added or subtracted before or after the value is assigned. In other words, the prefix form in the statement

```
    y = + + x;
```

determines that the variable *x* is first incremented and the result is assigned to the variable *y*. On the other hand, the postfix form

```
y = x + +;
```

determines that the original value of x is assigned to the variable y and then the variable x is incremented.

Indirection operator

[C] A *pointer* is a variable that holds the address of another variable. This address is obtained by means of the address-of operator (& symbol). However, pointers are special variables, which are managed differently than conventional ones. In the first place, pointer variables are declared using the C *indirection operator,* the * symbol. For example, the statement:

```
int *add1;
```

declares a *pointer variable* named add1. In the case of pointer variables the type does not refer to the type of the pointer, but to the type of the variable whose address the pointer stores. After this declaration, a variable, named add1, has been created and can be used as a pointer to any variable of int type. The actual operation of assigning an address to a pointer variable is performed by means of the address-of operator, as in the following statement:

```
add1 = &num1;
```

Now the pointer variable add1 holds the address of the variable num1.

But the pointer variable add1 would be of limited use if it served only as a shorthand for the expression &num1. A powerful feature of C is that it also allows the use of pointers to access, indirectly, the contents of a variable. Thus, once the pointer variable add1 holds the address of the variable num1, we can add 10 to the contents of num1 using the following statement:

```
*add1 = *add1 + 10;
```

The * symbol preceding a pointer variable indicates the contents of the variable whose address the pointer holds, num1 in this case.

Assuming that the pointer variable add1 holds the address of the variable num1, the following statements perform identical operations:

```
num1 = num1 + 10;
*add1 = *add1 + 10;
```

In this case there is no advantage to changing the value of a variable by using a pointer to its contents rather than by using the variable name. However, pointer variables become particularly useful in addressing array elements. The array declaration:

```
int array1[] = { 10, 20, 30, 4000, 5000 };
```

creates five integer variables that can be accessed by hard-coding the offset in the array brackets or by representing the offset with another variable:

```
num1 = array1[3];
```

or

```
count = 3;
num1 = array1[count];
```

In either case the value 4000 (stored in the fourth array element) could be assigned to the variable num1.

Another way of accessing array elements is by creating a pointer variable to hold the address of the first element of the array. For example, first declare a pointer variable to int type:

```
int *add1;
```

then set the pointer variable to hold the address of the first array element:

```
add1 = &array1[0];
```

As is the case with conventional pointer variables, an *array pointer* can be used to gain access to the contents of a variable by preceding it with the indirection operator symbol (*). For example, after initializing add1 with the address of array1[0], we can change the value of the first array element by coding:

```
*add1 = 100;
```

Input devices

[input/output] [**PC hardware and architecture**] Some PC configurations can receive and process input originating in devices different from the keyboard. The following are some alternative input devices:

1. Mouse
2. Track ball
3. Touchpad or digitizer
4. Scanner

The first three listed mechanisms are usually classified as *pointing devices*. Several independent vendors have developed and marketed pointing devices compatible with the IBM microcomputers of the PC line. These devices are typically packaged to include an interface card and the necessary software. One such device is the Microsoft mouse.

Input functions

[C] Most computer programs require some form of interaction with the user. The operation of furnishing data or instructions to a computer program is called *input*. The keyboard is the most common device by which the human operator communicates with the machine. Therefore, it is usually considered the *standard input device*.

int86() function

[C] PC implementations of C include a special library function called int86(), which allows using the BIOS services. Int86() is declared in the include file DOS.H. Note that the name int86() relates both to the word "interrupt" and to the 80x86 family of microprocessors; the use of BIOS services requires some knowledge of software interrupts and of the 80x86 internal registers.

Data is passed to the BIOS services in the 80x86 hardware registers. For example, the BIOS service that is used to change the current position of the screen cursor receives the new value for the cursor row in the DH register and the cursor column in the DL register. The most used registers for passing data to the BIOS services via the int86() library function are the general-purpose registers, although some services require the use of other registers.

The BIOS services provide many useful operations regarding input and output devices as well as system information. An MS-DOS C program can access these services by means of the int86() library function.

Not all BIOS services require data passed by the caller and not all of them return information. The service number is passed in the AH register. For example, service number 2 of interrupt 10H (video services) receives data in DH, DL, and BH, but returns nothing. On the other hand, service number 15 of this same interrupt requires no data passed to it and returns information in AL, AH, and BH. The following program uses BIOS service number 15 of interrupt 10H to obtain the current video mode:

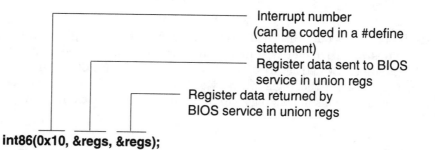

Interrupt number
(can be coded in a #define statement)
Register data sent to BIOS service in union regs
Register data returned by BIOS service in union regs

int86(0x10, &regs, &regs);

General Format of the C Function int86()

```
#include <stdio.h>
#define  VIDEO_INT  0x10
main()
{
    struct WORDREGS         /* General purpose registers as    */
        {                   /* word-size units                 */
        unsigned int ax;
        unsigned int bx;
        unsigned int cx;
        unsigned int dx;
        unsigned int si;
        unsigned int di;
        unsigned int flags;
        };
    struct BYTEREGS         /* General purpose registers as    */
        {                   /* byte-size units                 */
        unsigned char al, ah;
        unsigned char bl, bh;
        unsigned char cl, ch;
        unsigned char dl, dh;
        };
    union REGS              /* Union allows storage of either  */
        {                   /* byte-size or word-size units     */
        struct WORDREGS x;  /* x = word-size units             */
        struct BYTEREGS h;  /* h = byte-size units             */
        }
    union REGS regs;        /* union declaration of type REGS */
    unsigned char video_mode;
    regs.h.ah = 15;
    int86(VIDEO_INT, &regs, &regs);
    video_mode = regs.h.al;
    printf("\nActive video mode is: %u", video_mode);
return(0);
}
```

Note in this program that the video mode is recovered with the statement:

```
video_mode = regs.h.al;
```

In this case the data returned by the function (in the AL register) are stored in a byte-size variable of type unsigned char. The union tagged regs, of type REGS, defines two structures: WORDREGS and BYTEREGS. The first one allows addressing the registers as word-size units and the second one as byte-size units. This makes regs a *union of structures*. The expression

```
regs.h.al
```

which contains the membership operator twice, refers to the structure member al (in a structure of type BYTEREGS) within the regs union tag, of type h.

The structures WORDREGS and BYTEREGS, as well as the union of type REGS are declared in the include file dos.h. The programmer can save the effort of typing these elements by means of an include statement.

IRET

[Assembler] 8086 machine instruction. Mnemonic for Interrupt ReTurn. Transfers control to the instruction following an INT opcode by popping the far address from the stack as well as the flags. Since IRET restores all flags to the values at the time of the interrupt call, the interrupt handler need not be concerned with this element of the caller's context. IRET is also used to exit a hardware interrupt handler.

In protected mode if NT is clear then IRET returns from the interrupt routine without a task switch. In this case to code to which execution returns must be have equal or less privilege than the interrupt routine, as determined by the RPL bits of the CS selector. SP and SS are popped from the stack. If NT is set, then IRET reverses the effect of the CALL or INT instruction that caused the task switch. In this case the updated state of the task executing IRET is saved in the task state segment.

iteration

[General programming] The idea of a program *iteration* is often used in relation to loops and other repetitive structures. In this context to iterate means to perform repeatedly, and each transition through the statement or group of statements in the loop structure is considered an iteration. Thus, referring to a program loop that repeats a group of statements three times we can speak of the first, the second, and the third iteration. However, the concept of a program iteration is not limited to loop structures, but refers to any form of repetitive processing, independent of the logical means by which it is performed.

iterative statements

[General programming] Computer programs must often perform repetitive tasks. For example, a typical payroll program estimates wages and deductions by performing the same basic calculations on the data corresponding to each employee in the system. These repetitions are usually performed by means of special programming structures called *loops*.

The loop structure is merely a programming convenience that allows reusing the same program statements, with considerable savings in coding effort. Therefore, loops do not offer an original or singular function; repetitions that can be performed by means of a loop can also be specified by explicitly coding each processing step. Nevertheless, in some cases explicitly coding each program operation can be quite a cumbersome task.

All program loops, independently of the specific looping structures provided by a particular programming language, involve three characteristic steps.

1. The *initialization* step primes the logical elements and variables used by the loop structure to an initial, known state.

2. The *processing* step performs the repetitive processing operations. This step is repeated during each iteration.

3. The *testing* step evaluates the variables or conditions that determine the end of the loop. If the condition or conditions are met, the loop execution concludes, if not, the processing operation or operations are repeated. Note that these steps are more readily distinguishable in some loop structures than in others.

Instruction set

[PC hardware and architecture] At the assembler level, the 8086/8088 instruction set appears to have about 100 instructions. This simplification is possible by considering several machine operations as a single function; for example, the assembly language MOV mnemonic includes all 28 possible variants of the machine move operation. The assembler programs available for the IBM microcomputers translate these mnemonic operation codes and operands into the corresponding machine codes that can be executed by the CPU.

INT n instruction

[PC hardware and architecture] The INT n instruction generates an interrupt to the vector contained in the operand, independent of the nature of the original interrupt. For example, INT 00H generates a divide by zero interrupt as if this condition had actually occurred in the microprocessor.

Intel microprocessors

[PC hardware and architecture] All IBM microcomputers and compatible machines use an Intel microprocessors of the iAPX family. The Intel 8080 can be considered the immediate predecessor of the IAPX family. The 8080 was introduced in April 1974 as a general-purpose 8-bit microprocessor. The chip executes approximately 290,000 operations per second and addresses a memory area of 64K. An operational microcomputer using the 8080 could be built with only six additional chips.

Interrupt controller

[PC hardware and architecture] The Intel 8259A programmable interrupt controller (PIC) is an integrated circuit designed to manage the external interrupts in a microcomputer system. The 8259A is used in all IBM microcom-

Intel Microprocessor Architecture

FEATURES	8080	8086	8088	80186	80188	80286	80386	80386SX	486/Pentium
Address bus (in bits)	8	16	8	16	8	16	32	16	32
Internal data path (in bits)	8	16	16	16	16	16	32	32	32/64
Clock speed (in MHz)	2, 2.6, 6.3	5, 8, 10	5, 8	8, 10, 12.5	8, 10, 12.5	6, 8, 10, 12.5, 20	16, 20, 25, 33	16	25-66
Register to register (μs/data word)	1.3	0.3	0.38	0.2	0.3	0.125	0.125	0.125	0.04
Interrupt response time (μs)	7.3	6.1	8.6	3.36	6.2	2.52	3.5	2.52	3.5
Memory address range	64K	1 Mbyte	1 Mbyte	1 Mbyte	1 Mbyte	16 Mbytes	4 giga-bytes	4 giga-bytes	4 giga-bytes
Addressing modes	5	24	24	24	24	24	28	28	28
Coprocessor	No	8087	8087	8087	8087	80287	80287/80387	80287/80387	On chip
Number of general-purpose registers	6	8	8	8	8	8	8	8	8
Number of segment registers	0	4	4	4	4	4	6	6	6
Interrupt controller chip	8259-A	8259-A	8259-A	On chip	On chip	8259-A	8259-A	82335	μPLD
Timer-counter chip	8253	8253/54	8253/54	On chip	On chip	8253/54	8253/54	8253/54	On chip

Notes:
The 486 contains an integral cache controller and 8K of static RAM.
The Pentium contains a 16K static RAM cache.

puters of the PC and PS/2 lines and in many IBM-compatible machines. However, the hardware is not always configured in the same manner. For example, the IBM Personal Computer, the PC XT, the PCjr, and Models 25 and 30 of the PS/2 line use a single 8259A chip, while the PC AT, the Micro Channel models of the PS/2 line, and most IBM-compatible machines, use two 8259A controllers.

In operation, the 8259A can be described as consisting of four internal registers.

1. The *interrupt request register* (IRR) contains one bit for each interrupt channel (IRQ0 to IRQ7). The individual bits reflect which channels are requesting service. The IRR register can be read by the CPU.

2. The *interrupt mask register* (IMR) is an 8-bit register, one for each interrupt level. A bit set prevents the corresponding channel from generating an interrupt (masked).

3. The *priority resolver register* (PR) determines whether the interrupt's priority is sufficient to interrupt an executing interrupt service routine, according to the programmed priority scheme.

4. The *in-service register* (ISR) contains a bit for each interrupt level. This bit is set to indicate that the corresponding interrupt channel is being serviced. The ISR can be read by the CPU.

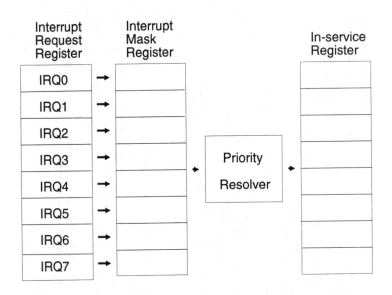

8259A Interrupt Controller Operation Diagram

Interrupt — nonmaskable

[PC hardware and architecture] The term *nonmaskable interrupt* is used to designate all interrupts that do not originate in the 8259A interrupt controller and are not affected by the processor's interrupt flag.

In IBM systems that use a single 8259A chip (such as the Personal Computer, the PC XT, the PCjr, and Models 25 and 30 of the PS/2 line), all external interrupts are mapped to eight lines, designated as IRQ0 to IRQ7. The PC AT and the Micro Channel models of the PS/2 line use two 8259A chips, designated as interrupt controllers 1 and 2. In this case there is a total of 16 interrupt lines, IRQ0 to IRQ15. Since IRQ2 is used to cascade the interrupts from controller number 2, it is not assigned to any specific interrupt.

Interrupt priorities

[PC hardware and architecture] Interrupts are processed according to priority assignments.

Interrupt Priorities

INTERRUPT	PRIORIY
Divide overflow	Highest
INT n instruction	
INTO (interrupt on overflow)	
NMI (nonmaskable interrupt)	
External interrupt on INTR line	
Single-step	Lowest

Interrupt processing

[PC hardware and architecture] Interrupt processing first tests whether the interrupt was triggered by a breakpoint or by an interrupt on overflow instruction. If it was triggered by a breakpoint, the CPU executes interrupt type 3, and it executes type 4 if the interrupt was triggered by an interrupt on overflow instruction. If the interrupt was triggered by neither a breakpoint nor an overflow condition, then the CPU uses the signature byte to calculate the address of the corresponding interrupt handler.

Interrupt vector table

[PC hardware and architecture] The special memory area that holds address pointers to each handler. The interrupt mechanism requires that the following conditions exist in the system:

1. The vector table in RAM, at segment 0000H, offset 0000H to 03FFH (1K), must have been initialized with the address of a service routine for each interrupt active in the system. The maximum number of entries is 256.

PC *Interrupt Types and Vectors*

ADDRESS	TYPE	INTERRUPT GROUP AND DESCRIPTION	
		NMI, Single-step, Breakpoint, Etc.	
0000H	0H	Divide by zero	
0004H	1H	Single-step	
0008H	2H	Nonmaskable interrupt (NMI)	
000CH	3H	Breakpoint	
0010H	4H	Interrupt on overflow (INTO)	
		Print Screen and Reserved	
0014H	5H	Print screen	
0018H	6H	Reserved by IBM	
001DH	7H	Reserved by IBM	
		Maskable External (8259 PIC)	
0020H	8H	System timer	IRQ0
0024H	9H	Keyboard handler	IRQ1
0028H	0AH	Reserved	IRQ2
002CH	0BH	Communications COM2	IRQ3
0030H	0CH	Communications COM1.....	IRQ4
0034H	0DH	Disk	IRQ5
0038H	0EH	Diskette	IRQ6
003CH	0FH	Printer	IRQ7
		BIOS Services and Data Areas	
0040H	10H	Video functions	
0044H	11H	Equipment check	
0048H	12H	Memory size	
004CH	13H	Diskette and disk	
0050H	14H	Communications	
0054H	15H	Cassette (AT extended services)	
0058H	16H	Keyboard	
005CH	17H	Printer	
0060H	18H	Resident BASIC language	
0064H	19H	Bootstrap	
0068H	1AH	Time-of-day	
006CH	1BH	Keyboard break	
0070H	1CH	User timer tick	
0074H	1DH	Video parameters ....Area	
0078H	1EH	Diskette parameters ....Area	
007CH	1FH	Graphic characters ....Area	
		DOS Services	
0080H	20H	DOS program terminate	
0084H	21H	DOS general service call	
0088H	22H	DOS terminate address	
008CH	23H	DOS control break exit address	
0090H	24H	DOS fatal error exit	
0094H	25H	DOS absolute disk read	
0098H	26H	DOS absolute disk write	
009CH	27H	DOS terminate and stay resident	
		DOS, BASIC, and User Software	
00A0H	28H	Reserved for DOS	
0100H	40H	Diskette BIOS revector	
0104H	41H	Hard disk parameters	
0108H	42H	Reserved by IBM	
0118H	46H	Hard disk parameters	
0128H	4AH	User alarm	
012CH	4BH	Reserved by IBM	
0180H	60H	Reserved for user software	
01C0H	70H	Real-time clock	
01C4H	71H	Reserved by IBM	
01D4H	75H	Math coprocessor	
01D8H	76H	Hard disk controller	
01DCH	77H	Reserved by IBM	
0200H	80H	Reserved or used by BASIC	
03C4H	F1H	Reserved for user software	

2. Each 4-byte entry stores a doubleword address in the standard segment:off-set form.

3. Interrupt types that do not have a service routine located at offset =type *4 must not be generated by the processor, by the hardware, or by an INT instruction.

Note that some vectors do not store pointers to service routines. For instance, address 0074H stores a pointer to a data area reserved for video parameters. The two addresses that follow also store pointers to data areas. Interrupts whose vectors do not contain pointers to service routines cannot be executed.

Interrupts

[**PC hardware and architecture**] Computer systems contain external devices that require the occasional attention of the central processor, such as keyboards, disk and diskette drives, and printers. One method of servicing external devices is to test them frequently to determine which, if any, require attention. This method, usually called *polling*, wastes considerable time in checking devices that do not need service. A more efficient method is to allow each device to *interrupt* the CPU. Compared with polling, the interrupt method substantially increases system performance.

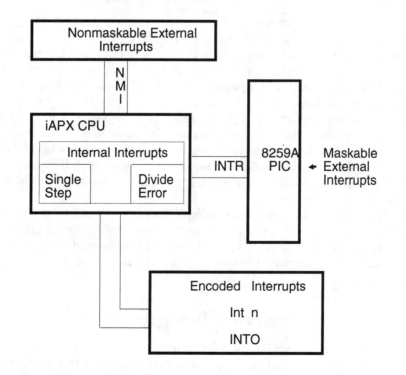

Interrupt Sources

The interrupt system in the PC is a mechanism that allows the central processing unit to respond to unpredictable events. When an interrupt signal is received, the CPU immediately diverts its attention from the task currently executing, but in a manner that allows the future resumption of this task. The processor then executes a routine that is specific to each particular interrupt. In the microprocessors of the Intel iAPX family, as used in IBM microcomputers, interrupts may be classified as follows:

1. *Internal interrupts* are those that originate inside the CPU, for example, the divide by zero or the single-step interrupt.

2. *External interrupts* are those initiated by external hardware. External interrupts are signaled to the CPU on the interrupt request line (INTR) or the nonmaskable interrupt line (NMI). On all IBM microcomputers the INTR line is driven by an Intel 8259A programmable interrupt controller.

3. *Software interrupts* are those initiated by an INT or INTO instruction.

Interrupt Encoding on Intel Systems

OPCODE	BYTES IN OPCODE	INTERRUPT TYPE
CCH	1	Type 3 interrupt (breakpoint)
CEH	1	Type 4 interrupt (INTO instruction)
CDH	2	Type 0 to 256 (interrupt type is encoded in the second byte)

Most internal, external, or software interrupts present to the CPU a specific signature, which is encoded in a byte that follows the interrupt opcode. This signature, sometimes called the *interrupt type*, serves to identify each interrupt to the CPU. However, interrupts generated by a breakpoint or by the INTO (interrupt on overflow) instruction do not contain a signature byte.

The breakpoint interrupt, typically used in debuggers, is planted at the location where execution is to be detained. The breakpoint handler is usually a routine to display registers and memory areas or perform other debugger functions. The breakpoint interrupt had to be designed as a 1-byte instruction so that it could be planted in the memory space occupied by even the shortest opcode in the instruction set.

The INTO instruction (interrupt on overflow) is triggered by the microprocessor's overflow flag (OF). The INTO instruction is used after an arithmetic or logical operation to detect if the signed result cannot be contained in the space of the destination operand. Because of its special nature, it does not require a signature byte.

Interrupts — Hardware interrupts

[**PC hardware and architecture**] Intel microprocessors of the iAPX line have two physical lines to signal interrupts, designated as INTR and NMI. The INTR line (interrupt request) is usually driven by an Intel 8259A interrupt controller.

All interrupt-driven external devices must be connected to the 8259A. The original purpose of an NMI line was to warn the microprocessor of an impending catastrophic event, like an imminent power failure, or of a parity error in memory. But some IBM systems use this line for other purposes; for instance, in the IBM PCjr, the NMI line is attached to the keyboard circuit, and in systems with an 8087 or 80287 math coprocessor, the NMI line is used to report an error exception.

The 8259A handles interrupts that originate in up to eight external devices by assigning a unique code to each interrupt source. This code, called the *interrupt type code*, is used by the CPU in locating, in the vector table, the address of the corresponding service routine. Interrupts that originate in the 8259A are maskable; that is, they can be individually enabled and disabled by programming the controller's interrupt mask register. In addition, all external interrupts can be temporarily disabled by clearing the processor's interrupt flag (IF) with a CLI instruction. The STI instruction resets IF, thus reenabling external interrupts.

INSERT

[MS-Pascal] Heading: (CONSTS S: STRING; VARS D: LSTRING;I: INTE-GER);A string intrinsic procedure. Inserts S starting just before D[I]. An error occurs if D is too small.

INTERRUPT attribute

[MS-Pascal] Applies only to procedures, not to functions or variables. It gives a procedure a special calling sequence that saves program status on the stack, which in turn allows a hardware interrupt to be processed, status restored, and control returned to the program, all without affecting the current state of the program.

Because procedures with the INTERRUPT attribute are intended to be invoked by hardware interrupts, they may not be invoked with a procedure statement. An INTERRUPT procedure can only be invoked when the interrupt associated with it occurs. INTERRUPT procedures take no parameters.

Declaring a procedure with the INTERRUPT attribute ensures that the procedure conforms to the constraints of an interrupt handler in which:

1. A special calling sequence saves all status on the stack

2. The status saved includes machine registers and flags, plus any special global compiler data such as the frame pointer

3. The saved status is restored upon exit from the procedure

All INTERRUPT procedures must be nested directly within a compiland.

Interrupts are not automatically vectored to INTERRUPT procedures nor are they enabled or disabled. Interrupt vectoring and enabling are too machine-dependent to be included in a machine-independent language like MS-Pascal.

J

JA

[Assembler] 8086 machine instruction. Mnemonic for Jump if Above. JNBE (Jump if Not Below or Equal) is an alternate mnemonic for the JA instruction. Relative jump to the target operand if CF and ZF = 0. The JA instruction usually follows a CMP, TEST, or an arithmetic or logical opcode, in order to direct execution to a target operand (usually a label) if the destination is a larger unsigned integer than the source.
Code sample:

```
            CMP     AL,20H      ; Compare AL and 20H
            JA      AL_BIGGER   ; Jump if AL > 20H
      ; At this point AL =< 20H
                .
                .
      AL_BIGGER:
```

In the context of Intel instruction mnemonics the terms *above* and *below* refer to unsigned integers while the terms *greater* and *less* refer to signed integers in two's complement form.
(See also: JNBE).
The range of a relative jump opcode is -128 to +127 bytes in 16-bit segments and -32768 to +32767 bytes in 32-bit segments.

JAE

[Assembler] 8086 machine instruction. Mnemonic for Jump if Above or Equal. JNB (Jump if Not Below) is an alternate mnemonic for the JAE instruction. Relative jump to the target operand if CF = 0. The JAE instruction usually follows a CMP, TEST, or an arithmetic or logical opcode, in order to direct execution to a target operand (usually a label) if the destination is an unsigned integer larger than or equal to the source.
Code sample:

```
            CMP     AL,20H       ; Compare AL and 20H
            JAE     AL_BIG_OR_EQ ; Jump if AL >= 20H
```

```
        ; At this point AL < 20H
                    .
                    .
        AL_BIG_OR_EQ:
```

In the context of Intel instruction mnemonics the terms *above* and *below* refer to unsigned integers while the terms *greater* and *less* refer to signed integers in two's complement form.

The range of a relative jump opcode is -128 to +127 bytes in 16-bit segments and -32768 to +32767 bytes in 32-bit segments.

JB

[Assembler] 8086 machine instruction. Mnemonic for Jump if Below. JNAE (Jump if Not Above or Equal) is an alternate mnemonic for the JB instruction. Relative jump to the target operand if CF = 1. The JB instruction usually follows a CMP, TEST, or an arithmetic or logical opcode, in order to direct execution to a target operand (usually a label) if the destination is a smaller unsigned integer than the source.

Code sample:

```
        CMP     AL,20H      ; Compare AL and 20H
        JB      AL_SMALLER  ; Jump if AL < 20H
        ; At this point AL => 20H
                    .
                    .
        AL_SMALLER:
```

In the context of Intel instruction mnemonics the terms *above* and *below* refer to unsigned integers while the terms *greater* and *less* refer to signed integers in two's complement form.

The range of a relative jump opcode is -128 to +127 bytes in 16-bit segments and -32768 to +32767 bytes in 32-bit segments.

JBE

[Assembler] 8086 machine instruction. Mnemonic for Jump if Below or Equal. JNA (Jump if Not Above) is an alternate mnemonic for the JBE instruction. Relative jump to the target operand if CF or ZF = 1. The JAE instruction usually follows a CMP, TEST, or an arithmetic or logical opcode, in order to direct execution to a target operand (usually a label) if the destination is an unsigned integer smaller than or equal to the source.

Code sample:

```
        CMP     AL,20H      ; Compare AL and 20H
        JAE     AL_SML_OR_EQ ; Jump if AL =< 20H
```

```
; At this point AL > 20H
        .
        .
AL_SML_OR_EQ:
```

In the context of Intel instruction mnemonics the terms *above* and *below* refer to unsigned integers while the terms *greater* and *less* refer to signed integers in two's complement form.

The range of a relative jump opcode is -128 to +127 bytes in 16-bit segments and -32768 to +32767 bytes in 32-bit segments.

JC

[Assembler] 8086 machine instruction. Mnemonic for Jump on Carry. Relative jump to the target operand if CF = 1. JC is an alternate mnemonic for the JB opcode. The JC instruction usually follows a CMP, TEST, or an arithmetic or logical opcode, in order to direct execution to a target operand (usually a label) if the destination is a smaller unsigned integer than the source. Code sample:

```
        CMP     AL,20H          ; Compare AL and 20H
        JC      CARRY_SET       ; Jump if AL < 20H
; At this point AL => 20H
        .
        .
CARRY_SET:
```

The range of a relative jump opcode is -128 to +127 bytes in 16-bit segments and -32768 to +32767 bytes in 32-bit segments.

JCXZ

[Assembler] 8086 machine instruction. Mnemonic for Jump if CX (or ECX) is Zero. The mnemonic JECXZ is used when the 32-bit ECX register is used. Transfer control to the target operand, usually a label, if CX (or ECX) = 0. This is the only relative jump instruction that is independent of the flags. One frequent use of JCXZ is to test for a zero value in CX (or ECX) on entering a loop in order to prevent an unexpected value in CX (or ECX) that makes the loop repeat 64K (or 32G) times. Code sample:

```
; Use of JCXZ to prevent a loop entry condition of
; CX = 0
        JCXZ    SKIP_LOOP       ; Test unexpected value
LOOP_LABEL:
```

```
            .
        LOOP    LOOP_LABEL
; Execution continues here if loop is exhausted or
; if CX = 0 on loop entry
SKIP_LOOP:
```

(See also: LOOP, LOOPE, LOOPZ, LOOPNE, and LOOPNZ).

The range of JCXZ and JECXZ is -128 to +127 bytes in either 16-bit segments or 32-bit segments.

JE

[Assembler] 8086 machine instruction. Mnemonic for Jump if Equal. JZ (Jump if Zero) is an alternate mnemonic for the JE instruction. Relative jump to the target operand if $ZF = 1$. The JE instruction usually follows a CMP, TEST, or an arithmetic or logical opcode, in order to direct execution to a target operand (usually a label) if the destination is an unsigned integer equal to the source.

Code sample:

```
        CMP     AL,20H        ; Compare AL and 20H
        JE      AL_EQUAL_20H  ; Jump if AL >= 20H
    ; At this point AL <> 20H
            .
            .
    AL_EQUAL_20H:
```

The range of a relative jump opcode is -128 to +127 bytes in 16-bit segments and -32768 to +32767 bytes in 32-bit segments.

JECXZ

(See JCXZ).

JG

[Assembler] 8086 machine instruction. Mnemonic for Jump if Greater. JNLE (Jump if Not Less or Equal) is an alternate mnemonic for the JG instruction. Relative jump to the target operand if (SF XOR OF) or $CF = 0$. The JG instruction usually follows a CMP, TEST, or an arithmetic of logical opcode, in order to direct execution to a target operand (usually a label) if the destination is a larger signed integer than the source.

Code sample:

```
        CMP     AL,-33        ; Compare AL and 33
        JG      AL_LARGER     ; Jump if AL > -33
```

```
; At this point AL =< -33
            .
            .

AL_LARGER:
```

In the context of Intel instruction mnemonics the terms *above* and *below* refer to unsigned integers while the terms *greater* and *less* refer to signed integers in two's complement form.

The range of a relative jump opcode is -128 to +127 bytes in 16-bit segments and -32768 to +32767 bytes in 32-bit segments.

JGE

[Assembler] 8086 machine instruction. Mnemonic for Jump if Greater or Equal. JNL (Jump if Not Less) is an alternate mnemonic for the JGE instruction. Relative jump to the target operand if (SF XOR OF) = 0. The JAE instruction usually follows a CMP, TEST, or an arithmetic or logical opcode, so as to direct execution to a target operand (usually a label) if the destination is an signed integer larger than or equal to the source.
Code sample:

```
        CMP     AL,-22        ; Compare AL and -22
        JAE     LARGER_OR_EQ  ; Jump if AL >= -22
; At this point AL < -22
            .
            .

LARGER_OR_EQ:
```

In the context of Intel instruction mnemonics the terms *above* and *below* refer to unsigned integers while the terms *greater* and *less* refer to signed integers in two's complement form.

The range of a relative jump opcode is -128 to +127 bytes in 16-bit segments and -32768 to +32767 bytes in 32-bit segments.

JL

[Assembler] 8086 machine instruction. Mnemonic for Jump if Less. JNGE (Jump if Not Greater or Equal) is an alternate mnemonic for the JL instruction. Relative jump to the target operand if (SF XOR OF) = 1. The JL instruction usually follows a CMP, TEST, or an arithmetic or logical opcode, in order to direct execution to a target operand (usually a label) if the destination is a smaller signed integer than the source.
Code sample:

```
        CMP     AL,-22        ; Compare AL and -22
        JB      AL_LESS       ; Jump if AL < 20H
```

```
; At this point AL => -22
        .
        .
        .
AL_LESS:
```

In the context of Intel instruction mnemonics the terms *above* and *below* refer to unsigned integers while the terms *greater* and *less* refer to signed integers in two's complement form.

The range of a relative jump opcode is -128 to +127 bytes in 16-bit segments and -32768 to +32767 bytes in 32-bit segments.

JMP

[Assembler] 8086 machine instruction. Mnemonic for JuMP. Unconditional transfer of execution to the target operand, usually a label, a procedure name, a general purpose register, or a memory operand. The JMP instruction does not save any return information on the stack so it cannot be used in place of CALL or INT.

Jumps to within the same segment are of type near, while jumps to addresses in other segment are of type far. The SHORT assembler directive can be used to force the assembler to generate a short jump when the distance cannot be calculated at assembly time, for example:

```
; At the time of the jump the assembler may not be able to
; determine the distance to the destination label. The SHORT
; operand forces the assumption of a destination within the
; range of a short jump
        JMP     SHORT DEST_S ; Force short jump
        .
        .
DEST_S:
; In this case code assumes that DEST_S is within the range
; of a relative jump (-128 to +127 bytes in 16-bit segments
; and -32768 to +32767 bytes in 32-bit segments.
```

Indirect jumps can be coded referencing a 16- or 32-bit general register or a memory operand. For example, a jump table in memory can provide word pointers to several the entry points. If a general purpose register is loaded with the base address of the jump table, another register or an immediate operand can serve as an index into the jump table. For example:

```
; Use of an indirect jump to an entry point defined in a
; data table
DATA    SEGMENT
JUMP_TABLE   DW      RNT_1 ; First routine offset
             DW      RNT_2 ; Second routine offset
             DW      RTN_3 ; Third routine offset
```

```
              ROUTINE_NO    DB      ?       ; Storage for routine number
              DATA    ENDS
              ;
              CODE    SEGMENT
                            .
                            .
              ; BX is used to calculate the number of the desired routine
                      MOV     BX,ROUTINE_NO
                      ADD     BX,BX           ; Double to get offset in table
                      JMP     JUMP_TABLE[BX]  ; Jump to routine
              RTN_1:
                            .
                            .
              RTN_2:
                            .
                            .
              RTN_3:
                            .
                            .
```

The CALL instruction can also be encoded using a table of pointers to several
destinations. A FAR jump can also use a memory operand to hold the doubleword pointer to the destination address. For instance, the address of a replaced
interrupt handler can be stored in a code segment variable so that execution
can be restored to it when required, as in the following code fragment:

```
              CODE    SEGMENT
              OLD_RN        DD      ?       ; Storage for routine far
                                            ; address
                            .
                            .
                      JMP     DWORD PTR CS:OLD_RTN    ; Jump to address
                                            ; stored in a variable
```

In protected mode far jumps consult the access right bytes (AR) of the
descriptor referenced by the long pointer. Depending on the AR byte a jump to
code segment with the same privilege level or a task switch takes place.
(See also: CALL).

JNAE

(See JB).

JNB

(See JAE).

JNBE

(See JA).

JNC

[Assembler] 8086 machine instruction. Mnemonic for Jump on Not Carry. Relative jump to the target operand if CF = 0. JNC is an alternate mnemonic for the JAE and JNB opcodes. The JNC instruction usually follows a CMP, TEST, or an arithmetic or logical opcode, in order to direct execution to a target operand (usually a label) if the destination is a larger unsigned integer than the source or if the range of the destination operand has been exceeded. Code sample:

```
        SUB     AL,20H       ; Perform AL - 20H
        JNC     NO_CF        ; Jump if AL > 20H
  ; At this point AL => 20H
        .
        .

    NO_CF:
```

The range of a relative jump opcode is -128 to +127 bytes in 16-bit segments and -32768 to +32767 bytes in 32-bit segments.

JNE

[Assembler] 8086 machine instruction. Mnemonic for Jump on Not Equal. Relative jump to the target operand if ZF = 0. JNZ is an alternate mnemonic for the JNE opcode. The JNE instruction usually follows a CMP, TEST, or an arithmetic or logical opcode, in order to direct execution to a target operand (usually a label) if the destination operand is equal to the source. Code sample:

```
        SUB     AL,20H       ; Perform AL - 20H
        JNE     NO_ZF        ; Jump if AL <> 20H
  ; At this point AL = 20H
        .
        .

    NO_ZF:
```

The range of a relative jump opcode is -128 to +127 bytes in 16-bit segments and -32768 to +32767 bytes in 32-bit segments.

JNG

(See JLE).

JNL

(See JGE).

JNLE

(See JG).

JNO

[Assembler] 8086 machine instruction. Mnemonic for Jump on Not Overflow. Relative jump to the target operand if OF = 0. The JNO instruction usually follows a CMP, TEST, or an arithmetic of logical opcode, in order to direct execution to a target operand (usually a label) if the overflow flag is clear. The overflow flag is used in signed arithmetic to indicate an operation that resulted in a carry into the high-order bit of the result. Therefore OF indicates an arithmetic or logical opcode which resulted in too large a positive number or too small a negative number. JNO, JO, and INTO instructions are typically used to trap this error.
Code sample:

```
            ADD     AL,+22          ; Perform AL + 22
            JNO     NO_OF           ; Jump if AL < +127 or
                                    ; AL > -127
        ; At this point AL is outside the range of an 8-bit number
        ; in two's complement form
                    .
                    .
        NO_OF:
```

The range of a relative jump opcode is -128 to +127 bytes in 16-bit segments and -32768 to +32767 bytes in 32-bit segments.

JNP

[Assembler] 8086 machine instruction. Mnemonic for Jump on Not Parity. Relative jump to the target operand if PF = 0. JPO is an alternate mnemonic for the JNP opcode. The JNP instruction usually follows a CMP, TEST, or an arithmetic or logical opcode, in order to direct execution to a target operand (usually a label) if the parity flag is clear. The parity flag (PF) is set when the low-order eight bits of the result of an arithmetic or logical instruction contain an even number of 1-bits. Otherwise PF is clear. PF was provided in the 8086 for compatibility with the Intel 8080 and 8085 CPU. JNP can be used to check for parity errors during the manipulation or transmission of ASCII characters.
Code sample:

```
; Use PF to determine parity odd or even condition
        AND     AL,01111111B ; Clear high bit
        JNP     PARITY_ODD   ; Go if odd number of 1-bits
; At this point AL parity is even
        .
        .
        .
PARITY_ODD:
```

The range of a relative jump opcode is -128 to +127 bytes in 16-bit segments and -32768 to +32767 bytes in 32-bit segments.

JNS

[**Assembler**] 8086 machine instruction. Mnemonic for Jump on Not Sign. Relative jump to the target operand if SF = 0. The JNS instruction usually follows a CMP, TEST, or an arithmetic of logical opcode, in order to direct execution to a target operand (usually a label) if the sign flag is clear. The sign flag is set by arithmetic or logical instructions that set the high-order bit (7, 15, or 30) of the result. In signed binary arithmetic SF indicates either the presence of a positive number (SF = 0) or a negative number (SF = 1). Therefore a conditional jump on the state of SF can be used to direct program flow according to the sign of the result. SF is usually ignored in unsigned arithmetic routines. Code sample:

```
; Branch to different handlers according to SF
        ADD     AL,+22      ; Perform AL + 22
        JNS     POS_RTN     ; Go to positive number
                            ; processing
; Routine here handles processing of negative results
        .
        .
        .
POS_RTN:
        .
        .
        .
```

The range of a relative jump opcode is -128 to +127 bytes in 16-bit segments and -32768 to +32767 bytes in 32-bit segments.

JNZ

(See JNE).

JO

[**Assembler**] 8086 machine instruction. Mnemonic for Jump on Overflow. Relative jump to the target operand if OF = 1. The JO instruction usually follows a CMP, TEST, or an arithmetic or logical opcode, in order to direct execution to a target operand (usually a label) if the overflow flag is set. The overflow flag is used in signed arithmetic to indicate an operation that resulted in a carry into the high-order bit of the result. Therefore OF indicates an arithmetic or logical opcode which resulted in too large a positive number or too small a negative number. JNO, JO, and INTO instructions are typically used to trap this error.

Code sample:

```
        ADD    AL,+22        ; Perform AL + 22
        JO     OF_SET        ; Jump if AL > +127 or
                             ; AL < -127
     ; At this point AL is in the range of an 8-bit number
     ; in two's complement form
               .
               .
OF_SET:
               .
               .
```

The range of a relative jump opcode is -128 to +127 bytes in 16-bit segments and -32768 to +32767 bytes in 32-bit segments.

JP

[Assembler] 8086 machine instruction. Mnemonic for Jump on Parity. Relative jump to the target operand if PF = 1. JPE is an alternate mnemonic for the JP opcode. The JP instruction usually follows a CMP, TEST, or an arithmetic or logical opcode, in order to direct execution to a target operand (usually a label) if the parity flag is set. The parity flag (PF) is set when the low-order eight bits of the result of an arithmetic or logical instruction contain an even number of 1-bits. Otherwise PF is clear. PF was provided in the 8086 for compatibility with the Intel 8080 and 8085 CPU. JNP can be used to check for parity errors during the manipulation or transmission of ASCII characters.

Code sample:

```
     ; Use PF to determine parity odd or even condition
        AND    AL,01111111B ; Clear high bit
        JP     PARITY_EVEN  ; Go if even number of 1-bits
     ; At this point AL parity is odd
               .
               .
PARITY_EVEN:
               .
```

The range of a relative jump opcode is -128 to +127 bytes in 16-bit segments and -32768 to +32767 bytes in 32-bit segments.

JPO

(see JNP).

JS

[Assembler] 8086 machine instruction. Mnemonic for Jump on Sign. Relative jump to the target operand if SF = 1. The JS instruction usually follows a CMP, TEST, or an arithmetic or logical opcode, in order to direct execution to a target operand (usually a label) if the sign flag is set. The sign flag is set by arithmetic or logical instructions that set the high-order bit (7, 15, or 30) of the result. In signed binary arithmetic SF indicates either the presence of a positive number (SF = 0) or a negative number (SF = 1). Therefore a conditional jump on the state of SF can be used to direct program flow according to the sign of the result. SF is usually ignored in unsigned arithmetic routines.

Code sample:

```
; Branch to different handlers according to SF
        ADD    AL,+22        ; Perform AL + 22
        JNS    NEG_RTN       ; Go to negative number
                             ; processing
; Routine here handles processing of positive results
        .
        .
        .

    NEG_RTN:
        .
        .
```

The range of a relative jump opcode is -128 to +127 bytes in 16-bit segments and -32768 to +32767 bytes in 32-bit segments.

JZ

(See JE).

K

KEY (statement)

[BASIC] [QuickBASIC] Sets or displays the function keys. The statement formats are:

```
KEY ON       displays function keys on screen line 25
KEY OFF      erases the function key display
KEY LIST     lists all 12 function keys on the screen
KEY n,x$     sets function key n to automatically type
             a string x$ of up to 15 characters
```

The action of the statement format:

```
KEY n,x$
```

is to assign the string x$ to function key n. The string must have length 15 or less. The value of n is in the range 1 to 10 for the first 10 function keys, and 30 or 31 for function keys F11 and F12 on the 101-key keyboards. After KEY n, a$ is executed; pressing the key Fn has the same effect as typing the characters in x$. Assigning a null string to a function key disables it as a function key. The statement KEY ON displays, on the last row of the output window, the first six characters of the assigned strings on the last row of the output window. The statement KEY OFF turns this display off. The statement KEY LIST displays all the assigned strings in vertical format.

There are six definable key traps. This capability allows trapping Ctrl, Shift, or super-shift key pressed.

These additional keys are defined by the statement:

```
KEY n,CHR$(KBflag)+CHR$(scan code)
```

where n is a numeric expression in the range 15 to 20. KBflag is a mask for the latched keys. The appropriate bit in KBflag must be set in order to trap a key that is shifted, Alt-shifted, or Ctrl-shifted. The KBflag values in hex are:

```
KEY          HEX           ACTION
```

Caps Lock	&H0	Caps Lock is not active
	&H40	Caps Lock is active
Num Lock	&H0	Num Lock is not active
	&H20	Num Lock is active
Alt	&H08	ALT key is pressed
Ctrl	&H04	Control key is pressed
Left Shift	&H02	Left Shift key is pressed
Right Shift	&H01	Right Shift is pressed
Scan code		Number identifying one of the 83 keys to trap

Trapped keys are processed in the following order:

1. Ctrl-PrtSc, which activates the line printer, is processed first. Even if Ctrl-PrtSc is defined as a trappable key, this does not prevent characters from being echoed to the line printer.

2. The function keys F1 to F10 and Cursor Up, Cursor Down, Cursor Right, and Cursor Left are processed. Setting scan codes 59 to 68, 72, 75, 77, or 80 as key traps has no effect, because these keys are considered to be predefined.

3. User-defined keys (range 15 to 20) are processed last.

KEY(n) statement

[BASIC] [QuickBASIC] Activates and deactivates trapping of the specified key. The statement formats are:

```
KEY(n) ON
KEY(n) OFF
KEY(n) STOP
```

where n is a numeric expression in the range 1 to 20, which indicates the trapped key, as follows:

n	ACTION
1-10	function keys F1 to F10
11	Cursor Up
12	Cursor Left
13	Cursor Right
14	Cursor Down
15-20	keys defined by the form: KEY n,CHR$(KBflag)+CHR$(scan code)

(See KEY).

KEY(n) ON must be executed to activate trapping of a function or cursor control key. If a nonzero line number is specified in the ON KEY(n) statement, then every time BASIC starts a new statement it checks to see if the specified key was pressed. If so, it performs a GOSUB to the line number (or label) specified in the ON KEY(n) statement. A KEY(n) statement cannot precede an ON KEY(n) statement. If KEY(n) is OFF, no trapping takes place and even if the key is pressed. Once a KEY(n) STOP statement has been executed, no trapping takes place. However, if the specified key is pressed the action is remembered, so that an immediate trap takes place when KEY(n) ON is executed. KEY(n) ON has no effect on the display of the soft key values are at the bottom of the screen.

Keyboard

[input/output] The keyboard has undergone substantial changes in the various models of the IBM microcomputers. These changes are related to the addition and deletion of certain keys, to the position of some control keys, and to the mechanical and electronic hardware components employed. The number of keys has gone from 83 in the Personal Computer keyboard, to 62 in the PCjr, 78 in the Convertible, 84 in the AT, and 101 in the keyboard for the PS/2 line. Other keys have been moved around several times; for instance, the escape key (labeled Esc), located at the left side of the top row in the Personal Computer and the PCjr, was moved to the right side of this row in the AT, and back to the top left on the PS/2 keyboard. The backslash key has also undergone several relocations.

All IBM keyboards use a dedicated microprocessor which monitors the mechanical key switches, thus freeing the main processor from this time-consum-

PC Keyboards

MACHINE	NUMBER OF KEYS	CONTROLLER	DESCRIPTION
PC PC XT Portable	83	Intel 8048	10 function keys in two columns on left side. Esc key at top left. Fixed typematic rate and keystroke delay.
PCjr	62	Intel 80C48	**Original model:** Battery-powered, cordless. Multistroke function keys. Typematic rate and delay can be increased. **Updated version:** Replacement for original PCjr keyboard. Improved mechanical design.
PC AT XT 286	84	Intel 8042	Relocated <Esc> key. Lighted indicators for lock keys. Sys Req key for protected mode. Programmable typematic rate and keystroke delay.
PS/2	101	Intel 8042	Relocated <Esc> key. Cursor control and editing keypads. 12 function keys. Lighted indicators for lock keys. Programmable typematic rate and keystroke delay.

ing task. This chip, called the *keyboard controller*, is an Intel 8048 in the PC, XT, and PCjr and an Intel 8042 in the AT and the PS/2 models.

The keyboard supplied with the original Personal Computer, also used in the PC XT and PC Portable, has 83 keys. The PC AT keyboard has 84 keys. It is characterized by relocated Esc, backslash (\), and Print Screen keys, by a new key labeled Sys Req (system request) intended for use in 80286 protected mode, and by light indicators that reflect the state of the lock keys. The microcomputers of the Personal System/2 line are equipped with a keyboard that has 101 keys in the version designed for use in the United States and 102 keys in the models sold outside the United States. This keyboard has a total of 12 function keys, a dedicated keypad for editing and cursor control, and a Pause/Break key. The Esc key was again repositioned, this time to the top left side, as in the original PC keyboard. In the PS/2 keyboard, the Sys Req key is an Alt function of the Print Screen. The Sys Req (system request) function is not used by Windows, OS/2 or by any other multitasking operating system presently available.

The various keyboards used in the different models of the IBM microcomputers are not interchangeable. The adapter hardware used for connecting the keyboards to the system units are incompatible, and the electronic components used in the various systems are also different.

Keyboard hardware

[PC hardware and architecture] [input/output] One of the innovations introduced by the Personal Computer AT and preserved in the PS/2 line is the use of the Intel 8042 keyboard controller in a programmable environment. The hardware appears to the programmer as follows:

1. A keyboard controller status register (read operations) at port 64H. This byte can be read at any time to determine the present condition of the keyboard hardware.

2. A keyboard controller command register (write operations) at port 64H. Output to this register is used to enable and disable the keyboard, to select the scan code translation mode, to set and reset the system flag bit, and to set the 8042 in the interrupt or poll mode.

3. An output buffer located at port 60H, which is used by the system to read the scan code received from the keyboard or a data byte that results from a system-to-keyboard command. Code that reads the output buffer should do so only if bit 0 of the status register equals one, indicating data in buffer.

4. An input buffer located at port 60H. Writing to port 60H sends a byte to the keyboard hardware or to the 8042 keyboard controller. 8042 access takes place if the controller is expecting a data byte following a command.

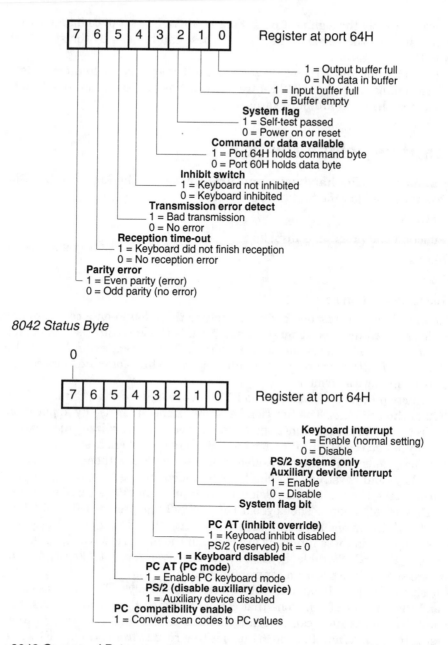

8042 Status Byte

8042 Command Byte

Code that writes to the input buffer should first test bit 0 of the status register to make sure that there is no data in the buffer.

Several command sets are active in the system. In one set are the commands that can be issued by the system to the 8042 keyboard controller through port 64H. In another set are the commands that can be issued to the keyboard hardware directly through port 60H. Finally, there is a set of commands that can be issued by the keyboard hardware. These can be read by the system at port 60H.

In programming the AT and PS/2 keyboard it is important to differentiate between commands to the 8042 controller, which is part of the system board, and those to the keyboard hardware.

Keyboard key classification

[input/output] [PC hardware and architecture] The keys on the IBM keyboard can be classified into five groups:

1. ASCII keys
2. Function and program control keys
3. Shift state keys
4. Lock state keys
5. Immediate action keys

The ASCII keys correspond approximately to those found on a conventional electric or electronic typewriter. One exception is the key with the symbol for the number one (1). This is due to the traditional use, in typewriter keyboards, of the letter l (ell) to represent the number one, while computer processing requires a numerical symbol.

The function keys are labeled F1 to F10 on keyboards of the PC line and F1 to F12 in the PS/2 line. The function keys are intended for use by application software; therefore, their functions have not been standardized. Application can freely assign roles to the function keys. By the same token, to avoid conflicts, system programs and memory-resident utilities should not them.

Other keys and keystroke combinations intended for use by applications are the arrow keys, the Insert (Ins), Delete (Del), Home, End, Page Up (PgUp), and Page Down (PgDn) keys. The keyboard of the PS/2 line provides an individual keypad with the arrow keys and another one with the editing keys. In the PC and AT keyboards these functions are found in the numeric keypad, while the PCjr and the PC Portable keyboards require two separate keystrokes to generate some of the program control functions.

The shift-state keys include the Shift, Ctrl, and Alt keys. Their purpose is to expand the number of functions that can be assigned to individual keys. For example, an application can assign a function to the code that results from pressing the F1 key, another one to the code that results from pressing F1 while holding the Shift key, a third one to pressing F1 while holding the Ctrl key, and a fourth operation to pressing F1 while holding the Alt key. The Shift key is also used more conventionally to generate uppercase alphabetical characters and the symbols associated with the number keys.

The Lock State Keys perform a similar function to that of the shift state keys; that is, they expand the range of possible interpretations of other keystrokes. The difference in their action is that the effect of a shift state key depends on its being held down while the principal key is pressed, while a lock state key enables a permanent interpretation of the principal keystrokes.

Since the effect of a lock state key persists after the key has been released, it is sometimes difficult for the user to determine which state is active. This explains the convenience of light indicators to reflect the state of the lock keys. These indicators [also called the keyboard light-emitting diodes (LEDs)] are found in the PC AT and PS/2 keyboards.

The lock state keys are labeled Caps Lock, Num Lock, and Scroll Lock. The Caps Lock key toggles the alphabetic keys, letters a through z, to upper- and lowercase. This action is similar to the shift lock function on a conventional typewriter keyboard, except that the Caps Lock affects the alphabetic keys only. The Num Lock key toggles between numbers and functions on the numeric keypad.

The Scroll Lock function was conceived as a toggle between cursor movements and text window scrolling. Although this action is assumed to refer to the arrow and editing keys, the implementation is left entirely to applications. The only action performed by the keyboard routine is to change the state of a control bit in the BIOS data area.

The BIOS interrupt service routine at INT 09H provides a few immediate services that are activated by specific keys or keystroke combinations, sometimes called the immediate action or hot keys. These functions are transparent to system and application software. For this reason they can be executed by the user at any time. The following hot keys are available in the PC:

1. The *reset function* is an immediate action that is activated by the combination keystroke Ctrl/Alt/Del. The keystroke causes a jump to the BIOS startup procedure known as the *warm boot routine*.

2. The *print screen function* is linked to a dedicated key in some systems and to a keystroke combination in others. The corresponding routine is located at BIOS INT 05H. This vector is in conflict with the 80286 BOUND instruction, which uses it to report a register value outside the specified limits.

3. The *pause function* is initiated by a dedicated key on the PS/2 keyboard but requires several keystrokes in other systems. The routine activated by this key consists of a wait-for-keystroke loop internal to the INT 09H handler. The key provides an application-independent wait.

4. The *break function* is a hot key whose action can be defined by the programmer. When the Ctrl/Break keystrokes are received by the keyboard interrupt handler, an INT 1BH is executed. In the default mode, this interrupt returns to the caller without any other action. The programmer can replace this vector with code to perform any desired action.

5. The *system request function* corresponds to a key labeled Sys Req in the AT keyboard. In the PS/2 keyboard this function is assigned as an Alt shift state of the Print Screen key, which is labeled SysRq on its front side. The system request function was conceived as an immediate action for interrupting the task executing in 80286 and 80386 protected-mode software. However, because not all keyboards have a dedicated key for the system request function, the designers of the OS/2

operating system preferred to assign the system request function to the Ctrl/Esc and Alt/Esc keystrokes.

Keyboard operation

[input/output] Certain fundamental principles of operation have been maintained in the various models of IBM keyboards. In general, the process can be described as follows:

1. Each key operates as a mechanical switch. The keyboard controller detects each time that a switch is closed (key pressed) or opened (key released). The controller, which can be an Intel 8048 or 8042, calculates and stores a code, specific for each key, in a register mapped to port 60H. This code, named the *scan code*, is unrelated to the key's ASCII value.

2. Once the scan code is stored, the keyboard controller generates an interrupt. All IBM systems point this interrupt to a handler located at interrupt 09H. In the PCjr, the interrupt is first directed to the nonmaskable interrupt (NMI) service routine, then to INT 48H for compatibility adjustments, and finally to INT 09H.

3. The service routine for INT 09H is part of the basic input/output system (BIOS). The routine first tests for keys that require special handling. If special handling is not required, INT 09H converts the scan codes into ASCII or extended ASCII characters. The ASCII code, as well as the original scan code, is stored in a BIOS buffer area named the keyboard or type-ahead buffer.

4. Some keystrokes require immediate action, for example, the Lock function keys, the Sys Req key, or Hot keys like the print screen or break functions. In these cases the keyboard handler performs the corresponding operations.

5. Other keystrokes not stored in the keyboard buffer are those used in interpreting previous or subsequent keystrokes, for instance, the shift state keys labeled Shift, Ctrl, and Alt, and the Caps Lock key. The INT 09H handler interprets these keys accordingly.

Keyboard scan codes

[input/output] The key codes stored by the keyboard hardware for processing by the Interrupt 09H handler, called *scan codes*, are not in ASCII or any other standard format. It is the INT 09H handler that must translate the scan codes into standardized ASCII values. For the same reason, routines that intercept the INT 09H handler to filter keystrokes or to provide customized handling will retrieve from port 60H the raw scan code.

All IBM systems provide the means for distinguishing between the action of closing or opening a key switch. The closing action is usually referred to as a *make code*, while releasing a key generates a code called the *break scan code*. In the PC XT the break code is the make code with the high bit set. In the PC AT the value F0H indicates that the following scan code corresponds to a break operation.

PC Make Codes for Scan Code Set No. 1

KEY	SCAN CODE	KEY	SCAN CODE
Esc	01H	1	02H
2	03H	3	04H
4	05H	5	06H
6	07H	7	08H
8	09H	9	0AH
0	0BH	-	0CH
=	0DH	Backspace	0EH
Tab	0FH	Q	10H
W	11H	E	12H
R	13H	T	14H
Y	15H	U	16H
I	17H	O	18H
P	19H	[	1AH
]	1BH	Enter	1CH
Ctrl	1DH	A	1EH
S	1FH	D	20H
F	21H	G	22H
H	23H	J	24H
K	25H	L	26H
;	27H	'	28H
`	29H	Left Shift	2AH
\	2BH	Z	2CH
X	2DH	C	2EH
V	2FH	B	30H
N	31H	M	32H
,	33H	.	34H
/	35H	Right Shift	36H
Print Screen	E0H 2AH	Alt	38H
Spacebar	39H	Caps Lock	3AH
F1	3BH	F2	3CH
F3	3DH	F4	3EH
F5	3FH	F6	40H
F7	41H	F8	42H
F9	43H	F10	44H
Num Lock	45H	Scroll Lock	46H
Home	47H	Up Arrow	48H
PgUp	49H	-	4AH

(continued)

PC Make Codes for Scan Code Set No. 1 (Continued)

KEY	SCAN CODE	KEY	SCAN CODE
Left Arrow	4BH	5 (keypad)	4CH
Right Arrow	4DH	+	4EH
End	4FH	Down Arrow	50H
PgDn	51H	Ins	52H
Del	53H		

Editing Keypad		Cursor Keypad	
Insert	E0H 52H	Left Arrow	E0H 4BH
Delete	E0H 53H	Up Arrow	E0H 48H
Home	E0H 47H	Down Arrow	E0H 50H
End	E0H 4FH	Right Arrow	E0H 4DH
Page Up	E0H 49H		
Page Down	E0H 51H		

New Keys In PS/2 Keyboard			
Right Alt	E0H 38H	F11	57H
Right Ctrl	E0H 1DH	F12	58H
Keypad Enter	E0H 1CH	Keypad /	E0H 35H
Pause	E1H 1DH 45H E1H 9DH C5H		

In the PS/2, and most PC-compatible keyboards, the programmer can select among three scan code sets. Although the system default is scan code set 2, the BIOS initializes scan code set 1 as active. In set number 1 the break codes are reported as for the PC and PC XT keyboard; that is, the break code is the make code with the high bit set. Several keys, which did not exist in previous keyboards, are preceded by the code E0H. The Pause key is not typematic and does not generate a break code. The scan codes for the Pause key are all generated on the make keystroke.

Keyboard typematic action

[input/output] Occasionally, a typist finds it necessary to repeat several keystrokes, for example, a succession of dashes to draw a horizontal line. With mechanical keyboards this repetition requires pressing and releasing the key for each character desired. With electronically controlled keyboards, like the ones used in computer terminals and in microcomputers, it is possible to detect when a key is being held down by the typist and proceed to automatically repeat the corresponding character. IBM refers to this operation as a *typematic action*. Several factors must be considered in implementing typematic action. In the first place, when a key is pressed, it makes and breaks the circuit several times before establishing a firm contact. This effect, called *key bounce*, is neutralized by waiting a few milliseconds for the key action to stabilize. Another factor to consider is that an average typist normally holds down each key a fraction of a second before releasing it. For this reason, the keystroke processing logic must be able to differentiate between the normal delay of individual keystrokes and a key that has been held down intentionally. This is achieved by measuring the time during which the key's circuit remains closed and by comparing the elapsed time with a norm for individual keystrokes.

In implementing typematic action, the processing logic first determines that a key is being held down intentionally, then starts repeating the character at a certain rate. The sequence of repeated characters is sometimes called a *typematic burst*. If the burst rate is too fast, the typist is not be able to release the key to end the sequence at the desired point. On the other hand, if the typematic burst is too slow, the typist has to wait excessively long for each character repetition. The initial delay and the burst rate are the two variables of typematic action. The ideal values of these variables are usually a matter of personal preference.

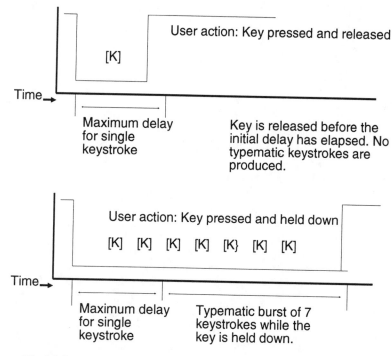

Typematic Action

KILL (command)

[BASIC] [QuickBASIC] Deletes a file from a disk. This command is BASIC's counterpart to the DOS ERASE command. The command format is:

```
KILL filespec
```

where filespec is a valid MS-DOS file specification string.

L

Label

[QuickBASIC] The language supports two mechanisms for identifying program lines that are the destinations of GOTO and GOSUB statements: line numbers and descriptive labels. Labels are names that follow the same rules as variable names, but are followed by a colon. When a label appears in a GOTO or GOSUB statement, execution jumps to the statement following the line containing the label.

Labels

[Assembler] Labels are place markers in an assembly language program. Like variable names, labels are used by the assembler to define a position in the program. A difference between variable names and labels is that variable names are used to identify data items, whereas labels are used to mark places in the program's code. Another difference is that labels must end in a colon symbol, whereas variable names do not. In the following code fragment the statement DOS_EXIT: is a label:

```
DOS_EXIT:
        MOV     AH,76        ; MS-DOS service request code
        MOV     AL,0         ; No error code returned
        INT     21H          ; TO DOS
```

LADDOK

[MS-Pascal] Heading: (A, B: INTEGER4;VAR C: INTEGER4) : BOOLEAN; Library routine of the no-overflow arithmetic group. Sets C equal to A plus B. One of two functions that do 32-bit signed arithmetic without causing a runtime error, even if the arithmetic debugging switch is on. LADDOK and LMULOK return TRUE if there is no overflow, and FALSE if there is. These routines are useful for extended-precision arithmetic, for modulo 2^{32} arithmetic, or arithmetic based on user input data.

LAHF

[Assembler] 8086 machine instruction. Mnemonic for Load register AF from Flags. Copies flags into AH register as follows:
SF to bit 7, ZF to bit 6, AF to bit 5, PF to bit 2, and CF to bit 0. AH bits 5, 3, and 1 are undefined.

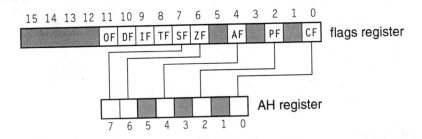

Bit Migration during LAHF
Initially, LAHF was provided to facilitate conversion of 8088 and 8085 assembler programs to run on the 8086 CPU.

LAN

(See local area networks).

LAR

[Assembler] 80286 machine instruction. Mnemonic for Load Access Right byte. Protected mode instruction. If the selector is visible at the current privilege level (CPL), LAR stores the access right byte of the descriptor into the high byte of the destination operand, and clears the low byte. If the descriptor privilege level (DPL) is >= CPL and DPL >= requested privilege level (RPL) then loading takes place and ZF is set. ZF is cleared otherwise.

32-bit operands can be specified in the 386 and later CPUs. The LAR instruction is not recognized in the real mode.

```
LAR Special Segment and Gate Descriptor Types
TYPE          NAME                    STATUS
0             invalid                 invalid
1             available 16-bit TSS    valid
2             LDT                     valid
3             busy 16-bit TSS         valid
4             16-bit call gate        valid
5             16/32-bit task gate     valid
6             16-bit trap gate        invalid
7             16-bit interrupt gate   invalid
8             invalid                 invalid
```

9	available 32-bit TSS	valid
A	invalid	invalid
B	busy 32-bit TSS	valid
C	32-bit call gate	valid
D	invalid	invalid
E	32-bit trap gate	invalid
F	32-bit interrupt gate	invalid

LBOUND (function)

[QuickBASIC] Returns the smallest subscript value that can be used in a one-dimensional array. For an array of any size the value of the function:

```
LBOUND(name, n)
```

is the smallest subscript value that may be used for the *n*th subscript of the array. For example, after the statement DIM sample(1 TO 31,1 TO 12,990 TO 999) is executed, the value of LBOUND(sample, 3) is the smallest value allowed for the third subscript of sample(), which is 990.

LCASE$ (function)

[QuickBASIC] Returns a string of all uppercase characters of the target string. The function format is:

```
LC$ = LCASE$(C$)
```

LDDRQQ

[MS-Pascal] Heading: (CONSTS A: REAL8): REAL8;
Arithmetic function that return the logarithm, base 10, of A. Both A and the return value are of type REAL8. This function is from the MS-FORTRAN runtime library and must be declared EXTERN.

LDS

[Assembler] 8086 machine instruction. Mnemonic for Load pointer using DS. Transfers a 32-bit address stored in a memory operand to the destination operand, which may be any 16-bit general register, and the DS segment register. The offset element of the address is transferred into the general register operand and the segment element into DS. Since string instructions assume that the source string (by SI) is in the current DS, LDS provides a convenient way of preparing for a string instruction when the source string is not in DS. This is accomplished by specifying SI as the destination operand. Code sample:

```
; Using LDS to load a pointer from a variable containing
; a far address to a memory operand
DATA    SEGMENT
BUF_A           DB      20 DUP ('?')  ; Buffer
ADD_BUF_A       DD      BUF_A         ; Far pointer
DATA    ENDS
;
CODE    SEGMENT
        .
        .
        .
        LDS     SI,ADD_BUF_A  ; Use LDS to set DS:SI
; At this point DS:SI point to the memory operand labeled
; BUF_A
```

LDSRQQ

[MS-Pascal] Heading: (CONSTS A: REAL4): REAL4;
Arithmetic function that return the logarithm, base 10, of A. Both A and the return value are of type REAL4. This function is from the MS-FORTRAN runtime library and must be declared EXTERN.

LEA

[Assembler] 8086 machine instruction. Mnemonic for Load Effective Address. Transfers the offset of the source operand, which must be a memory variable, to the destination operand, which must be a 16-bit general register. Although LEA is often considered to perform the same action as the OFFSET operator, there are important differences. In the first place LEA performs a dynamic calculation of the operand's current offset and allows the use of an index or base register. This feature allows the runtime calculation of the indexed address of a variable, for example:

```
        LEA     AX,ARRAY_1[BX]
```

In this case the offset loaded into AX is that of the variable (ARRAY_1) plus the index in register BX. This type of address calculation is not possible with the OFFSET operator. On the other hand, the entire address calculations performed by means of the OFFSET operator take place at assembly time. This explains why the form

```
        MOV     AX,OFFSET ARRAY_1
```

executes faster than the alternative:

```
        LEA     AX,ARRAY_1
```

For the same reasons, the MOV OFFSET form assembles in 4 bytes while the LEA form requires a 5-byte opcode. Intel recommends that the MOV OFFSET form be preferred when a runtime address calculation is not required.
In the 386 and later processors the LEA instruction allows the use of a 32-bit address either as the source, destination, or both source and destination operands.

LEAVE

[Assembler] 80286 machine instruction. Mnemonic for LEAVE procedure. The ENTER and LEAVE instructions are used mostly in the coding of high-level language compilers in order to create a stack frame that allows the creation and access to local variables. LEAVE deallocates all space reserved for local variables and restores SP and BP to the values at invocation time. LEAVE requires no operands. A RET instruction usually follows the LEAVE opcode. Code sample:

```
; Use of ENTER and LEAVE in a high-level procedure
DEMO   PROC   NEAR
; Assume that at access time to the procedure SS = 3FEH
; and SP = 000H
        ENTER  12,0   ; Allocation is 12 bytes
                      ; nesting level = 0
; At this point the following takes place:
;       BP -> stack (SP = 3FEH - 2H = 3FCH)
;       BP = SP (BP = 3FCH)
;       SP = SP - 12 (SP = 3FCH - CH = 3F0H)
; After the ENTER instruction code should not change the
; value of the base pointer register
         .
         .
        LEAVE
; At this point SP and BP are restored to the values
; before ENTER. Data in the local frame is destroyed.
        RET
DEMO   ENDP
```

(See also: ENTER).

LEFT$ (function)

[BASIC] [QuickBASIC] Returns the leftmost *n* characters of a string. The function format is:

```
v$ = LEFT$(x$,n)
```

where x$ is a string expression and *n* is a numeric value in the range 0 to 255. If *n* is greater than the number of characters in x$, then the value of the function is x$.

Example:

```
MSU$ = "MONTANA STATE UNIVERSITY"
A$ = LEFT$(MSU$, 7)
PRINT A$
```

Result: MONTANA

LEN (function)

[BASIC] [QuickBASIC] Returns the number of characters in a string. The function format is:

```
v = LEN(x$)
```

The value of LEN(var) where, var is not a string variable, is the number of bytes needed to hold the value of the variable in memory. That is, LEN(var) is 2, 4, 4, or 8 for integer, long integer, single-precision, and double-precision variables respectively. LEN(var), when var is a variable with a user-defined record type, is the number of bytes of memory needed to store the value of the variable.

LES

[Assembler] 8086 machine instruction. Mnemonic for Load pointer using ES. Transfers a 32-bit address stored in a memory operand to the destination operand, which may be any 16-bit general register, and the ES segment register. The offset element of the address is transferred into the general register operand and the segment element into ES. Since string instructions assume that the destination string (by DI) is in the current ES, LES provides a convenient way of preparing for a string instruction when the destination string is not in ES. This is accomplished by specifying DI as the destination operand.

Code sample:

```
; Using LES to load a pointer from a variable containing
; a far address to a memory operand
DATA    SEGMENT
BUF_B        DB    20 DUP ('?') ; Buffer
ADD_BUF_B    DD    BUF_B        ; Far pointer
DATA    ENDS
;
CODE    SEGMENT
```

```
        LES    DI,ADD_BUF_B ; Use LDS to set ES:DI
; At this point ES:DI point to the memory operand labeled
; BUF_B
```

LET (statement)

[BASIC] [QuickBASIC] Assigns the value of an expression to a variable. The statement format is:

```
[LET] variable = expression
```

If var is a fixed-length string variable with length n and LEN(exp) is greater than n, then the first n characters of exp are assigned to var. If LEN(exp) is smaller than n, then exp is padded on the right with spaces and assigned to var. If var is a user-defined type, then exp must be of the same type. The statement x = 10 is equivalent to LET x = 10.

LFS

[Assembler] 80386 machine instruction. Mnemonic for Load pointer using FS. Transfers a 32-bit address stored in a memory operand to the destination operand, which may be any 16-bit general register, and the FS segment register. The offset element of the address is transferred into the general register operand and the segment element into FS.
(See also: LDS, LES, LGS, LSS, and LEA).

LGDT

[Assembler] 80286 machine instruction. Mnemonic for Load Global Descriptor Table register. LGDT is used in operating system software to load the global descriptor table from a 6-byte memory operand into the global descriptor table register (LGTR). If the instruction references a 16-bit memory operand, then the register is loaded with a 16-bit limit and a 24-bit base. In this case the high-order eight bits of the six byte operand are not used. If the operand is 32-bits, then a 16-bit limit and a 32-bit base is loaded. In this case the high-order eight bits of the six byte operand are the high-order base address.

The storing of the global descriptor table register in a memory operand is performed by the SGTD instruction. In the 80286 the upper eight bits are undefined after SGTD.

LGS

[Assembler] 80386 machine instruction. Mnemonic for Load pointer using GS. Transfers a 32-bit address stored in a memory operand to the destination

operand, which may be any 16-bit general register, and the GS segment register. The offset element of the address is transferred into the general register operand and the segment element into GS.
(See also: LDS, LES, LFS, LSS, and LEA).

Library function

[C] The program lines

```
printf("Enter radius: ");
scanf("%f", &radius);
printf("\nArea is: %f", PI * (radius * radius));
```

contain the C library functions *printf()* and *scanf()*. The printf() function is generally used for video display output and the scanf() function to obtain keyboard input. Note that printf() and scanf() are not C keywords. This is because C does not contain commands to directly access input or output devices, but depends on library functions to perform these operations. Also note that the parentheses are part of the function name. This serves to indicate the presence of a C function, in contrast with keywords, variables, and other language elements that are not followed by parentheses.

Library Procedures and Functions

[MS-Pascal] The following routines are not predeclared, but are available in the MS-Pascal runtime library. They must be declared, with the EXTERN directive, before using in a program.

1. Initialization and termination routines. BEGOQQ and ENDOQQ are called during initialization and termination, respectively. You might use them to invoke a debugger or to write customized messages.

2. Heap management routines. Complement the standard NEW and DISPOSE procedures and include: ALLHQQ, FREECT, MARKAS, MEMAVL, and RELEAS

3. Interrupt routines. Handle interrupt processing, although the actual effect varies with the target machine: ENABIN, DISBIN, and VECTIN

4. Terminal I/O routines. Support direct input and output: GTYUQQ, PTYUQQ, and PLYUQQ

5. Semaphore routines. The procedures LOCKED and UNLOCK provide a binary semaphore capability. They can be used to ensure exclusive access to a resource in a concurrent system.

6. No-overflow arithmetic functions. Implement 16-bit and 32-bit modulo arithmetic. Overflow or carry is returned, instead of invoking a runtime error: LADDOK, LMULOK, SADDOK, SMULOK, UADDOK, and UMULOK

7. Clock routines. Provide operating system clock information: TIME, DATE, and TICS

LIDT

[Assembler] 80286 machine instruction. Mnemonic for Load Interrupt Descriptor Table register. LGDT is used in operating system software to load the interrupt descriptor table from a 6-byte memory operand into the interrupt descriptor table register (LGTR). If the instruction references a 16-bit memory operand, then the register is loaded with a 16-bit limit and a 24-bit base. In this case the high-order eight bits of the six byte operand are not used. If the operand is 32-bits, then a 16-bit limit and a 32-bit base is loaded. In this case the high-order eight bits of the six byte operand are the high-order base address.

The storing of the interrupt descriptor table register in a memory operand is performed by the SITD instruction. In the 80286 the upper eight bits are undefined after SITD.

LINE (statement)

[BASIC] [QuickBASIC] Draws a screen line or box. The statement format is:

```
LINE[(x1,y1)]-(x2,y2)[,[color][,B[F]][,style]]
```

where (x1,y1)(x2,y2) are the relative or absolute coordinates of the end points. Color is an integer that represents the color according to the video hardware and mode. Style is a 16-bit integer mask used to draw dots on the screen. The simplest form of the LINE statement is:

```
LINE -(x2,y2)
```

which draws a line from the current screen point to the pixel at screen coordinates (x2,y2). The statement LINE (x1,y1)-(x2,y2) draws a line connecting the two points. If the statement format is:

```
LINE (x1,y1)-(x2,y2),c
```

then the line is in color c of the current palette. The statement LINE (x1,y1)(x2,y2),,B draws a rectangle with the two points as opposite vertices. (If B is replaced by BF, a solid rectangle is drawn.) If s is a number in hexadecimal notation from 0 to &HFFFF, then LINE (x1,y1)-(x2,y2),,,s draws a styled line (with the pattern determined by s) connecting the two points. The pattern s is a 16-bit number in which the binary ones represent dots and binary zeros are the skips. For example, the s value &HAAAA produces the dot pattern:

```
1 0 1 0 1 0 1 0 1 0 1 0 1 0 1 0
```

LINE INPUT (statement)

[BASIC] [QuickBASIC] Reads a line from the keyboard into a string variable ignoring delimiters. The statement format is:

```
LINE INPUT[;]["prompt";]stringvar
```

where "prompt" is an optional prompt string, and stringvar is the name of the string variable to which the input is assigned.

The difference between LINE INPUT and INPUT is that the user may respond to LINE INPUT with any string, even one containing commas, leading spaces, and quotation marks. The entire string is assigned to the string variable.

LINE INPUT# (statement)

[BASIC] [QuickBASIC] Reads a line from a sequential file into a string ignoring delimiters. The statement format is:

```
LINE INPUT #filenum, stringvar
```

where filenum is the number assigned to the file with the OPEN statement, and stringvar is the name of the string variable to which the input is assigned. The statement LINE INPUT #n, a$ assigns to the string variable a$ the string of characters from the current location in the file up to the next pair of carriage return/line feed characters.

LLDT

[Assembler] 80286 machine instruction. Mnemonic for Load Local Descriptor Table register. LLDT is used in operating system software to load the local descriptor table register for a 16-bit source, which can be a register or a memory operand. This operand should contain a selector to the global descriptor table (GDT). The descriptor registers DS, ES, SS, FS, GS, and CS are not affected; neither is the local descriptor table (LDT) field in the task state segment. The LLDT instruction is not recognized in real mode.

LMSW

[Assembler] 80286 machine instruction. Mnemonic for Load Machine Status Word. LMSW is used in operating system software to load the machine status word part of the CR0 register from the 16-bit source operand. LMSW can be used to switch the CPU to protected mode but not back to real mode. When switching to protected mode code must perform an intrasegment jump to flush the instruction queue.

In the 80386 and later processors LMSW is provided for compatibility with 80286 code since in these processors the CR0 register can and should be loaded with a MOV instruction.

LMULOK

[MS-Pascal] Heading: (A, B: INTEGER4; VAR C: INTEGER4) : BOOLEAN;
Library routine of the no-overflow arithmetic group. Sets C equal to A times B. One of two functions that do 32-bit signed arithmetic without causing a runtime error on overflow. Normal arithmetic may cause a runtime error even if the arithmetic debugging switch is off. Both LMULOK and LADDOK return TRUE if there is no overflow, and FALSE if there is. These routines are useful for extended-precision arithmetic, or module 2^32 arithmetic, or arithmetic based on user input data.

LN

[MS-Pascal] Heading: (X: REAL): REAL;
Arithmetic function that returns the logarithm, base e, of X. Both X and the return value are of type REAL. To force a particular precision, declare LNSRQQ (CONSTS REAL4) and/or LNDRQQ (CONSTS REAL8) and use them instead. An error occurs if X is less than or equal to zero.

LNDRQQ

[MS-Pascal] Heading: (CONSTS A : REAL8): REAL8;
(See LN).

LNSRQQ

[MS-Pascal] Heading: (CONSTS A : REAL4): REAL4;
(See LN).

LOBYTE

[MS-Pascal] Heading: (INTEGER-WORD): BYTE;
Extend level intrinsic function that returns the least significant byte of an INTEGER or WORD. Depending on the target processor, the least significant byte may be the first or the second addressed byte of the word.
(See also: HIBYTE).

LOC (function)

[BASIC] [QuickBASIC] Returns the current location in a file. The statement format is:

```
v = LOC(filenum)
```

where filenum is the file number assigned with the OPEN statement. This function is valid for sequential, random-access, or binary files. For a sequential file with number n, LOC(n) is the number of blocks of 128 characters read from or written to the file since it was opened. For a random-access file, LOC(n) is the current record. In this case the current record can be either the last record read or written or the record identified in a SEEK statement. For a binary file, LOC(n) is the number of bytes from the beginning of the file to the last byte read or written.

Local area networks — topology

[PC hardware and architecture] LANs can assume different geometric patterns. These patterns, often called the network's *architecture* or *topology*, are unrelated to the cabling system used by the network and to other hardware components.

1. *The star*. The star design emulates the arrangement used in telephone networks in which a central switching station provides service to several customers or workstations. In the star topology all data are processed and controlled by a central computer. Since each workstation is cabled to the central computer, adding a new workstation requires a single cable. The STARLAN network, by AT&T, is an example of this technology.

2. *The bus*. In contrast with the individual cabling scheme used in the star topology, the bus network topology is based on a common line shared by all workstations. This design simplifies cabling and connections, but since all workstations share the network bus, each station must check all messages on the bus in order to identify those addressed to it. Although the bus topology is the least expensive to implement, it does suffer from signal interference and from inherent security flaws.

3. *The ring*. This third network topology, designed to combine the advantages of the star and bus designs, consists of a ring of interconnected workstations. The ring topology ensures that every workstation has equal access to the network. This plan is particularly convenient when the several workstations in the network are of approximately equal complexity and have the same access privileges. The IBM Token Ring Network is an example of this topology.

Local area networks — physical elements

[PC hardware and architecture] Because of the lack of protocols and standards it is difficult to make valid generalizations regarding LANs. However, the following elements seem to be present in most systems:

1. *Workstations*. A standard microcomputer is a typical LAN workstation. Although it is possible to configure a system using dedicated workstations with minimum processing resources, the greater practical use of LANs is in linking, for use within an organization, the already existing microcomputers, software, and peripherals. In this case, each network workstation is also capable of operating as an independent microcomputer. In many LAN systems the networking capabilities are provided in the form of a plug-in adapter card and a LAN software package.

2. *LAN servers*. A network server is a hardware-software device that controls and assigns the shared resources. LAN systems often use nondedicated servers; for example, a microcomputer equipped with a hard disk drive can perform the functions of a file server. In this case the file server manages the disk files and directories and controls access to the hard disk drive by the workstations. Typically, the fastest and most advanced microcomputer in a network is assigned the functions of a file server. Another type of server, called a *print* (or laser print) *server*, controls the spooling of documents to be printed and their eventual assignation to one or more printers.

3. *LAN cabling*. The workstations, servers, and peripherals in a LAN must be physically connected to each other. Several cable and connector options are available for LAN systems. The profusion of connecting hardware reflects the absence of standards in this field. The least expensive option is the *twisted pair cable* used for telephone systems. Twisting the wires distributes the environment noise evenly between the two elements in the pair but does not eliminate the noise. In network applications the cables are usually 22- or 24-gage. *Coaxial cable*, like that used for cable television, is also used in LANs. Although more expensive than twisted pair cable, coaxial cable can be used to transmit data faster and over longer distances. Finally, *fiber-optic cable* and hardware are also used to transmit network data. Although the most expensive option, fiber-optic technology is virtually immune from noise and interference. This makes transmissions over several miles of cable possible. In addition, the fiber-optic signal is protected from unauthorized reception, which can be a factor in networks that require absolute security.

4. *Baseband and broadband networks*. Coaxial cable network systems can be implemented in two forms: in the baseband design, supported by Xerox and Digital Equipment Corporation, the cable has a single, high-speed channel that is very efficient for data transmission but cannot carry integrated voice, data, and video signals. On the other hand, broadband systems can carry integrated signals but require amplifiers and the installation hardware is more complex and expensive.

Local Area Networks

[**PC hardware and architecture**] The benefit of sharing computer resources is related to the cost of computer hardware and to the need for sharing data and software. The concept of distributed processing, on the other hand, is based on the advantages of providing independent computing power to the individual human elements in a system. Microcomputer technology has made possible combining the best of both worlds in networks of workstations that have individual processing power and yet are able to share information and hardware.

A *local area network*, or LAN, is an arrangement of physically connected microcomputers, operating within a limited area for the purpose of sharing information and resources. The area of operation of a LAN is generally limited to less than one mile. Although there is presently very little standardization regarding LANs, the particular identity of a LAN is based on the fact that each unit is a "smart" terminal, equipped with its own processor, memory, and logic. A network of dumb terminals connected to a central processor does not satisfy the generalized definition of a LAN, even if the central processor is a microcomputer.

LOCATE (statement)

[BASIC] [QuickBASIC] Positions the cursor on the screen. Optionally this statement can be used to turn the cursor on and off and to define its size. The statement format is:

```
LOCATE [row][,[col],[cursor][,[start][,stop]]]]
```

where row is a number in the range 1 to 25 corresponding to a screen row, and col is a number in the range 1 to 80 (1 to 40 in low-resolution modes) corresponding to a screen column. Cursor is 0 to turn off the cursor and 1 to turn it on. Start is the first cursor scan line and stop is the last scan line (start and stop must be in the range 0 to 31). The operands cursor, start, and stop are not available in a graphics mode.

The statement:

```
LOCATE r, c
```

positions the cursor at screen row r, column c.

The statement:

```
LOCATE,, 0
```

turns off the display, while the statement

```
LOCATE,, 1
```

turns the display back on.

LOCK (command)

[QuickBASIC] This command is intended for use in a networking environment. The SHARE command enables file sharing and should be executed from DOS prior to using the LOCK statement. After a file has been opened with reference number n, the statement

```
LOCK #n
```

denies access to the file by any other process. For a random-access file, the statement

```
LOCK #n, r1 TO r2
```

denies access to records r1 through r2. For a binary file, this statement denies access to bytes r1 through r2. The statement

```
LOCK #n, r1
```

locks record or byte r1. Regarding sequential files all forms of the LOCK statement have the same effect as LOCK #n. The UNLOCK statement is used to remove locks from files. All locks should be removed before a file is closed or the program is terminated.

LOCK

[Assembler] 8086 instruction prefix. Mnemonic for LOCK bus. This instruction prefix is intended to prevent simultaneous access to a memory operand in a multiprocessor environment. The LOCK prefix asserts the lock bus signal for the duration of the instruction to which it refers. Since XCHG automatically locks to bus, the LOCK prefix is not necessary in this case.

The standard way of solving a possible memory contention conflict is by means of a dedicated memory switch, sometimes called a semaphore. This scheme is usually based on a bit that indicates that a certain contended resource is currently in use, thus preventing access by another processor or memory device. However, since setting the semaphore bit requires memory access time, it is possible that a second CPU could test the semaphore and find the resource available before the first one has had time to change the state of the semaphore bit.

One way to prevent this conflict is by implementing a single instruction to test and set the semaphore while the bus is locked. The method works because the memory hardware cannot grant two processors access to the same location, at the same time. The BTS instruction allows saving a bit in the carry flag and setting it in one single operation. Therefore it can be used in conjunction with the LOCK instruction to set a semaphore bit in a way that prevents a simultaneous access by another processor or device.

Code sample:

```
; Use of LOCK prefix to prevent simultaneous access to
; a semaphore
DATA    SEGMENT
SEMAPHORE      DB      0H      ; Bit 7 is semaphore bit
                               ; clear by default

DATA    ENDS
;
CODE    SEGMENT
        .

        .

BUSY_1:
LOCK  BTS    SEMAPHORE,7   ; Lock bus. Set bit 7
; In this case BTS returns the previous state of bit 7
; (semaphore bit) in the carry flag. If resource was in use
; then bit 7 was set, and CF = 1
      JC     BUSY_1         ; Repeat if resource in use
; At this point resource can be used by CPU
; Semaphore is set (bit 7 = 1)
        .

        .

; At the conclusion of its memory access, code should clear
; the semaphore bit
      AND    SEMAPHORE,01111111B ; Bit 7 = 0
```

(See also: BT, BTS, BTR, BTC, and XCGH).

LOCKED

[MS-Pascal] Heading: (VARS SEMAPHORE :WORD): BOOLEAN;
Library function of the semaphore group. If the semaphore was available, LOCKED returns the value TRUE and sets the semaphore unavailable. Otherwise, if it was already locked, LOCKED returns FALSE. UNLOCK sets the semaphore available.
(See also: UNLOCK).

LODS/LODSB/LODSW/LODSD

[Assembler] 8086 machine instruction. Mnemonic for LOaD String. Transfers the byte (LODSB), word (LODSW), or doubleword (LODSD) addressed by the source operand (DI register) to the AL, AX, or EAX register, and updates SI (or ESI) to point to the next element in the string. If DF = 0 then the source index is incremented. IF DF = 1 it is decremented. This instruction is not used with the REP prefix since the accumulator would be overwritten in each data transfer. However, LODS is often seen in software loops that perform string operations.

Code sample:

```
; Use of LODSB in a routine to output the accumulator
; to a port
DATA    SEGMENT
STRING_1       DB      '12345ABCDE',0
DATA    ENDS
;
CODE    SEGMENT
        .
        .
        MOV    SI,OFFSET STRING_1
        MOV    DX,PORT_X      ; Port to DX
        CLD                   ; Forward direction
SEND_IT:
        LODSB                 ; Character by DS:SI into AL
                            ; SI is bumped
        CMP    AL,0           ; Test for string terminator
        JE     BREAK_RTN      ; Go if AL = 0
        OUT    DX,AL          ; Send character to port
        JMP    SEND_IT        ; Continue
; At this point loop execution has concluded
BREAK_RTN:
        .
        .
```

LOF (function)

[QuickBASIC] [BASIC] Returns the length of a file, in bytes. The statement format is

```
v = LOF(filenum)
```

where filenum is the number assigned to the file with the OPEN statement.

LOG (function)

[BASIC] [QuickBASIC] Returns the natural logarithm (base e) of a numeric operand. The statement format is:

```
v = LOG(x)
```

Logical Operators

[C] The relational operators are used to evaluate if a condition relating two operands is true or false. The principal use of *logical operators* is in combining two or more conditional statements. Like relational expressions, expressions that contain logical operators return 1 if the expression is true or 0 if the expression is false.

C Logical Operators

OPERATOR	DESCRIPTION
&&	Logical AND
||	Logical OR
!	Logical NOT

For example, if $x = 4$, $y = 2$, and $z = 0$, the variable true_false evaluates to either 0 or 1, as in the following cases:

```
CASE       EXPRESSION                           VALUE OF true_false
1          true_false = x >> y && z == 0;       1 (true)
2          true_false = x >> y && z != 0;       0 (false)
3          true_false = x == 0 || z == 0;       1 (true)
4          true_false = x << y || z != 0;       0 (false)
5          true_false = !z == 1;                1 (true)
```

Note in case 1 that the variable true_false evaluates to 1 (true) because both relational elements in the statement are true. On the other hand, case 4 evaluates to 0 (false) because the OR connector requires that at least one of the relational elements be true and, in this case, both are false ($x >> y$ and $z = 0$). In case 5 the logical NOT operator is used to invert the value of the variable z, which becomes 1; therefore, the statement evaluates to 1 (true).

loop constructs

[C] C offers 3 different mechanisms for performing program iterations: the *for* loop, the *while* loop, and the *do while* loop constructs. The *for* loop provides, in a neat, self-contained structure, the three elements that are required for implementing a program iteration. These elements are usually called initialization, testing, and updating. This mode of operation makes the *for* loop useful in situations in which the programmer knows in advance the conditions for execution of the loop. For example, a routine to display the ASCII characters in the range 16 to 128 can be easily coded using a *for* loop by using the expression:

```
for (ascii = 16; ascii < 129; ascii ++)
```

The *while* loop is used to create an iteration structure that repeats while a certain terminating condition is not met. For example, the following loop displays and keeps count of the characters typed by the user until the <Enter> key is pressed:

```
count = 0;
```

```
while ( getche() != 0x0d )
        count ++
```

Due to this mode of operation the while loop is useful in creating loop structures in which the terminating condition is unpredictable.
In this case the *while* loop concludes when the user presses the <Enter> key. Therefore, the <Enter> key is not included in the character count performed by statement count ++. The *do while* loop provides an alternative mode of operation in which the terminating condition is processed in the loop; for example, the do while loop:

```
count = 0;
do
        count ++;
while ( getche() != 0x0d);
```

includes the <Enter> key in the keystroke count.
In many cases a program must use several loop constructs, often nested within other loops, in order to perform a complicated, repetitive task.

LOOP

[Assembler] 8086 machine instruction. Mnemonic for LOOP control. This instruction is intended to be used as an iteration control mechanism with conditional branching. LOOP decrements CX (or ECX) by one and transfers execution to the target operand (usually a label) if CX is not zero. If CX is zero loop execution breaks to the instruction following LOOP. Code must load the number of iterations into the CX register before executing LOOP.
Code Sample:

```
; Use of LOOP instruction in iteration control with
; conditional branching
DATA    SEGMENT
BUFF_1        DB      20 DUP ('?') ; 20-byte buffer
DATA    ENDS
;
CODE    SEGMENT
        .
        .
        .
; Use loop construct to initialize the first 10 bytes in
; BUFF_1
        MOV     CX,10           ; Counter for 10 iterations
        MOV     SI,OFFSET BUFF_1 ; Set SI as pointer
CLEAR_10:
        MOV     BYTE PTR[SI],' ' ; Place space in buffer
        INC     SI              ; Bump pointer
        LOOP    CLEAR_10        ; Iterate
```

```
; At this point the first 10 characters in BUFF_1 are
; spaces
```

LOOPE

[Assembler] 8086 machine instruction. Mnemonic for LOOP while Equal. LOOPZ is an alternate mnemonic for the LOOPE instruction. LOOPE is intended to be used as an iteration control mechanism based in the CX register and ZF, with conditional branching. LOOPE decrements CX (or ECX) by one and transfers execution to the target operand (usually a label) if CX is not zero and ZF is set. If CX is zero or ZF is clear, loop execution breaks to the instruction following LOOPE. Code must load the number of iterations into the CX register before executing LOOPE.

Code Sample:

```
; Use of LOOPE instruction in iteration control with
; conditional branching on ZF set and CX <> 0
DATA    SEGMENT
BUFF_1          DB      10 DUP (0H)     ; First buffer
BUFF_2          DB      10 DUP (0H)     ; Second buffer
DATA    ENDS
;
CODE    SEGMENT
        .
        .
        .
; Use loop construct to initialize the first 10 bytes in
; BUFF_1. Break if 10 bytes are transferred or if a character
; in BUFF_1 does not match the corresponding character in
; BUFF_2
; Code assumes that previous processing may have changed the
; initial buffer contents
        MOV     CX,10           ; Counter for 10 iterations
        MOV     SI,OFFSET BUFF_1 ; SI points to first buffer
        MOV     DI,OFFSET BUFF_2 ; DI points to second buffer
CLEAR_BUFF_1:
        MOV     BYTE PTR[SI],' ' ; Place space in buffer
        INC     SI              ; Bump buffer pointers
        INC     DI
        MOV     AL,[SI]         ; First buffer character to AL
        MOV     BL,[DI]         ; Second buffer character to BL
        CMP     AL,BL           ; Compare buffer characters
        LOOPE   CLEAR_BUFF_1    ; Iterate if CX <> 0 and if
                                ; buffers characters are equal
; At this point either 10 spaces have been stored in BUFF_1
; or two non-matching characters were found in the buffers
```

LOOPNE

[Assembler] 8086 machine instruction. Mnemonic for LOOP while Not Equal. LOOPNZ is an alternate mnemonic for the LOOPNE instruction. LOOPNE is intended to be used as an iteration control mechanism based in the CX register and ZF, with conditional branching. LOOPNE decrements CX (or ECX) by one and transfers execution to the target operand (usually a label) if CX is not zero and ZF is clear. If CX is zero or ZF is set, loop execution breaks to the instruction following LOOPNE. Code must load the number of iterations into the CX register before executing LOOPNE.

Code Sample:

```
; Use of LOOPNE instruction in iteration control with
; conditional branching on ZF clear and CX <> 0
DATA    SEGMENT
BUFF_1          DB      10 DUP (0H)    ; First buffer
BUFF_2          DB      10 DUP (0H)    ; Second buffer
DATA    ENDS
;
CODE    SEGMENT
        .
        .
        .
; Use loop construct to initialize the first 10 bytes in
; BUFF_1. Break if 10 bytes are transferred or if a character
; in BUFF_1 matches the corresponding character in BUFF_2
; Code assumes that previous processing may have changed the
; initial buffer contents
        MOV     CX,10           ; Counter for 10 iterations
        MOV     SI,OFFSET BUFF_1 ; SI points to first buffer
        MOV     DI,OFFSET BUFF_2 ; DI points to second buffer
CLEAR_BUFF_1:
        MOV     BYTE PTR[SI],' ' ; Place space in buffer
        INC     SI               ; Bump buffer pointers
        INC     DI
        MOV     AL,[SI]          ; First buffer character to AL
        MOV     BL,[DI]          ; Second buffer character to BL
        CMP     AL,BL            ; Compare buffer characters
        LOOPNE  CLEAR_BUFF_1     ; Iterate if CX <> 0 and if
                                 ; buffers characters are
                                 ; unequal
; At this point either 10 spaces have been stored in BUFF_1
; or two matching characters were found in the buffers
```

LOOPNZ

(See LOOPNE).

LOOPZ

(See LOOPE).

LOWER

[MS-Pascal] Heading: (EXPRESSION) : VALUE;
Extend level intrinsic function that takes a single parameter, which can be of type array, set, enumerated, or subrange, and returns the following:

1. The lower bound of an array
2. The first allowable element of a set
3. The first value of an enumerated type
4. The lower bound of a subrange

   LOWER uses the type, not the value, of the expression. The value returned by LOWER is always a constant.
(See also: UPPER).

LOWORD

[MS-Pascal] Heading: (INTEGER4): WORD;
Extend level intrinsic function that returns the low-order WORD of the four bytes of the INTEGER4.
(See also: HIWORD).

LPOS (function)

[BASIC] [QuickBASIC] Returns the current position of the print buffer pointer. The statement form is:

```
v = LPOS(n)
```

where *n* is the printer being tested, as follows:

```
n                 PRINTER
0 or 1 LPT1
2                 LPT2
3                 LPT3
```

LPRINT and LPRINT USING (statement)

[BASIC] [QuickBASIC] Prints data on the current printer. The statement formats are:

```
LPRINT [expression list[;]]
LPRINT USING v$; expression list[;]
```

Both statements print data on the printer in the same way PRINT and PRINT USING display data on the screen. LPRINT may be used to set various print modes, such as the width of the characters and the vertical spacing. This is accomplished by combining LPRINT and the CHR$() statement.
Example:

```
'send line feed code (10) to the printer
LPRINT CHR$(10)
```

LSET and RSET (statements)

[BASIC] [QuickBASIC] Formats data in a random file buffer in preparation for a PUT statement. The statement formats are:

```
LSET (or RSET) stringvar = x$
```

LSET left-justifies the string and RSET right-justifies it. If stringvar is a field variable of a random-access file, then the statement:

```
LSET a$ = x$
```

assigns the string x$ to a$, possible truncated or padded with spaces. If a$ is an ordinary variable, then the statement:

```
LSET a$ = x$
```

replaces the value of a$ with a string of the same length consisting of x$ truncated or padded on the right with spaces. LSET also can be used to assign a record of one user-defined type to a record of a different user-defined type.

LSL

[Assembler] 80286 machine instruction. Mnemonic for Load Segment Limit. Instruction to load a register with a segment limit and set ZF if the selector specified as a source operand is visible at the current privilege level and requested privilege level, and if the descriptor is of a type accepted by the LSL instruction. ZF is cleared if the descriptor is invisible or of the wrong type. The LSL instruction is not recognized in the processor's real mode.

```
LSL Special Segment and Gate Descriptor Types
TYPE           NAME                        STATUS
0              invalid                     invalid
1              available 16-bit TSS        valid
2              LDT                         valid
3              busy 16-bit TSS             valid
4              16-bit call gate            valid
5              16/32-bit task gate         valid
```

6	16-bit trap gate	invalid
7	16-bit interrupt gate	invalid
8	invalid	invalid
9	available 32-bit TSS	valid
A	invalid	invalid
B	busy 32-bit TSS	valid
C	32-bit call gate	valid
D	invalid	invalud
E	32-bit trap gate	invalid
F	32-bit interrupt gate	invalid

LSS

[Assembler] 80386 machine instruction. Mnemonic for Load pointer using SS. Transfers a 32-bit address stored in a memory operand to the destination operand, which may be any 16-bit general register, and the SS segment register. The offset element of the address is transferred into the general register operand and the segment element into SS.
(See also: LDS, LES, LFS, LGS, and LEA).

LTR

[Assembler] 80286 machine instruction. Mnemonic for Load Task state Register. Instruction used by operating system software to load the task state register (TSS) with the register of memory address specified in the operand. The loaded TSS is marked busy. A task switch does not take place. LTR is not recognized in the real mode.

LTRIM$ (function)

[QuickBASIC] Removes all spaces from the left end of a string. The value of the function:

```
LTRIM$(x$)
```

is the string obtained by removing all the spaces from the beginning of the string x$. The string a$ may be either of fixed or variable length.

lvalue and rvalue

[C] The implementors of C refer to *lvalue* (short for left value) and *rvalue* (short for right value). An lvalue (called a *modifiable lvalue* in ANSI C) is an expression that can be used to the left of the = sign. In an assignment expression the lvalue, sometimes called the left-hand operand, must represent a storage location. In other words, the element to the left of the = sign must be a variable name or a specific element of an array. If x and y are variables and arr[] is an array, the expressions:

```
x = 2 * y;
arr[1] = y;
```

are valid. However, since the identifier for the array does not refer to a specific storage location, the expressions:

```
arr[] = y;
arr = x * y;
```

are not valid. The unary increment and decrement operators (++ and —) give rise to lvalues and rvalues in expressions that do not have an = sign. Note that in this context, the word *unary* refers to a statement or operation that acts on a single object.

M

machine registers

[PC hardware and architecture] hardware elements in the CPU used for storing addresses and values. (See individual CPU architecture, for example, 8086 architecture, 80286 architecture, etc.)

macro — arguments

[C] In addition to the literal replacement of a numeric or string value for an identifier, C allows the use of an argument as the replacement element of a #define directive. This construction is usually called a macro. The most important element in the macro concept is the substitution or replacement that takes place when the macro is encountered during compilation. This substitution, sometimes called the *macro expansion*, is handled by a section of the compiler called the *preprocessor*.

The simplest version of a macro argument is a *macro formula*, for example

```
#define PI 3.1415927
#define DOUBLE_PI  2 * PI
```

In this case the macro formula DOUBLE_PI generates the product of the constant two times 3.1415927, which is represented by the identifier PI defined in another macro.

Finally, a macro can contain an argument that is replaced by a variable on expansion, as in the following program:

```
#include <stdio.h>
#define PI 3.1415926
#define CIRC(x) ((x + x) * PI)
main()
{
        float radius;
        printf("\nEnter radius of circle: ");
        scanf("%f", &radius);
        printf("\nCircumference is: %f", CIRC(radius));
        return(0);
}
```

In this example the macro named CIRC calculates the circumference of any variable (represented by x in the macro definition). For instance, the statement:

```
printf("\nCircumference is: %f", CIRC(radius));
```

uses the macro named CIRC to calculate the circumference of the variable named radius. Regarding the macro argument it is important to note that the replaced variable, which can be any legal C identifier, is enclosed in parentheses following the macro name. Also note that there can be no space between the macro name and the argument's left parenthesis. This use of spaces as separators in the macro definition creates a lexical peculiarity that sometimes confuses the novice programmer. A final point to keep in mind is that the macro definition does not end in a semicolon.

The use of parentheses in the argument makes macros somewhat reminiscent of C functions, to the point that some authors speak of *function-like macros*. However, there are differences between a macro and a function. Perhaps the most important one is that the macro expansion is the replacement of the identifier (the macro name) by its equivalent expression. Therefore, the code generated during a macro expansion is *in line*, while a function call requires that execution be transferred to the function body and then returned to the line following the call. The call/return operation associated with functions brings about an overhead in execution time. This determines that if identical processing is encoded as a macro and as a function, the function takes slightly longer to execute than the equivalent macro. On the other hand, the macro is expanded every time that its name is referenced in the code, whereas a function appears only once. This means that a macro that is referenced more than once adds more to the size of the executable file than an equivalent function.

macros

[C] The #define directive can be used to associate an identifier with a constant, for example, the program line

```
#define PI 3.1415927
```

thereafter assigns the constant value 3.1415927 to the identifier PI. By the same principle the #define directive can be used to assign a string value to an identifier; for example, the program line:

```
#define MSU "Montana State University\n"
```

assigns the string enclosed in double quotation marks to the identifier MSU. Thereafter any reference to MSU is replaced with the string "Montana State University\n". Note that it is conventional practice in C to use capital letters for identifiers associated with the #define directive.

main()

[C] All C programs must contain a function called main() at which execution always starts.

MARKAS

[MS-Pascal] Heading: (VAR HEAPMARK : INTEGER4) ;
Library procedure of the heap management group; similar to the MARK procedure in other implementations of Pascal. MARKAS marks the upper and lower limits of the heap. The DISPOSE procedure is generally more powerful, but MARKAS is useful for converting from other Pascal dialects.

In other Pascal implementations the parameter is of a pointer type. However, MS-Pascal needs two words to save the heap limits, since in some implementations the heap grows toward both higher and lower addresses. The HEAPMARK variable should not be used as a normal INTEGER4 number; it should only be set by MARKAS and passed to RELEAS.

To use MARKAS and RELEAS, pass an INTEGER4 variable, M for example, as a VAR parameter to MARKAS. MARKAS places the bounds of the heap in M. To release heap space, simply invoke the procedure with RELEAS (M). MARKAS and RELEAS work as intended only if DISPOSE is never called.

MC6845 CRT controller

[historical] [video systems] The 6845 CRTC is a special-purpose integrated circuit that serves as a link between the microprocessor and the CRT display. It allows interfacing with a character ROM generator chip. The following display adapters and systems of the IBM PC line use the Motorola 6845 CRT controller (CRTC) chip:

1. The Monochrome Display and Printer Adapter
2. The Color Graphics Adapter
3. The IBM PCjr
4. The Hercules Graphics Card

The Enhanced Graphics Adapter, EGA, and VGA video systems use chips that are similar to the Motorola 6845 CRTC.

MC6845 programmable registers

[video systems] The Motorola 6845 CRTC has 18 programmable registers that are accessible through two locations on the system's memory space.

The horizontal and vertical format registers are initialized by the BIOS start-up routines and normally require no other manipulation. The address of the 6845 CRT controller has a variable element, sometimes represented by the letter x.

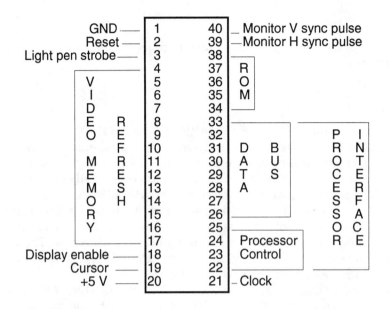

Function Groups:
Pins 4 to 17 — Access to 16K of video memory
Pins 34 to 38 — Row address for character generator ROMs
Pins 26 to 33 — 8-bit bidirectional data bus connection with the
　　　　　　　system microprocessor

MC6845 Pin Assignment

MC6845 CRT Controller Registers

BASE ADDRESS	REGISTER NAME	NUMBER	FUNCTION
3x4H	Address register		Select active register
3x5H	Horizontal format	0–3	Determine the horizontal display parameters
	Vertical format	4–8	Determine the vertical display parameters
	Interlace mode	9	Select normal sync, interlace sync, or interlace sync and video
	Cursor start	10	Determine the scan line for the start of the cursor and blink/no blink operation
	Cursor end	11	Determine the scan line for the end of the cursor
	Start address (high and low)	12–13	Determine the start address of display memory
	Cursor address (high and low)	14–15	Determine the display position for the cursor

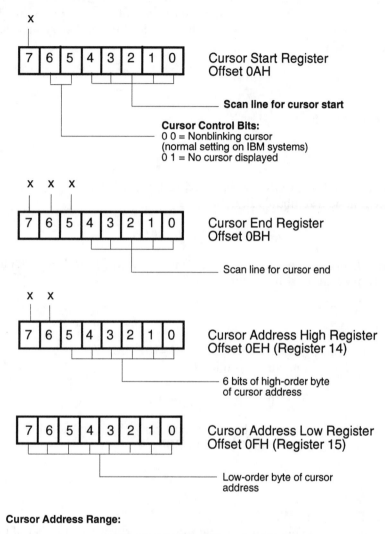

6845 CRT Controller Cursor Registers

One of the functions of the 6845 CRT controller is the display and control of the system cursor. Three 6845 registers are directly related to cursor management. The actual size of the cursor varies according to the vertical definition of the display hardware.

By setting the contents of the cursor address registers on the 6845 CRT controller, the cursor can be positioned anywhere on the video display. The cursor address registers are numbered 14 and 15, respectively. Register 15 (offset 0FH) holds the low byte of a 14-bit address that extends to the full 16K RAM addressed by the 6845. Register 14 (offset 0EH) holds the six significant bits of the high-order byte.

MDA

(See monochrome display adapter).

MDDRQQ

[MS-Pascal] Heading: (CONSTS A, B: REAL8) : REAL8; Arithmetic function. A modulo B, defined as:

```
MDDRQQ (A,B) = A - AIDRQQ (A/B) * B
```

Both A and B are of type REAL8. This function is from the MS-FORTRAN runtime library and must be declared EXTERN.

MDSRQQ

[MS-Pascal] Heading: (CONSTS A, B: REAL4) : REAL4; Arithmetic function. A modulo B, defined as:

```
MDSRQQ (A,B) = A - AISRQQ (A/B) * B
```

Both A and B are of type REAL4. This function is from the MS-FORTRAN runtime library and must be declared EXTERN.

MEMAVL

[MS-Pascal] Heading: :WORD; Library function of the heap management group. Returns the number of bytes available between the stack and the heap. MEMAVL acts like the MEMAVAIL function in UCSD Pascal. If you have previously used DISPOSE, MEMAVL may return a value less than the actual number of bytes available.

member of operator

(See structure — accessing its elements).

membership operator

(See structure — accessing its elements).

Memory

[PC hardware and architecture] Computer terminology equates memory with storage. In this sense it is correct to speak of disk or diskette memory. However, the more common use of the term limits the word *memory* to non-mechanical storage of digital information. Magnetic, optical, or other mechanical storage devices are therefore excluded. The terms *main* and *auxiliary* memory are also used in this context.

Main memory on IBM microcomputers is provided in semiconductor devices. A typical component consists of an array of cells contained in a silicon wafer and housed in a rectangular, integrated-circuit package. In operation, the memory chips can be classified as read-only memory (ROM) or read-and-write memory, RAM. The unit of data storage is called a *memory cell*. Each cell is a transistor flip-flop circuit capable of storing one bit of information.

Memory access

[PC hardware and architecture][Assembler] The byte (8 bits) is the unit of memory storage in IBM microcomputers. Therefore, in order to determine the state (set or clear) of a particular memory bit, the CPU must use one of the bit TEST instructions in conjunction with a corresponding mask. Bit masking is also required to write a specific memory bit without affecting the other bits in the byte.

The microprocessors of the Intel iAPX family implement addressing modes that permit direct access to memory. In the cases allowed, the CPU grants memory variables the same status as microprocessor registers. For example, if a memory byte is designated in the source with the variable name MEM_BYTE, it is possible to code in assembly language:

```
        MOV     AL,MEM_BYTE   ; Register loaded from
                              ; variable
or
        MOV     MEM_BYTE,CL   ; Variable loaded from
                              ; register
```

Since register and variable addressing imply that the instruction refers to the contents of the register or variable, the form MOV AL,[MEM_BYTE] is redundant and illegal.

Memory access

[PC hardware and architecture] All memory access in 80286 and later CPUs is based on three descriptor tables called the global descriptor table (GDT), the interrupt descriptor table (IDT), and the local descriptor table.

Global Descriptor Table Register (GDTR)

Base	Limit

39   15   0

Interrupt Descriptor Table Register (GDTR)

Base	Limit

39   15   0

Local Descriptor Table Register (LDTR)

Selector	Base	Limit

55   Visible   39   Invisible   0

80286 System Address Registers

(LDT). The address and length of these tables are stored in the system address registers. Each address register is named for its corresponding table: the global descriptor table register (GDTR), the interrupt descriptor table register (IDTR), and the local descriptor table register (LDTR). The address registers contain a 24-bit field (named the base) which holds the physical address for the beginning of the table and a 16-bit field (called the limit) which specifies the offset of the last valid entry. The LDTR also contains a *selector* portion that is visible to the application. This area is formatted exactly like a segment selector.

In 80286 protected mode, the value stored in the index field of the segment selectors (registers CS, DS, ES, and SS) serves as an index into the descriptor tables. The 13-bit index field allows from 1 to 8192 possible entries in each table. Table entries are formatted in 8-byte areas.

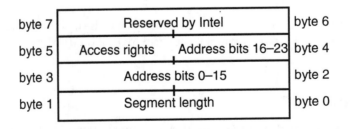

byte 7	Reserved by Intel	byte 6
byte 5	Access rights Address bits 16–23	byte 4
byte 3	Address bits 0–15	byte 2
byte 1	Segment length	byte 0

80286 Descriptor Table Entries Format

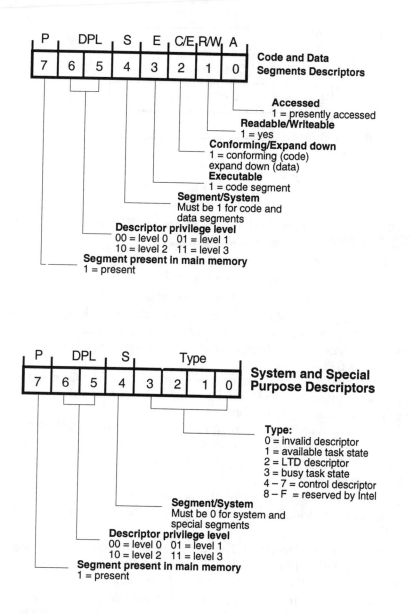

80286 Access Right Byte

The offset of a particular entry from the start of the descriptor table is calculated by multiplying the value in the index field by the eight bytes in each entry.

Byte 5 of the segment descriptor table entry is known as the *access rights byte*. The format of the access rights byte for code and data segment descriptors is different from that for system and special segment descriptors.

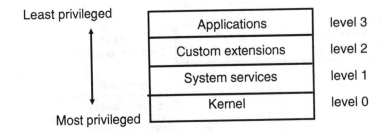

Applications	level 3
Custom extensions	level 2
System services	level 1
Kernel	level 0

Least privileged ↑ Most privileged ↓

80286 Privilege Levels

The hardware protection mechanisms in the 80286 serve to achieve the following functions:

1. System software is isolated from application programs
2. Tasks execute independently of one another
3. Segments are used according to their data types

Protection is implemented by establishing limitations on the use of memory and by restricting the instruction set available to applications. The degree of limitation is determined by a hierarchy of four privilege levels supported by the 80286 and later CPUs.

System programs do not have to enable all privilege levels; for example, the OS/2 operating system for the IBM microcomputers uses only three of the four privilege levels available in the chip.

The privilege level is controlled through three privilege-level indicators:

1. **DPL** (*descriptor privilege level*). The DPL is stored in bits 5 and 6 of the access rights byte of each descriptor. Its value indicates the privilege level of the entire segment.
2. **CPL** (*current privilege level*). The CPL is stored in bits 0 and 1 of the current *code segment* selector. It indicates the privilege level of the task currently executing.
3. **RPL** (*requested privilege level*). The RPL is stored in bits 0 and 1 of a segment selector. The RPL differs from the CPL in that the CPL refers to the code segment selector, while the RPL can refer to any segment.

The CPU follows specific rules for granting access to data and code segments. For instance, data access is granted if DPL >= CPL — in other words, if the privilege level of the data segment is lower than or equal to the privilege level of the current code segment. Note that the higher the privilege level, the lower the numerical value of DPL, CPL, and RPL. Regarding other code segments, access is granted if CPL = DPL, but more privileged code segments can be accessed via special descriptors called *call gates*.

The unit of execution for is called a task. The term thread of execution is sometimes used in a similar context. The microprocessor can execute only one task at a time. The CPU switches tasks as a result of an interrupt or a JMP,

CALL, or IRET instruction. The 80286 hardware provides complete isolation between tasks. This isolation is based on each task having its own independent address space, and on the protection mechanism.

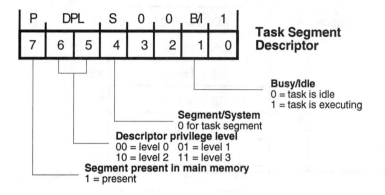

80286 Task Segment Access Rights Byte

The currently executing task is defined by the contents of the processor registers. This is known as the *task* or *processor state*. The task register, which is part of the 80286 CPU, contains a selector to the descriptor of the current task. The task segment descriptor has the same 8-byte structure and format as the other 80286 segment descriptors.

Bytes 2, 3, and 4 of the task segment descriptor contain the physical address of the task state segment (TSS). Each task has a unique TSS, which stores the task's address space and present state.

Memory — EMS

[PC hardware and architecture] In 1985, Lotus Development Corporation and Intel Corporation jointly announced a bank-switched memory expansion standard for the IBM microcomputers called expanded memory specification, or EMS. Shortly afterward Microsoft Corporation joined in the project, which was then designated as LIM EMS (Lotus, Intel, Microsoft expanded memory specification). Expanded memory allows applications to access up to 8 Mbytes of RAM in expanded memory boards through a software support product called the expanded memory manager, or EMM. This program is installed by the CONFIG.SYS file and thereafter becomes part of MS DOS. Expanded memory is available in blocks of 16K, called logical pages. Four logical pages reside in a 64K area called the *page frame*. The user can locate the page frame anywhere above the 640K block used by DOS.

Applications communicate with the expanded memory manager using the services of interrupt 67H. This process is quite similar to the DOS services of interrupt 21H; the service request number is loaded in the AH register and INT 67H is executed. Some services also require other registers to pass specific information.

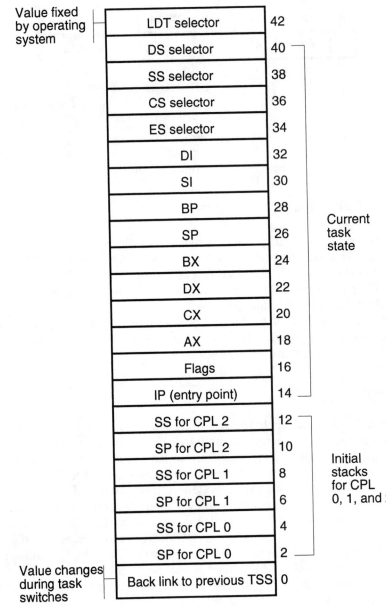

80286 Task State Segment

Note that, for expanded memory to be useful, applications must be designed to take advantage of this resource. Programs that are not equipped to manage expanded memory do not benefit by its presence.

MS DOS versions 4 and later include a driver program to support expanded memory. The driver, named XMA2EMS.SYS, is loaded by the CONFIG.SYS file. Once this driver is installed, applications can make use of expanded memory using the LIM specification. In addition, systems equipped with the 80386 or later CPUs can use a driver named EMM386.SYS, which allows memory beyond the 1-Mbyte DOS limit to be configured so as to emulate expanded memory.

Memory — expanded memory (LIM)

[PC hardware and architecture] Several techniques have been developed for expanding the memory resources in machines with a limited memory space. One of these techniques, called bank switching, assigns several blocks of memory to the same physical address space. A bank selection register determines which bank is active at the time of a memory access. By changing the value in the selection register, an application can address more memory than is visible to the CPU. Memory expansion methods based on bank switching require both hardware and software resources and must pay a considerable performance penalty.

Memory management (DOS)

[PC hardware and architecture] MS DOS can manage up to 1 Mbyte of RAM, but only the first 640K of this area are actually available for operating-system code and for user programs and data. This area (from 00000H to 9FFFFH) is sometimes called the *DOS memory area* or *conventional memory*.

Memory management — Windows and OS/2

[PC hardware and architecture] Windows and OS/2 memory management is based on the facilities provided by the 80286 and later CPUs. The manipulations are based on the protected-mode memory model and on the concept of segmented virtual memory. The idea of *virtual* memory stems from the fact that in protected mode, the segment registers contain a logical handle into a table (descriptor table).

In the real mode, the segment registers, which are directly accessible to the program, contain the base element of a physical address, while in protected mode, the memory structures are managed by the operating system; applications have limited access to them. If an application attempts to change the contents of a segment register directly, or to access memory in any illegal way, the CPU automatically generates an exception (protection fault) that serves to notify the operating system of an impending violation.

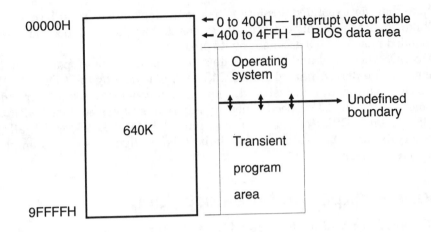

RAM Memory is DOS Systems

Protected-mode segments are accessed through selectors. These selectors, which are held in the segment registers CS, DS, SS, and ES, are an index into a descriptor table where the physical addresses are stored. The location of this table can be obtained only at the operating-system level. The segment descriptors stored in the descriptor table contain a 24-bit physical address for the segment base (See 80286). This 24-bit value allows operating system access to a minimum of 16 Mbytes of linear memory. Protected-mode selectors are also used in implementing virtual memory by swapping physical memory areas to disk files or other secondary storage devices.

Memory organization

[PC hardware and architecture] Memory cells are arranged in groups of eight bits, called *bytes*. The byte is the smallest addressable storage element in IBM microcomputers. This means that the CPU and other devices must read from and write to memory in groups of eight bits.

Memory — physical

[PC hardware and architecture] Memory is organized linearly; the sequential number assigned to each unit is called the *memory address*. The maximum number of memory units that can be addressed directly in a certain system depends on the internal architecture of the microprocessor.

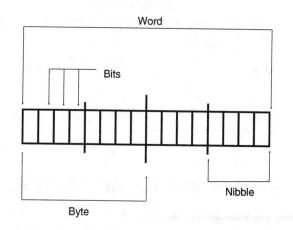

Bit, Byte, Nibble, and Word

Units of Memory

UNIT	EQUAL TO	NUMERICAL RANGE
Bit		2
Nibble	4 bits	16
Byte	8 bits 2 nibbles	256
Word	16 bits 2 bytes	65,535
Doubleword	32 bits 4 bytes 2 words	4,294,967,295
Quadword	64 bits 8 bytes 4 words	1.844670406 E19
Paragraph	128 bits 16 bytes 8 words	3.402823665 E38
Page	2048 bits 256 bytes 128 words 16 paragraphs	
Kilobyte	1024 bytes	
Megabyte	1,048,576 bytes 1024 kilobytes	
Gigabyte	1,073,741,824 bytes 1,048,576 kilobytes 1024 megabytes	
Terabyte	1,048,576 megabytes 1024 gigabytes	

Physical Memory

INTEL iAPX CPU	INTERNAL REGISTERS AND DATA PATHS	DIRECTLY ADDRESSABLE MEMORY
8088 8086 80286 80386 SX	20 bits	$2^{20} = 1,048,576$ bytes
80386 DX 486 Pentium	32 bits	$2^{32} = 4,294,967,295$ bytes

Memory — physical and logical address

[PC hardware and architecture] A memory address, expressed in terms of its segment base and offset component, is often referred to as the *logical address*. Logical addresses are conventionally written in the form segment:offset; for example, physical address AC214H can be expressed as logical address AC21:0004H or as logical address AC00:0214H.

Memory — segmented

[PC hardware and architecture] Intel microprocessors of the iAPX family use an addressing scheme known as *segmented memory*. In this scheme, memory is divided into segments, each corresponding to a linear space of 64K. Four segment registers are provided in the 8086 and 80286, and six in the 80386 and later CPUs. The memory address is obtained from two CPU registers; one of them (the segment register) designates the 16-bit base, and the second specifies the offset from the start of this base. The 20-bit address in physical memory is obtained by combining the two registers. This form of addressing allows access to 2^{20} bytes of memory (1 Mbyte).

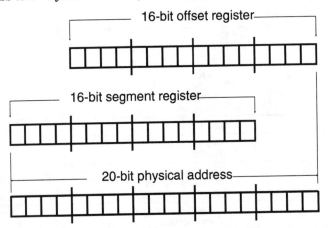

Segmented Memory Addressing

Since the low-order four bits of the physical address are always derived from the offset element, segment bases must start at paragraph boundaries (16 bytes). Thus, the first segment in memory starts at physical address 00000H (segment register = 0000H), and the next consecutive segment must begin at 00010H (segment register = 0001H). For the same reason, segments can overlap by multiples of 16 bytes. This means that a memory address can be reached using several segment-offset combinations. For example, the byte at physical address 00020H can be accessed using the following two sets of segment-offset values:

```
Set number           1           2
Segment              0000H       0001H
Offset               0020H       0010H
Physical address     00020H      00020H
```

The system may simultaneously address as many segments as there are segment registers in the CPU.

Memory storage of data

[PC hardware and architecture] Byte units of information are stored consecutively in memory. Units larger than a byte (words, doublewords, and quadwords) are conventionally stored by Intel iAPX microprocessors with the lower-order component in the lower-numbered memory address. This storage form is sometimes called the *little-endian* format.

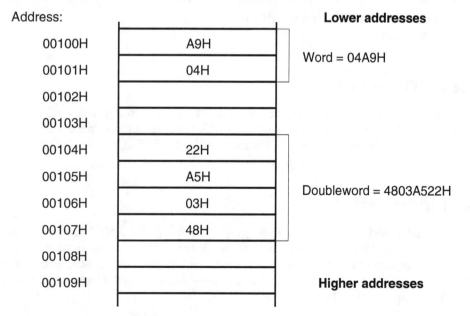

Words and Doublewords in Memory

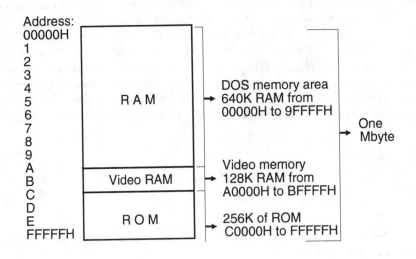

DOS General Memory Assignments

Memory use

[PC hardware and architecture] The use of memory resources by the IBM microcomputers can be classified as follows:

1. Storing nonvolatile programs and data (ROM)
2. System and user memory (RAM)
3. Video display memory

Memory — video

[PC hardware and architecture] IBM microcomputer video systems are memory-mapped. This means that the video image is stored in a dedicated area in RAM. This area is known by the names of video buffer, video memory, display buffer, and regen (regenerative) buffer.

Metacommand

[QuickBASIC] The statements $STATIC, and $DYNAMIC are called metacommands. Metacommands instruct the interpreter to insert certain code into the program or to treat certain statements specially. Since metacommands are not executed, they are preceded by the reserved word REM (or an apostrophe). For example, the statement:

```
REM $STATIC
```

tells the interpreter to store arrays in a special way.

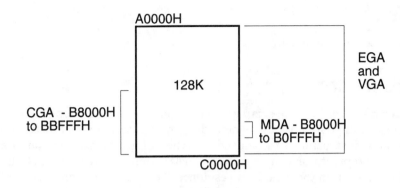

MDA = Monochrome Display Adapter
CGA = Color Graphics Adapter
EGA = Enhanced Graphics Adapter
VGA = Video Graphics Array (PS/2)

Video Memory

Microcomputer

[PC hardware and architecture] A system of miniature electronic devices, coupled to provide computer functions on a small scale. The fundamental elements of a microcomputer system are:

1. A central processing unit (microprocessor)

2. A primary storage facility (memory)

3. World interface devices (input and output facilities)

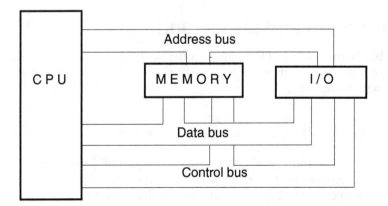

Elements of a Microcomputer System

Microdisk

(See diskette and microdisk).

Microprocessors

[PC hardware and architecture] An electronic semiconductor device capable of performing data operations according to an internal set of instructions. An individual instruction is recognized by its predefined code, called the *opcode*. Before a microprocessor can execute an instruction, it must first obtain the operation codes from their memory residence. This part of the process is called the *fetch cycle*. Once the instruction's codes have been fetched and decoded, then the CPU's internal circuitry can proceed to *execute* the opcode.

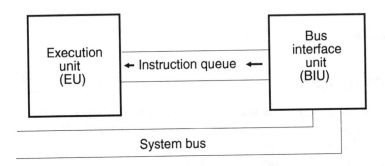

80x86 CPU Internal Architecture

MID$ (function and statement)

[BASIC] [QuickBASIC] Returns a requested substring within a string. When used as a statement, it replaces a portion of a string with a sub-string. The statement formats are:

```
v$ = MID$(x$,n[,m]) <= function
MID$(v$,n[,m]) = y$ <= statement
```

where n and m are integers in the range 1 to 255. The function form returns a string m characters long starting at the nth character. If m is omitted then all characters to the right beginning at the nth character are returned.

The statement form replaces the characters in v$ with the characters in y$, starting at position n. The optional m parameter refers to the number of characters in y$ to be used in the replacement.

MKDIR (command)

[BASIC] [QuickBASIC] Creates a disk directory. The statement format is:

```
MKDIR path
```

where path is a string (not more than 63 characters long) that defines the directive to be created.

MKI$, MKL$, MKS$, MKD$ (functions)

[BASIC] [QuickBASIC] Convert numeric to string types, as follows:

```
FUNCTION        CONVERSION                       LENGTH
MKI$            integer string                   2
MKL$            long integer to string           2
MKS$            single precision to string       4
MKD$            double precision to string       8
```

The numeric-to-string conversion is necessary with the buffer method of working with random-access files since any value placed in a buffer with LSET or RSET must be of string type.

MKSMBF$ and MKDMBF$ (functions)

[QuickBASIC] Convert single-precision, and double-precision numbers into strings of lengths four and eight, respectively, in the Microsoft Binary Format. This conversion is necessary before placing these numbers into random-access files to be read with Microsoft BASIC, GW-BASIC, BASICA, or early versions of QuickBASIC.

MNDRQQ

[MS-Pascal] Heading: (CONSTS A, B: REAL8): REAL8;
Arithmetic function that returns the value of A or B, whichever is smaller. Both A and B are of type REAL8. This function is from the MS-FORTRAN runtime library and must be declared EXTERN.
(See also: MXSRQQ and MXDRQQ).

MNSRQQ

[MS-Pascal] Heading: (CONSTS A, B: REAL4): REAL4;
Arithmetic function that returns the value of A or B, whichever is smaller. Both A and B are of type REAL4. This function is from the MS-FORTRAN runtime library and must be declared EXTERN.

(See also: MXSRQQ and MXDRQQ).

Modem

[PC hardware and architecture] Modems are optional components in most PC systems. They are either internal or external. Internal modems are furnished in the form of an adapter card. The modem card, which is installed in an expansion slot in the conventional manner, usually provides its own serial port. This port can be designated as serial port 1 to 4 (COM1, COM2, COM3, or COM4) according to the system configuration. In the PC line, and PC compatible machines, setting the serial port assignments may require changing mechanical connectors called jumpers. In the PS/2 line port assignments are performed by the programmable options select (POS) function of the system configuration software.

External modems usually require connection to an existing serial port. Both internal and external modems must also be connected to the telephone lines. The telephone system uses four connecting wires. The limited number of lines makes it necessary to use a serial communications protocol. This explains why modems normally access the computer through an RS-232-C port.

Modem communications

[PC hardware and architecture] Due to their convenience and availability, the telephone lines are often used as a data path in computer communications. But the telephone system is designed for voice communications. In order to transmit digital computer data through the telephone lines, the data must first be converted into an audio signal by a device called a *modulator*. By the same token, the receiving computer must use a demodulator to convert the audio signal into a digital signal. A device that can perform as a modulator/demodulator is called a *modem*.

Modem communications can take place according to different conventions and baud rates:

1. *300-Bd modems.* At 300 Bd/s the voltage signals are converted into audible tones following a convention known as *frequency key shifting,* or FKS. According to the Bell 103 protocol the originator logical 0 tone has a frequency of 1070 Hz, and the logical 1 tone, 1270 Hz. The answerer logical 0 tone has a frequency of 2025 Hz, and the logical 1 tone, 2225 Hz.

2. *1200-Bd modems.* The Bell 212A protocol establishes the conventions for modem communications at 1200 Bd/s. The communications techniques at this baud rate are based on phase modulation, which consists of manipulating the carrier signal so that two bits can be transmitted simultaneously in each direction. This accounts for a transmission speed rated at 1200 Bd, while the line frequency is of 600 Bd. The method, known as *phase shift keying,* or PSK, uses two carrier signals: the originator transmits at 1200 Hz and the answerer at 2400 Hz.

3. *2400-Bd modems*. Yet another protocol, known as CCITT V.22 (developed by the Cooperative Committee for International Telephony and Telegraphy of the United Nations) establishes the conventions for modem transmissions at 2400 Bd. This technique, based on creating 3 amplitudes and 12 phase angles, is known as *phase amplitude modulation,* or PAM. The resulting 36 states make possible the transmission of 6 simultaneous data bits. Consequently, although the line frequency is at 600 Bd, the transmission rate is rated at 2400 Bd/s.

4. *9600- and 19,200- Bd modems*. Techniques that combine data compression with PAM make possible modem transmissions at 9600 Bd and even higher rates. The present international standards for high-speed modem communications are CCITT V.29 and V.32.

Modem programming

[PC hardware and architecture] Programming the modem consists of transmitting and receiving specific codes and data through the modem's serial port. (See Serial communications).

Modem programming — AT command format

[PC hardware and architecture] Most modem command codes in the Hayes command set are preceded by the code letters AT (attention). The modem also uses these code letters to adjust the baud rate, word length, and parity values for the transmission. Commands are entered in a command line that can contain up to 40 characters (excluding spaces and AT codes).

A command line can include multiple commands and can contain embedded spaces and the conventional symbols commonly used in writing telephone numbers. For example, the parenthesis characters can be used to enclose the area code and the dash to separate the first three from the last four digits. The following command line instructs the modem to dial a telephone number using touch tones:

```
AT DT (406) 727-6319 >
```

Each AT command line must be terminated with a carriage return control code (0DH). In the above example the carriage return is represented by the characters.

Two modem commands in the Hayes command set do not require the AT preface and the carriage return terminator codes. The first one, the *escape* command, is used to instruct a modem, in the on-line mode, to return to the command mode. The command format consists of a 1-s initial guard time, followed by the Hayes escape code "+++" and another 1-s guard time wait. The guard times surrounding the escape code are designed to prevent the modem from accidentally interpreting the data values "+++" as an escape sequence.

The other command that does not require the standard preface and epilogue is the one to repeat the previous command line. The command code for the repeat command is A/.

Modem programming — Hayes command set

[PC hardware and architecture] In recent years, a company named Hayes Microcomputer Products has gained considerable recognition in the field of modem design and manufacturing. This has created a de-facto standard whereby most modems by other manufacturers are offered as being *Hayes-compatible*.

Frequently Used Modem Commands (Hayes System)

COMMAND	EXAMPLE	DESCRIPTION
A/	A/	Repeat last command (redial last number).
<w>+++<w>	+++	Escape sequence. Switch from on-line to command mode. <w> is 1-s wait
B<p>	AT B0<cr>	Enable communications protocol <p> can be: 0 = CCITT V.22 international 1 = Bell 212A protocol

D<s><n>	AT DT 727-6319	Dialing command. Subcommmands
		<s> can be:
		, = pause (default time 2 s)
		T = dial using touch tones
		P = dial using rotary (pulse) tones
		W = wait for dial tone
		; = return to command mode at end
		    of line (voice call dialing)
		<n> = telephone number with optional
		    "-" and "()" symbols

E<p>	AT E0 <cr>	Echo characters in command mode <p> can be: 0 = do not echo 1 = echo (default)
H<p>	AT H0<cr>	Hook control <p> can be: 0 = hang-up (on hook) 1 = pick-up (off hook)
O	AT O	Online. Return modem to on-line mode after escape or voice.
S<n>=<p>	AT S0=3 <cr>	Set modem register <n> = register number <p> = value installed in register
S <n>?	AT S0?<cr>	Report contents of modem register number <n>
V<p>	AT V1<cr>	Verbal response mode. <p> can be: 0 = numerical result codes 1 = verbal (text) result codes

Note:
    <cr> = carriage return code 0DH.

Modem programming — result codes

[PC hardware and architecture] In the Hayes system, commands that terminate in the carriage return code generate a standard modem response in the form of a numeric or text message. This response is sometimes called the *command result code*. The V command allows selecting a numeric or text mode for the screen message. The text response is often called the *verbal* response mode.

Result Codes to Hayes Modem Commands

CODE NO.	TEXT	DESCRIPTION
0	OK	Command line executed with no errors.
1	CONNECT	Modem connected.
2	RING	Incoming call detected.
3	NO CARRIER	Carrier signal not detected or lost.
4	ERROR	Error in command line. Invalid command or character limit exceeded.
5	CONNECT 1200	Modem connected at 1200 Bd/s.
6	NO DIALTONE	No dial tone detected.
7	BUSY	Busy signal.
8	NO ANSWER	Number dialed not answered.
9		Message not implemented.
10	CONNECT 2400	Modem connected at 2400 Bd/s.

Modem programming — states

[PC hardware and architecture] While in operation, the Hayes-compatible modem must be in one of two states. These states, or modes, are known as the on-line and the local command modes. While in the local command mode, the modem can receive command codes through its serial interface with the computer. The commands activate modem functions; for example, a command can make the modem dial a telephone number using touch tones. When the modem finishes executing a command, it sends a response message through the serial line.

Once a connection is established, the modem goes automatically into the on-line mode. In the on-line mode, data sent through the serial line is transmitted by the modem and is not interpreted as a command. A modem in the on-line mode can be either the originator or the answerer. To establish a connection between modems, one must be an originating modem and the other one an answering modem.

Modem registers

[PC hardware and architecture] The Hayes system uses a set of 28 internal registers, sometimes called the *S-registers*, which are accessible to the programmer via the S= and S? modem commands. The S-registers are numbered S0 to S27, and each register holds eight bits of data. Since the Hayes system is not a formal standard, the number of modem registers implemented and their default contents vary in modems by different manufacturers.

Modem Registers, Typical Use

NO.	RANGE	DEFAULT VALUE	CONTENTS
S0	0–255	0	Number of rings before answering. 0 = no auto answer
S1	0–255	0	Counter for incoming rings. Cleared automatically after 8 s
S2	0–127	"+"	Escape code character
S3	0–127	0DH	Command line and modem response terminator character
S4	0–127	0AH	Line feed character. Send after a verbal response string
S5	0–127	08H	Backspace character
S6	0–255	2	Wait time for dial tone (seconds)
S7	0–255	30	Wait time for carrier signal (seconds)
S8	0–255	2	Pause upon comma symbol in dial command (seconds)
S9	0–255	6	Response time after carrier detect signal (in one-tenths of a second)
S10	0–255	14	Wait time to hang-up after carrier is lost (in one-tenths of a second)
S11	0–255	70	Duration and spacing of touch tones (in one-hundreths of a second)
S12	0–255	50	Guard time before and after escape sequence (in one-fiftieths of a second)
S14	0–255	10001010B	7 6 5 4 3 2 1 0 Bits 1 = Echo ON 0 = Results ON 1 = Verbal results 0 = Use pulse tones 1 = Originate
S18	0–255	0	Duration of self-test (seconds)
S21	0–255	00000000B	7 6 5 4 3 2 1 0 Bits 00 = DTR ignored 0 = DCD always ON 0 = Long space disconnect OFF

(continued)

Modem Registers, Typical Use (Continued)

NO.	RANGE	DEFAULT VALUE	CONTENTS
S22	0–255	00001000B	
S23	0–255	00000101B	

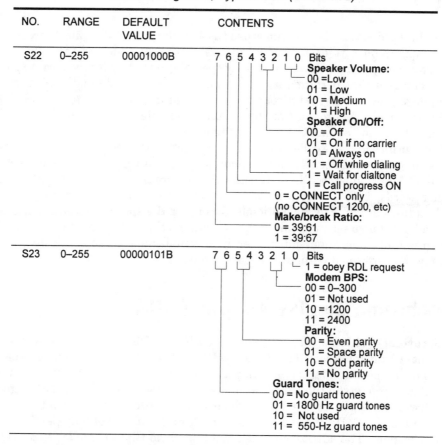

modular construction in C

[C] The idea behind modular construction is to break a processing task into smaller units that are easier to analyze, code, and maintain. A well-designed program is divided into a few fundamental functions that constitute its main modules. Since functions can contain other embedded functions, the process of dividing a program into individual modules can continue until processing reaches the simplest stage. In this manner the main modules may contain second-level modules, and the second-level modules may contain third-level modules, and so on.

A properly designed C function should perform a specific and well-defined set of processing operations. Each function contains a single entry and a single exit point. The individual functions should be kept within a manageable size. In practice, a well-conceived function rarely exceeds two or three pages of code. Except where program performance is an issue, it is a better programming practice to divide processing into several, smaller functions than to create a single, more complicated one.

module

[C] The word module is sometimes used as a synonym for a disk file. Since most C compilers operate on individual disk files, the disk files are also units of program compilation. However, strictly speaking, a module is any discrete part of a program that performs a self-contained task. If in managing a large C language program we find it convenient to separate the code into several disk files, we should refer to them as storage units, compilation units, or simply disk files, rather than equate the word "module" to a unit of storage.

Subroutines in C are called functions; it is these functions that constitute the true program modules. However, modular program construction is a design methodology and subroutines (functions) are mere programming facilities. In other words, both the concept of structured programming and the use of subroutines are, in a sense, optional. Except for the special procedure named main(), a C language program need not contain other functions. In fact, any C programming operation, no matter how complicated or sophisticated, can always be performed without using functions.

Monochrome Display Adapter (MDA)

[historical] [video systems] The Monochrome Display Adapter was the original text display card distributed by IBM. This card, sold as a monochrome display and printer adapter, can display the entire range of alphanumeric and graphic characters in the IBM character set. Hercules Computer Technologies produced a version of the MDA which could also operate in a bitmapped graphics mode. MDA is used with a monochrome monitor of long-persistence P39 phosphor. The adapter uses the Motorola 6845 CRT controller to provide the timing and control signals for the display. The MDA contains 4K of memory, starting at absolute address B0000H.

The adapter can address 4000 of its 4096 bytes (4K). The remaining 96 bytes, although not display memory, can be accessed by the CPU. VGA Monochrome mode number 7 is an emulation of the MDA card.

Mouse programming

[input/output] [PC hardware and architecture] The BIOS describes a pointing device interface associated with service number 194 of INT 15H. However, there are several difficulties associated with this service. In the first place, the IBM documentation dealing with this mouse service is not sufficient for programming the device. Another consideration is that the services are not compatible with different mouse hardware. Then there is the problem that various non-IBM versions of the BIOS do not include this service. Finally, the service is not recognized in the DOS mode of OS/2.

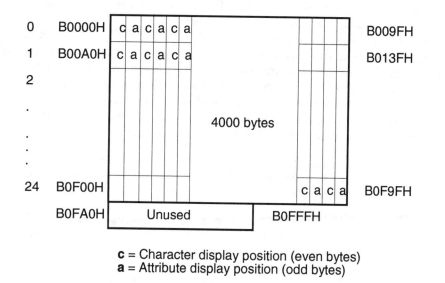

c = Character display position (even bytes)
a = Attribute display position (odd bytes)

Video Memory in Monochrome Mode

Due to these problems, the mouse driver software that has achieved more general acceptance is the one by Microsoft Corporation. The Microsoft mouse control software is installed as a system driver or as a TSR program. The system version is usually stored in a disk file with the extension .SYS and the TSR version in a file with the extension .COM. The Microsoft mouse interface services are documented in the book *Microsoft Mouse Programmer's Reference*, published by Microsoft Press.

Most manufacturers of mouse devices provide drivers that are compatible with the one by Microsoft. Therefore, the use of the Microsoft mouse interface is not limited to mouse devices manufactured by this company, but extends to all Microsoft-compatible hardware and software. The installation command for the mouse driver is usually included in the CONFIG.SYS or AUTOEXEC.BAT files. The Microsoft mouse interface attaches itself to software interrupt 33H and provides a set of 36 subservices. These mouse subservices are accessible by means of an INT 33H instruction.

Mouse programming — software installation

[input/output] [PC hardware and architecture] Applications that use the mouse device must adopt one of three alternatives regarding the support software: assume that the driver was installed by the user, load a driver program, or provide the low-level services within its code. By far, most applications adopt the first option, that is, assume that the user has previously loaded the mouse driver software. Although the more refined programs that use a mouse device include an installation utility that selects the appropriate driver and creates or modifies a batch file in order to insure that the mouse driver is resident at the time of program execution.

In any case, the first operation usually performed by an application that plans to use the mouse control services in interrupt 33H is to test the successful installation of the driver program. Since the driver is vectored to interrupt 33H, this test consists simply of checking that the corresponding slot in the vector table is not a null value (0000:0000H) or an IRET operation code. Either one of these alternatives indicates that no mouse driver is presently available. The following coding template shows the required processing:

```
; Code to check if mouse driver software is installed in the
; interrupt 33H vector. The check is performed by reading
; the interrupt 33H vector using MS-DOS service number 53,
; of INT 21H
        MOV     AH,53           ; MS_DOS service request
        MOV     AL,33H          ; Desired interrupt number
        INT     21H             ; MS-DOS service
; ES:BX holds address of interrupt handler, if installed
        MOV     AX,ES           ; Segment to AX
        OR      AX,BX           ; OR with offset
        JNZ     OK_INT33        ; Go if not zero
; Test for an IRET opcode in the vector
        CMP     BYTE PTR ES:[BX],0CFH   ; CFH is IRET
                                ; opcode
        JNE     OK_INT33        ; Go if not IRET
; At this point the program should provide an error handler
; to exit execution or to load a mouse driver
        .
        .
        .

; Execution continues at this label if a valid address was
; found in the interrupt 33H vector
OK_INT33:
        .
        .
        .
```

Mouse programming — subservices of Interrupt 33H

[input/output] [PC hardware and architecture] The Microsoft mouse interface was designed to provide control of the mouse device from high- and low-level languages. VGA alphanumeric programs can use the Microsoft mouse software by selecting one of two available text cursors. In the alpha modes the mouse driver manages the text cursor on a coarse grid of screen columns and rows, according to the active display mode. VGA programs that execute in graphics modes must provide their own cursor bitmap, which is installed by means of an interrupt 33H subservice. However, since the graphics cursor operated by the driver is limited to a size of 16-by-16 pixels, many graphics programs create and manage their own cursor. In this case the driver services are used to detect mouse movements, but the actual cursor operation and display are handled directly by the application. This is also the case of XGA programs that use the sprite functions to manage a mouse cursor image.

In addition to mouse cursor management and display, the subservices of interrupt 33H include functions to set the mouse sensitivity and rate, to read button press information, to select video pages, and to initialize and install interrupt handlers that take control when the mouse is moved or when the mouse buttons are operated. However, some of the services in the interrupt 33H drivers reprogram the video hardware in ways that can conflict with an application. For this reason, we have limited our discussion to those mouse services that are not directly related to the video environment. These services can be used from any VGA, XGA, or SuperVGA graphics modes without interference. However, in this case, it is the application's responsibility to perform all video updates.

Subservice 0 - Initialize Mouse
Subservice number 0 of interrupt 33H is used to reset the mouse device and to obtain its status. An application usually calls this service to certify that the mouse driver is resident and to initialize the device parameters.

Subservice 5 - Check Button Press Status
Programs that do not use interrupts can check mouse button press status by calling subservice number 5 of the Microsoft mouse interface. The call is typically located in a polling loop. The calling program passes the button code in the BX register; the value of 0 corresponds to the left mouse button and a value of 1 to the right button. The call returns the button status in the AX register; bit 0 is mapped to the left mouse button and bit 1 to the right mouse button. A value of 1 indicates that the corresponding button is down. The BX register returns the number of button presses that have occurred since this call was last made or since a driver software reset (see subservice 0 earlier in this section). The CX and DX registers hold the x and y cursor coordinates of the screen position where the last press occurred.

Subservice 11 - Read Motion Counters
The actual movement of the mouse-controlled icon is dependent on the state of two counters maintained by the mouse interface software. The Microsoft mouse interface at interrupt 33H stores the motion parameters in 1/200-in units called *mickeys*. The changes in the motion counters represent values from the last time the function was called. Subservice 11, of interrupt 33H, returns the values stored in the horizontal and vertical motion counters. The horizontal motion count is returned in the CX register and the vertical count in the DX register.

The values are signed integers in two's complement form. A negative value in the horizontal motion counter indicates mouse movement to the left, while a negative value in the vertical motion counter indicates a movement in the upward direction. Both the vertical and the horizontal counters are automatically reset by the service routine.

The detection of mouse action can be by a polling loop or by interrupts. Polling loops are often used in reading the motion counters so as to keep interrupt processing times to a minimum, specially considering that the Microsoft mouse interface does not allow the installation of more than one service routine. The processing inside a polling loop or a service routine takes place in similar fashion.

Subservice 12 - Set Interrupt Routine

The user action on the mouse hardware can be monitored by polling or by interrupt generation, as is the case with most other input devices. Polling methods are based on querying the device status on a time lapse basis, therefore polling routines as usually coded as part of execution loops. In the case of the mouse hardware the polling routine can check the motion counter registers and the button press and release status registers that are maintained by the mouse interface software.

The second and often preferred method of monitoring user interaction with the mouse device, particularly mouse button action, is by means of hardware interrupts. In this technique the program enables the mouse hardware actions that generate interrupts and installs the corresponding interrupt handlers. Thereafter, user action on the enabled hardware sources in the mouse automatically transfers control to the handler code. This frees the software from polling frequency constraints and simplifies program design and coding.

A typical application enables mouse interrupts for one or more sources of user interaction. For example, a program that uses the mouse to perform menu selection would enable an interrupt for movement of the trackball (or other motion detector mechanism) and another interrupt for the action of pressing the left mouse button. If the mouse is moved, the interrupt handler linked to trackball movement changes the screen position of the marker or icon according to the direction and magnitude of the movement. If the left mouse button is pressed, the corresponding interrupt handler executes the selected menu option.

Another frequently used programming method is to poll the mouse motion counters that store trackball movement and to detect button action by means of interrupts. This design reduces execution time inside the interrupt handler, which can be an important consideration in time-critical applications.

In the mouse interface software, the hardware conditions that can be programmed to generate an interrupt are related to an integer value called the *call mask*.

Subservice number 12 of the mouse interface at interrupt 33H provides a means for installing an interrupt handler and for selecting the action or actions that generate the interrupt.

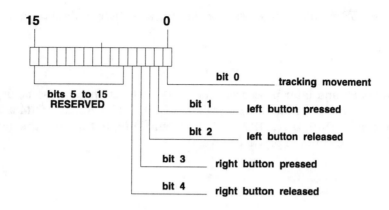

Mouse Interrupt Call Mask

MOV

[Assembler] 8086 machine instruction. Mnemonic for MOVe. Copies the source operand to the destination. Flags are not affected. In the 80286 and later processors, if the destination is a segment register, then the associated cache is also moved. A move into the SS register automatically inhibits interrupts until after the execution of the following instruction.

```
;   Addressing mode examples:
        MOV     AL,AH           ; Byte register to register
        MOV     SI,AX           ; Word register to register
        MOV     AL,21           ; Immediate operand to register
        MOV     CX,W_ITEM       ; Variable to CX
        MOV     AX,DATA         ; Segment name to register
        MOV     DS,BX           ; General register to segment
                                ; register
        MOV     SI OFFSET ITEM  ; Offset of variable to pointer
                                ; register
        MOV     AX SEG ITEM     ; Segment of variable to general
                                ; register
        MOV     BYTE PTR CS:[DI],AL ; General register stored
                                ; at memory location (with
                                ; segment override)
        MOV     CL,BYTE PTR [BX]; General register from memory
        MOV     BP,SS           ; BP register from SS segment
                                ; register
```

Since the MOV instruction does not affect the flags,

```
        MOV     AX,0
```

does not set ZF. An alternative way for clearing a register while setting the zero flag is:

```
XOR    AX,AX
```

In the 80386 and later processors the MOV instruction can also be used to move data to and from the control registers CR0, CR2, CR3, and CR4 and the debug registers DR0, DR1, DR2, DR3, DR6, and DR7. In this case the instruction must be executed at privilege level 0.

MOVEL

[MS-Pascal] Heading: (S, D: ADRMEM;N:WORD);
System level intrinsic procedure. Moves N characters (bytes) starting at S^ to D^, beginning with the lowest addressed byte of each array. Regardless of the value of the range and index checking switches, there is no bounds checking.

MOVER

[MS-Pascal] Heading: (S, D: ADRMEM; N: WORD);
System level intrinsic procedure similar to MOVEL, but starts at the highest addressed byte of each array. Use MOVER and MOVESR to shift bytes right. As with MOVEL, there is no bounds checking.
Example:

```
MOVER (ADR V[0], ADR V[4],12)
```

(See also: MOVESR).

MOVESL

[MS-Pascal] Heading: (S, D:ADSMEM;: N:WORD);
System level intrinsic procedure that moves N characters (bytes) starting at S^ to D^, beginning with the lowest addressed byte of each array. Regardless of the value of the range and index checking switches, there is no bounds checking.
Example:

```
MOVESL (ADS 'New String Value', ADS V, 16)
```

(See also: MOVEL).

MOVESR

[MS-Pascal] Heading: (S, D:ADSMEM;N: WORD);
System level intrinsic procedure similar to MOVESL, but starts at the highest
addressed byte of each array. Use MOVER and MOVESR to shift bytes right.
As with MOVESL, there is no bounds checking.
Example:

```
MOVESR (ADS V[O], ADS V[4], 12)
```

(See also: MOVER).

MOVS

[Assembler] 8086 machine instruction. Mnemonic for MOVe String. Transfers
the byte (MOVSB), word (MOVSW), or doubleword (MOVSD) addressed by the
source operand (SI register or ESI) to the destination operand (addressed by
DI or EDI), and updates SI (or ESI) and DI (or EDI) to point to the next element
in the string. If DF = 0 then the source and destination indexes are incremented.
IF DF = 1 they are decremented. When used with the REP prefix, MOVS
performs a memory-to-memory block transfer. Hardware assumes that the
source string is in the current data segment (DS) and the destination string is
in the current extra segment (ES). This assumption can be overridden for the
source string but not for the destination.
Code sample:

```
; Use of MOVSB in a routine to copy an area of memory to
; another one
DATA    SEGMENT
AREA_1 DB     '12345ABCDE' ; 10 bytes of source data
AREA_2 DB     '          ' ; Destination storage area
DATA    ENDS
;
CODE    SEGMENT
        .
        .
; Code assumes that DS --> the DATA segment
        PUSH    DS          ; Data segment to stack
```

This provides a mechanism for the sequential execution of POP SS and POP
SP instructions without danger of having an invalid stack. Nevertheless, the
LSS instruction is the preferred method of loading the SS and SP registers.

Loading a segment register while in protected mode results in several special
checks and actions described in the Intel Programmer's Reference manuals for
the respective CPUs.

Multicolor Graphics Array

[video systems] The Multicolor Graphics Array video system was introduced with the IBM Model 30 of the PS/2 line. The MCGA standard is also used in the PS/2 Model 25. Note that the IBM PS/2 line includes the video display hardware as part of the system board. But the PS/2 Model 25 and Model 30 are also compatible with the video cards used in the PC line. The MCGA standard was short-lived since the technology was soon replaced by the VGA.

MXDRQQ

[MS-Pascal] Heading: (CONSTS A, B: REAL8) : REAL8;
Arithmetic functions that return the value of A or B, whichever is larger. Both A and B are of type REAL8. This function is from the MS-FORTRAN runtime library and must be declared EXTERN.
(See also: MNSRQQ and MNDRQQ).

MXSRBQ

[MS-Pascal] Heading: (CONSTS A, B: REAL4) : REAL4;
Arithmetic functions that return the value of A or B, whichever is larger. Both A and B are of type REAL4. This function is from the MS-FORTRAN runtime library and must be declared EXTERN.
(See also: MNSRQQ and MNDRQQ).

N

NAME (command)

[BASIC] [QuickBASIC] Changes the name of a disk file. This is the BASIC counterpart of the DOS RENAME command. The statement format is:

```
NAME filespec1 AS filespec1
```

The action is change the name and/or the directory of filespec1 to the name and/or directory specified by filespec2. The two filespecs must refer to the same drive.

NDP

[PC hardware and architecture] [historical] In 1980, Intel introduced the 8087 mathematical coprocessor for the 8086 central processing unit. The 8087 chip is also known by the names numeric data processor (NDP), numeric data coprocessor, math coprocessor, and numeric processor extension (NPX). Numeric coprocessors are available for all iAPX central processors. However, the 80486 chip includes the floating-point operations of the NDP in its own instruction set. For this reason, it does not require a numerical processor extension. The designation 80x87 is sometimes used to refer generically to any member of the Intel family of mathematical coprocessors.

80x87 Coprocessors for the iAPX Processing Units

iAPX CPU	80x87 COPROCESSOR
8086	8087
8088/80C88	8087
80186/80188	8087
80286	80287
80386/486SX	80287 or 80387
486DX	No NDP required
Pentium	No NDP required

The 80x87 component can be imitated in software by a program called an 80x87 emulator. This software allows the programmer to do all the mathematical calculations using 80x87 instructions, even if the target system is not equipped with the physical coprocessor. If the emulator has been adequately designed and coded, the only difference between using the 80x87 chip and using its software version is that execution takes longer with the emulator than with the coprocessor. 80x87 emulators are available from Intel Corporation and from other software houses.

According to Intel, the 8087 component improves execution speeds of mathematical calculations by a factor of 10 to 100, compared with equivalent processing performed by 80x86 software. The 8087 extends the functions of the iAPX CPU by adding an instruction set of approximately seventy instructions and eight specialized registers for numerical operands.

NDP applications

[PC hardware and architecture] [Assembler] The mathematical coprocessor processes and stores numerical data encoded in seven different formats, but all internal calculations are performed in an 80-bit format that allows representation of nineteen significant decimal digits. The maximum precision available to the user is in the long real format, which encodes fifteen to sixteen significant decimal digits. The processing capability includes the following operations:

1. Data transfers, from memory into the processor's registers and vice versa, of all data formats; conversion from ASCII into the processor's floating-point formats and vice versa must be executed in external software
2. Arithmetic of integers and floating-point numbers
3. Square roots, scaling, absolute value, remainder, sign change, and extraction of the integer and fractional parts of a number
4. Direct loading of the constants 0, 1, p, and several logarithms
5. Comparison and testing of internal processor operands
6. Partial tangent and arctangent (from which other trigonometric functions can be calculated), and several exponential and transcendental bases
7. Control instruction to initialize the processor, to set internal operational modes, to store and restore the processor's registers and status, and to perform other housekeeping and auxiliary functions

NDP architecture

[PC hardware and architecture] The mathematical coprocessors of the 80x87 family have many common elements in their architecture. Internally, the NDP is divided into a control unit (CU) and a numeric execution unit (NEU). But the processor's internal structure is generally transparent to the programmer, who perceives the NDP as consisting of the following data areas:

1. A stack of eight operational registers
2. A control register
3. A status register
4. A tag word, consisting of two tag bits for each stack register
5. An instruction pointer
6. A data pointer

(See also: NDP register stack, NDP control registers, NDP status register, NDP tag register, NDP instruction and data pointers).

NDP control register

[PC hardware and architecture] The NDP operates in several modes. The programmer selects the mode of operation by loading a memory word into the control register.

A program can inspect or change the contents of the control register using the instructions FLDCW (load control word) or FSTCW (store control word).

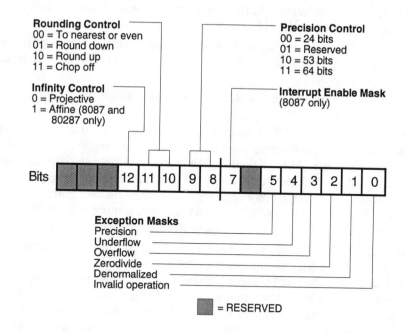

NDP Control Register

These NDP operational modes can be classified as computational and exception response modes. The exception response mode is determined by the settings of bits 0 to 5, and, in 8087 systems, also by bit 7 of the control register. Bits 0 to 5 (exception masks) define the error conditions that can generate an interrupt. If the exception mask for the condition is set (mask = 1), a default handling of the error condition automatically takes place inside the NDP. These on-chip responses to computational errors are usually adequate for most applications.

The error conditions determined by the NDP exception mask bits are the following:

1. *Invalid operation*. This error is usually a product of programming errors; for example, loading a nonempty register or popping an empty register, and also by stack overflow and underflow. Undefined operations can also generate an invalid operation error; for example, a division of zero by zero or the square root of a negative number. The invalid operation exception is frequently the only one that requires independent processing by means of an interrupt handler.

2. *Overflow*. Overflow occurs when a number exceeds the range of the destination data format.

3. *Underflow*. Underflow occurs when a number is too small for the destination data format.

4. *Zerodivide*. This error consists of a division by zero of a nonzero operand.

5. *Denormalized*. This error occurs if an operation is attempted when one or both operands are denormals.

6. *Precision*. This error indicates loss of numeric precision during the last operation. The most frequent cause of a loss of precision is internal rounding by the NDP.

The remaining fields of the control register determine the computational modes of operation.

7. *Precision control*. The NDP is designed to round the results of all floating-point operations before storing them in one of the stack registers. The setting of the precision control bits determines the format (temporary real, long real, or short real) to which the rounding takes place. The temporary real precision control mode (rounding to 64 bits) is the one best suited for most purposes. The other settings were added to provide compatibility with earlier processors and to meet a requirement of the IEEE 754 standard.

8. *Rounding control*. The rounding control field determines how the rounding takes place. Rounding to the nearest even number is the most common setting, since it is the least biased mode and is suitable for most applications. By changing the value in the rounding control field, a routine can be designed to execute the calculations twice, once rounding up and another time rounding down. Afterward, the two results can be compared and the upper and lower bounds of the exact result can be determined. This technique allows certifying that the result is correct within a certain interval.

9. *Infinity control*. The most common treatment of infinity recognizes the existence of infinitely large and infinitely small numbers. The IEEE standard supports only this treatment of infinity, known as *affine closure*, and so does the 80387. Nevertheless, the 8087 and 80287 also allow a treatment of infinity known as the *projective method of closure*. In this method, there is

no relation between infinity and ordinary signed numbers. The infinity control bit in the 8087 and 80287 control register permits the selection of either model of infinity. In the 80387, the infinity control bit is not active.

NDP/CPU interface

[**PC hardware and architecture**] The Intel 80x86 central processor and the 80x87 numeric data processor form a unit that has the combined instruction set and processing capabilities of both chips. To the programmer, the combination appears as a single device. The CPU and the mathematical coprocessor use the same clock generator, system bus, and interface components.

Instructions for the central processor and the math coprocessor are intermixed in memory in the instruction stream. The first five bits of the opcode identify a coprocessor escape sequence (bit code 11011xxx). This bit pattern identifies the 80x86 ESC (escape) operation code. All instructions that match these first five bits are executed by the coprocessor. However, the CPU distinguishes between escape instructions that reference memory and those that do not. If the instruction contains a memory operand, the CPU performs the address calculations on behalf of the coprocessor. On the other hand, if the escape instruction does not contain a memory operand, then the iAPX CPU ignores it and proceeds to execute the next instruction in line.

NDP data types

[**PC hardware and architecture**] The NDP operates on three different data types and a total of seven numeric formats. All numeric formats are stored in memory following the rule that the lowest significant element is located at the lowest-numbered memory address.

The NDP data types are classified as follows:

1. *Binary integers.* This data type corresponds to the word, doubleword, and quadword units of data storage. The sign bit is located at the highest numbered memory location; 1 = negative and 0 = positive. Negative numbers are represented in 2s complement form. The binary integer formats are named *word integer, short integer,* and *long integer.*

2. *Decimal integers.* This data type corresponds to the *packed decimal* format. The sign bit is located at the highest-numbered memory location; 1 = negative and 0 = positive. Two decimal digits are packed into each byte in binary-coded decimal form.

3. *Real numbers.* The NDP real-number formats are named *short real, long real,* and *temporary real.* As in the other formats, the sign bit is located at the highest memory address; 1 = negative and 0 = positive. In all real formats the number's digits are stored in the significand field. The logarithmic terms *mantissa* and *characteristic* are sometimes used to refer to the significand and exponent fields.

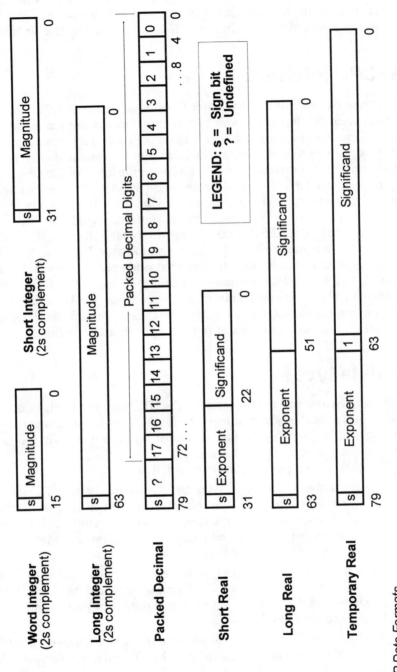

NDP Data Formats

Numerical Range of NDP Data Types

DESIGNATION	BITS	DIGITS	APPROXIMATE RANGE
Word integer	16	4–5	–32,768 to 32,767
Short integer	32	9	$-2x10^9$ to $2x10^9$
Long integer	64	18	$-9x10^{18}$ to $9x10^{18}$
Packed decimal	80	18	18 decimal digits
Short real	32	6–7	$8.43x10^{-37}$ to $3.37x10^{38}$
Long real	64	14–15	$4.19x10^{-307}$ to $3.37x10^{308}$
Temporary real	80	18–19	$3.4x10^{-4932}$ to $1.2x10^{4932}$

The exponent in the real formats is stored in bias form; bias 7FH for the short real format, bias 3FFH for the long real format, and bias 3FFFH for the temporary real format. The significand is stored in normalized form, that is, as a binary representation of a decimal number greater than 1 and less than 2. This form of normalization eliminates leading zeros when representing small values and maximizes the number of significant digits. The number of bits in the binary fraction is 23 in the short real, 52 in the long real, and 63 in the temporary real. The integer bit is implicit in the short and long real formats and explicit in the temporary real format. The implied binary decimal point follows the first digit of the significand.

Except for the temporary reals, all NDP numeric formats exist only in memory. When a number is loaded into an NDP stack register, it is automatically converted into a temporary real. All internal computations are carried out in temporary real numbers. The extended precision of this format provides a safety net for the computational errors that result from rounding, overflow, and underflow. This temporary real format can also be used for the storage of constants and intermediate results. However, it is better to refrain from using this format to increase the accuracy of computations, since this would compromise the safety features mentioned.

NDP detection

[PC hardware and architecture] The first step in configuring the numeric environment is to test for the presence of the physical numeric data processor. The following code fragment shows a simple way to detect the 8087, 80287, or 80387 chip. The test is based on the effect on the NDP status word of the initialization instruction FNINIT.

```
; PC program to detect the presence of the NDP
    STACK  SEGMENT stack
    DB     0100H DUP ('?')
    STACK  ENDS
    DATA   SEGMENT
```

```
                CTRL_87      DW      00H     ; NDP control word storage
                                            ; Initialized to zeros
                MSG_YES87    DB      '80x87 installed',0AH,0DH,'$'
                MSG_NO87     DB      'No 80x87 installed',0AH,0DH,'$'
DATA    ENDS
;
CODE    SEGMENT
        ASSUME CS:CODE
START:
; Establish data and extra segment addressability
        MOV     AX,DATA
        MOV     DS,AX
        ASSUME DS:DATA
; initialize NDP
        FNINIT                       ; Initialize NDP, no wait
        FNSTCW CTRL_87               ; Store control word in memory
        MOV     AX,CTRL_87           ; Control word to AX
        CMP     AH,03H               ; High byte will be 03H if
                                     ;   a coprocessor installed
        JNE     NO_87                ; No coprocessor in system
; At this point a NDP is detected
        MOV     AH,09H               ; DOS service request number
        LEA     DX,MSG_YES87 ; Message
        INT     21H                  ; DOS service
        JMP     DOS_EXIT                ; Exit
; No NDP in system
NO_87:
        MOV     AH,09H               ; DOS service request number
        LEA     DX,MSG_NO87             ; Message
        INT     21H                     ; DOS service
DOS_EXIT:
        MOV     AH,4CH               ; DOS service request code
        MOV     AL,0                    ; No error code returned
        INT     21H                     ; To DOS
CODE    ENDS
        END     START
```

NDP emulator

[PC hardware and architecture] Intel and other firms make available software products called 8087, 80287, or 80387 emulators. These programs are designed to offer a software alternative to the mathematical coprocessor hardware. Ideally, an emulator makes systems without the NDP chip execute all 80x87 instructions exactly as if there were a coprocessor installed. The vendors of software emulators often claim that the only difference between a system equipped with the coprocessor hardware and an emulated one is the slower execution of NDP instructions in the emulated version. In reality, emulator designers must make concessions, for the sake of performance, that determine small variations in emulator behavior in relation to the hardware counterpart.

This is particularly true in regard to computational precision and rounding. A limitation of the Intel emulator for 80x86/8087 systems is that the decision to use the software or the real component must be made at link time. Consequently, once a program has been linked with the emulator, it will not use the hardware component even if one is available in the host system.

The 80286 and 80386 CPU allow configuring of the numerics environment during system initialization. The MP (math present) and EM (emulate) bits in the processor's machine status word indicate whether an NDP is available in the system or not. If the MP bit is set (math coprocessor present), execution of the ESC instruction transfers control to the NDP in the normal manner. On the contrary, if the EM bit is set, an INT 7 is generated. Systems programmers can install the NDP emulator at this interrupt vector, thus making emulation transparent to applications. Note that the LMSW instruction, to change the machine status word, must be executed at the highest privilege level.

NDP implementations

[PC hardware and architecture] Three versions of the mathematical coprocessor have been released by Intel. The original chip, intended for use with the 8086/8088 and also compatible with the 80186 and 80188, is designated the 8087. The 80287 is the version designed to function with the 80286 CPU, and the 80387 is the version designed to function with the 80386 central processor. 8087 is Intel's designation for the original mathematical coprocessor chip. The chip was first offered to the public in 1980. It was developed simultaneously with the IEEE proposed standard for binary floating-point arithmetic, whose original version was published in 1979. For this reason, there are some minor differences between the 8087 chip and the standard; in most cases the difference consists of the 8087 exceeding the standard's requirements. The pertinent IEEE standard is number 754.

The 80287, introduced in 1983, is the version of the Intel mathematical coprocessor designed for the 80286 CPU. The 80287 extends numerical coprocessing to the protected-mode, multitasking environment of the 80286 CPU. When multiple tasks execute in the 80287, they receive the memory management and protection features of the central processor. According to Intel, the performance of the 80287 chip is 41 to 266 times that of equivalent software routines. The 80287 is also compatible with the 80386 central processor.

The internal architecture and instruction set of the 80287 are almost identical to those of its predecessor, the 8087. Most programs for the 8087 execute unmodified in the 80287 protected mode, except for the handling of numeric exceptions.

The Intel 80387 is a mathematical coprocessor intended for the 80386 central processing unit. The 80387 supports all 8087 and 80287 operations and instructions. Programs developed for the 8087 or the 80287 generally execute unmodified on the 80387. The 80387 conforms with the final version of the IEEE 754 standard for binary floating-point arithmetic, approved in 1985. This has made necessary the following changes in coprocessor behavior:

1. Automatic normalization of denormalized operands

2. Affine interpretation of infinity. Note that the 8087 and 80287 support both affine and projective infinities

3. Unordered compare instructions which do not generate an invalid operation exception if one operand is a NAN

4. A partial remainder instruction that behaves as expected in the IEEE 754 standard. The 80387 version of the FPREM instruction is named FPREM1

The 486DX and the Pentium CPU include the NDP hardware. In other words, the coprocessor functions are included with those of the main processor. To the programmer the 486 and Pentium appear as a CPU with a 387 mathematical coprocessor, although several minor modifications have been made to the NDP hardware and instruction set.

NDP instruction and data pointers

[PC hardware and architecture] These NDP registers have also been called the *exception pointers*. (See NDP Tag Register). After a computational instruction executes, the NDP automatically saves the instruction's operation code, its address, and, if included in the instruction, the operand address in the instruction and data pointer registers. This information can be examined by storing the processor's environment in memory through an FSTENV instruction or by storing the entire processor's state (environment and stack registers) by means of the FSAVE instruction. An exception handler can use this information to identify the instruction that generated an error.

In 80287 and 80387 systems, the storage format for the instruction and data pointers depends on the operating mode. In the real mode, the value stored is in the form of a 20-bit physical address and an 11-bit 8087 opcode. In protected mode, the value stored is the 32-bit virtual address of the last coprocessor instruction.

NDP instruction set

[PC hardware and architecture] [Assembler] NDP instructions are usually classified into the following groups:

1. Data transfer instructions

2 Arithmetic instructions

3. Comparison instructions

4. Transcendental instructions

5. Constant instructions

6. Processor control instructions

The instructions are described under their mnemonic codes, all of which start with the letter. The following is a list of the most used NDP operation codes:

Data transfer instructions:
FLD source (load real number)
FST destination (store real number)
FSTP destination (store real number and pop stack)
FXCH destination (exchange registers)
FILD source (integer load)
FIST destination (integer store)
FISTP destination (integer store and pop stack)
FBLD source (packed decimal load)
FBSTP destination (packed decimal store and pop)

Arithmetic Instructions:
FADD source
FADD destination, source (add real numbers)
FADDP destination, source (add real numbers and pop stack)
FIADD source (add integers)
FSUB source
FSUB destination, source (subtract real numbers)
FSUBP destination, source (subtract real numbers and pop stack)
FISUB source (subtract integers)
FMUL source
FMUL destination, source (multiply real numbers)
FMULP destination, source (multiply real numbers and pop stack)
FIMUL source (multiply integers)
FDIV source
FDIV destination, source (divide real numbers)
FDIVP destination, source (divide real numbers and pop stack)
FIDIV source (divide integers)
FDIVR source
FDIVR destination, source (reversed division of real numbers)
FDIVRP destination, source (reversed division and pop stack)
IDIVR source (reversed division of integers)
FSQRT

Other numeric operations:
FSCALE (scale)
FPREM (partial remainder)
FRNDINT (round to integer)
FXTRACT (extract exponent and significand)
FABS (absolute value)
FCHS (change sign)
Comparison Instructions:
FCOM source (compare real numbers)
FCOMP (compare and pop)
FCOMP source (compare real numbers and pop stack)
FCOMPP (compare reals and pop stack twice)
FICOM source (compare integers)

FICOMP source (compare integers and pop)
FUCOM, FUCOMP, and FUCOMPP are 80387 versions of the compare instruction
FIST (compare stack top with zero)
FXAM (examine register stack

Transcendental Instructions:
FPTAN (partial tangent)
FPATAN (partial arctangent)
F2XM1 (2 to the x minus 1)
FYL2X (log base 2 of x)
FYL2XP1 (log base 2 of x plus 1)

80387 transcendentals:
FSIN (sine)
FCOS (cosine)
FSINCOS (sine/cosine)

Constant Instructions:
FLDZ (load the value +0.0)
FLD1 (load the value +1.0)
FLDPI (load p)
FLDL2T (load log base 2 of 10)
FLDL2E (load log base 2 of e)
FLDLG2 (load log base 10 of 2)
FLDLN2 (load log base e of 2)

Processor Control Instructions:
FINIT (initialize processor)
FDISI (disable interrupts in 8087 systems)
FLDCW source (load control word)
FSTCW destination (store control word)
FSTSW destination (store the status word)
FCLEX (clear exceptions)
FSAVE destination (save NDP environment and register stack)
FRSTOR source (restore environment and register stack)
FSTENV destination (save environment only)
FLDENV source (restore environment)
FINCSTP (increment stack top pointer)
FDECSTP (decrement stack top pointer)
FFREE destination (change the register's tag to empty)

NDP limitations

[PC hardware and architecture] One limitation in programming the numerical data processor is that this chip must operate on encoded binary numbers in floating-point format. This means that the user's ASCII input must be converted into one of the machine's internal binary forms before calculation can take place. For the same reason, the results of the calculations must be converted from the internal formats into ASCII representations that can be interpreted by the user.

Another limitation is in relation to the calculation of trigonometric and logarithmic functions in 8087 and 80287 systems. In the trigonometric functions, for example, only the tangent can be obtained, and only for an angle in the range 0 to pi/4 radian. Sine and cosine functions must be calculated from the tangent, and the user's input must be previously scaled.

NDP programming

[PC hardware and architecture] [Assembler] To the programmer, the NDP appears as an extension to the internal registers and the instruction set of the central processor. Assembly language programs that use the NDP usually include opcodes from the instruction sets of both processors. NDP instruction mnemonics are identified in the source by the initial letter F. The addressing modes available in the NDP are a subset of those of the main CPU. For example, NDP addressing does not allow arithmetic operations on memory variables, as in the 80x86 instruction set.

Some NDP instructions allow the stack registers to be designated explicitly, in the ST(i) form, while in others the stack top operand is assumed. In addition, some instructions can have memory variables as operands; for example:

```
FADD                    ; Implicit destination operand
FADD    S_REAL ; Explicit source operand
FADD    ST,ST(3)        ; Destination and source operands
```

The leftmost operand is called the *destination*, and the rightmost operand is the *source*. Source operands supply data for the operation but are not altered during execution. The destination operand is replaced with the result.

The programmer must take into account that some NDP instructions change all previous ST designations; for example, loading data into a NDP stack register (FLD or FILD instructions) automatically pushes all previous values in the stack by one stack register.

NDP programming (conditional branching)

[PC hardware and architecture] [Assembler] All control transfer instructions are part of the main processor's instruction set. Conditional branching is a form of control transfer instruction that executes or not depending on the condition of the processor's status flags. Since conditional jumps depend on the state of the CPU flags, it is not possible to directly branch on the NDP's condition codes. However, the condition codes can be transferred to the CPU flag register, as in the following code fragment:

```
; Code to transfer the NDP condition codes onto the CPU flag
; register after comparing the third stack register (ST(2))
```

```
; with the stack top
      FCOM    ST(2)          ; Compare and set condition
                             ; code bits
      FSTSW   STATUS_87      ; Store NDP status register in
                             ; a memory variable (word)
      FWAIT                  ; Wait for NDP to conclude
      MOV     AX,STATUS_87   ; Status register to AX
      SAHF                   ; Move high byte of status
                             ; register (condition codes)
                             ; to CPU flags
; CPU conditional jump instruction can now be coded
```

NDP Condition Codes and CPU Conditional Jumps

INSTRUCTION	CONDITION CODES				INTERPRETATION
	C3	C2	C1	C0	
FCOM, FCOMP,	0	0	?	0	ST > source
FCOMPP, FICOM,	0	0	?	1	ST < source
FICOMP, FUCOM,	1	0	?	0	ST = source
FUCOMP, FUCOMPP	1	1	?	1	ST not comparable
	ZF	PF		CF	
	FLAGS AFTER SAHF				

OPCODE	FLAGS	TRANSFER CONDITION
JB	CF = 1	Taken if ST < source or not comparable
JBE	(CF or ZF) = 1	Taken if ST ≤ source or not comparable
JA	(CF or ZF) = 0	Taken if ST > source
JAE	CF = 0	Taken if ST ≥ source
JE	ZF = 1	Taken if ST = source or not comparable
JNE	ZF = 0	Taken if ST ≠ source

NDP programming (trigonometric functions)

A difficulty frequently encountered by programmers of 8087 and 80287 systems is that the trigonometric functions sine, cosine, and tangent cannot be obtained directly. The 80387 corrects this problem with the instructions FSIN, FCOS, and FSINCOS.

However, the 8087/80287 instruction set allows obtaining a sine-cosine ratio through the use of the partial tangent (FPTAN) or partial arctangent (FPATAN) instructions. All other trigonometric functions can be calculated from this ratio. One limitation is that the input value for these functions, in radian measure, must be previously scaled to the first octant.

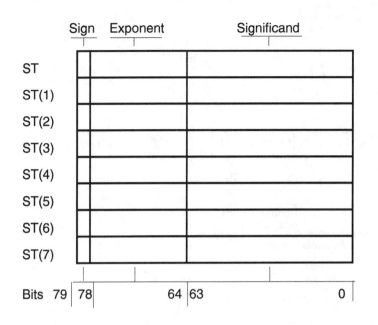

Register Stack

NDP register stack

[PC hardware and architecture] The numeric execution unit of the NDP contains eight internal registers for operational data. Many instructions allow these registers to be addressed explicitly, that is, according to their designation in the ST(i) form.

The explicit designation appears to the left of each register. Most assemblers allow the designations ST and ST(0) for the register at the stack top. For example, the instruction

```
FADD    ST,ST(2)
```

adds the third stack register (ST(2)) to the stack top register (ST). The sum replaces the previous value of ST.

Other NDP instructions operate implicitly on the register at the stack top. For example, the instruction FSQRT replaces the contents of the ST register with its square root.

Each of the stack registers is 80 bits wide. The data storage format corresponds to the NDP temporary real numeric format. This data format is used internally by the NDP in all its calculations.

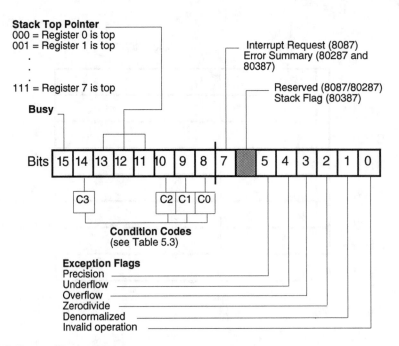

NDP Status Register

NDP status register

[PC hardware and architecture] The status register reflects the state of the NDP at the instant that it is accessed. The instruction FSTSW can be used to store the status register in a memory variable, where the program can inspect it. By coding FSTSW AX, 80287 and 80387 systems allow transferring the contents of the status register into the AX register.

Status register bits 0 to 5 reflect the error conditions of precision, underflow, overflow, division by zero, denormalized operand, and invalid operation. If one of these conditions has occurred, the corresponding bit in the status register is set. This action is independent of the setting of the exception masks of the control register. Once an error occurs, the corresponding error flag remains set until it is explicitly reset with a FCLEX (clear exceptions) instruction or until the coprocessor is reinitialized.

In 8087 systems, bit 7 of the status register is called the interrupt request bit. Intel literature on the 80287 refers to this bit as the error summary bit. In both cases, this bit is set if an unmasked exception bit is set in the status register. Therefore, bit 7 of the status register can be used to test whether an interrupt condition is pending.

The NDP condition code bits can be compared to the flag bits in the CPU. Their state is determined by NDP computational operations, and their setting reflects the outcome of these operations. The condition code bits can be tested by loading the status word into a CPU register. The test can be used in conditional branching.

NDP Condition Codes

INSTRUCTION	CONDITION CODE BITS				INTERPRETATION
	C3	C2	C1	C0	
FCOM, FCOMP,	0	0	?	0	ST >source
FCOMPP, FICOM,	0	0	?	1	ST < source
FICOMP	1	0	?	0	ST = source
	1	1	?	1	ST or source undefined
FTST	0	0	?	0	ST is positive and nonzero
	0	0	?	1	ST is negative and nonzero
	1	0	?	0	ST is zero (+ or -)
	1	1	?	1	ST is not comparable
FXAM	0	0	0	0	+Unnormal
	0	0	1	0	− Unnormal
	0	1	0	0	+Normal
	0	1	1	0	− Normal
	1	0	0	0	+0
	1	0	1	0	− 0
	1	1	0	0	+Denormal
	1	1	1	0	− Denormal
	0	0	0	1	+ NAN
	0	0	1	1	− NAN
	0	1	0	1	+Infinity
	0	1	1	1	− Infinity
	1	?	?	1	Empty
FUCOM,	0	0	?	0	ST > source
FUCOMP,	0	0	?	1	ST < source
FUCOMPP	1	0	?	0	ST = source
	1	1	?	1	Unordered

The condition code bits are also used to report the last three significant bits of the quotient generated by the partial remainder instruction, FPREM.

The field composed of bits 11, 12, and 13 encodes the number of the NDP register which is currently the stack top. After initialization, the value of this bit field is 000B. When a value is loaded onto the NDP stack, the stack top pointer field changes to 111B (7 decimal). Each successive operation that loads the NDP stack decrements the stack top pointer field, and each store increments it. One of the few practical uses of this bit field is in interpreting the tag register.

The busy bit indicates whether the NDP is idle or executing an instruction. This bit is of little practical use to applications.

NDP synchronization

[PC hardware and architecture] The coprocessor mechanism in microprocessor systems was pioneered by Intel with the 8087 NDP. The fundamental design allows a central processor and a coprocessor to execute simultaneously. The hardware elements that make possible coprocessor operation are a BUSY pin in NDP, connected to a TEST pin in the CPU. The NDP's BUSY pin sends a signal whenever the coprocessor is executing. The CPU's TEST pin, upon receiving a WAIT (or FWAIT) instruction, forces the central processor to detain execution until the coprocessor has finished.

Understanding processor and coprocessor synchronization is complicated by the fact that it is implemented differently in the 8087 than in the 80287 and 80387 hardware.

Configurations that use the 8087 must not present a new instruction to the NDP while it is still executing the previous one. This condition can be prevented by inserting a 80x86 WAIT instruction either before or after every coprocessor ESC opcode. If the WAIT follows the ESC, then the central processor does nothing while the NDP is executing. In order to allow concurrent processing by the CPU and the NDP, most assembler programs insert the WAIT instruction before the coprocessor ESC opcode. In this case, the CPU can continue executing its own code until it finds the next ESC in the instruction stream.

However, when the WAIT precedes the ESC, it becomes possible for the CPU to access a memory operand before the coprocessor has finished acting on it. If this possibility exists, the programmer must detect it and insert an additional FWAIT. The alternative mnemonic FWAIT is usually preferred in this case, since some emulator libraries do not recognize the WAIT opcode. The following code fragment shows a typical circumstance that requires the insertion of an FWAIT instruction.

```
FSTCW   CTRL_WORD     ; Store control word in memory
FWAIT                 ; Force the CPU to wait for NDP
                      ; to finish before
MOV     AX,CTRL_WORD  ; recovering the control word
                      ; into the AX register
```

Synchronization requirements are different in 80286/80287 and 80386/80387 systems. The 80286 and 80386 CPUs automatically check that the NDP has finished executing the previous instruction before sending it the next one. Unlike the 8087, the 80287 and 80387 do not require the WAIT instruction for synchronization. However, the possibility of both processors accessing the same memory operand simultaneously also exists in 80287/80387 systems and must be prevented as previously described for the 8087.

Some NDP processor control instructions have an alternative mnemonic that instructs the assembler not to prefix the instruction with a CPU FWAIT. This mnemonic form is characterized by the letters FN, signifying NO WAIT, for example, FINIT/FNINIT and FENI/FNENI. The no-wait form should be used only if CPU interrupts are disabled and the NDP is set up so that it cannot generate an interrupt that would precipitate an endless wait. In all other cases, the normal version of the instruction should be used.

NDP tag register

[PC hardware and architecture] Each 2-bit field of the tag register is associated with a stack register. The tag code defines the contents of each one of the eight stack registers.

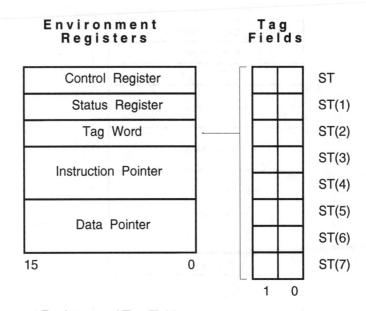

Environment Registers and Tag Fields

The tag code is used internally by the processor in optimizing performance. The tag codes are accessible to the program and can be used to determine the stack contents. It is necessary to inspect the stack top pointer field of the status register to determine which tag corresponds to which stack register. Stack register contents can usually be determined more precisely using the FXAM or FTST instructions and interpreting the resulting condition code bits.

NDP temporary real format

[PC hardware and architecture] The temporary real format is the internal data format used by the NDP for all values stored in the stack registers. All other data formats exist only in memory.

Nonzero real numbers are encoded in normalized form; that is, the high-order bit of the significand is set. This bit is explicit in the temporary real format. But, as a floating-point value approaches zero, the normalized form can no longer be used for encoding the significand.

Unnormal and denormal numbers are generically termed *nonnormals*. Denormals can be identified by all zeros in the exponent field. A denormal is the result of a masked underflow exception. It represents a number that is too small for the destination format. By gradually denormalizing the result, the NDP allows computations to continue at the expense of contaminating the final result with a rounding error. An unnormal is, generally, a descendant of a denormal, that is, a denormal that has grown bigger during numerical processing. The denormal format prevents a denormal from masquerading as a normal number.

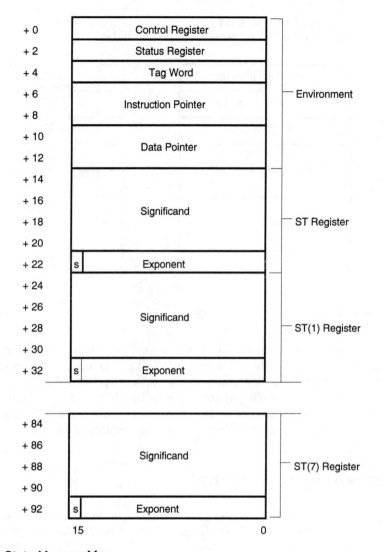

NDP State Memory Map

The *infinity* encoding can be produced intentionally by the programmer or can be the result of the masked response to the zerodivide or overflow exceptions. In the temporary real format, the infinities can be identified by all bits set in the exponent field while only the leading bit is set in the significand field. The encoding for infinity allows signed representations.

The encoding for *zero* can be positive or negative, according to the setting of the sign bit. Negative and positive zeros behave identically during computations. The FXAM instruction can be used to determine the sign of a zero value. An unnormal with a significand of all zeros and a nonzero exponent (but not all 1s) is sometimes called a *pseudo zero*.

NDP Encoding for Temporary Reals

CLASS			SIGN	BIASED EXPONENT	SIGNIFICAND
P O S I T I V E	R E A L	NAN	0 . . .	111 ... 111 . . .	1111 ...11 . 1000 ... 01
		Infinity	.	111 ... 111	1000 ... 00
		Normals	. . .	111 ... 110 . .	1111 ... 11 1000 ... 00
		Unnormals	. . .	. 000 ... 001	0111 ... 11 0000 ... 00
		Denormals	. .	000 ... 000 . .	0111 ... 11 0000 ... 01
		Zero	0	000 ... 000	0000 ... 00
N E G A T I V E	R E A L S	Zero	1	000 ... 000	0000 ... 00
		Denormals	. .	. .	0000 ... 01 0111 ... 11
		Unnormals	. . .	000 ... 001 . .	0000 ... 00 0111 ... 11
		Normals	. . .	. . 111 ... 110	1000 ... 00 1111 ... 11
		Infinity	.	111 ... 111	1000 ... 00
	NAN	Indefinite	.	. 111 ... 111	. 1100 ... 00
			1	111 ... 111	1111 ... 11
Bits			79	78 64	63 0

The designation *NAN* stands for not a number. A special type of NAN, called indefinite, is the masked response to an invalid exception. Whenever a NAN enters into a computation, it propagates and contaminates the result. A NAN can be identified in the temporary real format by all bits set in the exponent field and at least 1 bit set in the significand field. The special NAN called indefinite has the two high-order bits of the significand set, and all other significand bits clear.

NEC 765 Floppy Disk Controller Commands

NO.	DESCRIPTION	NO.	DESCRIPTION
1	SPECIFY CHARACTERISTICS	9	WRITE DATA
2	SENSE DRIVE STATUS	10	WRITE DELETED DATA
3	SENSE INTERRUPT STATUS	11	READ TRACK
4	SEEK (move to track)	12	READ ID
5	RECALIBRATE	13	SCAN EQUAL
6	FORMAT A TRACK	14	SCAN HIGH OR EQUAL
7	READ DATA	15	SCAN LOW OR EQUAL
8	READ DELETED DATA	16	INVALID (no operation)

NEC 765 commands

[**PC hardware and architecture**] The NEC 765 Floppy Disk Controller can execute 15 valid commands.

Commands to the FDC consist of several successive bytes transmitted through the FDC data register. The first byte contains the command codes. The remaining command bytes, which can make a total of two to nine bytes per command, contain data required for the operation. FDC commands can be described as consisting of three phases:

1. *Command Phase.* In this phase the FDC receives the sequence of bytes that constitutes a command. The controller enters the command phase after a RESET or following the conclusion of a previous command.

2. *Execution Phase.* In this phase the FDC performs the required operations. The controller enters the execution phase immediately after receiving the last byte in the command.

3. *Result Phase.* At the conclusion of the execution phase, some FDC commands report to the CPU the results of the performed operations. In these commands, the controller does not return to the command phase until these data are read by the CPU.

NEC 765 and other floppy disk controller commands can be obtained from the manufacturer's technical specification documents.

NEC 765 floppy disk controller

[**PC hardware and architecture**] IBM has used the same floppy disk controller chip in all the models of the PC and the PS/2 line. This floppy disk controller, or FDC, is the NEC 765. The Intel 8272A FDC is identical to the NEC chip.

The NEC 765 is capable of operating in single density (FM mode) and double-density (MFM mode), although all IBM microcomputer diskette drives use double-density recording. Data records can be of 128, 256, 512, and 1024 bytes (IBM systems under DOS use 512 bytes per sector). The controller chip can drive up to four drives of 8-, 5 1/4-, or 3 1/2-in media size.

Data transfers with the NEC 765 can take place using or not using direct memory access (DMA). In the non-DMA mode, the FDC interrupts the CPU as each data byte is transferred. In DMA operation, the CPU sends a command to the FDC and the data transfer takes place under the supervision of the DMA controller, while the CPU is free to perform other tasks. Note that the PCjr is the only IBM microcomputer that does not implement DMA.

NEC 765 — programming

Few programs require accessing the controller directly in order to perform diskette operations, since the services provided in the DOS and BIOS are usually sufficient and more convenient. The exceptions to this rule are operating system software and programs that use unconventional manipulations of the floppy disk controller (FDC) to obstruct unauthorized copying of diskettes.

Programming the NEC 765 FDC consists of issuing controller commands. These commands are executed by reading the main status register and by reading and writing to the data register. Read and write operations to the data register must be synchronized by examining bits 6 and 7 of the main status register. During write operations (command phase), the program must check that bit 6 of the main status register is clear (indicating flow from the CPU to the FDC) and that bit 7 is set (indicating that the data register is ready). This test must be performed before sending each byte in the command code. During read operations (result phase), the program must test that bit 6 of the main status register is set (indicating flow from the FDC to the CPU). This test must be performed before reading each result byte.

NEC 765 registers

[PC hardware and architecture] The transfer of information between the FDC and the system takes place through two 8-bit registers. One of these registers is designated as the *main status register* and the other one as the *data register*. The main status register, which is read-only, provides information regarding the status of each diskette drive in the system. The data register is used in issuing commands to the FDC and in obtaining command results.

The data register is used for issuing multiple-byte commands to the Floppy Disk Controller and for reading command results. During the command phase, the program sends all command bytes successively through the data register. After the last command byte is received, the controller automatically enters the execution phase. At the conclusion of the execution phase, the program must read all result bytes in the specific command. The FDC will not be ready for a new command until the last result byte is read from the data register.

Register address: 3F4H all IBM systems

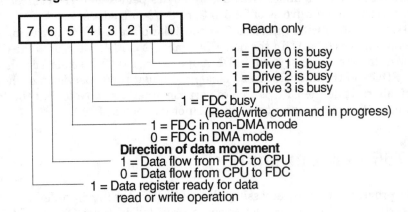

NEC 765 Main Status Register Bitmap

The result of an FDC command, except for those commands that do not have a result phase, is reported in one to seven bytes which are read by the CPU at the controller's data register port. The first 1, 2, or 3 of these result bytes correspond to the status registers. The status registers are numbered from 0 to 3 and are sometimes referred to as ST 0, ST 1, ST 2, and ST 3.

NEW

[MS-Pascal] Heading: (VARS P: POINTER);
Library procedure of the heap management, short form, group. Allocates a new variable V on the heap and at the same time assigns a pointer to V to the pointer variable P (a VARS parameter). The type of V is determined by the pointer declaration of P. If V is a super array type, use the long form of the procedure instead. If V is a record type with variants, the variants giving the largest possible size are assumed, permitting any variant to be assigned to P^.

```
Heading:(VARS P: POINTER; T1, T2,... TN: TAGS);
```

Allocates a variable with the variant specified by the tag field values T1 through TN. The tag field values are listed in the order in which they are declared. Any trailing tag fields can be omitted.

If all tag field values are constant, MS-Pascal allocates only the amount of space required on the heap, rounded up to a word boundary. The value of any omitted tag fields is assumed to be such that the maximum possible size is allocated.

If some tag fields are not constant values, the compiler uses one of two strategies:

1. It assumes that the first nonconstant tag field and all following tags have unknown values, and allocates the maximum size necessary.

2. It generates a special runtime call to a function that calculates the record size from the variable tag values available. This depends on the implementation. A similar procedure applies to DISPOSE and SIZEOF.

The programmer sets all tag fields to their proper values after the call to NEW and never changes them. The compiler does not do any of the following:

1. Assign tag values

2. Check that they are initialized correctly

3. Check that their value is not changed during execution

According to the ISO standard, a variable created with the long form of NEW cannot be any of the following:

1. Used as an expression operand

2. Passed as a parameter

3. Assigned a value

MS-Pascal does not catch these errors. Fields within the record can be used normally.

Assigning a larger record to a smaller one allocated with the long form of NEW would destroys part of the heap. Since this condition is difficult to detect at compile time, any assignment to a record in the heap that has variants uses the actual length of the record in the heap, rather than the maximum length. However, an assignment to a field in an invalid variant may destroy part of another heap variable or the heap structure itself. This error is not deleted, unless all tag values are explicit, the tag values are correct, and the tag checking switch is on.

The extend level allows pointers to super arrays. The long form of NEW is used, except that array upper bound values are given instead of tag values. All upper bounds must be given. Bounds can be constants or expressions; in any case, only the size required is allocated.

NEW (command)

[BASIC] Deletes the program in memory and clears all variables.

Non-IBM video systems

[historical] [video systems] Several independent companies have developed video systems for the PC which have achieved considerable prominence. In this context, the term "SuperVGA" refers to enhancements to the VGA standard developed.

NOT — bitwise operator

[C] Acts on a single operand by inverting all its bits. The NOT operation converts all 1-bits to 0 and all 0-bits to 1. The following example shows the result of a NOT operation:

```
                        0101 0101B
   BITWISE NOT          ----------
                        1010 1010B
```

NS-16450 and 16550 UART (See serial communications controllers).

Number systems

[PC hardware and architecture] Numbers are a cultural product, but one number system, called the decimal system, has gained almost universal acceptance. The symbols used in the decimal system are the Hindu-Arabic numerals. We are so familiar with the symbols of the decimal system (0, 1, 2, 3, 4, 5, 6, 7, 8, and 9) that we tend to consider them a natural phenomena, although, in reality, any system of numbers is an intellectual convention. It if often said that the decimal system of numbers resulted from the practice of counting with our fingers and that if humans had six fingers instead of ten our number system would have six symbols instead of ten.

The fundamental use of a system of numbers is counting. The simplest form of counting is by tallying, to which we all occasionally resort. Roman numerals probably derived from the tally system, since we can detect in some Roman numerals the vertical and diagonal traces used in tallying. The uncertainty in the positional value of the digits, the absence of a symbol for zero, and the fact that some digits required more than one symbol, complicate the rules of arithmetic using Roman numerals.

The Hindu-Arabic numerals were introduced into Europe during the 14th and 15th centuries. These numerals are used in a counting scheme where the value of each digit is determined by its column position (decimal positional system), as in this example:

```
   7 9 6 2
   | | | |_____     units
   | | |_____     10 units
   | |_____     100 units
   |_____     1000 units
```

The total value is obtained by adding the column weights of each unit

```
     7000 ——— 7 thousand units
      900 ——— 9 hundred units
+      60 ——— 6 ten units
        2 ——— 2 units
     _____
     7962
```

(See also: binary numbers).

Numeric data

[C] Numeric data are that with which we can perform mathematical operations. In other words, numeric data consist of number symbols used to represent quantities. This definition excludes the use of numbers as designators; for example, a telephone or a social security number. It is difficult to conceive a need for performing arithmetic operations on telephone or social security numbers.

Numeric data can appear in the form of variables or constants. C language numeric constants can be predefined by means of the #define directive, or they can be entered explicitly in the operations. Numeric variables are classified into two data types, *integral types* and *floating-point types*. The floating-point types are sometimes called *reals*.

Each data type corresponds to a specific category of numbers; for example, the integer data type allows representing whole numbers, while the real data type allows representing fractional numbers. For each data type C provides several *type specifiers* that further determine the characteristic and range of representable values.

C Numerical Data Types

TYPE	SPECIFIERS	STORAGE BYTES	RANGE
INTEGRAL			
	char	1	127 to -128
	unsigned char	1	0 to 256
	int - signed int	2	32,767 to -32,768
	unsigned - unsigned int	2	0 to 65,535
	short - short int	4	32,767 to -32,768
	long - long int	8	2,147,483,647 to -2,147,483,648
FLOATING-POINT			
	float	4	$8.43*10^{-37}$ to $3.37*10^{38}$
	double	8	$4.19*10^{-307}$ to $1.67*10^{308}$

Numeric Data Processor

(See NDP).

O

OCT$ (function)

[BASIC] [QuickBASIC] Returns a string that represents the octal value of the decimal argument. The function format is:

```
v$ = OCT$(n)
```

where *n* is a whole number between 0 and 2,147,483,647 and v$ is the base representation of *n*. If n is negative the two's complement form is used.

ODD

[MS-Pascal] Heading: (X: ORDINAL): BOOLEAN;
Data conversion function that tests the ordinal value X to see whether it is odd. ODD is TRUE only if ORD (X) is odd; otherwise it is FALSE.

ON COM(n) (statement)

[BASIC] [QuickBASIC] Sets up a trap for information coming into the communications buffer. The statement format is:

```
ON COM(n) GOSUB line (or label)
```

In BASIC the destination of the GOSUB operand is a program line number. In QuickBASIC the destination is program label. In either case *n* is the number of the communications port (1 or 2). The statement COM(n) ON must be first executed to activate communications line *n*. Thereafter information coming into the port causes a GOSUB action. The subroutine at line (or label) can be in the main body of the program or after its END statement. If COM(n) OFF is executed for the respective communications line then no trapping takes place. The communications trap handler should end with a RETURN statement. Example:

```
ON COM(10 GOSUB COM_RTN
COM(1) ON
```

.
.
```
COM_RTN:
```

ON ERROR (statement)

[BASIC] [QuickBASIC] Enables error trapping and specifies the line or label at which the error handler is located. The statement format is:

```
ON ERROR GOTO line (label)
```

After the ON ERROR statement executes, a program error causes a jump to an error-handling routine beginning at line (or label). The destination must be in the main body of the program.
(See also: RESUME).

ON KEY(n) (statement)

[BASIC] [QuickBASIC] Sets up a trap line (or label) that executes when the specified function key or cursor control key is pressed. The statement format is:

```
ON KEY(n) GOSUB line (label)
```

The subroutine at line or label can be in the main body of the program or after its END statement. A KEY(n) ON statement must be previously executed to activate keystroke trapping. The value n indicates the key to be trapped, according to the following:

```
n                KEY TRAPPED
1-10             function keys F1 to F10
11               Cursor Up
12               Cursor Left
13               Cursor Right
14               Cursor Down
15-20            keys defined by the form:
                 KEY n,CHR$( KBflag)+CHR$(scan code)
```

(See KEY).

ON TIMER (statement)

[BASIC] [QuickBASIC] Transfers control to a line or label when a predefined time period has elapsed. The statement format is:

```
ON TIMER(n) GOSUB line (label)
```

where n is an integer in the range 1 to 86400 (1 second to 24 hours). The statement ON TIMER(n) GOSUB line (label) sets up trapping of the computer's internal clock. After TIMER ON is executed, every n seconds the program directs execution to the subroutine beginning at line (or label).

ON...GOSUB and ON...GOTO (statement)

[BASIC] [QuickBASIC] Branches to one or several program lines (or labels) according to the value of an expression. The statement formats is:

```
ON n GOTO line[,line]...   <= BASIC
ON n GOTO label[,label]... <= QuickBASIC
ON n GOSUB line[,line]...   <= BASIC
ON n GOSUB label[,label]...<= QuickBASIC
```

The ON...GOSUB and ON...GOTO statements are typically used in branching according to the value selected from a displayed menu.
Example:

```
' use of ON...GOTO to branch from a screen menu
PRINT "1 = EXECUTE PROCESS A"
PRINT "2 = EXECUTE PROCESS B"
PRINT "3 = EXECUTE PROCESS C"
INPUT "ENTER SELECTION NUMBER: "; CHOICE
ON CHOICE GOTO PROA, PROB, PROC
  .
  .
  .
PROA:
  .
  .
  .
PROB:
  .
  .
  .
PROC:
  .
  .
  .
```

Opcode

[Assembler] Each instruction is represented in assembly language with a mnemonic word called the *operation code*, or *opcode*. The letters that form the opcodes are chosen so that they remind us of the operation that they represent; for example, the opcode MOV represents a move operation, the opcode INC represents increment, and the opcode DIV indicates an arithmetic division. 80x86 opcodes contain from two or more letters, which can be entered in uppercase or lowercase letters or in both.

OPEN "COM... (statement)

[BASIC] [QuickBASIC] Opens a communication file. The statement format is:

```
OPEN "COMn:b,p,d,s,L" AS #m LEN = g
```

the parameters are as follows:

```
PARAMETER     FUNCTION
n             communications line (1 or 2)
m             file number
g             block size (default = 128 bytes)
b             speed of transmission in bits per second
              (75, 110, 150, 300, 600, 1200, 1800, 2400,
              4800, or 9600)
P             parity:
                      S = parity bit received as space
                      O = odd parity
                      M = parity bit received as mark
                      E = even parity
                      N = no parity
d             number of data bits (5, 6, 7, or 8)
s             number of stop bits (1 or 2)
L             line parameters:
                      RS = supress RTS
                      CS[n] = control CTS
                      DS[n] = control DSR
                      CD[n] = control CD
                      LF = send line feed after carriage return
                      PE = enable parity checking
                      Note: n = wait period in ms before returning
                            device timeout error (range 0 to 65535)
```

OPEN (statement)

[BASIC] [QuickBASIC] Allows input or output to a file or device. The statement format is:

```
OPEN filespec [FOR mode] AS [#]filenum [LEN= recl]
```

or

```
OPEN mode2, [#lfilenum, filespec [,recl]
```

where mode can be OUTPUT, INPUT, APPEND, or BINARY. OUTPUT specifies sequential output mode. INPUT specifies sequential input mode. APPEND specifies sequential output mode where the file is positioned to the end of data on the file when it is opened. In BINARY mode information can be read or written in an arbitrary fashion. Mode must be a string constant, not enclosed in quotation marks. If mode is omitted, random access is assumed.

In the alternate form mode2 is a string expression with the first character being one of the following;

```
O          specifies sequential output mode
I          specifies sequential input mode
R          specifies random input/output mode
```

In either case filenum is an integer expression whose value is between 1 and the maximum number of files allowed. Filespec is a string expression for the file specification, which can contain a path. Recl is an optional integer expression which sets the record length for random files. It can range from 1 to 32767. The default record length is 128 bytes. Recl cannot exceed the value set by the /S: switch in the BASIC command line.

OPEN allocates a buffer for I/O to the file or device and determines the mode of access that is used with the buffer. Filenum is the number that is associated with the file or device for as long as it is open and is used by other I/O statements to refer to this file or device.

An OPEN must be executed before any I/O can be done to a device or file using any of the following statements, or any statement or function requiring a file number:

```
PRINT #                    WRITE#
PRINT # USING              INPUT$
INPUT#                     GET#
LINE INPUT #               PUT#
IOCTL #
```

GET and PUT are valid for random files or communications files. A disk file cay be either random or sequential, and a printer can be opened in either random or sequential mode; however, all other standard devices can be opened only for sequential operations.

BASIC normally adds a linefeed after each carriage return (CHR$(13)) sent to a printer. However, if you open a printer (LPTI:,LPT2:, or LPT3:) as a random file with width 255, this linefeed is suppressed.

APPEND is valid only for disk files. The file pointer is initially set to the end of the file, and the record number is set to the last record of the file. PRINT # or WRITE # then extends the file.
Example:

```
' either of the following statements opens the file
' named "DATA" for sequential output on the default
' device
OPEN 'DATA" FOR OUTPUT AS #1
OPEN "O", #1, DATA
```

DOS 3.0 and later support networking and make possible two enhancements to the OPEN statement. The DOS command SHARE enables file sharing and should be executed from DOS prior to the use of the enhanced variations of the OPEN statement. When several processes may utilize a file at the same time, accurate file handling requires that certain types of access be denied to anyone but the person who opened the file. The statement format:

```
OPEN filespec FOR mode LOCK READ AS #n
```

or

```
OPEN filespec FOR RANDOM LOCK READ AS #n LEN = g
```

opens the specified file and forbids any other process from reading the file. LOCK WRITE forbids any other process from writing to the file as long as the file is open. LOCK READ WRITE forbids reading or writing operations. LOCK SHARED grants full access to any other process.

Operand

[Assembler] Some 80x86 instructions contain a field called the *operand*. Whereas the opcode indicates an action to be performed by the instruction (verb element), the operand encodes the target, and sometimes the contents, of the action (noun element). In 80x86 assembly language operands can specify a CPU component (which can be either a *register* or a *port*), a location in the system's memory, or an immediate value. The operand of the instruction:

```
MOV    AH,76          ; MS-DOS service request code
```

specifies a register in the 80x86 CPU named AH and the immediate value 76. Once the instruction executes, the value 76 is loaded (moved) into register AH.

Although all 80x86 instructions must have an operation code (opcode), not all instructions have an explicit operand, because some 80x86 instructions perform such concrete operations that they do not require a distinct specification. For example, the instruction AAA (ASCII Adjust for Addition) is used in certain forms of 80x86 addition to modify the contents of the AL register. Because the action of the AAA instruction always takes place on the contents of the AL register, it does not require an operand.

A comma (,) divides the operand into two fields. The comma, as used in an instruction operand, is sometimes called a *delimiter*. The field to the left of the comma is called the destination. The destination holds the target of the action performed by the instruction. The field to the right of the comma is called the source; it holds the origin or the contents of this action. But not all 80x86 operands have a distinct source and destination field. Some instructions perform actions in which the source is implicit or which do not require a source. For example, the instruction INC (increment) adds the value 1 to the operand.

Because this added value cannot be changed, a source field is not required. Therefore the instruction to increment the AL register is coded as follows:

```
INC    AL                ; AL = AL + 1
```

Operation codes

[PC hardware and architecture] At the machine level, the 8086 CPU has about 300 possible operations in its instruction set. Each instruction can range in length from 1 to 6 bytes. For example, a move instruction (MOV) can be from 2 to 6 bytes long and can be encoded in 28 different forms.

Bits 2 to 7 of the first byte of the operation code form the *opcode field*. This 6-bit field is always associated with each encoding. Of these 2 bits, bit 1 is called the sign or direction bit and bit 0 the word/byte bit. The second byte of the instruction, if present, contains the mode (MOD), the register (REG), and the register/memory (R/M) fields. This byte is sometimes referred to as the Modrm byte; the MOD field occupies bits 7 and 6 of the Modrm byte. The REG field follows the MOD field and occupies bits 5, 4, and 3; and the R/M field takes up bits 2, 1, and 0.

Operators

[C] Programming languages use symbols, special characters, identifiers, and keywords to represent the operations to be performed. These words and symbols are called *operators*. Operators are used in expressions that produce program actions. For example, if a, b, and c are variables, the C expression:

```
c = a + b;
```

makes use of the = and the + operators to assign to the variable c the value that results from adding the variables a and b. The operators in this expression are the = (assignment) and + (addition) symbols.

C language operators must be used as elements of expressions; they are meaningless when used by themselves. For example, the term:

```
-a;
```

is a trivial expression that does not change the value of the variable. While the expression:

```
b = -b;
```

assigns a negative value to the variable b.

First Byte of 8086 Machine Codes

	LOW							
HI	0	1	2	3	4	5	6	7
0	ADD	ADD	ADD	ADD	ADD	ADD	PUSH	POP
1	ADC	ADC	ADC	ADC	ADC	ADC	PUSH	POP
2	AND	AND	AND	AND	AND	AND	SEG	DAA
3	XOR	XOR	XOR	XOR	XOR	XOR	SEG	AAA
4	INC	INC	INC	INC	INC	INC	INC	INC
5	PUSH	PUSH	PUSH	PUSH	PUSH	PUSH	PUSH	PUSH
6								
7	JO	JNO	JB	JNB	JE	JNE	JBE	JNBE
8	*	*	*	*	TEST	TEST	XCHG	XCHG
9	NOP	XCHG	XCHG	XCHG	XCHG	XCHG	XCHG	XCHG
A	MOV	MOV	MOV	MOV	MOVS	MOVS	CMPS	CMPS
B	MOV	MOV	MOV	MOV	MOV	MOV	MOV	MOV
C	**	**	RET	RET	LES	LDS	MOV	MOV
D	**	**	**	**	AAM	AAD		XLAT
E	LOOPNE	LOOPZ	LOOP	JCXZ	IN	IN	OUT	OUT
F	LOCK		REP	REP	HLT	CMC	TEST NOT NEG MUL	IMUL DIV IDIV

* = ADD, OR, ADC, SBB, AND, SUB, XOR, CMP
** = ROL, ROR, RCL, RCR, SHL, SHR, SAR

	LOW							
HI	8	9	A	B	C	D	E	F
0	OR	OR	OR	OR	OR	OR	PUSH	
1	SBB	SBB	SBB	SBB	SBB	SBB	PUSH	POP
2	SUB	SUB	SUB	SUB	SUB	SUB	SEG	DAS
3	CMP	CMP	CMP	CMP	CMP	CMP	SEG	AAS
4	DEC	DEC	DEC	DEC	DEC	DEC	DEC	DEC
5	POP	POP	POP	POP	POP	POP	POP	POP
6	PUSH	IMUL	PUSH	IMUL				
7	JS	JNS	JP	JNP	JL	JNL	JLE	JNLE
8	MOV	MOV	MOV	MOV	MOV	LEA	MOV	POP
9	CBW	CWD	CALL	WAIT	PUSHF	POPF	SAHF	LAHF
A	TEST	TEST	STOS	STOS	LODS	LODS	SCAS	SCAS
B	MOV	MOV	MOV	MOV	MOV	MOV	MOV	MOV
C			RET	RET	INT	INT	INTO	IRET
D	ESC	ESC	ESC	ESC	ESC	ESC	ESC	ESC
E	CALL	JMP	JMP	JMP	IN	IN	OUT	OUT
F	CLC	STC	CLI	STI	CLD	STD	INC DEC CALL	JMP PUSH

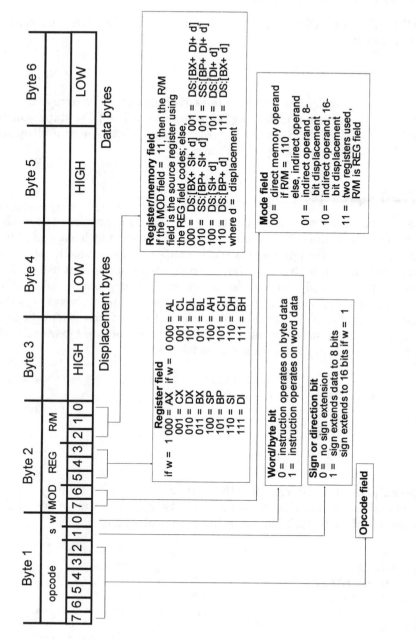

8086 Machine Code Format

OPTION BASE (statement)

[BASIC] [QuickBASIC] Declares the minimum value for array subscripts. Statement format is:

```
OPTION BASE n
```

where n is 0 or 1. The default is 0. A statement of the form DIM arrayname(n) defines an array with subscripts ranging from m to n. The DIM statement is preferable to OPTION BASE since it which permits both lower and upper subscript bounds to be specified for each array.

OR bitwise operator

[C] The OR bitwise operator (|) performs the Boolean inclusive OR of the operands. This determines that a bit in the result is set if at least one of the corresponding bits in the operands is set. Because the inclusive OR sets a bit in the result if either or both bits in the operands are set, a frequent use for this operation is to selectively set bits in an operand. This property of the OR operation can be described by saying that ORing with a 1-bit always sets the result bit, whereas ORing with a 0-bit preserves the value of the other operand. For example, to make sure that bits 5 and 6 of an operand are set we can OR it with a mask in which these bits are 1, as follows:

```
                  0001 0111B
BITWISE OR        0110 0000B
                  ----------
                  0111 0111B
```

ORD

[MS-Pascal] Heading: (X: VALUE): INTEGER;
Data conversion function that converts to INTEGER any value of one of the types shown in the following list according to the rules given.

```
Type                      Return Value
INTEGER           X
WORD <= MAXINT    X
WORD > MAXINT     X - 2 * (MAXINT + 1)
                       (i.e., same 16 bits as at start!)
CHAR              ASCII code for X
Enumerated            Position of X in the type definition,
                      starting with O
INTEGER4          Lower 16 bits (i.e., same as ORD(LOWORD)
                      (INTEGER4))
Pointer           Integer value of pointer
```

ORIGIN attribute

[MS-Pascal] ORIGIN tells the compiler where the procedure or function can be found directly, so the linker does not require a corresponding PUBLIC identifier. The ORIGIN attribute must be used with the EXTERN directive.

As with ORIGIN variables, the compiler uses the address to find the code and gives no directives to the linker. This permits calling routines at fixed addresses in ROM. In simple cases, it can substitute for a linking loader.

ORIGIN always implies EXTERN. Thus, procedures or functions that have previously been declared FORWARD cannot be declared with the ORIGIN attribute. ORIGIN cannot be used as an attribute after the module heading.

OUT (statement)

[BASIC] [QuickBASIC] Sends a byte to an output port. The statement format is:

```
OUT n,m
```

where n is a port number (range 0 to 65535), and m is the byte to be transmitted.

Overlay

(See storage — secondary).

P

PACK

[MS-Pascal] Heading: (CONSTS A: UNPACKED; I:INDEX; VARS Z:PACKED);

Data conversion procedure that moves elements of an unpacked array to a packed array. If A is an ARRAY [M..N] OF T and Z is a PACKED ARRAY [U..V] OF T, then PACK (A, I, Z) is the same as:

```
FOR J := U TO V DO Z [J] := A [J - U + I]
```

In both PACK and UNPACK, the parameter I is the initial index within A. The bounds of the arrays and the value of I must be reasonable; i.e., the number of components in the unpacked array A from I to M must be at least as great as the number of components in the packed array Z. The range checking switch controls checking of the bounds.

PAGE

[MS-Pascal] Heading: PAGE;

```
Heading: PAGE (VAR F);
```

File system procedure that causes skipping to the top of a new page when the textfile F is printed. PAGE with no parameter is the same as PAGE (INPUT).

PAINT (statement)

Fills in an area on the screen with the selected color. The statement format is:

```
PAINT (x,y) [[,paint] C,boundary] [,background]]
```

where (x,y) are the coordinates of a point within the area to be filled in. The coordinates can be given in absolute or relative form. This point is used as a starting point. Points specified outside the limits of the screen are not plotted, and no error occurs. Paint is a numeric or string expression used to fill a color or pattern in or around a bounded area. When paint is a numeric expression, it defines an attribute from the legal attribute range for the current video. In

medium resolution, the color is the current color (range 0 to 3) for that attribute
defined by the COLOR statement. In high resolution, two attributes (0-1) are
available. Zero is always the attribute for the background. The default foreground attribute is the maximum attribute for that screen mode: 3 in medium
resolution, 1 in high resolution. If paint is a string expression, then "tiling" is
performed. Boundary is a numeric expression that evaluates to an integer in
the legal attribute range of the current video mode. It defines the attribute for
the edges of the figure to be painted. Background is a 1-byte string expression
used in paint tiling.

Since there are only two attributes in high resolution, paint should not be
different from boundary. By default, boundary is equal to paint. A white area
can be painted black or a black area white.

PAINT fills any designated area no matter what the shape of the area;
however, the more complex the edges of a figure (jagged edges, for instance),
the more stack space BASIC uses.

The PAINT statement allows scenes to be displayed with very few statements.
Example:

```
'use the PAINT statement to fill in a box
'using the attribute in the current palette
SCREEN 1
LINE (0,0)-(100,150),2,B
PAINT (50,50),1,2
```

To use paint tiling, the paint attribute must be a string expression in the form:

```
CHR$ (&Hnn) +CHR$ (&Hnn) +CHRB (&Hnn)
```

The CHR$ sequence specifies a bit mask that is 1 byte wide. When the mask
is plotted all the way across and down the designated area defined by boundary,
a pattern is created rather than a solid color. The user designs the pattern. The
two hexadecimal numbers in the CHR$ expression correspond to eight bits. The
string expression can contain up to 64 bytes. The design created by the string
expression can be mapped as follows:

```
        x increases -->
        7 6 5 4 3 2 1 0
0,0     x x x x x x x x        Tile byte 0
0,1     x x x x x x x x        Tile byte 1
0,2     x x x x x x x x        Tile byte 2
  .
  .
0,63    x x x x x x x x        Tile byte 63 (maximum allowed)
```

The tile pattern is repeated uniformly over the area defined by boundary. If
you do not define an area, the whole screen is the designated area. Each byte
of the tile string masks eight bits along the x-axis when plotting points. Each

byte of the tile string is rotated as required to align the pattern along the y-axis. BASIC chooses the particular byte of the pattern to plot, using the formula y mod tile length.

Because there is only one bit per pixel in high resolution, a point is plotted at every position in the bit mask that has a value of 1. The length of this mask is eight. The pattern for the letter "x" is created as follows:

```
                          x increases -->
Tile byte 0          1 0 0 0 0 0 0 1      CHR$(&H81)
Tile byte 1          0 1 0 0 0 0 1 0      CHR$(&H42)
Tile byte 2          0 0 1 0 0 1 0 0      CHR$(&H24)
Tile byte 3          0 0 0 1 1 0 0 0      CHR$(&H18)
Tile byte 4          0 0 0 1 1 0 0 0      CHR$(&H18)
Tile byte 5          0 0 1 0 0 1 0 0      CHR$(&H24)
Tile byte 6          0 1 0 0 0 0 1 0      CHR$(&H42)
Tile byte 7          1 0 0 0 0 0 0 1      CHR$(&H81)
```

The method of designing patterns in each screen varies depending on the number of color attributes available in each screen mode. This is so because the number of bits per pixel is directly related to the number of color attributes available in each screen mode. In any screen, where X is the total number of color attributes for that screen:

$$LOG, (X) = Y$$

where Y is the number of bits per pixel. In high resolution, each byte of the string is able to plot eight points across the screen (1 bit per pixel), since:

$$LOG_2(2) = 1$$

In Screen 1, one medium-resolution tile byte describes four pixels, since medium resolution has only 2 bits per pixel:

$$LOG_2(4) = 2 \text{ bits per pixel}$$

Every two bits of the tile byte describe 1 of 4 possible color attributes associated with each of the four pixels to be plotted.

PALETTE and PALETTE USING (statements)

[QuickBASIC] Loads colors into the palette "jars" whose numbers range from 0 to 3, 0 to 15, 0 to 63, or 0 to 255. The statement requires a graphics monitor in an EGA, VGA, or MCGA display card. The statement format:

```
PALETTE m, n
```

assigns the nth color to the mth palette jar. The statement format:

```
PALETTE USING array(0)
```

specifies that each palette jar be filled with the corresponding color number stored in the array element: array(0) in jar 0, array(1) in jar 1, and so on.

Parallel port — control register

[PC hardware and architecture] The control register is located at the port's base address plus 2. This is a read-write register. The write function is used in setting the state of the signal lines that go from the computer to the printer or device. The read function can be used by the processor to obtain the value of the last byte written to the register.

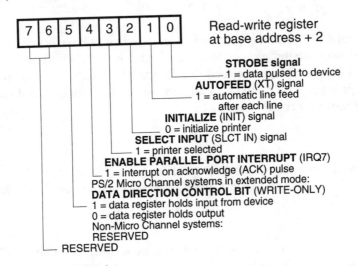

Parallel Port Control Register

Bit 5 of the control register, sometimes called the data direction control bit, is meaningful in Micro Channel systems only. The direction control bit is write-only; consequently, this bit does not report a meaningful value during read operations.

Parallel port — data register

[PC hardware and architecture] The data register is located at the port's base address. A write operation to the data register stores the data internally. This operation is sometimes called *latching* the data, and the register is referred to as the *data latch*. Note that latching data in the data register does not send it to an external device. The data transmission through the parallel port requires pulsing the Strobe line.

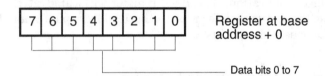

Parallel Port Data Register

In non-Micro Channel systems (the PC line and PS/2 Models 25 and 30) reading the data register produces the last byte that was written to the register. In Micro Channel systems operating in extended mode, reading the data register can produce a data byte latched by an external device. This form of read operation requires that bit 5 of the control register be set. If bit 5 of the control register is not set, the read operation produces the same result in extended mode as in the PC compatibility mode.

Parallel Port — extended mode

[**PC hardware and architecture**] In PS/2 systems with Micro Channel architecture, and in some PC compatible machines, the parallel port supports bidirectional communications. However, the parallel port in PC systems and non-Micro Channel models of the PS/2 line allow only unidirectional transmission on the Strobe and data lines. This limitation of PC and PS/2 non-Micro Channel systems probably results from the traditional notion that the parallel port is only a printer interface.

In the PS/2 Micro Channel systems the bidirectional operation of the parallel port, also called the *extended mode*, is selected during the programmable option select function (POS). POS register 2, at port I/O address 102H, contains the Option Select Data Byte 1. When bit 7 of this byte is set, the parallel port is unidirectional and emulates the parallel port in PC systems. When bit 7 of the Option Select Data Byte 1 is clear, the parallel port supports bidirectional operation and is said to be in extended mode.

In extended mode (bidirectional operation) the direction of data transmission is controlled by bit 5 of the parallel port control port. When this bit is set, the parallel port is in read mode and data from an external device is available in the port's data register. When the direction control bit is clear, the port is in the write mode and the read function is disabled. Bit 5 of the control register is not used in the unidirectional parallel port of non-Micro Channel systems.

Parallel port — hardware

[**PC hardware and architecture**] The parallel port appears as a set of three registers accessible to the programmer. The registers are designated as a *data* register, a *status* register, and a *control* register. The registers are mapped to a base port address that can take the values 3BCH, 378H, and 278H according to the system configuration. The data register is located at the base port address, while the status register is at the base address plus 1, and the control register at the base address plus 2.

Parallel port — implementations

[PC hardware and architecture] In the PC line the parallel port is supplied in the form of several optional adapters, while in PS/2 and PC-compatible machines the parallel port is often included in the motherboard hardware. The DOS designation for the parallel port uses the characters LPT (Line PrinTer) followed by the port number; for example, LPT1 and LPT2 designate the first and second parallel ports. A maximum of three parallel ports is allowed in a system. Address mapping of the parallel ports is not consistent with the DOS designation in LPTx form.

Parallel port — programming

[PC hardware and architecture] Programs that access the parallel port can do so using the services provided by the BIOS and DOS or by programming the port registers directly. Direct programming operations consist of obtaining the address of the available ports, initializing the parallel device (usually a printer), and sending and receiving data through the port.

The BIOS system initialization routines store the base address of the first parallel port (LPT1) at memory location 408H in the BIOS data area. The base addresses of the two possible additional parallel ports (LPT2 and LPT3) are stored at 40AH and 40CH, respectively. In the models of the PC line, the address of a fourth parallel port (LPT4) is at address 40EH, but this location in reserved in PS/2 systems. One or more of these fields is initialized to zero if the system contains fewer than the maximum number of allowed parallel ports; however, the BIOS does not initialize valid ports following a zero value.

Initializing the parallel port consists of setting the bit fields in the port's control register. In addition, bit 2 of the control register (INIT) initializes the parallel device. This line must be held low for a minimum of one-twentieth of a second.

Programs can initialize other functions on the parallel port by setting or clearing the corresponding bits in the control register.

Writing to the data register, located at the port's base address, stores a byte of data in the register. However, to actually transmit the latched data, the Strobe bit of the control register must be held high during a minimum of 5 ms. The following code fragment illustrates the process of latching the character byte, checking the device busy bit in the status register and pulsing the Strobe bit in the control register. The code assumes that a valid address for the first parallel port has been previously stored in the variable LPT1_BASE.

```
; Character to be sent to parallel port is already in AL
```

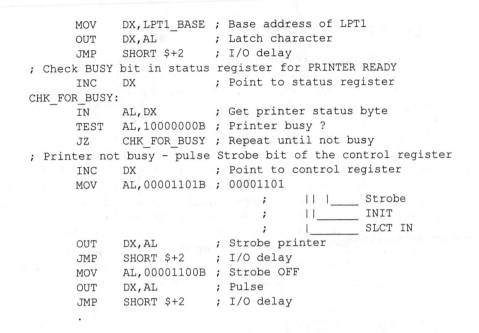

```
        MOV     DX,LPT1_BASE ; Base address of LPT1
        OUT     DX,AL        ; Latch character
        JMP     SHORT $+2    ; I/O delay
; Check BUSY bit in status register for PRINTER READY
        INC     DX           ; Point to status register
CHK_FOR_BUSY:
        IN      AL,DX        ; Get printer status byte
        TEST    AL,10000000B ; Printer busy ?
        JZ      CHK_FOR_BUSY ; Repeat until not busy
; Printer not busy - pulse Strobe bit of the control register
        INC     DX           ; Point to control register
        MOV     AL,00001101B ; 00001101
                          ;        || |____ Strobe
                          ;        ||_____ INIT
                          ;        |_____ SLCT IN
        OUT     DX,AL        ; Strobe printer
        JMP     SHORT $+2    ; I/O delay
        MOV     AL,00001100B ; Strobe OFF
        OUT     DX,AL        ; Pulse
        JMP     SHORT $+2    ; I/O delay
        .
        .
```

Parallel port — status register

[PC hardware and architecture] The status register is located at the port's base address plus 1. This is a read-only register which can be used by the CPU to obtain the current status of the signal lines that go from the printer or device to the computer.

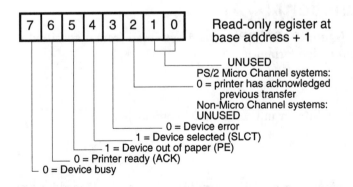

Read-only register at base address + 1

UNUSED
PS/2 Micro Channel systems:
0 = printer has acknowledged previous transfer
Non-Micro Channel systems: UNUSED
0 = Device error
1 = Device selected (SLCT)
1 = Device out of paper (PE)
0 = Printer ready (ACK)
0 = Device busy

Parallel Port Status Register

Note bits 3, 6, and 7, which correspond with the busy, ACK, and error lines. Because these lines are implemented using a negative voltage, their active condition is reported with a 0 bit.

Pascal — programming language

[Pascal] [General programming] Procedure-oriented programming language designed by Niklaus Wirth in 1968. Pascal is a member of the Algol family of programming languages. The notion underlying Pascal's design was a language that promoted a style consistent with the principles of structured programming.

Pascal is a small language with a limited syntax and not many built-in functions. Therefore it is easy to implement and learn. One significant limitation of traditional Pascal is the absence of an exponentiation operator, which forces the programmer to repeated multiplications or to the use of logarithmic functions in the calculations of exponentials. Among its strong points is that it provides a pointer data type which is useful in the definition and manipulation of linked lists, and that it supports programmer-defined data types.

During the 1970's and 1980's Pascal gained considerable popularity in American colleges and universities. Therefore it has exerted a major influence in the habits of programmer's trained during this period.

PCOPY (statement)

[QuickBASIC] Copies the content of screen pages. The statement format is:

```
PCOPY m, n
```

where *m* is the source screen page and *n* is the target screen page. The use of the PCOPY statement depends on the video mode.
(See also: SCREEN).

PEEK (function)

[BASIC] [QuickBASIC] Returns a byte read from a specified memory location. The function format is:

```
v = PEEK(n)
```

where *n* is an integer in the range 0 to 65535.

Pentium

[PC hardware and architecture] In 1993 Intel released its newest member of the 80x86 line, named the Pentium processor. Soon thereafter IBM-compatible microcomputers using the Pentium CPU appeared on the market.

The most important claims made by Intel regarding the Pentium CPU are related to the chip's architecture and performance. Pentium programming is virtually identical to that of the 486. Intel literature states that the Pentium processor contains over 3.1 million transistors, compared to 1.2 million in the 486. As with the 486, the internal architecture of the Pentium is 32 bits wide; however, the data bus used by the new chip is 64 bits. The result is a considerable performance gain in data read and write operations; performance is estimated to be 3.3 times that of the 486.

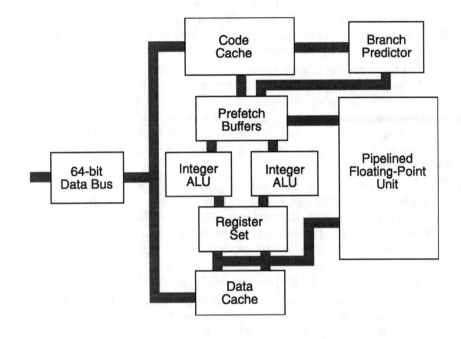

Pentium Processor Architecture

In general, the performance of the Pentium-based machine can be compared with that of many present-day workstation platforms and local-area network servers. The following are the most important features of the Pentium:

1. The chip's *superscalar architecture* makes it capable of parallel execution of two integer operations in a single clock cycle. The notion of a superscalar design is based on the presence of more than one execution unit. The Pentium contains two processing pipelines, each with its own arithmetic-logic unit (ALU), address generation logic, and data cache. The result of this design is that the Pentium processor can execute more instructions in the same amount of time than any of its predecessors. Intel documentation claims that the resulting performance is 1.9 times that of a comparable 486 CPU.

2. Another performance-improvement element in the Pentium chip is the presence of separate internal caches for code and data. A cache is a fast memory area used as temporary storage for frequently used code and data

items. The 486 contains an 8K on-chip cache that handles both code and data operations. In the Pentium there are two 8K cache areas, one for code and another one for data. In addition, the Pentium caching operation is based on a "writeback" algorithm based on the MESI protocol (Modified, Exclusive, Shared, Invalid). This method improves cache performance by preventing bottlenecks and improving system consistency. The MESI protocol also makes feasible the use of the Pentium in a multiprocessing environment. In this manner a system can be designed in which two or more Pentium chips share a processing task while ensuring that the data cached and sub-sequently modified by one processor is correctly accessed by the other ones.

3. The Pentium uses a "branch prediction" technique that improves perform-ance by providing a dedicated code buffer to hold the instructions most likely to be repeated in a program loop. This method, which has often been used in mainframe machines, is based on the assumption that the branch of execution last taken in a program loop is the most likely one to be used again. The boost to performance is based on keeping these instructions in the execution pipelines.

4. The floating-point unit of the Pentium also uses a pipeline architecture that is capable of executing two 80x87 instructions in a single clock cycle. The three-stage floating-point instruction pipelines are connected to the system's integer pipelines. Intel states that the performance of the floating-point unit of the Pentium is five to ten times that of a comparable 486 CPU. This substantial performance improvement will be evident in calculation-inten-sive applications, such as graphics and CAD programs.

5. Other features, usually associated with mainframe computers, that have been incorporated into the Pentium are related to error detection and functional redundancy checking (FRC). This feature is particularly useful when the Pentium-based machine serves as a hub in a client/server environ-ment.

To fully exploit the performance gains of the Pentium requires software designed to take advantage of the new features offered by this chip. At the present time Windows 95, Windows NT, and the OS/2 operating system already provides 32-bit processing environment. Applications will have to be recompiled to take advantage of the Pentium superscalar architecture, which in turn requires compilers and language products that address the chip's charac-teristics.

PIDRQQ

[MS-Pascal] Heading: (CONSTS A: REAL8; CONSTS B: INTEGER4) : REAL8;
  Arithmetic function whose return value is A**B (A to the INTEGER power of B). A is of type REAL8. B is always of type INTEGER4. This function is from the MS-FORTRAN runtime library and must be declared EXTERN.

PISRQB

[MS-Pascal] Heading: (CONSTS A: REAL4; CONSTS B: INTEGER4) : REAL4;

Arithmetic function whose return value is A**B (A to the INTEGER power of B). A is of type REAL4. B is always of type INTEGER4. This function is from the MS-FORTRAN runtime library and must be declared EXTERN.

PLAY (function)

[BASIC] [QuickBASIC] Returns the number of notes in the music background buffer which are waiting to be played. The function format is:

```
v = PLAY(n)
```

where *n* is a dummy argument that can have any value.

PLAY (statement)

[BASIC] [QuickBASIC] Plays music as specified by string. Statement format is:

```
PLAY string
```

PLAY implements a concept similar to DRAW by embedding a "tune definition language" into a character string. String is an expression consisting of single or double-character music commands, as follows:

Commands A to G with optional #, +, or -:

Plays the indicated note in the current octave. A number sign (#) or plus sign (+) afterward indicates a sharp; a minus sign (-) indicates a flat. A #, +, or - is not allowed unless it corresponds to a black key on a piano. For example, B# is an invalid note.

```
O n  Octave:
```
Sets the current octave for the notes that follow. There are seven octaves, numbered 0 to 6. Each octave goes from C to B. Octave 3 starts with middle C. Octave 4 is the default octave.

```
> n:
```
Go up to the next higher octave and play note *n*. Each time note *n* is played, the octave goes up, until it reaches octave 6. For example:

```
PLAY ">A"
```

raises the octave and plays note A. Each time PLAY ">A" is executed, the octave goes up until it reaches octave 6; thereafter, each time PLAY ">A" executes, note A plays at octave 6.

< n:

Go down one octave and play note n. Each time note n is played, the octave goes down, until it reaches octave 0. For example:

```
PLAY "<A"
```

lowers the octave and plays note A.

N n:

Plays note n, which can range from 13 to 84. In the seven possible octaves, there are 84 notes. The statement format

```
PLAY n = 0
```

means "rest." This is an alternative way of selecting notes besides specifying the octave (*n*) and the note name (A-G).

Ln:

Sets the length of the notes that follow. The actual length of the note is 1/n, where *n* can range from 1 to 64, as follows:

```
LENGTH          EQUIVALENT TO
L1              whole note
L2              half note
L3              one of a triplet of three half notes
                    (1/3 of a 4-beat measure)
L4              quarter note
L5              one of a quintuplet
                    (1/5 of a measure)
L6              one of a quarter-note triplet
  .
L64             sixty-fourth note
```

The length can also follow the note when you want to change only the length of the note. For example, A16 is equivalent to L16A.

Pn:
Pause (rest). *n* can range from 1 to 64, and figures the length of the pause in the same way as L (length).

(dot or period):
When placed after a note, causes the note to be played as a dotted note. A dot increases the duration of a note by half the duration of the note. A note can

have more than one dot. Each dot increases the total value of the note by one-half the value of the previous dot. For example, a double-dotted halfnote is equivalent in duration to a half note plus a quarter note plus an eighth note.

`Tn:`

Tempo. Sets the number of quarter notes in a minute. *n* can range from 32 to 255. The default is 120.

`MF:`

Music foreground. Music (created by SOUND or PLAY) runs in foreground. Each subsequent note or sound does not start until the previous note or sound is finished. Press Ctrl-Break to exit PLAY. Music foreground is the default state.

`MB:`

Music background. Music (created by SOUND or PLAY) runs in background instead of foreground. Each note or sound is placed in a buffer, allowing the BASIC program to continue executing while music plays in the background. The music background buffer can hold up to 32 notes at one time.

`MN:`

Music normal. Each note plays seven-eighths of the time specified by L (length). This is the default setting of MN, ML, and MS.

`ML:`

Music legato. Each note plays the full period set by L (length).

`MS:`

Music staccato. Each note plays three-fourths of the time specified by L.

```
X variable;
```

Executes specified string.

In all of these commands the *n* argument can be a constant or a variable. The semicolon (;) is required when you use a variable in this way, and when you use the X command. Otherwise a semicolon is optional between commands, except that a semicolon is not allowed after MF, MB, MN, ML, or MS. Also, any blanks in string are ignored.

PLYUQQ

[MS-Pascal] Library routine of the terminal I/O group. Writes an end-of-line character to the terminal screen. Is useful for doing terminal I/O in a low-overhead environment. These functions are part of a collection of routines called Unit U, which implements the MS-Pascal file system.

PMAP (function)

[BASIC] [QuickBASIC] Maps physical coordinates to world coordinates and vice versa. The function format is:

```
v = PMAP(x,n)
```

where x is the coordinate of the point to be mapped. n can take any of the following values:

```
n                COORDINATE MAPPING
0                x world to x physical
1                y world to y physical
2                x physical to x world
3                y physical to y world
```

The statement is often used in relation to the WINDOW statement.

POINT (function)

[BASIC] [QuickBASIC] In the first form returns the attribute of a screen pixel. In the second form returns the value of the current x or y graphics coordinate. Statement format is:

```
v = POINT (x,y)   <= attribute form
v = POINT (n)     <= coordinate form
```

where (x,y) are the pixel coordinates in absolute form. n returns the value of the x or y graphics coordinate and can have the following values:

```
n                RETURNS
0                current x physical coordinate
1                current y physical coordinate
2                current x world coordinate if
                 WINDOW active, else the current
                 x physical coordinate
3                current y world coordinate if
                 WINDOW active, else the current
                 y physical coordinate
```

pointer-member operator

[C] Accessing individual structure members by means of a pointer requires a special symbol called the *pointer-member operator*. This operator symbol consists of a dash and an angle bracket combined to simulate an arrow (->). For instance, if one member of the structure tr1 is named side_a, we can use the pointer-member operator as follows:

```
        tr_ptr -> side_a
```

Note that the pointer-member operator (->) is combined with the structure pointer in a similar manner as the membership operator (.) is combined with the structure name.

Pointer

(See indirection operator; address-of operator).

Pointer arithmetic

[C] It is possible to use pointers to gain access to the various elements within an array. C follows special rules regarding arithmetic with pointer variables.

The first array element is accessed by initializing the pointer variable to its address. The next element of the array is accessed by the pointer, C automatically takes into account the size of the array elements. For example, the statement:

```
    add1++;
```

or

```
    add1 = add1 + 1;
```

bumps the pointer variable to the next array element, whatever its size. In other words, C language pointer arithmetic is scaled to the size of the elements in the array.

POKE (statement)

[BASIC] [QuickBASIC] Writes a byte into a memory location. Statement format is:

```
    POKE n,m
```

where *n* indicates the offset address in the current segment (range is 0 to 65535). The segment base can be selected with DEF SEG. *m* is the data byte to be written. The complement to POKE is PEEK.

POPA

[Assembler] 80286 machines instruction. Mnemonic for POP All registers. Pops all eight 16-bit registers from the stack while discarding the stored value for SP. The registers are POPed in the order: DI, SI, BP, SP (discarded), BX, DX, CX, AX. The alternate mnemonic POPAD was introduced with the 80386

for SP. The registers are POPed in the order: DI, SI, BP, SP (discarded), BX, DX, CX, AX. The alternate mnemonic POPAD was introduced with the 80386 to perform a 32-bit register version of the original opcode. POPA and POPAD are usually preceded by PUSHA and PUSHAD.
(See also: PUSHA, PUSHAD).

POPAD

(See POPA).

POPF

[Assembler] 8086 machine instruction. Mnemonic for POP Flags. Transfers the word at the top of the stack into the 80x86 flags register overwriting the previous values. After the transfer is performed, SP is incremented by two. The combination of PUSHF and POPF allows a procedure to save the caller's flags so that they can later be restored. The PUSHF/POPF sequence is the only means for changing the value of the trap flag (TF). This is accomplished by pushing the flags, changing the contents of the memory image, then popping the flags, as in the following code fragment:

```
; Use of PUSHF and POPF to set the trap flag, located in
; bit 8 of the flags register
      PUSHF                    ; Flags to stack top
      POP    AX                ; Stack top to AX
; Flag bits are now in AX. AH bit 0 is trap flag
      OR     AH,00000001B ; Set trap flag
      PUSH   AX                ; Flags back to stack
      POPF                     ; Trap flag is now set
```

(See also: PUSHF).

POS (function)

[BASIC] [QuickBASIC] Returns the current column position of the cursor. The function format is:

```
v =   POS(n)
```

where n is a dummy argument.

POSITN

[MS-Pascal] Heading: (CONSTS PAT: STRING;CONSTS S: STRING; I: INTE-GER) : INTEGER;
    String intrinsic function that returns the integer position of the pattern PAT in S, starting the search at S[I]. If PAT is not found or if I > upper (S), the return

value is 0. If PAT is the null string, the return value is 1. There are no error conditions.

PRDRQQ

[MS-Pascal] Heading: A, B :REAL8): REAL8;
Arithmetic function that returns A ** B (A to the REAL power of B). Both A and B are of type REAL8. An error occurs if A < 0 (even if B happens to have an integer value). This function is from the MS-FORTRAN runtime library and must be declared EXTERN.

PRED

[MS-Pascal] Heading: (X : ORDINAL): ORDINAL;
Data conversion function that determines the predecessor to X. The ORD of the result returned is equal to ORD (X) - 1. An error occurs if the predecessor is out of range or overflow occurs. These errors are detected if appropriate debug switches are on.

Preprocessor directive

[C] A C language lexical element that indicates a command to be performed at compile time. The term "preprocessor" relates to multipass compilers, but has been preserved in single-pass compilers for consistency. The # sign indicates the presence of a preprocessor directive when it occurs as the first non-whitespace character of a program line. The most frequently used preprocessor directives are #include and #define.
(See also: #include; #define).

PRINT (statement)

[BASIC] [QuickBASIC] Displays data on the screen. The statement format is:

```
PRINT [expression][;]
```

PRINT expression displays the value of the expression at the current position of the cursor and moves the cursor to the beginning of the next row of the screen. Negative numbers are displayed with a trailing space and positive numbers with a leading space. If the statement is followed by a comma, then the cursor moves to the next print zone. If followed by a semicolon, then the cursor moves to the next position. Several expressions may be placed in the same PRINT statement if separated by semicolons or by commas. If no expression is contained in the PRINT statement, a blank line is displayed.

PRINT USING (statement)

[BASIC] [QuickBASIC] Prints strings of numbers using a specific format. The statement format is:

```
PRINT USING a$; expression list [;]
```

the action is to display the values of the expressions (possibly interspersed with text from a$) in the format or formats specified by a$. The statement can be used to align and display numeric expressions with dollar signs, commas, asterisks, two decimal places, and preceding or trailing signs. Numbers are formatted via the symbols #, +, $, $$, *, **, ^^^^, comma, and period. Strings are formatted with the symbols &, !, and \ \. To use one of the special symbols for text in a format string the symbol must be preceded it with an underscore (_).

SYMBOL	MEANING	n	string	RESULT
#	Each symbol stands for one digit in a numeric field	1234.6	"######"	1235
		123	"######"	123
		123.4	"######"	123
		12345	"####"	%12345
.	Denotes the placement of the decimal point	123.4	"######.#"	123.4
,	Causes commas to be displayed left of every third digit to the left of the decimal point	12345	"#######,"	12,345
$	Displays a $ sign as the First character of the field	23.45	"$####.##"	$ 23.45
$$	Displays a $ sign immediately before the first digit displayed	23.45	"$$####.##"	$23.45
**	Inserts asterisks in place of leading blanks	23.45	"**######"	*****23
*	Displays an asterisk as the first character of the field	23.45	"*#######"	* 23
^^^^	(at end) Displays the number in exponential notation	12345	"##.#^^^^"	1.2E+04
		-12	"#.##^^^^"	-12E+01
+	Reserves a space for the sign of the variable	12	"+#######"	+12
		12	"#######+"	12-
&	Display entire string		"Montana"	Montana
!	Display first letter of string		"Montana"	M
\ \	Display first n letters of string (where the are n-2 spaces between the slashes)		"Montana"	Mont

PRINT# and PRINT# USING (statements)

[BASIC] [QuickBASIC] Writes data sequentially to a file opened as a sequential file for output or append. The statement format is:

```
PRINT# filenum,[USING x$] exp list [;]
```

where filenum is the number assigned to the file with the OPEN statement, x$ is a string expression containing the format characters described in PRINT USING, and exp list is a list of the numeric or string expressions to be written to the file.

printf() — conversion specifications

[C] The presence of the percent (%) symbol in the format string denotes the beginning of a *conversion specification*. For example, in the program line:

```
printf("\nArea is: %f", PI *(radius * radius));
```

the conversion specification consists of the percent symbol followed by the f *conversion operator*, which generates the display of a floating point number in decimal form. Each conversion specification refers to a specific subargument. These subarguments, which can be in the form of constants, variables, or formulas, are separated by commas from each other and from the format string. The following figure shows the relation between the conversion specifications and the subarguments in the printf() function.

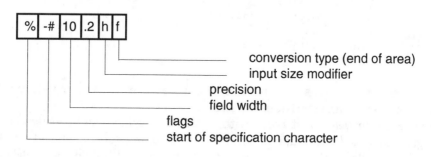

Conversion Specification Fields

A conversion specification can contain several optional elements. The first one is the *conversion specification code* (%). This symbol indicates the start of a conversion specification area. The optional *flags field* serves to format or modify the conversion operation by introducing signs, decimal point, blanks, and the octal or hexadecimal prefix.

The *width field* is an integer value that determines the number of characters displayed. If the value has fewer characters than those specified in the width field, the output is padded to the requested width. If the - flag is present, then the value is padded to the right of the field; if not, it is padded to the left. If the width value is preceded with a 0 digit, then padding is done with a 0 character; otherwise the blank character is used. The width field never causes a value to be truncated. If the value exceeds the width, all characters are displayed.

If the width specification is an asterisk (*), then the width value is supplied as a subargument to the format string, as in the following example:

Format Flags For printf()

FLAG CODE	FLAG ACTION	DEFAULT ACTION
-	Result is left-justified withn the field	Result is right-justified within the field
+	Prefix result with + or 1 sign	Only negative values have sign
space	Prefix unsigned results with a space	No space is prefixed to unsigned values

#	Output is modfied according to the conversion operator as follows:
	Operator Action
	  o Prefix value with 0
	  x Prefix value with 0x
	  X Prefix value with 0X
	  f,e, or E Format value with decimal point
	  g or G Format value with decimal point if there are invalid digits to the right. Do not truncate trailing zeros	

```
main()
{
    int width_value;
    double number1 = 1234.56;
    width_value = 20;
    printf("%0*f\n", width_value, number1);
}
```

In this case the width is determined by the value of variable width_field, which is represented by an asterisk in the format string.

The *precision field* must begin with a period (.) symbol and consists of an integer value that determines the number of characters displayed or the number of decimal places in the result. Unlike the width field, the precision field can cause the truncation of a number or the rounding of a floating-point result. The action of the precision field depends on the conversion type.

Like the width field, the precision field can contain an asterisk (*) . In this case the precision value is supplied as a subargument to the format string, in a similar manner as for the width field.

The *input-size modifier* determines how printf() interprets certain data types according to the addressing conventions determined by the storage model of the program. The use of these modifiers lies beyond the scope of this book.

Precision Field In printf()

CONVERSION TYPE	ACTION	DEFAULT
i,d,u,o,x,X	Number of digits displayed	1 digit
f,e,E	Number of digits to the right of the decimal point	6 decimal places
g,G	Maximum number of significant digits displayed	All significant digits displayed
s	Maximum number of characters displayed	Characters displayed until NULL found

The conversion specification area ends with the *conversion type code*. This code, which is a required element of the specification, consists of a single letter that determines the output format, as well as the parameters permitted on the other specification fields.

C Conversion Type Codes

CODE	DATA TYPE	VALID FLAGS	OUTPUT FORMAT
d,i	integer	- + 0 space	signed decimal
o	integer	- + 0 # space	signed octal integer
x	integer	- + 0 # space	signed hexadecimal integer using lowercase letters
X	integer	- + 0 # space	signed hexadecimal integer using uppercase letters
f	floating point	- + 0 # space	signed decimal in the form [-]mmm.nnnnn. The number of n digits is determined by the precision field. Default value is 6 n digits.
e,E	floating point	- + 0 # space	decimal number in scientific notation, as follows: e = [-]m.sssssse[]xx E = [-]m.ssssssE[]xx where m is a single digit. n is the number of digits (default value is 6 digits).
g	floating point	- + 0 # space	uses %f or %e, whichever is shorter. No trailing zeros.
G	floating point	- + 0 # space	same as g but exponent is preceeded by E
c	character	-	single character
s	pointer to char	-	string displayed until first NULL or until character count determined by the precision field
n	pointer to int		stores count of characters so far displayed at the location pointed by the argument (see text)
p	pointer		displays a far pointer argument as a logical address (SSSS:OOOO) and a near pointer as an offset (OOOO) (see text)

Note that the conversion type codes n and p, are available only in ANSI C implementations. These codes may behave differently in implementations of C that do not comply with the ANSI standard.

printf() — escape sequences

[C] In the printf() format string the characters \n is a *newline escape sequence.* An escape sequence is a combination of special characters used to specify a control code to the output device or to display a reserved character. The first symbol of the escape sequence is the backslash (\ ).

Escape Sequences (ANSI C Standard)

ESCAPE CODE	VALUE	ASCII	ACTION
CONTROL CODES:			
\a	0x07	BEL	Audible keyboard beep
\b	0x08	BS	Backspace
\f	0x0C	FF	Form feed (new page)
\n	0x0A	LF	Line feed (new line)
\r	0x0D	CR	Carriage return (start of line)
\t	0x09	HT	Horizontal tab
\v	0x0B	VT	Vertical tab
DISPLAY CODES:			
\\		\	Display backslash
\"		"	Display double quote
\'		'	Display single quote
\ddd			Display octal string
\xddd			Display hexadecimal string

printf() — library function

[C] The *printf()* library function provides the programmer with a way for formatting, converting, and displaying numbers and displaying text. printf() transmits data to the standard output device, which is designated in C as *stdout.* On the PC the standard output device is the video display. However, both UNIX and MS-DOS allow the redirection of input and output to other devices.

For example, a C program that contains the printf() function can be executed under MS-DOS so that output to the video display is redirected to the printer. The MS-DOS command:

```
AREA >> PRN
```

redirects output of the program named AREA to the printer device. The program line:

```
printf("Enter radius: ");
```

contains the simplest mode of the printf() function. After this line executes, the words enclosed in quotation marks are sent to the standard output device (normally the video display). In this case the phrase "Enter radius: " is called a *character string argument*. Note that the double quotation marks serve to delimit the character string.

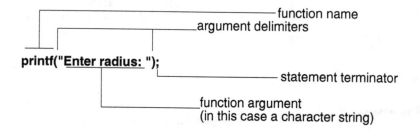

prinf() Function Elements

The fundamental elements of the printf() function are the function name and the function arguments (enclosed in parentheses).

Printf() can contain other arguments in addition to character strings. For example, in the program line:

```
printf("\nArea is: %f", PI * (radius * radius));
```

we can detect a more elaborate argument than in the printf() function of printf() line.

The function argument in a printf() function can consist of an elaborate format string. The compiler reads this format string left to right in search of subarguments and escape sequences.

Procedure format

[MS-Pascal] The general format for procedures includes three parts: the heading, declaration, and body. The heading is followed by:

1. Declarations for labels, constants, types, variables, and values
2. Local procedures and functions
3. The body, which is enclosed by the reserved words BEGIN and END

When the body of a procedure finishes execution, control returns to the program element that called it.

At the standard level, the order of declarations must be as follows:

1. LABEL
2. CONST
3. TYPE

4. VAR

5. Procedures and functions

At the extend level any number of LABEL, CONST, TYPE, VAR, and VALUE sections are allowed, as well as procedure and function declarations, in any order. Although data declarations (CONST, TYPE, VAR, VALUE) can be intermixed with procedure and function declarations, it is usually clearer to give all data declarations first. Putting variable declarations after procedure and function declarations ensures that these variables are not used by any of the procedures or functions.

Procedures and functions

[MS-Pascal] Pascal procedures and functions are subprograms that execute under the main program. Procedures and functions can be nested and can call themselves (recursion). Procedures are always invoked as program statements. Functions that return a value can also be invoked in program statements.

Predeclared common procedures and functions do not have to be declared in a program, since they are predefined. Pascal also includes library procedures and functions that you must declare EXTERN in order to use.

Procedures and Functions in MS-Pascal

CATEGORY	PURPOSE
File system	Operate on files
Dynamic	Dynamically allocate and deallocate data structures
allocation	On the heap at runtime
Data conversion	Convert data from one type to another
Arithmetic	Perform common numeric and transcendental functions
Extend level intrinsics	Provide additional procedures and functions at the extend level of MS-Pascal
System level instrinsics	Provide additional procedures and functions at the system level of MS-Pascal
String instrinsics	Operate on STRING and LSTRING type data
Library	Not predeclared; you must declare them with the EXTERN directive

Protected mode

[PC hardware and architecture] The 80286 and later Intel processors start up in the real address mode. This mode is also activated also upon a system RESET. In the real mode, the 286 CPU performs identically to the 8086. In general, the 80286 and later CPUs execute RAM and ROM resident programs written for the 8086 or the 8088 CPU. Protected address mode is initiated by loading the machine status word (LMSW instruction) with the protection enable (PE) flag set. Once the protected mode is attained, the system must be reset in order to return to real address mode execution. Protected mode provides the following features:

1. On-chip memory management of a virtual address space of up to 1 gigabyte in the 80286 and 4 gigabytes in 386 and later CPUs

2. A hierarchy of up to four privilege levels to improve system reliability and to separate multiple users

3. Support for multiple tasks with separate address spaces and task switching

PRSRQQ

[MS-Pascal] Heading: A, B :REAL4): REAL4;
Arithmetic function that returns A ** B (A to the REAL power of B). Both A and B are of type REAL4. An error occurs if A < 0 (even if B happens to have an integer value). This function is from the MS-FORTRAN runtime library and must be declared EXTERN.

PSET and PRESET (statement)

[BASIC] [QuickBASIC] Draws a point at the specified screen position. The statement format is:

```
PSET (x,y) [,foreground color]
PRESET (x,y), [,background color]
```

In graphics modes, the statement PSET (x,y) displays the point with coordinates (x,y) in the foreground color and the statement PRESET (x,y) displays it in the background color. The statement PSET (x,y),c or the statement PRESET(x,y),c causes the point (x,y) to be displayed in color c of the current palette.

PTYUQQ

[MS-Pascal] Heading: (LEN : WORD; LOC: ADSMEM);
Library routine of the terminal I/O group. Writes LEN characters, beginning at LOC in memory, to the terminal screen.
Example:

```
PTYUQQ (8, ADS 'PROMPT: ');
```

PUBLIC attribute

[MS-Pascal] Indicates a procedure or function that can be accessed from other modules. Code can access PUBLIC procedures and functions from other loaded modules by declaring them EXTERN in the modules that call them. Thus, declare a procedure PUBLIC and define it in one module, and use it in another by declaring it EXTERN.

As with variables, the identifier of the procedure or function is passed to the linker. PUBLIC and ORIGIN are mutually exclusive; PUBLIC routines need a following block, and ORIGIN routines must be EXTERN.

Any procedure or function with the PUBLIC attribute must be directly nested within a program or implementation. A higher level way to link MS-Pascal routines is by linking separately compiled units.

PUSH

[**Assembler**] 8086 machine instruction. Mnemonic for PUSH onto stack. Decrements the stack pointer according to the operand size and then places the operand on the new stack top. The single operand can be a machine register or a memory variable. If the operand is a 16-bit value then the stack pointer is decremented by 2. Starting with the 80386 the PUSH instruction can be used with 32-bit operands, for example:

```
PUSH    EAX          ; PUSH 32-bit register
PUSH    MEM_DWORD    ; or 32-bit variable
```

In this case the stack pointer is decremented by 4 before the operand is stored in the stack.

In the 8086 the action of PUSH SP is consistent with the other PUSH operands, that is, the stack pointer is first decremented and then the value of SP is stored in the stack. This behavior was changed starting with the 80286 so that the value stored is the contents of SP as it existed before the instruction. (See also: POP).

PUSHA

[**Assembler**] 80286 machines instruction. Mnemonic for PUSH All registers. Pushes all eight 16-bit registers into the stack. The registers are POPed in the order: AX, CX, DX, BX, SP, BP, SI, and DI. The alternate mnemonic PUSHAD was introduced with the 80386 to perform a 32-bit register version of the original opcode. PUSHA and PUSHAD are usually followed by POPA and POPAD.
(See also: POPA, POPAD).

PUSHF

[**Assembler**] 8086 machine instruction. Mnemonic for PUSH Flags.
PUSHF decrements the stack pointer by 2 and copies the FLAGS register to the new top of stack. PUSHFD is a 32-bit version of PUSHF introduced with

the 80386. PUSHFD decrements the stack point by 4 and copies the 80386 EFLAGS register to the new top of stack, which is pointed to by SS:ESP. (See also: POPF, POPFD).

PUT

[MS-Pascal] Heading: (VAR Fl;
File system procedure that writes the value of the file buffer variable F^ to the currently pointed-to component of F and advances the file pointer.

PUT (statement (files))

[BASIC] [QuickBASIC] Write a record from the random buffer to a random file. The statement format is:

```
PUT [#]filenum y[, recnum]
```

where filenum is the number assigned to the file with the OPEN statement, and recnum is the record number, in the range 1 to 16Mb. If recnum is omitted, the record after the one most recently accessed by a GET or PUT statement is filled.

The PUT statement is also used to place data into a binary file. In this case, var is a variable that holds a value consisting of b bytes. For example, if var is an integer variable, then b is 2. If var is an ordinary string variable, then b equals the length of the string currently assigned to it. In this case, the statement:

```
PUT #n,p,var
```

writes the successive bytes of var into the b consecutive locations beginning with position p in the binary file with reference number n. If p is omitted, then the current file position is used as the beginning position.

PUT (statement (graphics))

[BASIC] [QuickBASIC] Plots an image on a specified screen area. The statement format is:

```
PUT (x,y), array [,action]
```

where (x,y) are the coordinates of the top left corner of the image to be transferred, array is a numeric array containing the data, and action is one of the following:

```
CODE            ACTION
PSET            Store array data onto screen
PRESET          Same as PSET but image complement is
                displayed
AND, OR, XOR    Specifies the logical operation performed
                on each image pixel on the screen and the
                data array
```

Object animation can be performed using the XOR mode of the PUT statement since consecutively XORing an object restores the original image. The sequence of steps can be as follows:

1. PUT the object on the screen using the XOR mode

2. Recalculate object position

3. PUT object in XOR mode on present location to erase and restore screen

4. Change display location and go to step 1

putc() — library function

[C] The *putc()* function (which is available in most PC implementations) performs identically as putchar(). However, putc() is defined as a stream function. In C a stream can be visualized as a sequence of data items flowing to an output device or from an input device.

Standard Stream Devices

DEVICE NAME	STREAM	DEFAULT I/O
stdin	standard input	keyboard
stdout	standard output	video display
stderr	standard error	video display
stdprn	standard printer	parallel port (LPT1)
stdaux	standard auxiliary	serial port (COM1)

putc() requires an explicit designation of the stream device, while putchar() assumes that the destination is the standard output stream (stdout). For example:

```
putchar(0xdb);
putc(0xdb, stdout);
```

Because of this difference in their operation putchar() is often considered more convenient when the programmer is addressing the video display, while putc() comes in handy when it is necessary to direct the output to a different stream device. For example, the following line outputs the character 0xdb to the printer device:

```
putc(0xdb, stdprn);
```

putchar() — library function

[C] The character display function of the standard C library is *putchar()*. This function, which is part of the stdio.h include file, sends a single character to the standard output device (stdout).
(See putc()).

puts() — library function

[C] The *puts()* function is a library facility, part of the stdio.h include file, that displays a string of characters to the standard output device (stdout). The PC the default output device is the video screen. An important characteristic of puts() is that the function automatically adds a newline escape sequence at the end of the displayed string. This mode of operation make the puts() function convenient when the programmer intends to display a string on a separate screen line. On the other hand, puts() cannot be used with variables and does not admit the conversion specifications used with printf(). However, puts() does recognize the escape sequence code.

R

RAM

[**PC hardware and architecture**] Although the letters RAM stand for "random-access memory," it is often considered that this type of memory would be better described as "read-and-write memory." In contrast with read-only memory (see ROM), the principal characteristic of RAM is that it allows both storage and retrieval of data.

In the PC, RAM is used for storing system data, operating systems, and applications programs, as well as user and application data. Video memory is also RAM. On power-up, all RAM is blank or contains irrelevant data, called *garbage*. Programs and data are loaded into RAM from ROM or from permanent storage devices, like floppy and hard disk drives.

Two areas of RAM are reserved for system use in all IBM microcomputers: the interrupt vector table, from 0 to 400H, and the BIOS data area, from 400 to 4FFH. Specific systems may also have other reserved areas.

Random-access files

[**BASIC**] [**QuickBASIC**] The two methods for writing records to and reading records from random-access files are the "record variable method" and the "buffer method." With the buffer method, a portion of memory referred to as a buffer is set aside for the file. A FIELD statement specifies fixed-length string field variables whose values are held in the buffer. LSET and RSET statements assign values to the field variables, and PUT and GET statements move the contents of the buffer into a record of the file, and vice versa, respectively. The functions CKI, CKL, CKS, and CKD are used to convert numbers to fixed-length strings prior to being placed into the buffer by LSET and RSET statements. After a GET statement places a record in the buffer, the functions MKI, MKL, MKS, and MKD are used to convert the these strings back into numbers of the appropriate type.

RANDOMIZE (statement)

[**BASIC**] [**QuickBASIC**] Reseeds the random number generator. The statement formats are:

```
          RANDOMIZE [n]
```

or

```
          RANDOMIZE TIMER
```

In the first form *n* is numeric expression used as random number seed. The statement RANDOMIZE TIMER automatically uses the computer's clock to seed the random number generator. RANDOMIZE by itself requests a seed. If the random number generator is not seeded, the same list of numbers is generated by RND each time it executes.

RCL/RCR

[**Assembler**] 8086 machine instructions. Mnemonic for Rotate through carry Left (RCL) and Rotate through carry Right (ROR). The rotate-through-carry opcodes shift the bits of the register or memory operand. In RCL and RCR, the carry flag is part of the rotation. RCL shifts the carry flag into the low-order bit and shifts the high-order bit into the carry flag; RCR shifts the carry flag into the high-order bit and shifts the low-order bit into the carry flag.

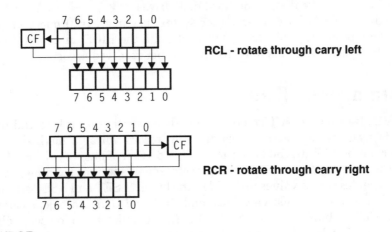

RCL/RCR

The rotate is repeated the number of times indicated by the second operand, which is either an immediate number or the contents of the CL register. For example:

```
     RCL    AX,5          ; Rotate-through-carry-left AX bits
                          ; 5 times
     RCL    BX,CX         ; Rotate-through-carry-left BX bits
                          ; CX times
     RCR    AL,CL         ; Rotate-through-carry-right AL bits
```

```
                                  ; CL times
        RCR     MEM_WORD,1        ; Rotate-through-carry-right bits stored
                                  ; in variable MEM_WORD, one time
```

To reduce the maximum instruction execution time, the 80386 does not allow rotation counts greater than 31. If a rotation count greater than 31 is attempted, only the bottom five bits of the rotation are used. The overflow flag is defined only for the single-rotate forms of the instructions (second operand = 1). It is undefined in all other cases.

RDMSR

[Assembler] Pentium machine instruction. Mnemonic for ReaD from Model Specific Register. The value in ECX specifies one of the 64-bit Model Specific Registers of the Pentium processor. The content of that Model-Specific Register is copied into FDX:EAX. EDX is loaded with the high-order 32 bits, and FAX is loaded with the low-order 32 bits. This instruction must be executed at privilege level O or in real-address mode; otherwise, a protection exception is generated.

The following values are used to select model specific registers on the Pentium processor:

```
VALUE (IN HEX)   REGISTER NAME         DESCRIPTION
    00H          Machine Check Address  Stores address of cycle
                                        causing exception
    01H          Machine Check Type     Stores cycle type of
                                        cycle causing exception
```

An exception #GP(0) is generated if the current privilege level is not 0 or the value in ECX does not specify a Model-Specific Register of the Pentium processor.

READ

[MS-Pascal] Heading: (VAR F; P1, P2,...PN);
File system procedure that reads data from files. Both READ and READLN are defined in terms of the more primitive GET.

READ (statement)

[BASIC] [QuickBASIC] Reads values from DATA statements and assigns them to variables. The statement format is:

```
READ var1 [,var2...]
```

where var1 and var2 are data items stored in a DATA statement. READ statement variables can be numeric or string.

READFN

[MS-Pascal] Heading: (VAR F; P1, P2,...PN);
File system procedure of the extend level I/O group. Is the same as READ with two exceptions:

1. File parameter F should be present (INPUT is assumed but a warning is issued).
2. If a parameter P is of type FILE, a sequence of characters forming a valid filename is read from F and assigned to P in the same manner as ASSIGN.

Parameters of other types are read in the same way as the READ procedure.

READLN

[MS-Pascal] Heading: (VAR F; P1, P2,... PN);
Textfile I/O procedure. At the primitive GET level, without parameters, READLN (F) is equivalent to the following:

```
BEGIN
        WHILE NOT EOLN (F) DO GET (F);
        GET (F)
END
```

READLN is very much like READ, except that it reads up to and including the end of line.

READSET

[MS-Pascal] Heading: (VAR F;VAR L: LSTRING; CONST S: SETOFCHAR);
File system procedure of the extend level I/O group. READSET reads characters and puts them into L, as long as the characters are in the set S and there is room in L.

Records

[General programming] In computer programming a record is defined as a set of related data items. A typical example is the record for an individual employee in an organization's computer information system. In this case the record would hold the employee's name, address, Social Security number, mailing address, base salary or wage, number of dependents, and other pertinent information.

Many practical programming problems require operating on data records in which the individual items belong to different data types. For example, if C were used to code a payroll program, the employee data would be stored in variables of different types. String items, such as the employee's name, Social Security number, and mailing address, would go into arrays of type char. Decimal data items, such as wages and deductions, would be stored in variables of type real. Finally, integral data items, such as the number of dependents, would probably be encoded using the unsigned char or int data types.

In general, arrays are defined as a collection of data items of the same type. For this reason a data record that consists of data items of different type cannot be stored in a single array. A *structure* is a data storage unit that contains one or more variables of the same or of different types. The concept of a structure allows treating a group of related items as a unit, such as the employee record previously mentioned, thus helping the programmer to organize and manage the more complicated data processing operations.

REDIM (statement)

[**QuickBASIC**] Redimension a dynamic array. The statement format is:

```
REDIM arrayname (...)
```

The action of the REDIM instruction is to erase the array from memory and recreate it. The information inside the parentheses has the same form and produces the same result as that in a DIM statement. After the REDIMensioning, all elements are restored to their default values. Although the ranges of the subscripts may be changed, the number of dimensions must be the same as in the original DIMensioning of the array. Inserting SHARED right after REDIM in a REDIM statement in the main body of a program, allows all procedures in the program to share the array.

Relational operators

[C] Relational operators, as the name suggests, are used to evaluate if a certain relationship between operands is true or false. The result of an expression that contains a relational operator is 1 (if the expression is true) or 0 (if the expression is false).

C Relational Operators

>	Greater than
<	Less than
<=	Less than or equal
>=	Greater than or equal
==	Equal
!=	Not equal

For example, if $x = 4$ and $y = 2$, the variable true_false evaluates to either 0 or 1, as shown in the following cases:

CASE	EXPRESSION	VALUE OF true_false
1	true_false = x >> y;	1 (true)
2	true_false = x << y;	0 (false)
3	true_false = x == 0;	0 (false)
4	true_false = x != 0;	1 (true)
5	true_false = x <<= 4;	1 (true)

Note in case 3, the difference between the assignment operator (=) and the equal to (==) relational operator. The assignment operator is used in this expression to ascribe to the variable true_false the result of comparison $x == 0$. In case 3 this value is 0 (false) because the value of the variable x is 4. However, the relational operator == does not change the value of the variable x, as would the statement x = 0. The programmer must be aware of this difference between the simple assignment operator (=) and the equal to relational operator (==), because this type of error is often not detected by the compiler.

RELEAS

[MS-Pascal] Heading: (VAR HEAPMARK: INTEGER4) ;
Library routine of the heap management group. Similar to RELEASE in other implementations of Pascal. RELEAS disposes of heap space past the area set with a previous MARKAS call. The DISPOSE procedure in MS-Pascal is generally more powerful, but RELEAS may be useful for converting from other Pascal dialects.

In other Pascals, the parameter is of a pointer type. However, MS-Pascal needs two words to save the heap limits. The HEAPMARK variable should not be used as a normal INTEGER4 number; it should only be set by MARKAS and passed to RELEAS.

REM (statement)

[BASIC] [QuickBASIC] Insert program remark. The statement format is:

```
REM comment
```

or

```
' comment
```

The statement REM allows a statement to be placed in a program. A line of the form REM comment is ignored during execution. The REM statement is also used to place metacommands into the program. The REM statement may be abbreviated as an apostrophe.

RENUM (command)

[BASIC] Renumber program lines. This command is not available in Quick-BASIC.

REP/REPE/REPZ/REPNE/REPNZ

[Assembler] Prefix byte for 8086 string instructions. Mnemonic for REPeat (REP), REPeat while Equal (REPE), REPeat while Zero (REPZ), REPeat while Not Equal (REPNE), and REPeat while Not Zero (REPNZ). The prefix byte controls subsequent string instruction repetition. The different mnemonics are provided to improve program clarity; REP, REPE, and REPZ are synonymous, as well as REPNZ and REPNE. The repeat prefixes do not affect the flags. REP is used in conjunction with the MOVS (Move String) and STOS (Store String) instructions and is interpreted as "repeat while not end-or-string" (CX not 0). REPE and REPZ operate identically and are physically the same prefix byte as REP. REPE and REPZ are used with the CMPS (Compare String) and SCAS (Scan String) instructions and require ZF to be set before initiating the next repetition. REPNE and REPNZ are mnemonics for the same prefix byte. These instructions function the same as REPE and REPZ except that the Zero flag must be cleared or the repetition is terminated. ZF does not need to be initialized before executing the repeated string instruction.

Repeated string sequences are interruptable; the processor recognizes the interrupt before processing the next string element. System interrupt processing is not affected. Upon return from the interrupt, the repeated operation is resumed from the point of interruption. However, execution does not resume properly if a second or third prefix (i.e., segment override or LOCK) has been specified in addition to any of the repeat prefixes. At interrupt time, the processor "remembers" only the prefix that immediately precedes the string instruction. After returning from the interrupt, processing resumes, but any additional prefixes specified are not in effect. If more than one prefix must be used with a string instruction, interrupts may be disabled for the duration of the repeated execution. However, this does not prevent a nonmaskable interrupt from being recognized. Also, the time that the system is unable to respond to interrupts may be unacceptable if long strings are being processed.

```
; Sample encodings using the REP prefix:
REP    MOVSB           ; Repeat MOVSB instruction while CX not
                       ; zero
REPE   SCASB           ; Repeat SCASB instructions until
                       ; CX = 0 or ZF = 1.
```

Reserved words

[C] A C identifier cannot be a word used for other purposes by the language. The special words, called *reserved words*, recognized in C are the following:

```
                     C LANGUAGE RESERVED WORDS
  asm        default      float       register      switch
  auto       do           for         return        typedef
  break      double       fortran     short         union
  case       else         goto        signed        unsigned
  char       entry        if          sizeof        void
  const      enum         int         static        volatile
  continue   extern       long        struct        while
```

RESET

[MS-Pascal] Heading: (VAR F)
File system procedure that resets the current file position to its   beginning and does a GET (F).

RESET (command)

[BASIC] [QuickBASIC] Closes all open files and clears the system buffer. The command format is:

```
        RESET
```

Using RESET is equivalent to using CLOSE with no file reference numbers.

RESET operation

[PC hardware and architecture] The designers of a microcomputer chip must make provision for ways to start or restart the system. This means that the processor must begin execution in an identical manner every time power is applied to the corresponding lines. The 8086 responds to POWER-ON or RESET by executing the instruction located at FFFF:0000H.

CPU State on Power-up and RESET

CPU ELEMENT	STATE
Flags	All clear
Instruction pointer	0000H
CS register	FFFFH
DS register	0000H
SS register	0000H
ES register	0000H
First opcode at	FFFF:0000H

In IBM microcomputers, logical address FFFF:0000H contains a jump to the first instruction in a BIOS routine, called the power-on self-test (or POST), which tests and initializes the system hardware.

RESTORE (statement)

[BASIC] [QuickBASIC] Allows DATA statement to be reread from a specified line or program label. The statement format is:

```
RESTORE [line (or label)]
```

If line or label is omitted, the first DATA statement in the program is accessed. Subsequent READ statements continue selecting data from that point.

RESULT

[MS-Pascal] Heading: (FUNCTION-IDENTIFIER) : VALUE ;
An extend level intrinsic function. Used to access the current value of a function; can only be used within the body of the function itself or in a procedure or function nested within it.

RESUME (statement)

[BASIC] [QuickBASIC] Continues execution after an error handler has executed. The statement format is:

```
RESUME [0] [label] [NEXT]
```

The action is for the program to branch back to the statement in which the error was encountered. The variations RESUME label and RESUME NEXT cause the program to branch to the statement at the indicated label or to the statement following the statement in which the error occurred, respectively. The combination of ON ERROR and RESUME NEXT is similar to the combination GOSUB and RETURN.

RET

[Assembler] 8086 machine instruction. Mnemonic for RETurn from procedure. Transfers control from a procedure back to the instruction following the CALL that activated the procedure. The assembler generates an intrasegment RET if the programmer has defined the procedure NEAR, or an intersegment RET if the procedure has been defined as FAR. RET pops the word at the top of the stack (pointed to by register SP) into the instruction pointer and increments SP by two. If RET is intersegment, the word at the new top of stack is popped into the CS register, and SP is again incremented by two.

The optional numeric parameter to RET gives the number of stack bytes (OperandMode = 16) or words (OperandMode= 32) to be released after the return address is popped. These items are typically used as input parameters to the procedure called.

In real mode, CS and IP are loaded directly. In Protected Mode, an interseg-ment return causes the processor to check the descriptor addressed by the return selector. The AR byte of the descriptor must indicate a code segment of equal or lesser privilege (or greater or equal numeric value) than the current privilege level. Returns to a lesser privilege level cause the stack to be reloaded from the value saved beyond the parameter block.

DS, ES, FS, and GS segment registers can be set to 0 by the RET instruction during an interlevel transfer. If these registers refer to segments that cannot be used by the new privilege level, they are set to 0 to prevent unauthorized access from the new privilege level.

```
; Sample encodings
      RET              ; Return from procedure
      RET    4         ; Return and add 4 to SP
```

return keyword

[C] The *return* keyword is used to end the execution of a function and return control to the line following the function call. A return statement can contain an expression, conventionally enclosed in parentheses, that represents the value returned to the caller. For example, the statement:

```
return((r + r) * PI);
```

If no value is associated with the return statement then the returned value is undefined. If no return statement appears in a function body, then the function concludes at its last statement; that is, when it encounters the closing brace (}). In this case programmers sometimes say that the function "fell off the edge." Functions that return no values should be prototyped and declared with a return value of type void.

The return statement can also be used to return a constant to the calling program, as in the following trivial program:

```
#include <stdio.h>
unsigned int dummy(void);
main(){
      printf("\nConstant value returned is: %u", dummy());
}
unsigned int dummy(void)
{
      return (6);
}
```

In this case the function named dummy returns a constant to the calling routine. The value of the constant (6) is displayed by the printf() statement. A return statement can appear anywhere in the function body. A function can contain more than one return statement, and each one can return a different value to the caller; for example:

```
if ( program_error >> 0 )
        return (1);
else
        return (0);
```

In conclusion, a C function can contain no return statement, in which case execution concludes at the closing brace (function falls of the edge) and the returned value is undefined. On the other hand, a function can contain one or more return statements. A return statement can appear in the form:

```
return;
```

In this case no value is returned to the caller. Or a return statement can return a constant, optionally enclosed in parentheses:

```
return 0;
```

or

```
return (1);
```

Finally, a return statement can return a variable or include a formula; for example:

```
return (error_code);
return((r + r) * PI);
return 2 * radius;
```

If a function returns no value it should be prototyped and declared of void type. In this case the return statement, if used, does not contain an expression.

RETURN (statement)

[BASIC] [QuickBASIC] Ends execution of a subroutine and returns to the statement following the last GOSUB. The statement format is:

```
RETURN [line (or label)]
```

The variation RETURN line (or label) causes the program to branch back to the statement following the indicated line or label.

RETYPE

[MS-Pascal] Heading: (TYPE-IDENT, EXPRESSION) : TYPE-IDENT;
System level intrinsic function that provides a generic type escape; returns the value of the given expression as if it had the type named by the type identifier. The types implied by the type identifier and the expression should have the same length, but this is not required. There are two other ways to change type in MS-Pascal:

1. Declare a record with one variant of each type needed, assign an expression to one variant, and then get the value back from another variant. (This is an error not detected at the standard level. Note that the relative mapping of variables changes between different versions of the compiler.)

2. Declare an address variable of the type wanted and assign to it the address of any other variable (using ADR).

Each of these methods has its own subtle differences and should be avoided whenever possible.

REWRITE

[MS-Pascal] Heading: (F);
File system procedure. Resets the current file position to its beginning.

RIGHT$ (function)

[BASIC] [QuickBASIC] Returns the rightmost n characters in a string. The function format is:

```
v$ = RIGHT$(x$,n)
```

where x$ is a string expression, and n is an integer that specifies the number of characters to be extracted from the target string. If n is greater than the number of characters of a$, then the value of the function is a$.
(See also: MID$, and LEFT$).

RMDIR (command)

[BASIC] [QuickBASIC] Removes a directory from the specified disk. The statement format is:

```
RMDIR path
```

where path is a valid MS-DOS pathname.

RND (function)

[BASIC] [QuickBASIC] Returns a random number between 0 and 1. The function format is:

```
v = RND[(x)]
```

where *x* is a numeric expression. The value of:

```
v = INT(RND * (n+1)
```

is a random whole number from 1 to n.

ROL/ROR

[Assembler] 8086 machine instructions. Mnemonic for Rotate Left (ROL), and Rotate Right (ROR). The left rotate instructions shift all the bits right-to-left. The high-order bit is copied to the low-order bit position and to the carry flag. The right rotate instruction shifts the bits right-to-left. The low-order bit is copied into the high-order bit position and into the carry flag. Note that in the ROL and ROR instructions, the original value of the carry flag is not a part of the result, but the carry flag receives a copy of the bit that was shifted from one end to the other.

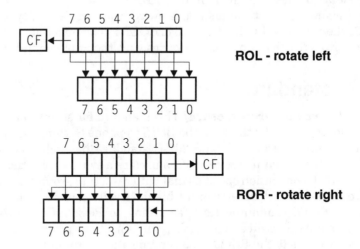

ROL/ROR

The rotate is repeated the number of times indicated by the second operand, which is either an immediate number or the contents of the CL register. For example:

```
ROL     AX,3            ; Rotate-left AX bits 3 times
```

```
ROL     BX,CX          ; Rotate-left BX bits CX times
ROR     AL,CL          ; Rotate-right AL bits CL times
ROR     MEM_WORD,1     ; Rotate-right bits stored in variable
                       ; MEM_WORD, one time
```

ROM

[PC hardware and architecture] The contents of ROM are fixed at the time the chips are manufactured. In the PC, ROM is used to store the system initialization and testing routines, as well as a collection of input and output services. This program is called the basic input/output system, or BIOS. Some systems also store a version of the BASIC program in ROM.

ROUND

[MS-Pascal] Heading: (X: REAL): INTEGER;
Arithmetic function that rounds X away from zero. X is of type REAL4 or REAL8; the return value is of type INTEGER. The effect of ROUND on a number with a fractional part of 0.5 varies with the implementation.

ROUND4

[MS-Pascal] Heading: (X: REAL): INTEGER4;
Arithmetic function that rounds real X away from zero. X is of type REAL4 or REAL8; the return value is of type INTEGER4. The effect of ROUND4 on a number with a fractional part of 0.5 varies with the implementation.

RS-232-C standard

[PC hardware and architecture] This standard for serial communications was developed jointly by the EIA, the Bell Telephone System, and modem and computer manufacturers. The RS-232-C standard has achieved such widespread acceptance that its name is often used as a synonym for the serial port.

The RS-232-C convention specifies that with respect to ground, a voltage more negative than -3V is interpreted as a 1-bit and a voltage more positive than +3V as a 0-bit. Serial communications according to RS-232-C require that the transmitter and the receiver agree on a communications protocol. The following terminology refers to the RS-232-C communications protocol:

1. *Baud period*. The rate of transmission measured in bits per second. The transmitter and the receiver clocks must be synchronized to the same baud period. The word *baud* was chosen to honor the nineteenth-century French scientist and inventor J.M.E.Baudot.

2. *Marking state*. The time period during which no data is being transmitted. During the marking period the transmitter holds the line at a steady high voltage.

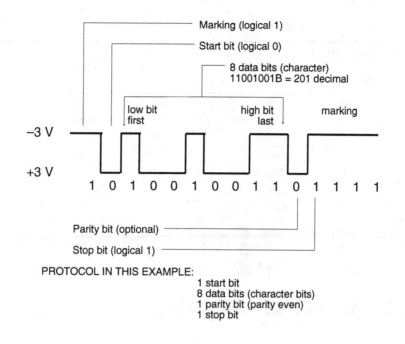

Bit Stream in Serial Communications

3. *Start bit*. The low-bit which indicates that data transmission is about to start. The low state that occurs during the start bit is called the *spacing state*.

4. *Character bits*. The data stream composed of 5, 6, 7, or 8 bits that encode the character transmitted. The least significant bit (LSB) is the first one transmitted.

5. *Parity bit*. An optional bit, transmitted following the character bits, used to check for transmission errors. If *even parity* is chosen, the transmitter sets or clears the parity bit so as to make the sum of the character's 1-bits and the parity bit an even number. In *odd parity* the parity bit makes the sum of 1-bits an odd number. If parity is not correct, the receiver sets an error flag in a special register. This register can be read by the central processing unit.

6. *Stop bits*. One or more high-bits inserted in the stream following the character bits or the parity bit, if there is one. The stop bit or bits ensure that the receiver has enough time to get ready for the next character.

The time period separating characters is variable. The transmitter holds the line voltage high (marking state) until it is ready to send. The start bit (spacing state) is used to signal the start of a new character. This mode of operation, in which the characters are independent from each other, is called *asynchronous communications*. The start bit is also used by the receiver to resynchronize with the transmitter. This compensates for drifts and small errors in the baud rate.

Definition of Common RS-232-C Lines

CONNECTOR			FUNCTION	CODE NAME	DIRECTION
DB-25	DB-9	BERG			
1		B2	Ground	G	
2	3	A4	Transmit data	TD	Output
3	2	A8	Receive data	RD	Input
4	7	A3	Request to send	RTS	Output
5	8	A7	Clear to send	CTS	Input
6	6	A6	Data set ready	DSR	Input
7	5	B1	Chassis ground	G	
8	1	A5	Carrier detect	CD	
20	4	A2	Data terminal ready	DTR	Output
22	9		Ring indicator	RI	Input

RS-232-C connectors and wiring

[PC hardware and architecture] The RS-232-C standard requires a specific hardware connector with 25 pins, called a *D-shell connector*, or DB-25. But not all IBM serial ports use the DB-25 connector. The PCjr serial port uses a 16-position BERG connector and the PC AT Serial/Parallel Adapter uses a 9-pin D-shell connector.

The RS-232-C standard has earned the reputation of being excessively flexible. This flexibility has determined that interfacing with RS-232-C devices often requires customized wiring. However, in connecting devices that correspond to the DTE and DCE designation, respectively — for instance, a computer to a modem — the required wiring is straight-through. This means that pin number 2 in the computer is connected to modem pin number 2, pin 3 to pin 3, and so forth.

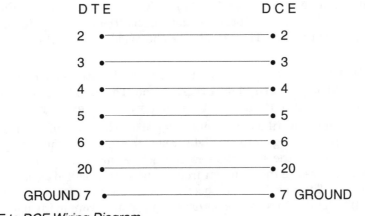

DTE to DCE Wiring Diagram

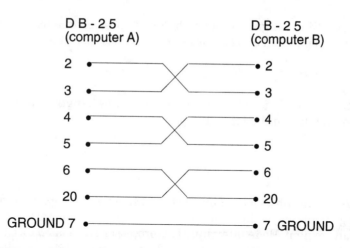

PC Null Modem Wiring Diagram (HB)

Connecting similar devices, for example, a computer to a computer or a terminal to a terminal, requires crossed wiring. This connecting scheme, which ensures that the receiving lines are coupled to the transmitting lines, is known as a *null modem*.

RS-232-C protocol

[**PC hardware and architecture**] In the RS-232-C protocol the transmission-reception parameters are selected from a range of standard values. The following are the most common ones in the PC:

Baud rate: 50, 110, 300, 600, 1200, 2400, 4800, 9600, and 19200

Data bits: 5, 6, 7, or 8

Parity bit: Odd, even, or no parity

Stop bits: 1, 1.5, or 2

RS-232-C defines data terminal equipment (DTE) and data circuit-terminating equipment (DCE), sometimes called data communications equipment. According to the standard the DTE designation includes both terminals and computers, and DCE refers to modems, transducers, and other devices. The serial port in IBM microcomputers is defined as DTE.

RSET (statement)

[**QuickBASIC**] Assigns a string to the field variable of a random-access file. The statement format is:

```
RSET af$ = b$
```

In this case RSET assigns the string b\$ to af\$, possibly truncated or padded on the left with spaces. If a\$ is an ordinary variable, then the statement:

```
RSET a$ = b$
```

replaces the value of a\$ with a string of the same length consisting of b\$ truncated or padded on the left with spaces.

RSM

[Assembler] Pentium machine instruction. Mnemonic for Resume from System Management mode. Resume operation of a program interrupted by a System Management Mode interrupt. The processor state is restored from the dump created upon entrance to SMM. The contents of the model-specific registers are not affected. The processor leaves SMM and returns control to the interrupted application or operating system. If the processor detects any invalid state information, it enters the shutdown state. This happens in any of the following situations:

1. If the value stored in the State Dump Base field is not a 32 Kbyte aligned address

2. If any reserved bit of CR4 is set to 1

3. If any combination of bits in CR0 is illegal; namely, (PG=1 and PE=0) or (NW=1 and CD=0)

A protected mode exception #UD is generated if an attempt is made to execute this instruction when the processor is not in System Management Mode

RTRIM\$ (function)

[QuickBASIC] Trims all spaces from the end of a string. The function format is:

```
v$ = RTRIM$(a$)
```

where v\$ is the string obtained by removing all the spaces from the end of the string a\$. The string a\$ may be either fixed- or variable-length.

RUN (command)

[BASIC] [QuickBASIC] Begins execution of a program. The command format is:

```
RUN [line (or label)]
```

All values previously assigned to variables are deleted. The variation RUN filespec loads the specified program from a disk and executes it. The specified program must be a BASIC program. The statement RUN line (or label) restarts the current program at the point referenced.

rvalue

(See lvalue and rvalue).

S

SADDOK

[MS-Pascal] Heading: (A, B: INTEGER; VAR C : INTEGER) : BOOLEAN;
Library routine of the no-overflow arithmetic group. Sets C equal to A plus B.
One of two functions that do 16-bit signed arithmetic without causing a runtime
error on overflow. Normal arithmetic may cause a runtime error even if the
arithmetic debugging switch is off. Both SADDOK and SMULOK return TRUE
if there is no overflow, and FALSE if there is. These routines can be useful for
extended-precision arithmetic, or modulo 2^{16} arithmetic, or arithmetic based on
user data.

SAHF

[Assembler] 8086 machine instruction. Mnemonic for Store AH registers into
Flags. Copies the contents of bits 7, 6, 4, 2, and 0 from the AH register into SF,
ZF, AF, PF, and CF respectively. OF, DF, IF, and TF are not defined following
SAHF. The instruction is provided mainly for compatibility with the 8080
processors, but it also finds use in transferring the math coprocessor's condition
code bits into the flags register so that a conditional branch can be used
accordingly.

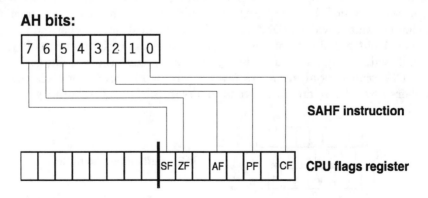

SAHF Instruction

SAL/SHL

[Assembler] 8086 machine instruction. Mnemonic for Shift Arithmetic Left (SAL), or Shift Logical Left (SHL). SAL and SHL are different mnemonic for the same instruction. SAL (or its synonym, SHL) shifts the bits of the operand from the low-order bit to the high-order bit. The high-order bit is shifted into the carry flag, and the low-order bit is set to O.

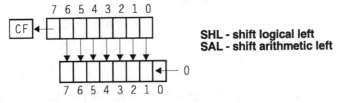

SHL - shift logical left
SAL - shift arithmetic left

SHL/SAL Instruction

The shift is repeated the number of times indicated by the second operand, which is either an immediate value or the contents of the CL register. The 80386 does not allow shift counts greater than 31. If a shift count greater than 31 is attempted, only the bottom five bits of the shift count are used. The overflow flag is set only if the single-shift forms of the instructions are used. OF is set to 0 if the high bit of the answer is the same as the result of the carry flag (i.e., the top two bits of the original operand were the same); OF is set to 1 if they are different.

SAR

[Assembler] 8086 machine instruction. Mnemonic for Shift Arithmetic Right (SAR). Shifts the bits in the destination operand (byte, word, or doubleword) to the right by the number of bits specified in the count operand. Bits equal to the original high-order (sign) bit are shifted in on the left, preserving the sign of the original value. Note that SAR does not produce the same result as the dividend of an equivalent IDIV instruction if the destination operand is negative and 1-bits are shifted out. For example, shifting -5 right by one bit yields -3, while with integer division -5 by 2 yields -2. The difference is due to the fact that IDIV truncates all numbers toward zero, while SAR truncates positive numbers toward zero and negative numbers toward negative infinity.

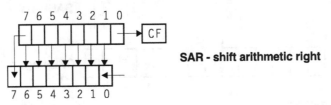

SAR - shift arithmetic right

SAR Instruction

The shift is repeated the number of times indicated by the second operand, which is either an immediate value or the contents of the CL register. The 80386 does not allow shift counts greater than 31. If a shift count greater than 31 is attempted, only the bottom five bits of the shift count are used. The overflow flag is set only if the single-shift forms of the instructions are used. OF is set to 0 if the high bit of the answer is the same as the result of the carry flag (i.e., the top two bits of the original operand were the same); OF is set to 1 if they are different.

SBB

[Assembler] 8086 machine instruction. Mnemonic for SuBtract with Borrow. Adds the source operand to the carry flag and subtracts the sum from the destination operand. Both operands may be bytes, words, or doublewords. An immediate value is first sign-extended when it is subtracted from a word operand.

```
; Sample encodings:
        SBB     AX,7            ; Immediate from AX register
        SBB     ECX,231         ; Immediate from EAX
        SBB     BX,CX           ; Register from register
        SBB     MEM_WORD,CL     ; Register from memory variable
```

SCANEQ

[MS-Pascal] Heading: (LEN : INTEGER; PAT: CHAR; CONSTS S: STRING; I: INTEGER) : INTEGER;

String intrinsic function that scans, starting at S[I], and returns the number of characters skipped. SCANEQ stops scanning when a character equal to pattern PAT is found or LEN characters have been skipped. If LEN 0, SCANEQ scans backwards and returns a negative number. SCANEQ returns the LEN parameter if it finds no characters equal to pattern PAT found or if I UPPER(S). There are no error conditions.

scanf()

[C] C contains no specific input or output facilities since these operations are performed by means of library functions. The scanf() function (pronounced scan-ef) is the most used input function in these library facilities. It can be considered the input counterpart of the printf() function. The scanf() function reads data from the standard input device (normally the keyboard) into a variable.

Each scanf() function call contains one or more arguments. Each argument consists of a specification string, enclosed in double quotes, and one or more destination variables. The specification string and format operators are similar to those of the printf() function.

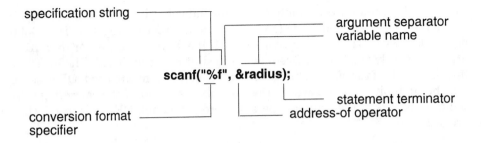

A new program element noticeable in scanf() is the ampersand (&) preceding the variable name. The ampersand, called the *address-of operator*, calculates the memory address of a variable. To understand the action of this symbol it is important to recall the definition of a variable as a labeled container for storing a data object. In C language the variable name is used to retrieve the value stored in the container (the *value of the variable*) and the ampersand is used to indicate the location of the container in the computer's memory space (the *address of the variable*).

In scanf() the address-of operator indicates where the input value is to be placed. If this symbol is omitted, the function fails and the program generates a runtime error.

The characters input during the scanf() function can be classified as *whitespace characters*, such as a blank space, tab, or newline (enter) characters, and *nonwhitespace characters* such as letters, numbers, or other valid keyboard symbols. The first whitespace character encountered by the scanf() function is interpreted as the end of the input field.

scanf() – input specifications

[C] The presence of the percent (%) symbol in the format string denotes the beginning of *input specification*. As in the printf() function, the percent symbol marks the start of a specifications field. Each input specification refers to a specific subargument, which is usually a variable preceded by the address-of operator. If the function contains more than one subargument, they will be separated by commas from each other and from the format string.

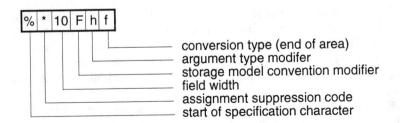

scanf() Input Specification Fields

scanf() Conversion Type Code

CODE	EXPECTED INPUT	VARIABLE OF TYPE
NUMERIC TYPES		
d D	decimal integer	int long
o O	octal integer	int long
x X	hexadecimal integer	int long
i I	Decimal, hex or octal integer	int long
u U	unsigned integer	unsigned int unsigned long
f	floating point in decimal format	float
e, E	floating point in exponential format	float
g, G	floating point in decimal or exponential format	float
ALPHANUMERIC TYPES		
c	character (including whitespace characters)	char
s	string (use "%1s" to input first non-whitespace character)	array of char
POINTER TYPES		
n	no input read	int
p	logical address in hex format (OOOO or SSSS:OOOO)	far or near pointer according to memory model or variable type

The action of the various elements in the input specification fields is as follows:

1. The first element is the *conversion specification code* (%). This symbol, which is the same one used in the printf() function, indicates the start of the input specification area.

2. The asterisk is optionally used as an assignment suppression code. If this symbol is present, the input operation takes place normally, according to the conversion type code described below, but the entered value is discarded.

3. The *field width* is an integer value that determines the maximum number of characters read by the function. If a whitespace character is encountered in the input field, then fewer characters than determined by the width field are stored.

4. The *storage model convention modifier field* determines how scanf() interprets certain data types according to the addressing conventions determined by the storage model of the program.

5. The *argument type modifier field* is used to override some default argument types. The prefix letter l indicates a long version of the int variable type and

h indicates the short version. The prefix letter L indicates *long double* in floating-point conversions.

6. The input specification area ends with the *conversion type code*. This code, which is a required element of the specification, consists of a single letter that determines the input format and limits the parameters allowed on the other specification fields.

SCANNE

[MS-Pascal] Heading: (LEN : INTEGER; PAT: CHAR; CONSTS S; STRING; I:INTEGER):INTEGER;

String intrinsic function. Similar to SCANEQ, but stops scanning when a character not equal to pattern PAT is found.

Scans, starting at S[I], and returns the number of characters skipped. SCANNE stops scanning when a character not equal to pattern PAT is found or LEN characters have been skipped. If LEN < 0, SCANNE scans backwards and returns a negative number. SCANNE returns LEN parameter if it finds all characters equal to pattern PAT found or if I UPPER (S). There are no error conditions.

SCAS/SCASB/SCASW/SCASD

[Assembler] 8086 machine instruction. Mnemonic for SCAn String, Byte, Word, or Doubleword. Subtracts the memory byte or word at the destination register from the AL, AX, or EAX register. The result is discarded; only the flags are set. The operand must be addressable from the ES segment. No segment override is allowed.

If the size attribute is 16 bits, DI is used as the destination register. If it is 32 bits then EDI is used.

The address of the memory data being compared is determined solely by the contents of the destination register, not by the operand to SCAS. The operand validates ES segment addressability and determines the data type. Code must load the correct index value into DI or EDI before executing SCAS.

After the comparison is made, the destination register is automatically updated. If the direction flag is 0 (CLD was executed), the destination register is incremented; if the direction flag is 1 (STD was executed), it is decremented. Increments and decrements are 1 for byte operands, 2 for word operands, and 4 for doublewords. In block searches SCAS is preceded by the REPE or REPNE prefix. In this case CS or ECX serves as a repetition counter.

(See also: REP).

Screen resolution

[video systems] The resolution of a video graphics system is measured in the total number of separately addressable elements per unit area, called screen pixels. Resolution is measured in pixels per inch. The maximum resolution of a VGA system is approximately 80 pixels per inch, both vertically and horizontally.

Not all video systems output a symmetrical pixel density. For example, the maximum resolution of the EGA standard is the same as that of the VGA on the horizontal axis (80 pixels per inch) but only 58 pixels per inch on the vertical axis. The asymmetrical pixel grid of the EGA and of other less refined video standards introduced programming complications. For example, in a symmetrical VGA screen a square figure can be drawn using lines of the same pixel length, but these lines would produce a rectangle in an asymmetrical system. By the same token, the pixel pattern of a circle in a symmetrical system appears as an ellipse in an asymmetrical one.

SCREEN (function)

[BASIC] [QuickBASIC] Returns the ASCII code for the character at the specified screen position, expressed in row/column form. The function format is:

```
v = SCREEN (r,c [,z])
```

where r,c are the row and column coordinates. z is a numeric expression. If z is nonzero then the number of the palette jar being used to color the character is returned.

SCREEN (statement)

[BASIC] [QuickBASIC] Sets the screen attributes. The statement format is:
SCREEN [mode]][,burst][,apage][,vpage]
where mode is a numeric expression, as follows:

```
FORM                SETS VIDEO SYSTEM IN
SCREEN 0            text mode
SCREEN 1            medium-resolution graphics mode
SCREEN 2            high-resolution graphics mode
SCREEN 3            720x348 Hercules graphics mode, two colors
SCREEN 7            320x200 16-color EGA, VGA adapters
SCREEN 8            640x200 16-color EGA, VGA adapters
SCREEN 9            640x350 4-to-16 color EGA, VGA adapters
SCREEN 10           640x350 monochrome EGA adapters
SCREEN 11           640x480 2-color MCGA, VGA adapters
SCREEN 12           640x480 16-color VGA only
SCREEN 13           320x200 256-color MCGA, VGA adapters
```

Burst is a numeric expression representing true (nonzero) or false (zero) which enables and disables color. When a graphics adapter is used in text mode, the computer can store the contents of several different screens, called pages. The number of pages allowed, call it n, depends on the graphics adapter and selected mode. At any time, the page currently displayed is called the visual page and the page currently being written to is called the active page. If a and v are numbers from 0 to n-1 then the statement:

```
SCREEN ,,a,v
```

designates page a as the active page and page v as the visual page.

SEEK

[MS-Pascal] Heading: (VAR F; N : INTEGER4);
File system procedure of the extend level I/O group. In contrast to normal sequential files, DIRECT files are random access structures. SEEK is used to randomly access components of such files.

SEEK (statement)

[QuickBASIC] Sets the current file pointer position. The statement format is:

```
SEEK #n,p
```

In this case SEEK sets the current file position in binary or random access mode, referenced by n, to the pth byte or record. The next GET or PUT statement reads or writes bytes, respectively, beginning with the pth byte or record. The value of the function SEEK(n) is the current file position either in bytes or by record number. After a PUT or GET statement is executed, the value of SEEK(n) is the number of the next byte or record.

Segment registers

(See machine registers).

SELECT CASE (statement)

[QuickBASIC] Provides a compact method for selecting the execution of one of several blocks of statements, as in a displayed menu. Typically, a SELECT CASE block begins with a line of the form SELECT CASE expression and ends with the statement END SELECT. In between are statements of the form:

```
CASE valuelist
```

and perhaps the statement:

```
CASE ELSE
```

The items in valuelist may be individual values, or ranges of values such as "a TO c" or "IS x". Each of these CASE statements is followed by a block of one or more statements. The block of statements following the first CASE valuelist statement is the only one executed. If none of the value lists includes the value of expression and a CASE ELSE statement is present, then the block of statements following the CASE ELSE statement is executed.

Sequential evaluation operator

(See comma operator).

Serial communications — interrupts

[**PC hardware and architecture**] Serial communications programs that make use of hardware interrupts allow greater freedom of operation to the transmitting and receiving devices. Interrupt-driven communications programs can operate more efficiently and use higher baud rates than programs that rely on polling or handshaking techniques. All serial communications controllers used in the IBM microcomputers support hardware interrupts.

Without some form of synchronization during data transmission, communications programs on the PC lose characters when operating at speeds above 1200 Bd. The reason is that monitoring the serial line for new characters is left to the receiver, therefore the program must remove the received character from the data register before the next one arrives. Failure to do so results in an overrun error, as the old data byte is overwritten by the new one.

The frequency with which the program must monitor the line for new data can be estimated by dividing the baud rate by the number of bits in each character transmitted. In a typical encoding each character contains one start bit, seven data bits, one parity bit, and one stop bit. This makes a total of ten bits per character. Dividing the baud rates by the ten bits required to represent each character gives the following approximate transmission speeds, in characters per second (cps):

Baud rate	Speed
300	30
600	60
1200	120
2400	240
4800	480

Consequently, a receiver operating at 2400 Bd has to monitor the communications line at a minimum frequency of 240 times per second to prevent reception errors. This leaves the CPU with less than 1/240 of a second in which to store, display, or otherwise manipulate the received character.

The PC serial communications controllers make possible the generation of several hardware interrupts during the communications cycle. Of these, the received data available interrupt is probably the most used one. This interrupt can be described as a way of giving the microprocessor a "tap on the shoulder" to let it know that data is available on the serial line. The CPU can then interrupt whatever it is doing long enough to remove the character from the receiver data register and store it in a dedicated buffer. The characters can remain in the buffer until the CPU has time to perform the required processing.

Serial communications — software handshake

[PC hardware and architecture] Some serial communications setups do not use the control lines required for hardware handshaking. For example, the null modem wiring connecting two PCs through the serial port uses only the transmit data and receive data lines. Several software handshake protocols have been developed to allow serial communications when the RS-232-C control signals are not available.

The XON/XOFF convention uses the character 13H (XOFF) to signal to the transmitting device to stop sending characters and the character 17H (XON) to signal that transmission can take place.

Serial communications controller — architecture

[PC hardware and architecture] The internal architecture of the various serial communications controllers used in the PC (8250 UART, NS-16450, and NS-16550) appears almost identical to the programmer. The CPU can gain access to the controller registers through the corresponding ports.

Serial communications controller — Baud Rate Divisor Registers

[PC hardware and architecture] The baud rate divisor registers, also called the *divisor latch registers*, are used to program the baud rate generator in the serial communications controller. One baud rate divisor register (BRDL) stores the least significant byte, and the following register (BRDH) stores the most significant byte. The following formula calculates the value of the divisor that generates a given baud rate:

```
                    clock speed (in Hz)
        Divisor = -----------------------
                    16 * desired Baud rate
```

Divisor Values for the Baud Rate Generator

BAUD RATE	PCAT and PS/2 CLOCK SPEED, 1.8432 MHz			CLOCK SPEED, 1.7895 MHz		
	DECIMAL	HEX	% ERROR	DECIMAL	HEX	% ERROR
50	2304	900H	0	2337	8BDH	0.008
75	1536	600H	0	1491	5D3H	0.017
110	1047	417H	0.026	1017	3F9H	0.023
134.5	857	359H	0.058	832	340H	0.054
150	768	300H	0	746	2EAH	0.050
300	384	180H	0	373	175H	0.050
600	192	C0H	0	186	BAH	0.218
1200	96	60H	0	93	5DH	0.218
1800	64	40H	0	62	3EH	0.218
2000	58	3AH	0.690	56	38H	0.140
2400	48	30H	0	47	2FH	0.855
3600	32	20H	0	31	1FH	0.218
4800	24	18H	0	23	17H	1.291
7200	16	10H	0	– NOT RECOMMENDED –		
9600	12	CH	0	– NOT RECOMMENDED –		
19200	6	6H	0	– NOT RECOMMENDED –		

The clock speed (Ck) is 1,843,200 Hz in all IBM microcomputers except the PCjr. In the PCjr the clock speed is 1,789,500 Hz.

Setting the baud rate in the serial communications controllers requires programming the baud rate divisor registers. However, the baud rate divisor least significant byte register is mapped to the same address as the transmitter holding register and the receiver data register, while the baud rate divisor most significant byte is mapped to the same address as the interrupt enable register. In order to select the baud rate divisor registers, it is first necessary to set bit 7 of the line control register. Due to this, its high bit is often called the *divisor latch access bit*, or DLAB. When the DLAB bit of the line control register is clear (bit equals zero), access can be gained to the transmitter holding register, the receiver data register, and the interrupt enable register.

The following code fragment illustrates setting the baud rate of the first serial port (COM1) to 1200 baud (Bd) in a non-PCjr system. The code assumes that a valid address for the first serial port has been previously stored in a variable named COM1_BASE:

```
MOV    DX,COM1_BASE ; See previous code fragment
ADD    DX,3              ; Line control register is at
                         ; base address + 3
IN     AL,DX         ; Read contents of LC register
```

```
    JMP    SHORT $+2           ; I/O delay
    OR     AL,80H              ; To set the divisor latch access
                               ; bit (DLAB)
    OUT    DX,AL               ; To line control register
    JMP    SHORT $+2           ; I/O delay
    MOV    AL,60H              ; LSB for 1200 Bd (Table 7.7)
    MOV    DL,0F8H                ; Address of divisor's LSB
    OUT    DX,AL               ; AL to baud rate divisor LSB
    JMP    SHORT $+2              ; I/O delay
    MOV    AL,0H               ; MSB for 1200 Bd (see table)
    MOV    DL,0F9H                ; Address of divisor's MSB
    OUT    DX,AL               ; AL to Bd rate divisor MSB
    JMP    SHORT $+2              ; I/O delay
; Bd rate is now set for 1200 Bd
```

Serial communications controller — Interrupt Enable Register

[**PC hardware and architecture**] The serial communications controller allows four types of interrupts. The interrupt enable register (IER) permits activating one or more of these interrupt sources. Serial communication interrupts also require setting bit 3 of the modem control register and that the CPU's interrupt system be active.

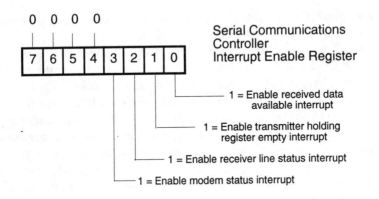

Interrupt Enable Register

In IBM microcomputer systems the communications interrupt, originating in the serial line designated as COM1, is linked to the hardware interrupt line IRQ4. This line is vectored through interrupt 0CH. The interrupts originating in the serial line designated COM2 are linked to IRQ3 and to interrupt vector 0BH.

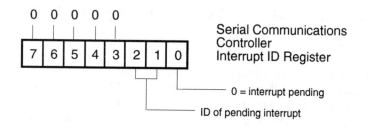

Interrupt Identification Register

Serial communications controller — Interrupt Identification Register

[PC hardware and architecture] The interrupt identification register (IID) stores a priority code that makes possible the identification of one or more pending interrupts. The possible interrupt sources depend on setting the IER. Bit 0 of the interrupt ID register will be clear if there si a pending interrupt. Polling routines can use this bit to determine whether there is an interrupt condition that requires service.

Bits 1 and 2 of the interrupt ID register contain the priority code that permits the identification of the pending interrupt. This code is also called the *interrupt priority level*.

Interrupt Priority, Type, Cause, and Reset Action in the Serial Communications Controller

INTERRUPT ID BITS		INTERRUPT PRIORITY LEVEL	TYPE	POSSIBLE CAUSES	RESETTING ACTION
2	1				
1	1	1	Receiver line status.	Overrun error. Parity error. Framing error. Break interrupt.	Read the line status register.
1	0	2	Received data available.	Data in register.	Read receiver data register.
0	1	3	Transmitter holding register empty.	No data in register.	Read interrupt ID register or write THR.
0	0	4	Modem status.	Clear to send. Data set ready. Ring indicator. Received line signal detect.	Read modem status register.

Serial communications controller — Line Control Register

[**PC hardware and architecture**] The high bit of the line control register (LCR), often called the divisor latch access bit (DLAB), is used to select between various registers mapped to the same address. If the DLAB bit is set, then read or write operations to the registers mapped to the base address (3F8H or 2F8H) access the baud rate divisor LSB register. Also, read and write operations to the base address plus one (3F9H or 2F9H) access the baud rate divisor LSB register. On the other hand, if the DLAB bit is clear, write operations to the base address access the transmitter holding register and read operations will access the receiver data register. In this case read and write operations to the base address plus one access the interrupt enable register.

The other bit fields in the LCR are used in relation to the RS-232-C communications protocol.

The break control bit can be used to selectively enable and disable terminals in a communications network.

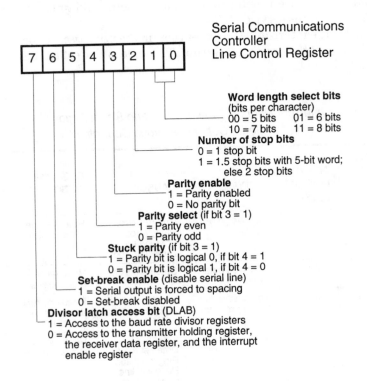

Serial Communications
Controller
Line Control Register

Word length select bits
(bits per character)
00 = 5 bits   01 = 6 bits
10 = 7 bits   11 = 8 bits
Number of stop bits
0 = 1 stop bit
1 = 1.5 stop bits with 5-bit word;
    else 2 stop bits
Parity enable
1 = Parity enabled
0 = No parity bit
Parity select (if bit 3 = 1)
1 = Parity even
0 = Parity odd
Stuck parity (if bit 3 = 1)
1 = Parity bit is logical 0, if bit 4 = 1
0 = Parity bit is logical 1, if bit 4 = 0
Set-break enable (disable serial line)
1 = Serial output is forced to spacing
0 = Set-break disabled
Divisor latch access bit (DLAB)
1 = Access to the baud rate divisor registers
0 = Access to the transmitter holding register,
    the receiver data register, and the interrupt
    enable register

Line Control Register

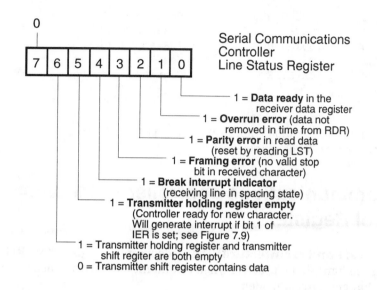

Line Status Register

Serial communications controller — Line Status Register

[PC hardware and architecture] Provides the CPU with information regarding the state of the data transfer operations.

Bits 1, 2, 3, and 4 reflect specific error conditions that can occur during serial communications. The error bits of the LSR are reset when the receiver data or the line status registers are read by the CPU. Bit 0 of the LSR can be used to determine if a character is ready at the receiver data register. Bit 0 is reset when the character is removed from the receiver data register. Bit 5 indicates that the transmitter holding register is ready to accept a new character. No new character should be input until bit 5 equals 1. This bit is reset when the transmitter holding register is loaded. If bit 1 of the interrupt enable register is set, an interrupt is generated when bit 5 of the LSR changes to a logical 1.

The following code fragment tests the LSR for error conditions, data ready, and transmitter holding register empty, and then branches to the corresponding routine:

```
        MOV     DX,COM1_BASE
CHECK_LINE:
        MOV     DL,0FDH         ; Line status register offset
        IN      AL,DX           ; Read byte
        JMP     SHORT $+2       ; I/O delay
        TEST    AL,00011110B    ; Test error bits 1, 2, 3 or 4
        JNZ     ERROR           ; Error condition, take action
```

```
TEST    AL,00000001B        ; Data ready ?
JNZ     RECEIVE             ; Take action
TEST    AL,00100000B        ; THR empty ?
JNZ     SEND                ; Yes, take action
JMP     CHECK_LINE          ; Continue looping
    .
    .
    .
; Code at labels ERROR, RECEIVE, and SEND will handle
; processing in each case
```

Serial communications controller — Modem Control Register

[PC hardware and architecture] The modem control register (MCR) is used in setting the handshake protocol when communicating with a modem or with a device that emulates a modem.

Bits 0 and 1 of the MCR control the data-terminal-ready (DTR) and the request-to-send (RTS) signals that appear on pin numbers 20 and 4 of the connector. When these bits are set, the DTR and RTS signals become active. Bit 3 of this register controls the output 2 signal. This signal allows the interrupts generated by the communications controller to reach the interrupt controller. Programs that use communications interrupts must set this bit. Bit 4 provides a loopback feature that can be used in testing the communications controller or the operation of portions of a serial communications program.

Serial communications controller — Modem Status Register

[PC hardware and architecture] The modem status register (MSR) provides the CPU with information regarding the state of the control lines from the modem or modem-like device. The first four bits of this register are set to logical 1 whenever a modem control line changes state.

When set, bits 0, 1, 2, and 3 of the MSR generate a modem status interrupt if bit 3 of the interrupt enable register is also set.

Serial communications controller — Receiver Data Register

[PC hardware and architecture] The receiver data register, also called the *receiver buffer register*, holds the character received.

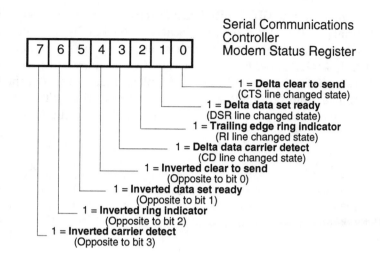

Modem Status Register

Serial communications controller — Transmitter Holding Register

[PC hardware and architecture] The transmitter holding register contains the character ready to be sent. During a transmission operation the LSB in the holding register is the first one sent.

Serial communications controllers — programming

[PC hardware and architecture] The serial communications controllers 8250 UART, NS-16450, and NS-16550 appear to the programmer as 10 internal registers. These registers are accessible to the CPU through as many ports. IBM systems allow the use of more than one serial communications device by mapping each device to a different set of seven ports. In all IBM microcomputers, except the PCjr, if the serial communications controller is mapped to ports 3F8H to 3FEH, it is said to be configured as communications port number 1, or COM1. If it is mapped to ports 2F8H to 2FEH, then it is said to be configured as COM2.

Some PC hardware allows more than one serial port in a system. For example, changing jumper J1 on the AT's Serial/Parallel Adapter determines the mapping and designation of the serial port. In one setting, the serial port becomes COM1 and the first digit of the port's address becomes 3. In the alternate setting the port is designated as COM2 and the first digit of the address becomes 2. These possible variations in the serial port can be the source of uncertainty regarding the number of serial ports installed in a system and their address mapping. In any case, the BIOS initialization routines store the base address of the first serial port (COM1) at memory locations 400H in the BIOS data area. If additional ports are implemented, their base addresses are stored at memory locations 402H, 404H, and 406H, respectively. One or more of these fields is initialized to zero if the system contains less than four serial ports, but the BIOS does not initialize valid ports following a zero address value.   The following code fragment shows how to obtain and save the address of the four possible serial ports:

```
DATA    SEGMENT
COM1_BASE    DW      0000H  ; Storage for COM1 base address
COM2_BASE    DW      0000H  ; Storage for COM2 base address
COM3_BASE    DW      0000H  ; Storage for COM3 base address
COM4_BASE    DW      0000H  ; Storage for COM4 base address
DATA    ENDS
CODE    SEGMENT
        ASSUME CS:CODE
        .
        .

; Obtain base address of serial ports from BIOS data area
        PUSH    DS           ; Save program's DS
        XOR     AX,AX        ; AX = 0
        MOV     DS,AX        ; Data segment zero for BIOS
        MOV     DX,DS:0400H  ; Base address of COM1
        MOV     CX,DS:0402H  ; Base address of COM2
        MOV     BX,DS:0404H  ; Base address of COM3
        MOV     AX,DS:0406H  ; Base address of COM4
        POP     DS           ; Restore program's DS
        MOV     COM1_BASE,DX ; Store COM1
        MOV     COM2_BASE,CX ; Store COM2
        MOV     COM1_BASE,BX ; Store COM3
        MOV     COM2_BASE,AX ; Store COM4
; The code can now check each stored port address for a zero
; value to determine the number of valid ports
        .
        .
```

Serial communications — handshake

[PC hardware and architecture] Handshake techniques make it possible for the receiver to suspend the transmission when the characters cannot be processed faster than the transmission rate. A typical example of handshaking is in the communications setup between a computer and a serial printer. In this case, the printer may force the computer into a wait state until the previous character has been printed or if other circumstances require it, such as an out-of-paper condition. Handshaking can be implemented using hardware or software techniques.

In serial communications, hardware handshaking is based on the RS-232-C control signals. A simple handshake protocol can be established using the data-set-ready and data-terminal-ready signals. For example, a serial printer (DTE) raises the data-terminal-ready line to inform the computer (DCE) that it is ready to receive. If the printer wants to suspend transmission, it lowers data terminal ready to a negative voltage. The clear-to-send (CTS) and request-to-send (RQS) lines can be used as a subsidiary handshake.

Handshaking between data communications equipment (DCE) and data terminal equipment (DTE) usually requires straight-through connections. This means that in the case of a serial printer, the printer's DTR signal becomes DSR at the computer and the printer's RQS becomes the computer's CTS.

Serial communications — programming character and file transfers

[PC hardware and architecture] According to the RS-232-C standard, serial communications programs can transfer data encoded in units of 5- to 8-bit lengths. In the PC only the 7- and 8-bit word lengths are in use. The ASCII encoding of character data comprises the range from 20H to 7FH. This makes it possible to encode all the ASCII characters in seven bits.

Programs that operate exclusively with character data can improve their performance by adopting a protocol that uses seven data bits per character word. The usual control codes, in the range 00H to 1FH, can also be transmitted with this convention. For example, the XON/XOFF software handshaking protocol can be used with a 7-bit transmission format.

On the other hand the transmission of program code, graphic symbols, and other binary data, requires the full range of the 8-bit encoding. This fact prohibits the use of embedded control codes, since all possible values can be present in the data stream. The simplest solution to this problem consists of adopting protocols that transmit data, not as individual characters, but in blocks of a predefined size. The blocks usually include headers with handshake characters, which are used to establish the communications line, and conclude with checksum characters used in detecting transmission errors.

The XMODEM file transfer protocol, developed in 1977 by Ward Christensen and later modified by Keith Petersen, has gained considerable popularity in the microcomputer field. In the XMODEM convention, data is transferred in 132-byte blocks.

The XMODEM convention also implements handshaking. According to the protocol, data transmission cannot begin until the sender receives a character 15H (called *NAK*, or *negative acknowledge*) from the receiver. At this time the sender can transmit one 132-byte block. The code 06H (called *acknowledge*, or *ACK*) is issued by the receiver to acknowledge each block received correctly. If the receiver detects errors, it uses the code 15H (NAK) to request from the transmitter to resend the block. At the end of the transmission the transmitter sends the code 04H (called *EOT*, or *end of transmission*).

Serial Communications Controllers

[PC hardware and architecture] The fundamental element of the serial port is an integrated circuit communications controller. The 8250 universal asynchronous receiver and transmitter (UART), or a functionally equivalent chip, is used in the IBM Asynchronous Communications Adapter of the PC line, in the PCjr, and in the non-Micro Channel computers of the PS/2 line (Models 25 and 30). The Serial/Parallel Adapter in the PC AT is equipped with the NS-16450 chip, and the Micro Channel models of the PS/2 line with the NS-16550. The various serial communications controllers listed have similar architectures and appear almost identical to the programmer.

In operation, the transmitter portion of the controller converts an 8-bit data value, placed by the processor in the adapter's output port, into a serial bit stream formatted according to the RS-232-C protocol. During the transmission operation the controller inserts the necessary start, stop, and parity bits. On the other hand, the controller can also decode an incoming bit stream and place the data byte in the adapter's input port, where it can be read by the processor. During the reception operation the chip uses the start, stop, and parity bits to synchronize the transmission, to identify the data bits, and to check for errors.

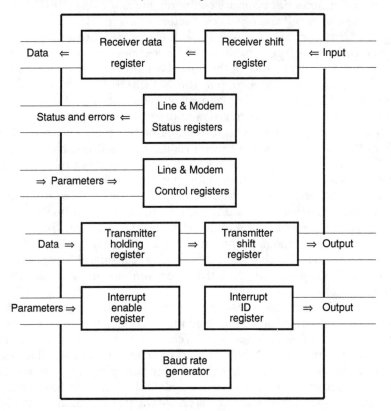

Registers and Functions of the Serial Communications Controller

Serial Communications — programming

[**PC hardware and architecture**] The asynchronous serial communications controllers used in the IBM microcomputers can be initialized, set up, and controlled in many different ways. However, the fundamental problem that must be solved by the communications software is frequently related to the synchronization of sender and receiver. Synchronization techniques can be based on polling, handshake, or interrupts.

Polling techniques consist of a time loop during which the receiving device checks the status of the data register. The polling frequency must be short enough to ensure that the transmitting device does not send a new character before the previous one has been removed by the receiver. Consequently, the slower the baud rate, the longer the polling frequency that satisfies this requirement. The processing tasks that the receiver must perform between polling cycles is another factor to be considered in polling. Failure to remove the received data results in an overrun error, as the old data byte in the receiver register is overwritten by a new one.

At sufficiently slow baud rates it is possible to design communications routines based on polling that will satisfactorily perform simple operations. However, programs that execute at the higher baud rates or that must perform more elaborate processing, require other means of synchronization. In addition, polling techniques need an *intelligent* receiver and are usually not possible in regard to *dumb* devices, such as printers and terminals.

Serial port implementations

[**PC hardware and architecture**] In the various models of the PC line the serial port is furnished in an optional adapter card known as the Asynchronous Communications Adapter. The PCjr comes equipped with a built-in serial port. In the PC AT the serial port is furnished as an optional adapter card, known as the Serial/Parallel Adapter, while in all models of the PS/2, and in most PC-compatible machines, one or more serial ports are furnished on the motherboard. The usual serial port hardware on the PC conforms to the RS-232-C standard.

SETcc

[**Assembler**] 80386 machine instruction. Mnemonic for SET on condition. This group of instructions was introduced with the 80386 CPU to allow conditionally setting a byte-size operand. Intel and others have documented that the purpose of this group of instructions is to aide in the implementation of boolean expressions in high-level languages such as Pascal and BASIC. The following table lists the available operation codes for SETcc:

OPCODE	DESCRIPTION
SETA	Set byte if above (CF=0 and ZF=0)
SETAE	Set byte if above or equal (CF=0)
SETS	Set byte if below (CF=1)
SETBE	Set byte if below or equal (CF=1 or (ZF=1)
SETC	Set if carry (CF=1)
SETE	Set byte if equal (ZF=1)
SETG	Set byte if greater (ZF=0 or SF=OF)
SETGE	Set byte if greater or equal (SF=OF)
SETL	Set byte if less (SF<>OF)
SETLE	Set byte if less or equal (ZF=1 and SF<>OF)
SETNA	Set byte if not above (CF=1)
SETNAE	Set byte if not above or equal (CF=1)
SETNB	Set byte if not below (CF=0)
SETNBE	Set byte if not below or equal (CF=0 and ZF=0)
SETNC	Set byte if not carry (CF=0)
SETNE	Set byte if not equal (ZF=0)
SETNG	Set byte if not greater(ZF=1 or SF<>OF)
SETNGE	Set if not greater or equal (SF<>OF)
SETNL	Set byte if not less (SF=OF)
SETNLE	Set byte if not less or equal (ZF=1 and SF<>OF)
SETNO	Set byte if not overflow (OF=0)
SETNP	Set byte if not parity (PF=0)
SETNS	Set byte if not sign (SF=0)
SETNZ	Set byte it not zero (LF=0)
SETO	Set byte if overflow (OF=1)
SETP	Set byte if parity(PF=1)
SETPE	Set byte if parity even (PF=1)
SETPO	Set byte if parity odd (PF=0)
SETS	Set byte if sign (SF=1)
SETZ	Set byte if zero (ZF=1)

SGDT/SIDT

[Assembler] 80286 machine instruction. Mnemonic for Store Global Descriptor Table register and Store Interrupt Descriptor Table register. Copies the contents of the descriptor table register referenced in the opcode to the six bytes of memory indicated by the operand. The LIMIT field of the register is assigned to the first word at the effective address. If the operand-size is 32 bits, then the next three bytes are assigned to the BASE field of the register and the fourth byte is written with zero. In this case the last byte is undefined. If the operand-size is sixteen bits, the next four bytes are assigned the 32-bit BASE field of the register. SGDT and SIDT are used solely in system software.

SGN (function)

[BASIC] [QuickBASIC] Returns the sign of x. The function format is:

```
v = SGN(x)
```

The value of the function SGN(x) is 1 (*x* positive), 0 (*x* is zero), or -1 (*x* is negative).

SHARED (statement)

[QuickBASIC] In a procedure specifies the variables that are shared with the main body of the program. The statement format is:

```
SHARED varl,uar2,...
```

The type of each variable is either determined by a type-declaration tag, a DEFtype statement, or an AS clause. If an AS clause is used, then it must declare the type of the variable in the main body of the program. Any change made to a shared variable by the procedure changes the variable of the same name in the main body, and vice versa. Declaring a variable as SHARED in a procedure allows the variable to be used by both the main body and the procedure without passing it as an argument, in other words, the variable is public. Arrays dimensioned in the main body of the program may be shared with procedures by listing their names followed by empty parentheses.

SHDRQQ

[MS-Pascal] Heading: (CONSTS A: REAL8): REAL8;
Arithmetic function that return the hyperbolic sine of A. A is of type REAL8. This function is from the MS-FORTRAN runtime library and must be declared EXTERN.

SHELL (statement)

[BASIC] [QuickBASIC] Loads an executes a child process or transfers control to the MS-DOS command interpreter. If c$ is a DOS command, then the statement SHELL c$ suspends execution of the BASIC program, executes the DOS command specified by c$, and then resumes execution of the BASIC program. The statement SHELL by itself suspends program execution and invokes the MS-DOS command mode. After a SHELL command execution can be resumed with the EXIT command.

Shift-left and Shift-right bitwise operators

[C] The shift left (<) and shift right (>) operators are used to transpose to the left or right all the bits in the operand. The operators require a second operand that specifies the number of bits to be shifted. For example, the following expression shifts left, by 2 bit positions, all the bits in the variable bit_pattern:
bit_pattern = bit_pattern < 2;

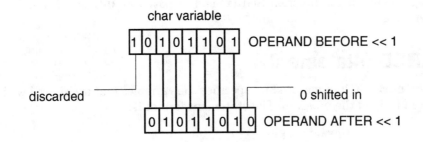

Left Shift of a Char Variable

SHLD

[Assembler] 80386 machine instruction. Mnemonic for Shift Left Double precision. Shifts the first operand as many bits as specified by the count operand. The second operand provides the bits to shift in from the left (starting with bit 31). The result is stored back in the destination. The source register remains unaltered. The count operand is provided by either an immediate byte or the contents of the CL register. These operands are taken MODULO 32 to provide a number between 0 and 31 by which to shift. Because the bits to shift are provided by the specified register, the operation is useful for performing multiprecision shifts. SF, ZF, and PF are set according to the result of the operation. CF holds the value of the last bit shifted out. OF and AF are undefined.

The double precision shift instructions (SHLD and SHRD) require three operands. The left-most operand is the destination of the shift. The right-most operand is the bit count to be used. The center operand is the source. Source and destination must be of the same size: for example, if the destination is a word-size register then the source has to be a word size register or memory variable. By the same token, if the destination is a doubleword register or memory location then the source must also be 32-bits wide. Either source or destination may be a memory operand, but at least one of them must be a machine register. The count operand can be an immediate byte or the value in the CL register. The limit of the shift count is 31 bits. See SHRD for sample code of a double-precision shift.

SHR

[Assembler] 8086 machine instruction. Mnemonic for Shift logical right. Shifts the bits in the destination operand (byte, word, or doubleword) to the right by the number of bits specified in the count operand. Zeros are shifted into the high-order bit. If the sign bit retains its original value, then OF is cleared.

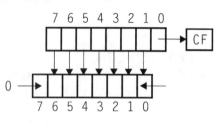

SHR - shift logical right

SHR

SHRD

[**Assembler**] 80386 machine instruction. Mnemonic for Shift Right Double precision. Shifts the first operand as many bits as specified by the count operand. The second operand provides the bits to shift in from the right. The result is stored back in the destination. The source register remains unaltered. The count operand is provided by either an immediate byte or the contents of the CL register. These operands are taken MODULO 32 to provide a number between 0 and 31 by which to shift. Because the bits to shift are provided by the specified register, the operation is useful for performing multiprecision shifts. SF, ZF, and PF are set according to the result of the operation. CF holds the value of the last bit shifted out. OF and AF are undefined.

The double precision shift instructions (SHLD and SHRD) require three operands. The left-most operand is the destination of the shift. The right-most operand is the bit count to be used. The center operand is the source. Source and destination must be of the same size, for example, if the destination is a word-size register then the source has to be a word size register or memory variable. By the same token, if the destination is a doubleword register or memory location then the source must also be 32-bits wide. Either source or destination may be a memory operand, but at least one of them must be a machine register. The count operand can be an immediate byte or the value in the CL register. The limit of the shift count is 31 bits. The following code fragment shows a double precision bit shift:

```
; Demonstration of a double procession shift
    XOR    AX,AX        ; Clear destination
    MOV    BX,1234H      ; Load BCD digits 1 2 3 4
    SHRD   AX,BX,8       ; Shift right BX digits 8 bits and
                         ; store result in AX
    ;At this point AX = 3400H. BX is unchanged
```

Note that the SHRD instruction has been used to shift four packed BCD digits from right end of the BX register into the AX register. The digit shift is accomplished by selecting a bit count that is a multiple of 4, since each digit takes up four bits. In this manner a bit count of eight has shifted 2 packed BCD digits. Note that the source register is unchanged by the double precision shift.

SHSRQQ

[MS-Pascal] Heading: (CONSTS A: REAL4): REAL4;
Arithmetic function that returns the hyperbolic sine of A. A is of type REAL4.
This function is from the MS-FORTRAN runtime library and must be declared
EXTERN.

Simple assignment operator

[C] The = sign is used in C as a *simple assignment operator*. The result of the
statement

```
a = a + 2;
```

is that the variable a is assigned the value that results from adding 2 to its own
value. Note that the term simple is related to the fact that C, in order to permit
more compact coding, also allows compound assignments.

Note that this use of the = sign in C is limited to assigning a value to a storage
location referenced by a variable or by an array element. It cannot be interpreted as an algebraic equation, because C is not capable of simplification
operations involving elements to the left of the = sign. For example, in elementary algebra we learn to solve an equation by isolating a variable on the
left-hand side of the = sign, as follows:

```
2x = y
x = y/2
```

However, in a C program, the line:

```
2 * x = y;
```

generates a compile-time error, because the language is not designed to perform
even this simple algebraic manipulation.

SIN

[MS-Pascal] Heading: (X: NUMERIC): REAL;
Arithmetic function that returns the sine of X in radians. Both X and the
returned value are of type REAL4. To force a particular precision, declare
SNSRQQ (CONSTS REAL4) or SNDRQQ (CONSTS REAL8) instead.

SIN (function)

[BASIC] [QuickBASIC] Calculates the sine function. The function format is:
v = SIN(x)

The angle x is in radians.

Sizeof operator

[C] Is used to determine the size of a data item. The result is offered in bytes. The operand can be a variable name or a data type. If reference is to a data type, the data type name must be enclosed in parentheses. The following statement displays the length in bytes of the variable x:

```
printf("the variable x is %u bytes," sizeof x);
```

while the following statement displays the storage allocation, in bytes, of an int data type:

```
printf("an int data type has %u bytes", sizeof (int));
```

The sizeof operator is particularly useful in porting C language programs to a new machine or compiler.

SIZEOF

[MS-Pascal] Heading: (VARIABLE): WORD;

```
        Heading: (VARIABLE, TAG1, TAGB,...TAGN): WORD;
```

An extend level intrinsic function that returns the size of a variable in bytes. Tag values or array upper bounds are set as in the NEW and DISPOSE functions. If the variable is a record with variants (first form) the maximum size possible is returned. If the variable is a super array, the second form must be used.

SLDT

[Assembler] 80286 machine instruction. Mnemonic for Store Local Descriptor Table register. Stores the contents of the Local Descriptor Table Register (LDTR) in the two-byte register or memory variable indicated in the operand. LDTR is a selector register that points to the Global Descriptor Table. This instruction is used solely in protected mode code.

SMSW

[Assembler] 80286 machine instruction. Mnemonic for Store Machine Status Word. Stores the machine status word, located in the CR0 register, in the 2-byte register or memory location indicated in the operand.

SMULOK

[MS-Pascal] Heading: (A,B: INTEGER; VAR C: INTEGER): BOOLEAN;
Library routine of the no-overflow arithmetic group. Sets C equal to A times B.
SMULOK is one of two functions that perform 16-bit signed arithmetic without
causing a runtime error on overflow. Normal arithmetic may cause a runtime
error, even if the arithmetic debugging switch is off. Each routine returns TRUE
if there is no overflow, and FALSE if there is. These routines can be useful for
extended-precision arithmetic, modulo 2^{16} arithmetic, or arithmetic based on
user input data.

SNDRQQ (CONSTS A: REAL8): REAL8;

(See SIN).

SNSRQB

[MS-Pascal] Heading: (CONSTS A: REAL4): REAL4;
(See SIN).

SORT

[MS-Pascal] Heading: (X): REAL
Arithmetic function that returns the square root of X, where X is of type REAL.
Declare SRSRQQ (CONSTS REAL4) or SRDRQQ (CONSTS REAL8) to force
a particular precision. An error occurs if X is less than 0.

Sound systems

[PC hardware and architecture] All IBM microcomputers are capable of generating sound through an on-board speaker. Although the individual hardware
components vary in different systems, IBM has maintained software compatibility in sound generation from the original Personal Computer to the PS/2 line.
The sound generation hardware can be combined to produce sound by two
different methods.

In *method number 1*, the CPU programs timer channel 2 to generate a square
wave, which is gated to the speaker through bits 0 and 1 of port 61H. The tone
is determined by the frequency to which timer channel 2 is set. In *method
number 2*, the CPU generates a wave by toggling bit 1 of port 61H on and off .
A software delay loop for the on and off cycles determines the frequency of the
waves, and consequently, the tone produced by the speaker. When method
number 2 is used, the speaker is disconnected from timer channel 2 by clearing
bit 0 in port 61H.

Method Number 1

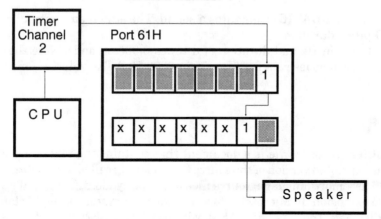

Method Number 2

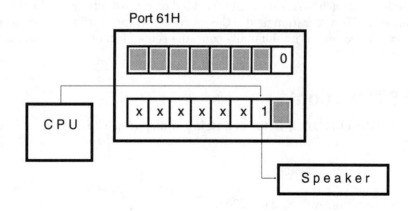

Sound Generation Diagrams

Although method number 2 of sound generation is more flexible than method number 1, it has some important drawbacks. In the first place, in method number 2, the processor takes a direct part in the sound generation process and cannot attend to other matters. In the second place, method number 2 uses the CPU as a timing device for generating the sound wave. Since different processors operate at different speeds, the frequency and duration of the tone change in different systems. Compensating for these differences requires elaborate programming. Finally, in method number 2, interrupts must be disabled while the sound is being produced. If they are not, the system timer interrupt creates considerable interference with the generated sound. Disabling interrupts can affect the system clock count and its dependent functions.

SOUND (statement)

[BASIC] [QuickBASIC] Generates a sound. The statement format is:
SOUND pitch, duration
where pitch is in Hz and duration of d times 0.055 seconds. Note that piano
keys have frequencies ranging from 55 to 8372 Hz.) The value of *f* must be at
least 37.

Source file

[Assembler] A *source file* is a document that contains the text of a computer
program. A printed version of the source file is usually called a *source file listing*.
In 80x86 assembly language, source files are usually identified by a distinctive
filename extension. In Microsoft's Macro Assembler system assembly language
source files have the extension .ASM, whereas Intel's ASM 86 system uses the
extension .SRC.

An assembly language source file consists of a series of individual program
lines called *statements*. A statement is divided into two fields, labeled operation
and comment. The operation field of the source statement performs a processing
function. The comment field usually contains some form of explanation of the
statement.

SPACE$ (function)

[BASIC] [QuickBASIC] Returns a string of n spaces. The statement format
is:

```
v$ = SPACES$(n)
```

where n is an integer from 0 to 32767.

spaghetti code

(See goto statement).

SPC (function)

[BASIC] [QuickBASIC] Skip *n* spaces in a PRINT statement. The statement
format is:

```
PRINT SPC(n)
```

The function SPC can be used in PRINT, LPRINT, and PRINT# statements,
For example, the statement:

```
PRINT a$; SPC(n); b$
```

skips *n* spaces between the displays of the two strings.

SQR

[MS-Pascal] Heading: (X: NUMERIC): NUMERIC;
Arithmetic function that returns the square of X, where X is of type REAL,
INTEGER, WORD, or INTEGER4.

SQR (function)

[BASIC] [QuickBASIC] Returns the square root. The function format is:

```
v = SQR(x)
```

where *x* is a non-negative number *x*.

SRDRQB

[MS-Pascal] Heading: (CONSTS A: REAL8): REAL8;
(See SORT).

SRSRQQ

[MS-Pascal] Heading: (CONSTS A: REAL4): REAL4;
(See SORT).

Stack

[PC hardware and architecture] [Assembler] The stack area is an auxiliary data structure located in a reserved portion of the system's memory. Its
mode of operation is said to be *last in, first out* (LIFO), that is, the last element
stored in the stack is the first one retrieved. A stack is used for the temporary
storage of memory addresses and data items. In assembler programming the
stack area is set up by the programmer but it is also used by the microprocessor
and by the system software. Not all programs have their own stack. The
following statements are used to create a 1K stack in an 80x86 assembler
program:

```
STACK    SEGMENT stack
         DB      1024 DUP ('?')   ; Default stack is 1K
STACK    ENDS
```

statement blocks in loops

[C] Roster symbols ({}) are used in C language to group statements into a structure usually called a statement block. Statement blocks can also be used in loop constructs so that more than one statement are included in the processing operation. For example, the following factorial calculation program prints a partial product after each loop iteration

```
main()
{
    unsigned int number, fac_pro, cur_fac;
    printf("FACTORIAL CALCULATION\nEnter positive integer: ");
    scanf("%u", &number);
    fac_pro = number;
      for (cur_fac = number - 1; cur_fac  1; cur_fac - -) {
          fac_pro = cur_fac * fac_pro;
          printf("partial product is: %u", fac_pro);
        }
    printf("Factorial is: %u", fac_pro);
}
```

Statement blocks

[C] A way for grouping statements so that they are treated as a unit by the compiler. This grouping is performed by means of brace ({}) symbols. The statements enclosed in braces are called a *compound statement* or a *statement block*.

The following code fragment shows the use of a statement block in an if statement so that more than one statement executes when the test condition evaluates to true:

```
if (typed_key == BIG_B || typed_key == LIT_B)  {
        printf("Keystroke was letter B");
        printf("\a\a\a");
        }
```

Here the brace symbols ({ and }) associate more than one statement with the *if* construct. Therefore, both printf statements execute if the conditional clause evaluates to true and both are skipped if it evaluates to false.

static

(See: variables — lifetime).

STATIC (statement)

[QuickBASIC] Specifies that variables are local (static). The statement format is:

```
STATICA var1, var2, ...
```

It is used at the beginning of the definition of a procedure. Memory for static variables is permanently set aside by BASIC. This allows static variables to retain their values between successive calls of the procedure. The type of each variable is either determined by a DEFtype statement, a type-declaration tag, or an AS clause. Static variables have no connection to variables of the same name outside the procedure. For this reason they may be named without concerns regarding possible name duplication. Arrays may be declared static by listing their names followed by empty parentheses in a STATIC statement, and then dimensioning them in a subsequent DIM statement.

STC

[Assembler] 8086 machine instruction. Mnemonic for SeT Carry flag. Sets the carry flag (CF).

STD

[Assembler] 8086 machine instruction. Mnemonic for SeT Direction flag. Sets the direction flag so that subsequent string operations decrement the index registers, SI, ESI, DI, or EDI.

STI

[Assembler] 8086 machine instruction. Mnemonic for SeT Interrupt-enable flag. Sets IF thus enabling processor recognition of maskable interrupt requests appearing on the INTR line. Note that a pending interrupt is not recognized until the instruction following STI has executed. STI does not affect any other flags.

STOP (statement)

[BASIC] [QuickBASIC] Suspends the execution of a program. By pressing F5 execution can be resumed beginning with the first statement after the STOP .

Storage devices — direct access

[**PC hardware and architecture**] Direct access storage devices can be compared to a turntable record player in which the user rapidly accesses any portion of a recording by positioning the tone arm on the desired point of the recorded surface. Sequential access storage devices, on the other hand, can be compared to a cassette recorder, in which the user must cross over previous recordings in order to access a specific part of the tape. The main advantage of a direct access device is the greater average access speed to individual data items.

Direct access storage devices can use magnetic or optical technologies. Although magnetic devices are still by far more popular, optical technology is no longer limited to compact disk (CD ROM) playback systems. Currently available are write-once–read-many-times (WORM) optical drives, which furnish an alternative mass storage medium, as well as erasable optical disks, which may evolve as an alternative to the diskette drive.

Storage devices — sequential access

[**historical**] [**PC hardware and architecture**] The original IBM PC and the PCjr have a connector for a conventional cassette recorder. The BIOS in these machines, as well as in the AT, provides the following services:

1. *BIOS service number 0, INT 15H*. Cassette motor ON.
2. *BIOS service number 1, INT 15H*. Cassette motor OFF.
3. *BIOS service number 2, INT 15H*. Read data blocks from cassette.
4. *BIOS service number 3, INT 15H*. Write data blocks to cassette.

However, the cassette interface never obtained commercial significance and was discontinued with the PC XT.

Another sequential access magnetic storage device sometimes used in IBM microcomputers is known as a *streaming tape drive*. The most common use of streaming tape drives is as a fast and relatively inexpensive means for backing up hard disk drives. At a typical rate of 5 Mbytes/min, a streaming tape drive can back up or restore a 60-Mbyte hard disk in approximately 12 min. The sequential access feature of this device severely limits its use in other forms of data storage.

Storage — hard disk

[**PC hardware and architecture**] The hard disk system is a direct access, magnetic storage device with nonremovable media. The hard disk device differs from a diskette drive in the following ways:

1. The hard disk drive uses several magnetically coated, metal disks as recording media, instead of the individual plastic media used by diskette

systems. The individual disks are usually called *platters* in hard disk systems.

2. The metal disks of a hard disk form part of the drive mechanism and normally are not removable from the drive.

3. The drive motor in a hard disk rotates constantly, while the diskette drive motor is turned on prior to every data access operation and off after the data have been read or written.

4. Most hard disk drives are formatted by the manufacturer.

The advantages and disadvantages of hard disks over diskette systems are a direct result of their different structures. One substantial advantage of diskette storage is that the recording media can be easily moved to other compatible devices and machines, which provides a convenient method of data exchange. On the other hand, the metal-based, nonremovable media used in hard disk drives allow a design in which the platters rotate constantly and at a higher rate than is possible in diskette mechanisms. This, in turn, makes possible more compact magnetic storage patterns, higher data transfer speeds, and faster access times.

The differences between hard disks and diskette systems can be summarized by stating that hard disk drives offer better performance than diskette systems at the price of lesser portability of the stored data. The typical performance improvement of hard disks over diskette drives is in the ratio of 10:1. An additional mechanical advantage of hard disk over diskette systems is that the recording heads of a hard disk drive do not touch the magnetic surface of the platters.

Hard disk drives are usually called *fixed disk drives* in IBM literature. The term *Winchester drive* refers to an external hard disk drive. The original version of the Winchester drive was equipped with 8-in-diameter platters. The word "Winchester" probably originated in the fact that the device had two 30-Mbyte platters, reminiscent of the Winchester 30-30 rifle.

Storage — hard disk hardware

[PC hardware and architecture] [historical] A hard disk drive was offered as an option for the first time with the introduction of the Personal Computer XT. But not all models of the IBM microcomputers that followed the XT can support the hard disk option. For example, the PC Portable, the PCjr, and the PC Convertible cannot normally be equipped with an internal hard disk drive. Nevertheless, third-party manufacturers have offered internal and external hard disk options for some of these models.

Non-IBM sources have proliferated in the hard disk market. Companies like Seagate (formerly Shugart), Computer Memories Incorporated (CMI), and Tandon Corporation have gained considerable popular favor in this field. Alternative options for the conventional hard disk drive are external drives, drives mounted on adapter cards, and platterless drives with battery-operated RAM memories.

Storage — hardware

[PC hardware and architecture] In the PC auxiliary storage devices are based, almost exclusively, on magnetic and optical technology, while main memory consists of read-only memory (ROM) and random-access memory (RAM) storage. Magnetic storage devices can be subclassified into two groups: devices that can access an individual data item directly (*direct access*) and those in which it is necessary to cross over other stored data in order to reach the desired item (*sequential access*). A typical example of a direct access device is a disk or diskette system, and an example of sequential storage is a magnetic tape storage system. Optical devices store information on concentric disk areas, somewhat similar to those of magnetic disks. For this reason they should be considered direct access devices. At the present stage of technological development, access time is usually greater in optical drives than in their magnetic counterparts.

Storage — secondary

[PC hardware and architecture] Because that part of main memory (primary storage) which can be accessed by the user is volatile, scarce, and costly, computer systems often require other means of data storage. The alternatives to storing data in the system's main memory are usually called *auxiliary* or *secondary storage*. Larger computer systems can trace auxiliary storage hardware to mechanical encoding and decoding devices, such as those employed in the punched card and punched tape systems used extensively in the 1950s and 1960s. By the advent of microcomputers in the late 1970s, magnetic storage had almost totally superseded mechanical storage, the reason being that magnetic data storage technology often provides greater convenience and faster access to the information.

It is conventionally accepted that auxiliary storage serves as an extension of the system's main memory and that programs and data residing in auxiliary storage devices must be moved into main memory for manipulation and execution. This notion is based on the idea that auxiliary storage serves as a long-term, nonvolatile information storage medium, but not as a substitute for main memory. However, as data storage devices have become more efficient, the conventional concepts of auxiliary storage have changed. Fast access technologies allow software to move portions of code and data to main memory as needed. These blocks, sometimes called *overlays*, can reside successively in the same area of main memory. By overlaying code and data, a program is able to reduce the main memory area required for its execution.

STOS/STOSB/STOSW/STOSD

[Assembler] 8086 machine instructions. Mnemonic for STOre String, Byte, Word, or Doubleword. Transfers the contents of the AL, AX, or EAX register to the memory byte or word given by the destination register relative to the ES segment. The destination register is DI for a size attribute of 16 bits or EDI for a size attribute of 32 bits. The destination operand must be addressable from the ES register. A segment override is not allowed.

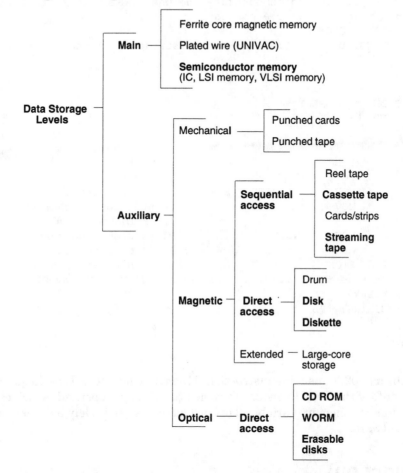

Note: Bold letters indicate storage technologies used in the IBM microcomputers.

Main and Auxiliary Data Storage

The address of the destination is determined by the contents of the destination register, not by the explicit operand of STOS. This operand is used only to validate ES segment addressability and to determine the data type. Code must load the correct index value into the destination register before executing STOS. After the transfer is made, DI is automatically updated. If the direction flag is 0 (CLD was executed), DI is incremented; if the direction flag is 1 (STD was executed), DI is decremented. DI is incremented or decremented by 1 if a byte is stored, by 2 if a word is stored, or by 4 if a doubleword is stored.

STOS can be preceded by the REP prefix for a block fill of CX or ECX bytes, words, or doublewords. This is a convenient method for initializing a string to a constant value, for example, to blank a text line or initialize a memory area.

```
; Sample code to demonstrate the use of STOS in initializing
; a memory area to a constant
DATA      SEGMENT
STRING1 DB      'This is a test string' ; 21-character string
.
.
.
CODE      SEGMENT
.
.
.
        PUSH    DS                ; DS to stack
        POP     ES                ; and to ES
        MOV     DI,OFFSET STRING1 ; Set-up pointer
        MOV     CX,10             ; Counter for 10 characters to
                                  ; blank in the target string
        MOV     AL,' '            ; Blank code (constant) to AL
        CLD                       ; Forward direction
REP     STOSB                     ; Store byte and repeat
; At this point first 10 characters of STRING1 have been
; blanked, thus:
; STRING1  DB  "            test string"
```

STR

[Assembler] 80286 machine instruction. Mnemonic for Store Task Register. The contents of the Task Register are copied to the 2-byte operand, which can be a register or a memory variable. This instruction is used solely by operating system software.

STR$ (function)

[BASIC] [QuickBASIC] Returns the string representation of a numeric variable. The statement format is:

```
v$ = STR$(x)
```

VAL is complementary to STR$.

String intrinsics

[MS-Pascal] [Turbo Pascal] String intrinsics provide procedures and functions that operate on strings. The following are available:

```
CONCAT          DELETE          INSERT          COPYLST
COPYSTR         POSITN          SCANEQ          SCANNE
```

Turbo Pascal string functions are:

```
Delete          Insert          Str             Val
Concat          Copy            Length          Pos
```

STRING$ (function)

[BASIC] [QuickBASIC] Returns a string of repeated characters. The statement formats are:

```
v$ = STRING$(n,m)
```

or

```
v$ = STRING$(n,x$)
```

If n is a whole number from 0 to 32767, then the value of STRING$(n,a$) is the string consisting of the first character of a$ repeated n times. If m is a whole number from 0 to 255, then the value of the function STRING$($n,m$) is the string consisting of the character with ASCII value m repeated n times.

structure

[C] Although C structures share some of the properties of functions and of arrays, they constitute a distinct programming concept. In fact, C structures contain lexical elements that have become characteristic of the language.

structure — accessing its elements

[C] Individual array elements are accessed by means of a subscript that encodes the relative position of each item in the array. In accessing a particular member of a structure both the type declaration and the variable declaration must taken into account. C provides a *membership operator* symbol, represented by a dot (.), which is also called the *dot operator* or the *member-of* operator. By means of the membership operator, a structure member (defined in the structure type declaration) and a variable name can be connected, as in the statement:

```
machinist_1.wage = 14.55;
```

which creates an addressable variable by relating the structure variable "machinist_1" with the structure element "wage."

structure — initializing variables

[C] Like conventional variables, structure variables can be initialized at the time they are declared. The initialization of a structure variable, which is reminiscent of the initialization of an array variable, can be seen in the following statement:

```
static struct employee_data machinist_1 =
    { "Joe Smith", "234-43-274", 14.55, 40.2, 5 };
```

Note that as is the case with arrays, a structure variable must be declared static if it is to be initialized inside a function. By the same token, function variables declared external do not require the static keyword. An alternative style for initializing function variables is to place each item on a separate line, as follows:

```
static struct employee_data machinist_2 =
    {
    "Jim Jones",
    "200-12-345",
    16.00,
    10.5,
    2
    };
```

structure — type declaration

[C] Like other elements of C, structures must be predeclared. This operation usually requires two distinct steps: the *structure type declaration* and the *structure variable declaration*.

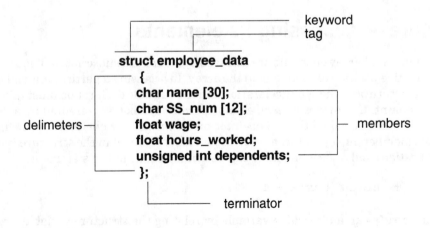

Elements of a C Structure Type Declaration

In the structure type declaration the programmer defines the structure name, sometimes called the *structure tag*, and lists one or more associated variables, called the *structure members*. These members that be of different data types. Note the following program elements in the structure type declaration:

1. It starts with the keyword *struct*.

2. The identifier following the struct keyword is the structure tag. The tag refers to the structure type.

3. The elements of the structure are enclosed in braces, in a similar manner as the body of a function.

4 The structure type declaration ends in a semicolon.

Since the structure is a pattern of data objects to be associated in storage, the structure tag is not a variable name, but a type name. In other words, a structure is a programmer-defined data type. The type declaration can be visualized as a description of a *template* to be used in grouping several data objects, frequently of different type. The type declaration, which is reminiscent of the function prototype, serves as a mere description of a structure and, therefore, assigns no physical storage space; it creates a structure template.

structure — variable declaration

[C] Once the structure type declaration has defined the tag and data format for a structure, the program can allocate storage space for one or more structures by means of the *structure variable declaration*. For example, once the type of structure for employee data has been declared, the program can assign storage space for five employees, as follows:

```
struct employee_data shop_foreman;
struct employee_data machinist_1;
struct employee_data machinist_2;
struct employee_data welder_1;
struct employee_data welder_2;
```

Hereafter the program will have reserved storage for five structures, of the type declared. In this particular example each structure requires the following memory space, including the string terminator codes:

MEMBER	BYTES
char name [30]	31
char SS_num [12]	13
float wage	4
float hours_worked	4
unsigned int dependents	2
	-------
total storage	54 bytes

Note that each structure variable declaration statement performs a similar operation as a variable declaration; that is, it reserves storage for a data item and assigns to it a particular identifier (name).

C language also allows declaring a structure variable at the same time as the type declaration; for example:

```
struct employee_data
          {
          char name [30];
          char SS_num [12];
          float wage;
          float hours_worked;
          unsigned int dependents;
          } welder_1, welder_2;
```

In this case the variables welder_1 and welder_2, of the structure tag employee_data, are declared at the time of the type declaration.

Structured programming

[historical] In the past twenty years there has been a movement that favors the creation of better-structured, easier to understand computer programs. This movement, usually called *structured programming*, proposes a tactical methodology for designing and coding computer programs. It is based on the following fundamental elements:

1. *Modular program construction*. The program is subdivided into segments that represent a complete logical unit.

2. *Use of control structures*. Processing is performed by means of elementary control structures in the programming language. These are classified as sequence, decisions, and iteration structures.

3. *Predeclaration of subprograms, constants, and other data*. Program elements should not be introduced unexpectedly but predeclared or listed separately so that they can be examined as a group.

4. Abundant program comments. The program should include embedded comments that serve to isolate and identify the modules and structures and to explain the program's logic. However, the programmer should avoid comments that are trivial, redundant, or in bad taste.

5. *Top-down program design*. The programmer's creative process follows a series of progressive steps, starting with a purely lexical description of the program's task, which is gradually refined into a final version coded in the chosen computer language.

6. *Scientific verification of program correctness*. In order to ascertain its reliability and correctness, the program should be tested and verified following established techniques of software engineering.

structures — passing to functions

[C] Because of the limitation that structures cannot be accessed as a unit, a C program cannot pass a structure to a function directly. Nevertheless, as in the case of bit fields, we can get around this limitation by storing the address of the structure in a pointer variable and passing this address to the function. However, keep in mind that the value of a structure variable (the structure member) can be passed as a parameter.

The declaration, initialization, and passing of structure pointers are quite similar to that of conventional pointer variables. Nevertheless, the handling of structure pointers requires special symbols and operators. In the first place, the pointer declaration must specify that the object of the pointer is a structure.

For example, the statement:

```
struct triangle *tr_ptr;
```

creates a pointer to a structure of the tag triangle. But the structure pointer must be initialized to a particular structure, not to a template. For example, if triangle is the tag for a structure template, the statement:

```
tr_ptr = &triangle;
```

is illegal. However, the statement:

```
struct triangle tr1;
```

creates a structure variable named tr1, according to the tag triangle. Thereafter we can initialize a pointer to the structure tr1 as follows:

```
tr_ptr = &tr1;
```

Structures, like other variables, can be declared external in order to make them visible to all functions in a program. Local structures (declared inside a function) can be passed to other functions by means of structure pointers, which then can use the pointer-member operator to gain access to the data stored in the structure.

(See also: pointer-member operator).

SUB

[Assembler] 8086 machine instruction. Mnemonic for SUBtract. Subtract the source from the destination operand and the result replaces the destination. The operands may be bytes, words, or doublewords. When an immediate byte value is subtracted from a word operand the immediate value is first sign-extended to the size of the destination. Both operands may be signed or unsigned binary digits. AF, CF, OF, PF, and ZF are updated.

```
; Sample encodings:
        SUB     BX,CX           ; BX minus CX
        SUB     ECX,1234        ; ECX minus immediate value
        SUB     MEM_WORD,CL     ; Memory word minus register
        SUB     [BP+2],CL       ; Register plus offset, minus
                                ; register
```

SUB/END SUB (statement)

[QuickBASIC] A subprogram is a multistatement block beginning with a statement of the form:

```
SUB SubProgramName(parlist)
```

followed on subsequent lines by one or more statements for carrying out the task of the subprogram, and ending with the statement END SUB. Parlist is a list of variables through which values will be passed to the subprogram whenever it is called.

Subroutines

[QuickBASIC] A subroutine is a sequence of statements beginning with a label and ending with a RETURN statement. A subroutine is meant to be branched to by a GOSUB statement and is usually placed so that it cannot be entered inadvertently. For example, subroutines might appear after an END statement.

SUCC

[MS-Pascal] Heading: (X : ORDINAL): ORDINAL;
Data conversion function that determines the successor to X. The ORD of the returned result is equal to ORD (X) + 1. An error occurs if the successor is out of range or overflow occurs. These errors are detected if appropriate debug switches are on.

SuperVGA

[historical] [video systems] SuperVGA boards are characterized by graphics features that exceed the VGA standard in definition, color range, or both. A typical SuperVGA graphics board is capable of executing, not only the standard VGA modes, but also other modes that provide higher definition or greater color range than VGA. These are usually called the SuperVGA Enhanced Modes.

The proliferation of SuperVGA hardware was the cause of many compatibility problems, due to the fact that the enhanced features of the SuperVGA cards were not originally standardized. For this reason, the SuperVGA enhancements in the card produced by one manufacturer were often incompatible with the enhancements in a card made by another company. In 1989, several manufacturers of SuperVGA boards formed the Video Electronics Standards Association (VESA) in an attempt to solve this lack of standardization. The VESA SuperVGA standard defines several enhanced video modes and implements a BIOS extension designed to provide a few fundamental video services in a compatible fashion.

SWAP (statement)

[BASIC] [QuickBASIC] Exchanges the values of two variables. The statement format is:

```
SWAP var1, var2
```

where var1 and var 2 are two variables of the same type.

Switch construct

[C] Programs often contain routines that select between processing options according to the value of an integer variable. For example, the user is presented with a labeled menu and asked to type the number or letter code that corresponds to the desired alternative, as in the following example:

```
*********************************
|      GEOMETRICAL CALCULATIONS    |
|               PROGRAM            |
*********************************
| Figure:                          |
|              1. circle           |
|              2. parallelogram    |
|              3. triangle         |
|              4. ellipse          |
*********************************
| Type number desired:             |
*********************************
```

In this case the program can input the user's keystroke into an integer variable and then use several nested *if* statements to test the value of the variable and to direct execution to the corresponding processing option. On the other hand, the C *switch* statement provides a simpler construct that allows multiple decisions based on an integer value.

The *switch* construct consists of the following elements:

1. The *switch* keyword

2. A controlling expression, of integral type, enclosed in parentheses (usually a variable name)

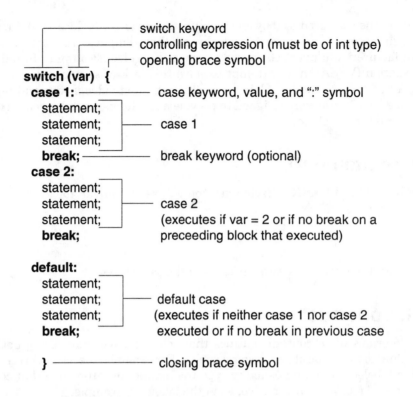

Structure of the C switch Construct

3. One or more *case* statements followed by an integer or character constant (or an expressions that evaluates to a constant). These statements are terminated by a colon symbol

4. An optional *break* statement at the end of each case block that allow exiting the *switch* structure immediately

5. An optional *default* statement that executes if none of the preceding case statements has executed. The default statement is also terminated with a colon symbol

The *controlling expression* in the *switch* construct, enclosed in parentheses, must evaluate to an int or shorter data type. Although the control expression is typically a variable name, it is possible to have a control expression that includes other int or char variables or that performs integer arithmetic. For example, if ctrl and val_two are two unsigned integer variables, the following is a legal and valid control expression:

```
switch ((ctrl - 1)/val_two)
```

The *case* keyword serves to create a label-like statement to which execution is directed. It is followed by an integer or character constant or an expression that evaluates to an integer or character constant. If the control statement is a char type, then the case constant is enclosed in single quotes, as in the following code fragment:

```
main()
{
        char sw_var1;
        switch (sw_var1)  {
              case 'A':
                      printf("\nA";
                      break;
              case 'B':
                      printf("\nB");
                      break;

    .
    .
    .

        }
}
```

If the control statement evaluates to an int or unsigned int type, then the case constant does not require quotes, as in the following code fragment:

```
main()
{
        int sw_var2;
        switch (sw_var2)  {
              case 1:
                      printf("\n1";
                      break;
              case 2:
                      printf("\n2");
                      break;

    .
    .
    .

        }
}
```

The *break* keyword is optional in the *switch* construct, but if it is not present at the end of a case block, then the following *case* or *default* blocks also execute until a break keyword or the end of the construct is encountered. In any case, if a break keyword is encountered, execution is immediately directed to the end of the *switch* construct. A *break* statement is not required on the last block (*case* or *default*) of a *switch* construct, but it is usually typed to improve readability.

All execution blocks within a switch construct must be enclosed in braces, but the *case* and the *default* keywords automatically block the statements that follow them. For this reason braces are not necessary to indicate the main execution block within a case or default block.

System level intrinsics

[MS-Pascal] Provides several intrinsic procedures and functions which are available at the system level:

```
FILLC         MOVESL        FILLSC        MOVESR
MOVEL         RETYPE        MOVER
```

The MOVE and FILL procedures perform low-level operations on byte strings. RETYPE arbitrarily changes the type of an expression.

SYSTEM (command)

[BASIC] [QuickBASIC] Exits BASIC and returns to MS-DOS. The command format is:

```
SYSTEM
```

In QuickBASIC SYSTEM closes all open files and returns control to the QuickBASIC environment.

T

TAB (function)

[BASIC] [QuickBASIC] Tabulates to the position n. The function format is:

```
PRINT TAB(n)
```

The function TAB(n) is used in PRINT, LPRINT, and PRINT# statements to move the cursor to the current position plus n spaces.

TAN (function)

[BASIC] [QuickBASIC] Returns the trigonometric tangent of x. The function format is:

```
v = TAN(x)
```

where x must be an angle in radians for which the tangent is defined.

TEST

[Assembler] 8086 machine instruction. Mnemonic for TEST (logical compare). Updates the flags as if a logical AND of the operands had been performed. The operand size can be bytes or words. If a TEST instruction is followed by JNZ (jump if not zero) the jump is taken if there are corresponding 1-bits in both operands.

```
; Sample code for determining if the high-order bit of AL
; is set using TEST
      TEST   AL,10000000B ; Test operand against mask
      JNZ    HIGH_BIT_SET ; Go if true
; Execution drops if high-order bit of AL is clear
      .
      .
      .
; Code at the destination label handles processing if test is
```

```
                ; true, that is, if high-order bit of AL is set
                HIGH_BIT_SET:
                    .
                    .
```

Texas Instruments Graphics Architecture

(See TIGA).

THDRQQ

[MS-Pascal] Heading: (CONSTS A: REAL8): REAL8;
Arithmetic function that returns the hyperbolic tangent of A. Both A and the
return value are of type REAL8. These functions are from the MS-FORTRAN
runtime library and must be declared EXTERN.

THSRQQ

[MS-Pascal] Heading: (CONSTS A : REAL4) : REAL4;
Arithmetic function that returns the hyperbolic tangent of A. Both A and the
return value are of type REAL4. These functions are from the MS-FORTRAN
runtime library and must be declared EXTERN.

TICS

[MS-Pascal] Heading: :WORD;
A library routine of the clock function group. TICS returns the value of an
operating system timing location. The result is in a time interval, such as
hundredths of a second, depending on operating system and on hardware.

TIGA video system

[historical] [video systems] A line of graphics coprocessor chips and associated software developed by Texas Instruments. The TI hardware is designated
as the TMS340 line of graphics coprocessors and the support software is named
the Texas Instruments Graphics Architecture, or TIGA. TMS340/TIGA-based
systems are usually found in high-end video adapters.

TIME

[MS-Pascal] Heading: (VAR S : STRING);
Library routine of the clock function group. Assigns the current time to its
STRING (or LSTRING) variable. If the parameter is an LSTRING, the program

must set the length before calling the TIME procedure. The format depends on the operating system.

(See also: DATE).

TIME$ (variable and statement)

[BASIC] [QuickBASIC] Sets or retrieves the system time. The format is:

```
variable     v$ = TIME$
statement    TIME$ = x$
```

The value of the function TIME$ is expressed as a string of the form hh:mm:ss. Hours range from 0 to 23, as in military time. The variable form is used to retrieve the current time. The statement form sets the computer's internal clock to the corresponding time.

TIMER (function)

[BASIC] [QuickBASIC] Returns a single-precision number representing the number of seconds elapsed since midnight in the system clock or since a reset. The function format is:

```
v = TIMER
```

Timers — programmable

[PC hardware and architecture] Many computer operations require some form of synchronization. All IBM microcomputers contain a dedicated IC (or equivalent circuits in a larger electronic device) that provides various timing services. For instance, the PC, the PC XT, the PCjr, and the PS/2 Model 25 and Model 30 use the Intel 8253 programmable interval timer, while many AT-class machines employs a similar component designated as the Intel 8254-2. The Micro Channel computers of the PS/2 line are equipped with proprietary IBM circuits. However, these circuits are software-compatible with the 8253 and 8254-2 chips.

TMS340

[historical] [video systems] TMS340 is a line of general-purpose chips optimized for graphics processing in a 32-bit environment. The technology was developed by Texas Instruments and has its predecessors in the TI's 320 line of digital signal processing chips. The first member of the TMS340 line, designated the TMS34010, was introduced in 1986 as a Graphics System Processor. TMS34020 was unveiled in 1990 as an object-code compatible upgrade to the TMS34010.

In order to simplify the programming task and to standardize communications between applications and TMS340 hardware, Texas Instruments developed a software interface called the Texas Instruments Graphics Architecture, or TIGA. The first version of the TIGA-340 interface, designated version 1.1, was released in June 1989. To the programmer the TIGA appears as a library of graphics primitives for the TMS340 graphics processors. Since each routine in the TIGA is rigorously defined in the standard, a program developed using the TIGA interface runs satisfactorily in any TIGA-compatible board.

At the present time Texas instruments is no longer encouraging the development of new products based on the TMS340 chips.

TNDRQQ

[MS-Pascal] Heading: (CONSTS A : REAL8) : REAL8;
Arithmetic functions that return the tangent of A. Both A and the return value are of type REAL8. This function is from the MS-FORTRAN runtime library and must be declared EXTERN.

TNSRQB

[MS-Pascal] Heading: (CONSTS A: REAL4) : REAL4;
Arithmetic functions that return the tangent of A. Both A and the return value are of type REAL4. This function is from the MS-FORTRAN runtime library and must be declared EXTERN.

Transient program area (TPA)

[PC hardware and architecture] DOS memory can be divided into an operating-system area and a transient program area, or TPA. The portion located in lower memory is always the operating-system part, but exact boundaries depend on the DOS version, on the installed device drivers, on memory-resident utilities, on the number of disk buffers reserved, and on other factors. (See memory management DOS).

At load time, the transient program area is dynamically allocated to applications by DOS. There are also DOS services to request memory, to release allocated memory, and to modify existing allocations. Programs should make use of these services to manage their own execution space and should not make use of memory resources without notifying DOS.

TRON and TROFF (commands)

[BASIC] [QuickBASIC] Turn the debug trace function on and off. The statement formats are:

```
TRON
```

```
TROFF
```

These statements, which are abbreviations of "trace on" and "trace off," are used to debug programs. The statement TRON causes the program to execute slower than normal and for each statement to be highlighted on the screen as it executes. TROFF terminates this tracing.

TRUNC

[MS-Pascal] Heading: (X: REAL) : INTEGER;
Arithmetic function that truncates X toward zero. X can be of type REAL4 or REAL8. The return value is of type INTEGER.
Examples:

```
TRUNC (2.4) is 2
TRUNC (-3.7) is -3
```

An error occurs if ABS (X - 1.0) >= MAXINT.

TRUNC4

[MS-Pascal] Heading: (X: REAL) : INTEGER4;
Arithmetic function that truncates real X towards zero. X is of type REAL4 or REAL8, and the return value is of type INTEGER4.
Examples:

```
TRUNC4 (1.6) is 1
TRUNC4 (-1.6) is -1
```

An error occurs if ABS (X - 1.0) >= MAXINT4.

U

UADDOK

[MS-Pascal] Heading: (A, B: WORD; VAR C: WORD): BOOLEAN;
Library routine of the no-overflow arithmetic group. Sets C equal to A plus B. One of two functions that do 16-bit unsigned arithmetic without causing a runtime error or overflow. Normal arithmetic may cause a runtime error even if the arithmetic debugging switch is off. The following is the binary carry resulting from this addition of A and B:

```
WRD (NOT UADDOK (A, B, C))
```

Both UADDOK and UMULOK return TRUE if there is no overflow and FALSE if there is. These routines are useful for extended-precision arithmetic, or modulo 2^{16} arithmetic, or arithmetic based on user input data.

UART

(See serial communications controllers).

UBOUND (function)

[QuickBASIC] For a one-dimensional array UBOUND Returns the largest subscript value that may be used. The value of the function:

```
UBOUND(arrayName, n)
```

is the largest value that may be used for the nth subscript of the array.

UCASE$ (function)

[QuickBASIC] Returns a string in which all characters are changed to uppercase. The function format is:

```
v$ = UCASE$(a$)
```

UMULOK

[MS-Pascal] Heading: (A, B: WORD; VAR C: WORD): BOOLEAN;

Library routine of the no-overflow arithmetic group. Sets C equal to A times B. One of two functions that do 16-bit unsigned arithmetic without causing a runtime error on overflow. Normal arithmetic may cause a runtime error even if the arithmetic debugging switch is off. Each routine returns TRUE if there is no overflow and FALSE if there is. These routines are useful for extended-precision arithmetic, or module 2^{16} arithmetic, or arithmetic based on user input data.

union

[C] A *union* is a variation on the concept of structure in which the member variables can hold different data types at different times. The union type declaration consists of a list of data types matched with the variable names in a similar manner as in the structure type declaration. The union variable declaration is similar to a structure variable declaration except that the structure declaration causes the compiler to reserve storage for all the members listed, whereas in the union declaration the compiler reserves space for the largest member in the aggregate. In other words, the members of a structure variable have their own memory space, while the members of a union variable share a common memory space. For this reason, in relation to unions, the programmer must keep track of the current occupant of the common memory space. The following program demonstrates the use of a union to hold three different data items of type double, float, and int:

```
#include <stdio.h>
    union vari_data
            {
            double num_type1;
            float num_type2;
            int num_type3;
            };
main()
{
union vari_data first_set;   /* Declare the union variable   */
                             /* named first_set              */
first_set.num_type3 = 12;    /* Store an integer in union    */
printf("\nCurrent occupant is integer %d", first_set.num_type3);
first_set.num_type2 = 22.44; /* Store a float in union       */
printf("\nCurrent occupant is float %f", first_set.num_type2);
first_set.num_type1 = 0.023; /* Store a double in union      */
printf("\nCurrent occupant is float %E", first_set.num_type1);
return(0);
}
```

UNLOCK

[MS-Pascal] Heading: (VARS SEMAPHORE : WORD) ;

Library routine of the semaphore procedure. UNLOCK sets the available semaphore. As a binary semaphore, there are only two states. UNLOCK can be called any number of times and can be used to initialize the semaphore. (See also: LOCKED).

UNPACK

[MS-Pascal] Heading: (CONSTS Z: PACKED;VARS A: UNPACKED; I: IN-DEX) ;

Data conversion procedure that moves elements from a packed array to an unpacked array. If A is an ARRAY [M..N] OF T, and Z is a PACKED ARRAY [U..V] OF T then the call is the same as:

```
FOR J := U TO V DO A [J - U + I] := Z [J]
```

In both PACK and UNPACK, the parameter I is the initial index within A. The bounds of the arrays and the value of I must be reasonable, that is, the number of components in the unpacked array A from I to M must be at least as great as the number of components in the packed array Z. The range checking switch controls checking of the bounds.
(See also: PACK).

UPPER

[MS-Pascal] Heading: (EXPRESSION) : VALUE;

Extend level intrinsic function. Takes a single parameter of one of the following types: array, set, enumerated, or subrange, and returns one of the following:

1. The upper bound of an array
2. The last allowable element of a set
3. The last value of an enumerated type
4. The upper bound of a subrange

The value returned by UPPER is always a constant, unless the expression is of a super array type. In this case, the actual upper bound of the super array type is returned. Note that the type and not the value of the expression is used for UPPER.
(See also: LOWER).

V

VAL (function)

[BASIC] [QuickBASIC] Returns the numerical value of a string containing a numeric expression. The function format is:

```
v = VAL(x$)
```

where x$ is a number in string form. If the leading characters of the string x$ corresponds to a number, then VAL(x$) is the number represented by these characters. For any number n:

```
VAL(STR$(n))
```

is n.

Variable

[C] In computer terminology a variable is a memory structure for holding program data. The program line

```
float radius = 0;
```

is a *variable declaration*. In C all variables must meet the following requirements:

1. A variable is assigned a name, which must meet the requirements for identifiers.

2. A variable must be of a certain *variable type* which defines the category of stored information. For example, a C variable can be an integer, a character, a floating-point number, or a character string, among others.

3. A variable must be declared before it is used in a C program. The variable declaration must include the variable name and the assigned data type. The declaration can optionally initialize the variable to a value.

Variable declaration

[C] In C the predeclaration of constants, although strongly recommended, is not strictly required by the language. However, every variable used by a C program must be predeclared by separately specifying its name and type. This declaration serves a double purpose:

1. To inform the compiler of a variable name and type so that it reserves a memory space in which to store it

2. To provide a central area so the variables used by the program can be examined by the programmer

A variable declaration must include the variable name and type, for example:

```
int num1;
```

C allows the declaration of several variables of the same type by separating the variable names with commas; for example:

```
int num2, num3, num4;
```

A variable declaration can also include its initialization. In this case the value assigned to the variable is preceded by the equal sign; for example:

```
float radius = 1.22;
```

C Language Data Types

NAME	OTHER NAME	BYTES	VALUE RANGE
CHARACTER TYPES:			
char	signed char	1	127 to -128
unsigned char		1	0 to 255
INTEGER TYPES:			
int	signed int	2	32,767 to -32,768
unsigned	unsigned int	2	0 to 65,535
short	short int	4	32,767 to -32,768
long	long int	8	2,147,483,647 to -2,147,483,648
FLOATING-POINT TYPES:			
float		4	$8.43*10^{-37}$ to $3.37*10^{38}$
double		8	$4.19*10^{-307}$ to $1.67*10^{308}$

Variable name

(See assembler directive).

Variable — name, contents, and address

[C] We can visualize a C variable as a labeled container in the computer's memory space. The label associated with the variable is the identifier that was assigned as a name at the time of variable declaration. For example, in the variable declaration

```
float radius = 0;
```

the label for the variable is "radius."

The content of a variable is the string or numeric value that it currently holds. After the initialization line of the previous paragraph the variable named radius will have a content (or value) of zero. While a program is executing, the contents of variables can change due to user input or as the result of processing operations. For example, if the variable num1 has a content of 4, the statement:

```
num1 = num1 * 2;
```

changes its contents to 8.

The third element of a C variable is its *address*, which is a number representing its location in the computer's *memory space*. While the programmer assigns the variable its name and can initialize and change its contents, the *address of the variable* is determined by C and system software (compiler, linker, and loader).

Variables

[MS-Pascal] The initial values of variables are not defined. The VALUE section, which should follow the VAR section, is an MS-Pascal extension that lets you explicitly initialize program, module, implementation, STATIC, and PUBLIC variables. If the initialization switch ($initck) is on, all INTEGER, INTEGER subrange, REAL, and pointer variables are set to an uninitialized value. File variables are always initialized, regardless of the setting of the initialization switch.

Variables and constants

[C] Using mathematical terminology we often classify computer data as *variables* and *constants*. In C variables are assigned names and stored in a memory structure determined by the variable type. The contents of a variable can be changed anywhere in the program. For this reason a variable can be visualized as a labeled container, defined by the programmer, for storing a data object. Constants, on the other hand, represent values that do not change in the course of program execution. Constants are often created by means of the #define directive.

In C it is also possible to enter constant values directly. For example, it is possible to code:

```
area = (radius * radius) * 3.1415927;
```

However, except for display message strings and other simple data items, the use of undefined constants is generally considered a bad programming practice because *hard coded constants,* introduced unexpectedly, decrease the readability of the code and violate the principles of structured programming.

Variables — automatic

[C] Automatic variables are declared inside a function body (after the opening brace). The name automatic is related to the fact that these variables automatically disappear when the function concludes its execution. For this reason the scope of an automatic variable is limited to the function in which it is declared, as in the following example:

```
main()
{
    .
    .
    .
{
user_1()
{
    int alpha;
    .
    .
    .
}
```

In this case the variable alpha is visible to the user_1() function but not the main() function.

Variables — lifetime

[C] A variable's lifetime refers to the time span of program execution over which the variable retains its value. The lifetime of automatic variables is the execution time of the function that contains it. In other words, automatic variables are created when the function in which they are located executes and disappear when the function concludes. External variables, on the other hand, have a lifetime that extends through the course of program execution. An external variable retains its value at all times.

The *static* keyword is used in C to modify the scope and lifetime of variables. For instance, a static variable declared inside a function has the same scope as an automatic variable and the same lifetime as an external variable. For example:

```
main()
{
    .
    .
{
user_1()
{
    static int alpha;
    .
    .
}
```

In this case the *internal static* variable alpha is visible only inside the function user_1(), but the value of alpha is preserved after the function concludes. In this manner, when execution returns to the user_1() function alpha still holds its previous value.

External static variables are useful in programs that contain more than one source module, because external static variables are visible only to the program module in which they are declared, while nonstatic external variables are visible to any other program module.

Variables — scope

[C] At the time it is declared, a variable assumes certain attributes. The two principal ones are called the variable's *scope* and *lifetime*. The term scope refers to the part of a program over which the variable is recognized. Regarding scope C variables are classified as *external* and *automatic*. In other programming languages the term *global* is used to represent external variables and the term *local* to represent automatic variables.

External variables are declared outside all functions, often at the beginning of the program. The scope (also called the *visibility*) of an external variable starts at the point it is declared and extends to the end of the program. For this reason if an external variable is declared between two functions it will be visible to the second function, but not to the first one, as in this example:

```
main()
{
    .
    .
{
int alpha;
user_1()
{
    .
    .
}
```

In this case the variable alpha is visible and can be referenced by the user_1() function but not by main().

VARPTR (function)

[BASIC] [QuickBASIC] Returns the offset of a variable in the current segment. The function format is:

```
v = VARPTR(variable)
```

where the value of var (if it is a numeric or a fixed-length string) or of the descriptor of var (if it is a variable-length string or an array variable).

VARPTR$ (function)

[BASIC] [QuickBASIC] Returns a 5-character string that specifies the form and location of a variable. The function format is:

```
v$ = VARPTR$(variable)
```

The first character indicates the variable type, as follows:

```
2 = integer
3 = string
4 = single precision
8 = double precision
```

This function is often used in conjunction with DRAW and PLAY.

VARSEG (function)

[QuickBASIC] Returns the segment address of a variable.

VECTIN

[MS-Pascal] Heading: (V : WORD ; PROCEDURE I [INTERRUPT]);
Library procedure of the interrupt handling group. One of three procedures for processing interrupts. VECTIN sets an interrupt vector, so that interrupts of type V are connected to procedure I. (ENABIN enables interrupts and DISBIN disables interrupts.) The effect of these procedures and the meaning of V varies with the target machine.

VERR/VERW

[Assembler] 80286 machine instruction. Mnemonic for VErify segment for Reading or Writing. VERR and VERW expect the 2-byte register or memory operand to contain the value of a selector. The instructions determine whether the segment denoted by the selector is reachable from the current privilege level; also whether it is readable or writable. If the segment is determined to be accessible, the zero flag is set. Otherwise it is clear. For the instructions to set ZF the following conditions must be met:

1. The selector must denote a descriptor within the bounds of the table (GDT or LDT). The selector must be "defined."
2. The selector must denote the descriptor of a code or data segment.
3. If the instruction is VERR, the segment must be readable. If the instruction is VERW, the segment must be a writable data segment.
4. If the code segment is readable and conforming, the descriptor privilege level (DPL) can be any value for VERR. Otherwise, the DPL must be greater than or equal to (have less or the same privilege as) both the current privilege level and the selector's RPL.

The validation performed is the same as if the segment were loaded into DS or ES and the indicated access (read or write) were performed. The zero flag receives the result of the validation. The selector's value cannot result in a protection exception. This enables the software to anticipate possible segment access problems.

The only faults that can occur are those generated by illegally addressing the memory operand which contains the selector. The selector is not loaded into any segment register, and no faults attributable to the selector operand are generated.

VESA

(See SuperVGA).

VGA

(See also: video graphics array).

VGA architecture

[**video systems**] The VGA system is divided into three separate components: the VGA chip, video memory, and a digital-to-analog converter (DAC).

VGA attribute byte

[**video systems**] In the alphanumeric modes 0, 1, 2, 3, and 7 the VGA video buffer is structured to hold character codes and attribute bytes. The VGA standard allows redefining two of the attribute bits in the color alphanumeric modes: bit 7 can be redefined to control the background intensity, and bit 3 can be redefined to perform a character-set select operation.

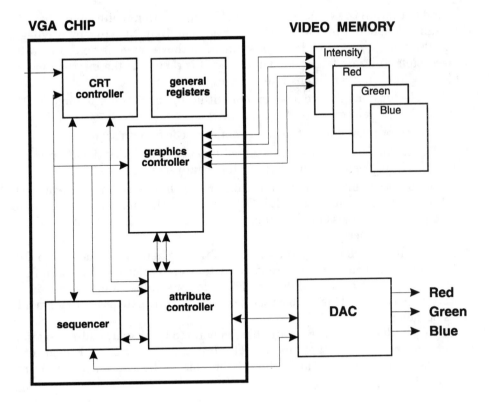

VGA Component Diagram

Bit 3 of the attribute byte controls the foreground intensity in both monochrome and color systems. Alternatively this bit can be used to select one of the character sets provided in the BIOS. The default function of bit 7 is the blink function. However, bit 3 can be reprogrammed to control the foreground intensity. The programmer can toggle the functions assigned to bits 3 and 7 of the attribute byte by means of BIOS service calls or by programming the VGA registers directly.

VGA attribute controller

[video systems] The Attribute Controller receives color data from the Graphics Controller and formats it for the video display hardware. Input to the Attribute Controller is in the form of attribute data in the alphanumeric modes and in the form of serialized bit plane data in the graphics modes. The data is converted into 8-bit digital color output to the DAC. Blinking, underlining, and cursor display logic are also controlled by this register. In VGA systems the output of the Attribute Controller goes directly to the video DAC and the CRT.

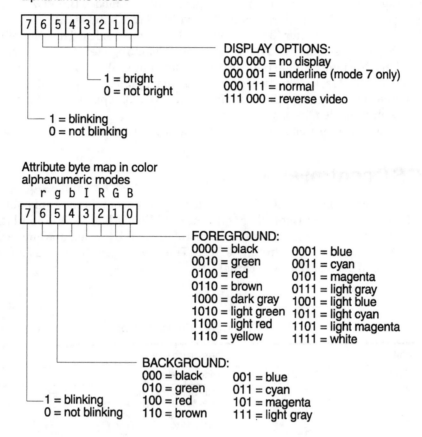

Bitmaps of VGA Attribute Byte

VGA Attribute Controller Registers

PORT	OFFSET	DESCRIPTION
3C0H		Attribute Address and Palette Address register
3C1H		Read operations
3C0H	0–15	Palette registers
	16	Attribute Mode Control
	17	Screen Border Color Control (overscan color)
	18	Color Plane Enable
	19	Horizontal Pixel Panning
	20	Color Select

VGA border color

[video systems] In some alphanumeric and graphics modes the VGA display area is surrounded by a colored band. The width of this band is the same as the width of a single character (8 pixels) in the 80-column modes. The color of this border area is determined by the Overscan Color register of the Attribute Controller. Normally the screen border is not noticeable, since the default border color is black. The border color is not available in the 40-column alphanumeric modes or in the graphics modes with 320 pixel rows, except for VGA graphics mode number 19.

(See also: VGA programming -- the attribute controller).

VGA CRT controller

[video systems] The VGA CRT Controller register group is the equivalent of the Motorola 6845 CRT Controller chip of the PC line. When VGA is emulating the MDA, the port address of the CRT Controller is 3B4H; when it is emulating the CGA, then the port address is 3D4H. These ports are the same as those used by the MDA and the CGA cards.

VGA CRT Controller Registers

PORT	OFFSET	DESCRIPTION
03x4H		Address register
03x5H	0	Total horizontal characters minus 2 (EGA)
		Total horizontal characters minus 5 (VGA)
	1	Horizontal display end characters minus 1
	2	Start horizontal blanking
	3	End horizontal blanking
	4	Start horizontal retrace pulse
	5	End horizontal retrace pulse
	6	Total vertical scan lines
	7	CRTC overflow
	8	Preset row scan
	9	Maximum scan line
	10	Scan line for cursor start
	11	Scan line for cursor end
	12	Video buffer start address, high byte
	13	Video buffer start address, low byte
	14	Cursor location, high byte
	15	Cursor location, low byte
	16	Vertical retrace start
	17	Vertical retrace end
	18	Last scan line of vertical display
	19	Additional word offset to next logical line
	20	Scan line for underline character
	21	Scan line to start vertical blanking
	22	Scan line to end vertical blanking
	23	CRTC mode control
	24	Line compare register

Notes: 3x4H/3x5H = 3B4H/3B5H when emulating the MDA
3x4H/3x5H = 3D4H/3D5H when emulating the CGA

Most registers in the CRT Controller are modified only during mode changes. Since this operation is frequently performed by means of a BIOS service, most programs do not access the CRT Controller registers directly. One exception is in the code required to set VGA mode X. Since mode X is not standard, it must be set by programming the VGA registers directly. In this case the code has to access registers in the CRT Controller group in order to expand the vertical scanning range.

The CRT Controller registers related to cursor size and position are also occasionally programmed directly.

Another group of registers within the CRT Controller that are occasionally programmed directly are those that determine the start address of the screen window in the video buffer. This manipulation is sometimes used in scrolling and panning text and in graphics mode manipulations. In VGA systems the CRT Controller Start Address High and Start Address Low registers (offset 0CH and 0DH) locate the screen window within a byte offset, while the Preset Row Scan register (offset 08H) locates the window at the closest pixel row. Therefore the Preset Row Scan register is used to determine the vertical pixel offset of the screen window. The horizontal pixel offset of the screen window is programmed by changing the value stored in the Horizontal Pixel Pan register of the Attribute Controller.

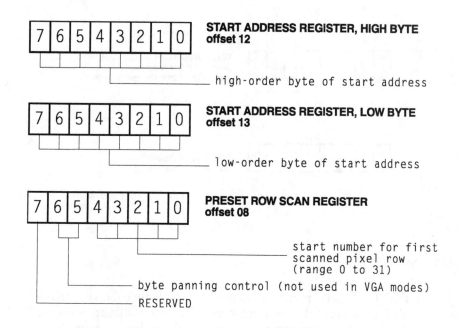

VGA Start Address and Preset Row Scan Register

VGA Video Digital-to-Analog Converter Addresses

REGISTER	OPERATIONS	ADDRESS
Pixel Address (write operations)	Read-Write	3C8H
Pixel Address (read operations)	Write only	3C7H
DAC State register	Read only	3C7H
Pixel Data register	Read-Write	3C9H
Pixel Mask register	Read-Write	3C6H

VGA Digital-to-Analog Converter (DAC)

[video systems] The Digital-to-Analog Converter, or DAC, provides a set of 256 color registers, sometimes called the color look-up table, as well as three color drivers for an analog display. The DAC register set permits displaying 256 color combinations from a total of 262,144 possible colors.

Each of the DAC's 256 registers uses six data bits to encode the value of the primary colors red, green, and blue. This design determines that each DAC register is 18 bits wide. It is the possible combinations of 18 bits that allow 262,144 DAC colors. Note that the VGA color registers in the DAC duplicate the color control offered by the Palette registers of the Attribute Controller.

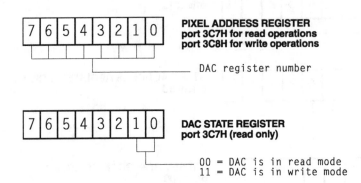

VGA DAC Registers

In fact, the VGA Palette registers are provided for compatibility with the EGA card, which does not contain DAC registers. When compatibility with the EGA is not an issue, VGA programming can be simplified by ignoring the Palette registers and doing all color manipulations in the DAC. Furthermore, the Palette registers are disabled when VGA is in the 256-color mode 19, since mode 19 has no EGA equivalent.

The DAC Pixel Address register holds the number (also called the address) of one of the 256 DAC registers. Read operations to the Pixel Address register are performed to port 3C7H and write operations to port 3C8H. A write operation changes the 18-bit color stored in the register (in red/green/blue format). A read operation is used to obtain the RGB value currently stored in the DAC register.

The DAC State register encodes whether the DAC is in read or write mode. A mode change takes place when the Pixel Address register is accessed: if the Pixel Address register is set at port 3C7H; then the DAC goes into a read mode, if it is set at port 3C8H, then the DAC goes into a write mode. Notice that although the Pixel Address register for read operations and the DAC State register are both mapped to port 3C7H there is no occasion for conflict, since the DAC State register is read only and the Pixel Address register for read operations is write only.

The Pixel Data register in the DAC is used to hold three six-bit data items representing a color value in RGB format. The Pixel Data register can be read after the program has selected the corresponding DAC register at the Pixel Address read operation port 3C7H. The Pixel Data register can be written after the program has selected the corresponding DAC register at the Pixel Address write operation port 3C8H. The current read or write state of the DAC can be determined by examining the DAC State register.

VGA general registers

[video systems] The General registers are used primarily in initialization of the video system and in mode setting. Most applications let the system software handle the initialization of the video functions controlled by the General registers. For example, the easiest and most reliable way for setting a video mode is BIOS service number 0, of interrupt 10H. On the other hand, the code has to access the General registers when setting a nonstandard VGA mode, such as VGA mode X.

Note that bit number 7 of Input Status Register 0, at port 3C2H is used in determining the start of the vertical retrace cycle of the CRT controller. This operation is sometimes necessary to avoid interference when updating the video buffer.

The Feature Control Register and the Video Subsystem Enable Register in the General Register group are reserved. IBM recommends that applications use subservice 12H of BIOS interrupt 10H to disable address decoding by the video subsystem. The DAC State Registers are discussed separately.

VGA graphics controller

[video systems] The registers in the Graphics Controller group serve to interface video memory with the Attribute Controller and with the system microprocessor. The Graphic Controller is bypassed in the alphanumeric modes.

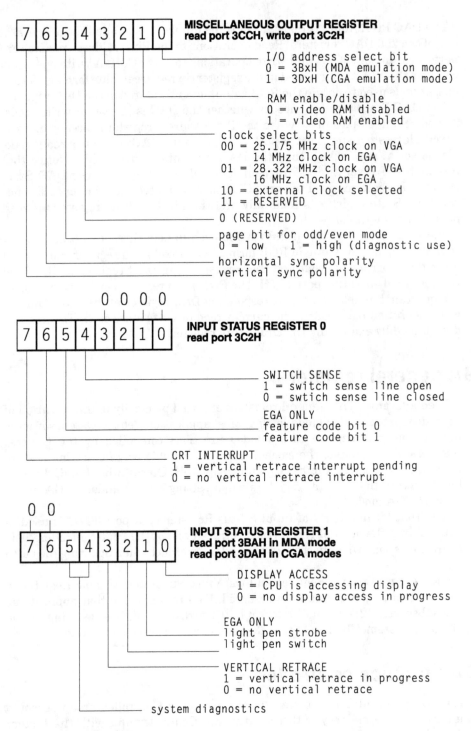

MISCELLANEOUS OUTPUT REGISTER
read port 3CCH, write port 3C2H

7 6 5 4 3 2 1 0

I/O address select bit
0 = 3BxH (MDA emulation mode)
1 = 3DxH (CGA emulation mode)

RAM enable/disable
0 = video RAM disabled
1 = video RAM enabled

clock select bits
00 = 25.175 MHz clock on VGA
     14 MHz clock on EGA
01 = 28.322 MHz clock on VGA
     16 MHz clock on EGA
10 = external clock selected
11 = RESERVED

0 (RESERVED)

page bit for odd/even mode
0 = low   1 = high (diagnostic use)

horizontal sync polarity

vertical sync polarity

0 0 0 0

7 6 5 4 3 2 1 0

INPUT STATUS REGISTER 0
read port 3C2H

SWITCH SENSE
1 = switch sense line open
0 = swtich sense line closed

EGA ONLY
feature code bit 0
feature code bit 1

CRT INTERRUPT
1 = vertical retrace interrupt pending
0 = no vertical retrace interrupt

0 0

7 6 5 4 3 2 1 0

INPUT STATUS REGISTER 1
read port 3BAH in MDA mode
read port 3DAH in CGA modes

DISPLAY ACCESS
1 = CPU is accessing display
0 = no display access in progress

EGA ONLY
light pen strobe
light pen switch

VERTICAL RETRACE
1 = vertical retrace in progress
0 = no vertical retrace

system diagnostics

VGA General Registers

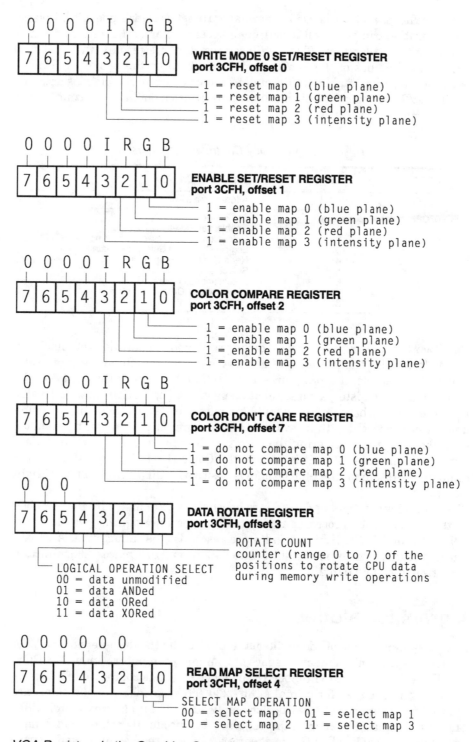

```
0 0 0 0 I R G B
7 6 5 4 3 2 1 0
```

WRITE MODE 0 SET/RESET REGISTER
port 3CFH, offset 0

1 = reset map 0 (blue plane)
1 = reset map 1 (green plane)
1 = reset map 2 (red plane)
1 = reset map 3 (intensity plane)

```
0 0 0 0 I R G B
7 6 5 4 3 2 1 0
```

ENABLE SET/RESET REGISTER
port 3CFH, offset 1

1 = enable map 0 (blue plane)
1 = enable map 1 (green plane)
1 = enable map 2 (red plane)
1 = enable map 3 (intensity plane)

```
0 0 0 0 I R G B
7 6 5 4 3 2 1 0
```

COLOR COMPARE REGISTER
port 3CFH, offset 2

1 = enable map 0 (blue plane)
1 = enable map 1 (green plane)
1 = enable map 2 (red plane)
1 = enable map 3 (intensity plane)

```
0 0 0 0 I R G B
7 6 5 4 3 2 1 0
```

COLOR DON'T CARE REGISTER
port 3CFH, offset 7

1 = do not compare map 0 (blue plane)
1 = do not compare map 1 (green plane)
1 = do not compare map 2 (red plane)
1 = do not compare map 3 (intensity plane)

```
0 0 0
7 6 5 4 3 2 1 0
```

DATA ROTATE REGISTER
port 3CFH, offset 3

ROTATE COUNT
counter (range 0 to 7) of the
positions to rotate CPU data
during memory write operations

LOGICAL OPERATION SELECT
00 = data unmodified
01 = data ANDed
10 = data ORed
11 = data XORed

```
0 0 0 0 0 0
7 6 5 4 3 2 1 0
```

READ MAP SELECT REGISTER
port 3CFH, offset 4

SELECT MAP OPERATION
00 = select map 0   01 = select map 1
10 = select map 2   11 = select map 3

VGA Registers in the Graphics Controller Group

The Set/Reset register is used to permanently set or clear a specific bit plane. This operation can be useful in writing a specific color to the entire screen or in disabling a color map. The Set/Reset register affects only write mode 0 operations. The use of the Set/Reset register requires the use of the Enable Set/Reset register. Enable Set/Reset determines which of the maps is accessed by the Set/Reset register. This mechanism provides a double-level control over the four maps.

VGA Graphics Controller Registers

PORT	OFFSET	DESCRIPTION
03CEH		Address register
03CFH	0	Set/Reset
	1	Enable Set/Reset
	2	Color Compare for read mode 1 operation
	3	Logical Operation Select and Data Rotate
	4	Read Operation Map Select
	5	Select Graphics Mode
	6	Miscellaneous Operations
	7	Read Mode 1 Color Don't Care
	8	Bit Mask

The Color Compare register is used during read mode 1 operations of some VGA modes to test for the presence of memory bits that match one or more color maps. For example, if a program sets bit 0 (blue) and bit 3 (intensity) of the Color Compare register, a subsequent memory read operation shows a 1-value for those pixels whose intensity and blue maps are set, while all other combinations are reported with a 0-value. One or more bit planes can be excluded from the compare by clearing the corresponding bit in the Color Don't Care register. If the intensity bit is zero in the Color Don't Care register, a color compare operation for the blue bitmap is positive for all pixels in blue or bright blue color.

The Data Rotate register determines how data is combined with data latched in the system microprocessor registers. The possible logical operations are AND, OR, and XOR. If bits 3 and 4 are reset, data is unmodified. A second function of this register is to right-rotate data from 0 to 7 places. This function is controlled by bits 0 to 2.

VGA graphics modes

[video systems] One of the problems confronted by the designers of the VGA system was the limited memory space of IBM microcomputers under MS-DOS. Recall that in VGA mode number 18 the video screen is composed of 480 rows of 640 pixels per row, for a total of 307,200 screen pixels. If eight pixels are encoded per memory byte, each color map would take up approximately 38K. This means that the four maps required to encode 16 colors would need approximately 154K. The VGA designers were able to reduce this memory space by using a latching mechanism that maps all four color maps to the same memory area.

In VGA mode 18 the color attribute of a single screen pixel is stored in four memory maps. Logically, the four maps are located at the same address. The base address for all four video maps is A0000H. Which map is active depends on which of the four latches is open. Note that the color codes for the first eight screen pixels are stored in the four maps labeled Intensity, Red, Green, and Blue. The first screen pixel has the intensity bit and the green bit set; therefore, it appears light green.

VGA memory mapping is different in the various alphanumeric and graphics modes. In VGA mode number 18 the color of each screen pixel is determined by the bit settings in four memory maps. However, in mode number 19, in which VGA can display 256 colors, each screen pixel is determined by one video buffer byte. Although, to the programmer, the buffer appears as a linear space starting at address A000H, in reality VGA uses all four bit planes to store video data in mode 19. The color value assigned to each pixel in the 256-color modes depends on the DAC register setting.

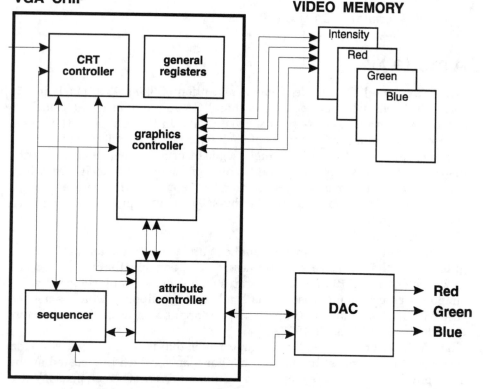

Memory Structure in VGA Mode 18

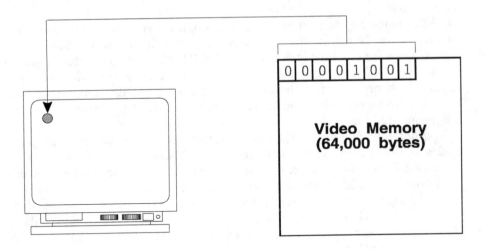

Memory Structure in VGA Mode 19

VGA mode X

[video systems] VGA mode X has a resolution of 320-by-240 pixels in 256 colors. It displays 40 more pixel rows than VGA standard mode 19. But these additional 40 pixel rows are not achieved easily. In the first place the screen space in mode number 19 consists of 64,000 pixels (320 by 200). This number of pixels can be contained in a single segment or video map. Expanding the display to 240 rows raises the total number of screen pixels to 76,800, which exceeds the capacity of a processor segment register, and, therefore, of a single video map. On the other hand, the 320-by-240 resolution provides a symmetrical drawing grid.
(See screen resolution).

Several features of VGA mode X make it attractive to the animations programmer. In the first place it offers a better resolution than the only other mode in 256 colors (mode 19). Mode X operates on a symmetrical pixel grid, which simplifies programming. Also, mode X allows page flipping, which is not the case with modes 18 and 19. Finally, the performance of mode X considerably exceeds that of VGA mode 19.

Like VGA mode 18, mode X is a planar mode; that is, video data is stored in several planes or maps. In mode X the four planes, which are located at the same physical address, are mapped to a different range of screen pixels. Video data in map 0 (plane 0) is mapped to pixel number 0, and all successive pixels in an arithmetic sequence with a common difference of 4. Map 1 contains video data for pixel number 1, and all successive pixels in a sequence with a common difference of 4. The same applies to maps 2 and 3. Which pixel map is active depends on the latching mechanism, controlled by the VGA Map Mask register. Mode X resembles mode 19 in that the color of a screen pixel is determined by a memory byte. This simplifies and speeds up processing since the time-consuming bit-masking operations necessary in mode 19 are not required in mode X.

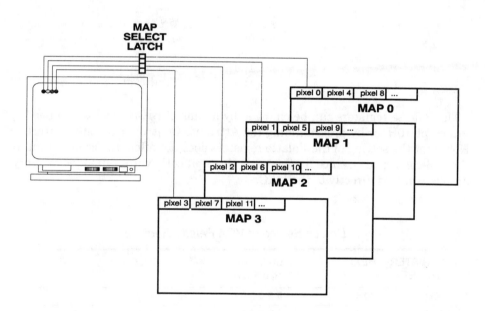

Memory Structure in VGA Mode X

VGA nonstandard video modes

[historical] [video systems] Graphics and animation programmers have tinkered with the VGA in an effort to create display modes that better suit their own purposes and requirements. The best known nonstandard VGA mode is the one called Mode X. Although this mode has been in use by graphics and animations programmers for some time, it was fist documented in an article by Michael Abrash published in *Dr. Dobb's Journal* in July 1991. This mode is not documented or supported in IBM's technical documents for VGA or by other major VGA manufacturers.

VGA palette registers

[video systems] In 16-color modes, the 16 Palette registers of the Attribute Controller determine how the 16 color values in the IRGB bit planes are displayed.

Each VGA Palette register consists of six bits, allowing 64 color combinations in each register. Each color is represented by two bits, and each one can have four possible levels of saturation; for example, the levels of saturation for red are:

```
Saturation          rgbRGB          Interpretation
    0               000000          no red
    1               100000          low red
    2               000100          red
    3               100100          high red
```

The Palette registers can be changed by means of BIOS service number 16, interrupt 10H, or by programming the Attribute Controller registers directly. Note that the setting of the Palette registers does not affect the color output in the 256-color modes, since, in this case, the 8-bit color values in video memory are transmitted directly to the DAC.

Default Setting of VGA Palette Registers

REGISTER OFFSET	HEX	BITS 0–5 rgbRGB	COLOR
00H	00H	0 0 0 0 0 0	Black
01H	01H	0 0 0 0 0 1	Blue
02H	02H	0 0 0 0 1 0	Green
03H	03H	0 0 0 0 1 1	Cyan
04H	04H	0 0 0 1 0 0	Red
05H	05H	0 0 0 1 0 1	Magenta
06H	14H	0 1 0 1 0 0	Brown
07H	07H	0 0 0 1 1 1	White
08H	38H	1 1 1 0 0 0	Dark grey
09H	39H	1 1 1 0 0 1	Light blue
0AH	3AH	1 1 1 0 1 0	Light green
0BH	3BH	1 1 1 0 1 1	Light cyan
0CH	3CH	1 1 1 1 0 0	Light red
0DH	3DH	1 1 1 1 0 1	Light magenta
0EH	3EH	1 1 1 1 1 0	Yellow
0FH	3FH	1 1 1 1 1 1	Intensified white

VGA programming (pixel masking)

[video systems] All read and write operations performed by the VGA take place at a byte level. However, in certain graphics modes, such as mode 18, video data is stored at a bit level in four color maps. In this case, the code must mask out the undesired color maps in order to determine the state of an individual screen pixel or to set a pixel to a certain color. The TEST instruction provides a convenient way for determining an individual screen pixel following a read operation. The Bit Mask register permits setting individual pixels while in write modes 0 and 2.

In the execution of write operations while in VGA mode 18, the bit mask for setting an individual screen pixel can be found from a look-up table or by right-shifting a unitary bit pattern (10000000B). The following code fragment calculates the offset into the video buffer and the bit mask required for writing an individual pixel using VGA write modes 0 or 2:

```
; Mask and offset computation from x and y pixel coordinates
; Code is for VGA mode number 18 (640 by 480 pixels)
; On entry:
;               CX = x coordinate of pixel (range 0 to 639)
;               DX = y coordinate of pixel (range 0 to 479)
; On exit:
;               BX = byte offset into video buffer
;               AH = bit mask for the write operation using
;                    write modes 0 or 2
; First calculate address
        PUSH    AX              ; Save accumulator
        PUSH    CX              ; Save x coordinate
        MOV     AX,DX           ; y coordinate to AX
        MOV     CX,80           ; Multiplier (80 bytes per row)
        MUL     CX              ; AX = y times 80
        MOV     BX,AX           ; Free AX and hold in BX
        POP     AX              ; x coordinate from stack
; Prepare for division
        MOV     CL,8            ; Load divisor
        DIV     CL              ; AX / CL = quotient in AL and
                                ; remainder in AH
; Add in quotient
        MOV     CL,AH           ; Save remainder in CL
        MOV     AH,0            ; Clear high byte
        ADD     BX,AX           ; Offset into buffer to BX
        POP     AX              ; Restore AX
; Compute bit mask from remainder
        MOV     AH,10000000B    ; Unitary mask for 0 remainder
        SHR     AH,CL           ; Shift right CL times
; The byte offset (in BX) and the pixel mask (in AH) can now
; be used to set the individual screen pixel
```

VGA programming (setting a pixel)

[video systems] Once a write mode is selected, code can access video memory to set the desired screen pixels, as in the following code fragment:

```
; Write mode 2 pixel setting routine
; On entry:
;                 ES = A000H
;                 BX = byte offset into the video buffer
;                 AL = pixel color in IRGB format
;                 AH = bit pattern to set (mask)
;
; Note: this procedure does not reset the default read or
; write modes or the contents of the Bit Mask register.
; The code assumes that write mode 2 has been set previously
        PUSH    AX          ; Color byte
        PUSH    AX          ; Twice
; Set Bit Mask register according to value in AH
        MOV     DX,3CEH     ; Graphic controller address
        MOV     AL,8        ; Offset = 8
        OUT     DX,AL       ; Select Bit Mask register
        INC     DX          ; To 3CFH
        POP     AX          ; Color code once from stack
        MOV     AL,AH       ; Bit pattern
        OUT     DX,AL       ; Load bit mask
; write color
        MOV     AL,ES:[BX]  ; Dummy read to load latch
                            ; registers
        POP     AX          ; Restore color code
        MOV     ES:[BX],AL  ; Write the pixel with the
                            ; color code in AL
        .
        .
        .
```

VGA programming (setting the write mode)

[video systems] The write mode is selected by setting bits 0 and 1 of the Graphic Controller's Graphic Mode register. It is a good programming practice to preserve the remaining bits in this register when modifying bits 0 and 1. This is performed by reading the Graphic Mode register, altering the write mode bits, and then resetting the register without changing the remaining bits. The following code fragment sets a write mode in a VGA system. The remaining bits in the Select Graphics Mode register are preserved.

```
; Set the Graphics Controller's Select Graphic Mode register
; to the write mode in the AH register
        MOV     DX,3CEH             ; Graphic Controller Address
```

```
MOV     AL,5                ; Offset of Mode register
OUT     DX,AL               ; Select this register
INC     DX                  ; Point to Data register
IN      AL,DX               ; Read register contents
AND     AL,11111100B        ; Clear bits 0 and 1
OR      AL,AH               ; Set mode in AL low bits
MOV     DX,3CEH             ; Address register
MOV     AL,5                ; Offset of Mode Register
OUT     DX,AL               ; Select again
INC     DX                  ; Point to Data register
OUT     DX,AL               ; Output to Mode Register
```

VGA programming (the attribute controller)

[video systems] Because the VGA Attribute Controller does not have a dedicated bit to control the selection of its internal address and data registers, programming this register group is different from that of the other VGA registers. The Attribute Controller uses an internal flip-flop to toggle the address and data functions. This explains why the Index and the Data registers of the Attribute Controller are both mapped to port 3C0H.

The first operation consists of accessing Input Status register 1 of the General register in order to clear the flip-flop. The address of the Status register 1 is 3BAH in monochrome modes and 3DAH in color modes. The complete sequence of operations for writing data to the Attribute Controller is as follows:

1. Issue an IN instruction to address 3BAH (in color modes) or to address 3DAH (in monochrome modes) to clear the flip-flop and select the address function of the Attribute Controller.

2. Disable interrupts.

3. Issue an OUT instruction to the address register, at port 3C0H, with the number of the desired data register.

4. Issue another OUT instruction to this same port to load a value into the Data register.

5. Enable interrupts.

The Attribute Mode Control register serves to select the characteristics associated with the video mode. Bit 0 selects whether the display is in an alphanumeric or in a graphics mode. Bit 1 determines if VGA operates in a monochrome or color emulation. Bit 2 is related to the handling of the ninth screen dot while displaying the graphics characters in the range C0H to DFH. If this bit is set, the graphics characters in this range generate unbroken horizontal lines. This feature refers to the MDA emulation mode only, since other character fonts do not have the ninth dot. BIOS sets this bit automatically in the modes that require it.

Bit 5 of the Attribute Mode Control register in the Attribute Controller group relates to independently panning the screen sections during split-screen operation. Bit 6 of the Attribute Mode Control register is set to 1 during operation in

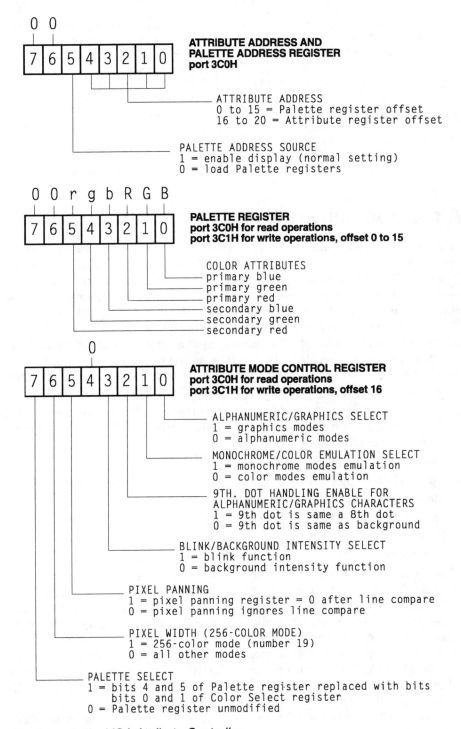

ATTRIBUTE ADDRESS AND PALETTE ADDRESS REGISTER
port 3C0H

ATTRIBUTE ADDRESS
0 to 15 = Palette register offset
16 to 20 = Attribute register offset

PALETTE ADDRESS SOURCE
1 = enable display (normal setting)
0 = load Palette registers

PALETTE REGISTER
port 3C0H for read operations
port 3C1H for write operations, offset 0 to 15

COLOR ATTRIBUTES
primary blue
primary green
primary red
secondary blue
secondary green
secondary red

ATTRIBUTE MODE CONTROL REGISTER
port 3C0H for read operations
port 3C1H for write operations, offset 16

ALPHANUMERIC/GRAPHICS SELECT
1 = graphics modes
0 = alphanumeric modes

MONOCHROME/COLOR EMULATION SELECT
1 = monochrome modes emulation
0 = color modes emulation

9TH. DOT HANDLING ENABLE FOR
ALPHANUMERIC/GRAPHICS CHARACTERS
1 = 9th dot is same a 8th dot
0 = 9th dot is same as background

BLINK/BACKGROUND INTENSITY SELECT
1 = blink function
0 = background intensity function

PIXEL PANNING
1 = pixel panning register = 0 after line compare
0 = pixel panning ignores line compare

PIXEL WIDTH (256-COLOR MODE)
1 = 256-color mode (number 19)
0 = all other modes

PALETTE SELECT
1 = bits 4 and 5 of Palette register replaced with bits
    bits 0 and 1 of Color Select register
0 = Palette register unmodified

Registers in the VGA Attribute Controller

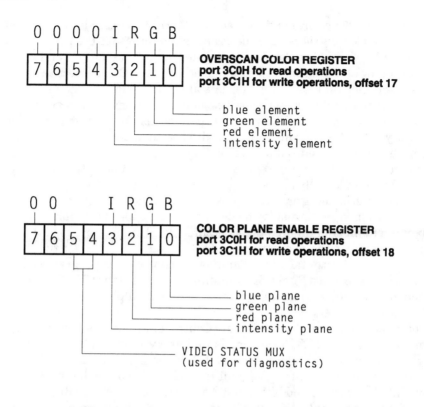

OVERSCAN COLOR REGISTER
port 3C0H for read operations
port 3C1H for write operations, offset 17

    blue element
    green element
    red element
    intensity element

COLOR PLANE ENABLE REGISTER
port 3C0H for read operations
port 3C1H for write operations, offset 18

    blue plane
    green plane
    red plane
    intensity plane

VIDEO STATUS MUX
(used for diagnostics)

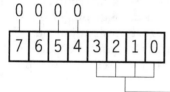

HORIZONTAL PIXEL PANNING REGISTER
port 3C0H for read operations
port 3C1H for write operations, offset 19

    number of pixels to left-shift
    video data

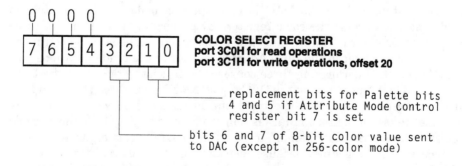

COLOR SELECT REGISTER
port 3C0H for read operations
port 3C1H for write operations, offset 20

    replacement bits for Palette bits
    4 and 5 if Attribute Mode Control
    register bit 7 is set

    bits 6 and 7 of 8-bit color value sent
    to DAC (except in 256-color mode)

Other VGA Registers in the Attribute Controller Group

mode number 19 (256 colors) and cleared for all other modes. Finally, bit 7 of the Attribute Mode Control register determines the source for the bits labeled r and g (numbers 4 and 5) in the Palette register. If bit 7 is set, the r and g bits in the Palette register are replaced by bits 0 and 1 of the Color Select register. If bit 7 is reset, then all Palette register bits are sent to the DAC.

The Color Plane Enable register allows excluding one or more bit planes from the color generation process. The main purpose of this function is to provide compatibility with EGA systems equipped with less than 256K of memory. Bits 4 and 5 of this register are used in system diagnostics.

The Horizontal Pixel Panning register of the Attribute Controller is used to shift video data horizontally to the left, pixel by pixel. This feature is available in the alphanumeric and graphics modes. The number of pixels that can be shifted is determined by the display mode. In the VGA 256-color graphics mode the maximum number of allowed pixels is three. In alphanumeric modes 0, 1, 2, 3, and 7, the maximum is eight pixels. In all other modes the maximum is seven pixels. The Horizontal Pixel Panning register can be programmed in conjunction with the Video Buffer Start Address registers of the CRT Controller to implement smooth horizontal screen scrolling in alphanumeric and in graphics modes.

The Color Select register of the Attribute Controller provides additional color selection flexibility to the VGA system, as well as a way for rapidly switching between sets of displayed colors. When bit 7 of the Attribute Mode Control register is clear, the 8-bit color value sent to the DAC is formed by the six bits from the Palette registers and bits 2 and 3 of the Color Select register. If bit 7 of the Attribute Mode Control register is set, then the 8-bit color value is formed with the lower four bits of the Palette register and the four bits of the Color Select register. Since these bits affect all Palette registers simultaneously, the program can rapidly change all displayed colors by changing the value in the Color Select register. The Color Select register is not used in the 256-color graphics mode 19.

VGA programming (the DAC registers)

[video systems] Once the DAC is in a specific mode (read or write), an application can access the color registers by performing a sequence of three operations, one for each RGB value. The read sequence consists of selecting the desired DAC register in the Pixel Address register at the read operations port (3C7H) and then performing three consecutive IN instructions. The first one loads the 6-bit value stored in the DAC register for the color red, the second one loads the green value, and the third one loads the blue value. The write sequence takes place in a similar fashion. This mode of operation allows rapid access to the three data items stored in each DAC register as well as to consecutive DAC registers. Because each entry in the DAC registers is six bits wide, the write operation is performed using the least significant six bits of each byte. The order of operations for the WRITE function is as follows:

1. Select the starting DAC color register number by means of a write operation to the Pixel Address write mode register at port 3C8H.

2. Disable interrupts.

3. Write the 18-bit color code in RGB encoding. The write sequence consists of three bytes consecutively output to the Pixel Data register. Only the six low-order bits in each byte are meaningful.

4. The DAC transfers the contents of the Pixel Data register to the DAC register number stored at the Pixel Address register.

5. The Pixel Address register increments automatically to point to the subsequent DAC register. Therefore, if more than one color is to be changed, the sequence of operations can be repeated from step 3.

6. Reenable interrupts.

Read or write operations to the video DAC must be spaced 240 ns apart. Assembly language code can meet this timing requirement by inserting a short JMP instruction between successive IN or OUT opcodes. The instruction can be conveniently coded in this manner:

```
        JMP        SHORT $ + 2        ; I/O delay
```

VGA programming (the Read Map Select Register)

[video systems] VGA video memory in the graphics modes is based on encoding the color of a single pixel into several memory maps. The Read Map Select register is used to determine which map is read by the system microprocessor. The following code fragment shows the use of the Read Operation Map Select register:

```
; Code to read the contents of 4 color maps in VGA mode 18
; Code assumes that read mode 0 has been previously set
; On entry:
;                   ES = A000H
;                   BX = byte offset into video map
; On exit:
;                   CL = byte stored in intensity map
;                   CH = byte stored in red map
;                   DL = byte stored in green map
;                   DH = byte stored in blue map
;
; Set counter and map selector
        MOV        CX,4        ; Counter for 4 maps to read
        MOV        DI,0        ; Map selector code
READ_IRGB:
; Select map from which to read
        MOV        DX,3CEH     ; Graphic Controller Address
                               ; register
        MOV        AL,4        ; Read Operation Map Select
```

```
        OUT     DX,AL           ; register
        INC     DX              ; Graphic controller at 3CFH
        MOV     AX,DI           ; AL = map selector code (in DI)
        OUT     DX,AL           ; IRGB color map selected
; Read 8 bits from selected map
        MOV     AL,ES:[BX]      ; Get byte from bit plane
        PUSH    AX              ; Store it in the stack
        INC     DI              ; Bump selector to next map
        LOOP    READ_IRGB       ; Execute loop 4 times
; 4 maps are stored in stack
; Retrieve maps into exit registers
        POP     AX              ; B map byte in AL
        MOV     DH,AL           ; Move B map byte to DH
        POP     AX              ; G map byte in AL
        MOV     DL,AL           ; Move G map byte to DL
        POP     AX              ; R map byte in AL
        MOV     CH,AL           ; Move R map byte to CH
        POP     AX              ; I map byte in AL
        MOV     CL,AL           ; Move I map byte to CL
        .
        .
        .
```

VGA Programming (setting several adjacent pixels)

[video systems] VGA programs executing in mode 18 must access the VGA Map Mask register in order to set one or more screen pixel. The following code fragment shows typical operations:

```
; Code to set 8 bright-red pixels in VGA mode number 18
; The code assumes that video mode number 18 is selected,
; that ES is set to the video segment base, and that BX points
; to the offset of the first pixel to be set
; First select register
        MOV     DX,3C4H         ; Address register of Sequencer
        MOV     AL,2            ; Offset of Map Mask
        OUT     DX,AL           ; Map Mask selected
        MOV     DX,3C5H         ; Data to Map Mask
        MOV     AL,00001100B    ; Intensity and red bits set
                                ; in IRGB encoding
        OUT     DX,AL           ; Map Mask = 0000 IR00
; Setting the pixels consists of writing a 1 bit in the
; corresponding buffer address.
        MOV     AL,ES:[BX]      ; Dummy read operation
        MOV     AL,11111111B    ; Set all bits
        MOV     ES:[BX],AL      ; Write to video buffer
; Restore the Map Mask to the default state
```

```
MOV     DX,3C4H          ; Address register of Sequencer
MOV     AL,02H           ; Offset of Map Mask
OUT     DX,AL            ; Map Mask selected
MOV     DX,3C5H          ; Data to Map Mask
MOV     AL,00001111B     ; Default IRGB code for Map Mask
OUT     DX,AL            ; Map Mask = 0000 IRGB
  .
  .
  .
```

VGA read and write modes

[video systems] VGA systems allow several ways for performing memory read and write operations, usually known as the read and write modes. The Select Graphics Mode register of the Graphics Controller group allows the programmer to select which of two read and four write modes is active. The four VGA write modes can be described as follows:

Write mode 0 is the default write mode. In this write mode, the Map Mask register of the Sequencer group, the Bit Mask register of the Graphics Controller group, and the CPU are used to set the screen pixel to a desired color.

In *write mode 1* the contents of the latch registers are first loaded by performing a read operation and then copied directly onto the color maps by performing a write operation. This mode is often used in moving areas of memory.

Write mode 2, a simplified version of write mode 0, also allows setting an individual pixel to any desired color. However, in write mode 2 the color code is contained in the CPU byte.

In *write mode 3* the byte in the CPU is ANDed with the contents of the Bit Mask register of the Graphic Controller.

(See also: VGA programming the graphic mode register).

The VGA also provides two read modes. In read mode 0, the default, the CPU is loaded with the contents of one of the color maps. In read mode 1, the contents of the maps are compared with a predetermined value before being loaded into the CPU. The active read mode depends on the setting of bit 3 of the Graphic Mode Select register, in the Graphics Controller.

The Miscellaneous register is used in conjunction with the Select Graphics Modes register to enable specific graphics function. Bits 2 and 3 of the Miscellaneous register control the mapping of the video buffer in the system's memory space.

VGA registers

[video systems] VGA systems include a chip containing several registers, a memory space dedicated to video functions, and a digital-to-analog converter, or DAC. (See VGA architecture). The VGA registers are mapped to the system's address space and accessed by means of the central processor. The VGA programmable registers (excluding the DAC) belong to five groups:

1. The General registers. This group is sometimes called the external registers due to the fact that on the EGA, they were located outside the VLSI chip. The General registers provide miscellaneous and control functions.

2. The CRT Controller registers. This group of registers controls the timing and synchronization of the video signal and also the cursor size and position.

3. The Sequencer registers. This group of registers controls data flow into the Attribute Controller, generates the timing pulses for the dynamic RAMs, and arbitrates memory accesses between the CPU and the video system. The Map Mask registers in the Sequencer allow the protection of entire memory maps.

4. The Graphics Controller registers. This group of registers provides an interface between the system microprocessor, the Attribute Controller, and video memory, while VGA is in a graphics mode.

5. The Attribute Controller registers. This group of registers determines the characteristics of the character display in the alphanumeric modes and the pixel color in the graphics modes.

VGA Register Groups

GENERAL REGISTERS				
1. Miscellaneous output	Write			03C2H
	Read			03CCH
2. Input status 0	Read			03C2H
3. Input status 1	Read	03BAH	03DAH	
4. Feature control	Write	03BAH	03DAH	
	Read			03CAH
5. Video subsystem enable	R/W			03C3H
6. DAC state	Read			03C7H
ATTRIBUTE CONTROLLER REGISTERS				
1. Address	R/W			03C0H
2. Other	Write			03C0H
	Read			03C1H
CRT CONTROLLER REGISTERS				
1. Index	R/W	03B4H	03D4H	
2. Other CRT controller	R/W	03B5H	03D5H	
SEQUENCER REGISTERS				
1. Address	R/W			03C4H
2. Other	R/W			03C5H
GRAPHICS CONTROLLER REGISTERS				
1. Address	R/W			03CEH
2. Other	R/W			03CFH

VGA Sequencer Registers

03C4H		Address register
03C5H	0	Synchronous or Asynchronous Reset
	1	Clocking Mode
	2	Map Mask
	3	Character Map Select
	4	Memory Mode

VGA sequencer

[video systems] The VGA Sequencer register group controls memory fetch operations and provides timing signals for the dynamic RAMs. This allows the microprocessor to access video memory in cycles inserted between the display memory cycles.

The Address register of the Sequencer group is used to select which one of the Data registers is currently accessed. Only the three low-order bits of the Address register are used. The Data register at offset 0 is used during system reset. The Clocking Mode register is also used mostly during mode setting, except for bit 5, which can be used to turn off the display. Turning off the display assigns all memory access time to the CPU, which can be used to perform a rapid full screen update. The most used registers of the Sequencer group are the Map Mask, Character Map Select, and Memory Mode.

The Map Mask register in the Sequencer group allows the protection of any specific memory map by masking it from the microprocessor and from the Character Map Select register. If VGA is in a color graphics mode, the Map Mask can be used to select the color at which one or more pixels are displayed. The color is encoded in the IRGB format. To access the Map Mask register, first load the value 2 into the address register of the Sequencer, at port 3C4H, which is the offset of the Map Mask register.

The Character Map Select register of the Sequencer is used in selecting one of the BIOS character maps. This operation is related to reprogramming bit 3 of the attribute byte. In this case bit 3 serves o select one of two character sets. Normally the character maps, named A and B, have the same value and bit 3 of the attribute byte is used to control the bright or normal display of the character foreground. When the Character Map Select register is programmed so that character maps A and B have different values, then bit 3 of the attribute byte is used to toggle between two sets of 256 characters each. Multiple VGA character sets ares used mostly when programming in VGA alphanumeric modes.

The Memory Mode register of the Sequencer is related to the display modes. Most programs leave the setting of this register to the BIOS mode select services.

VGA standard modes

[video systems] In the VGA standard the video modes are not dependent on the monitor. For example, a VGA equipped with a direct drive color monitor can execute in monochrome mode 7.

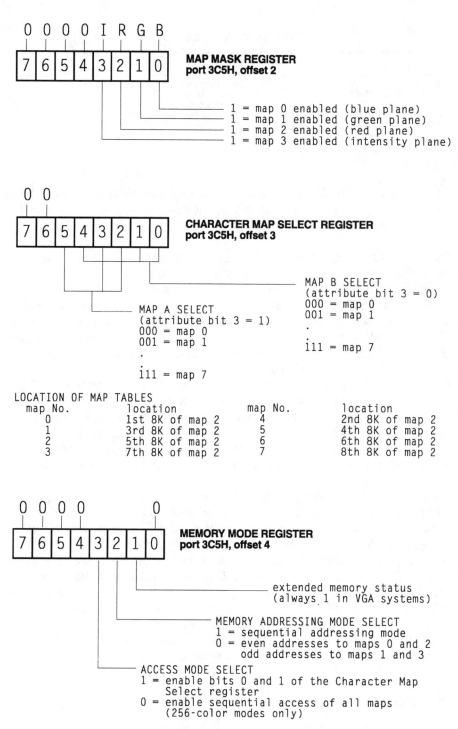

VGA Registers in the Sequencer Group

VGA video buffer

[video systems] The VGA buffer can start in any one of three possible addresses: B0000H, B8000H, and A0000H. Address B000H is used only when mode 7 is enabled; in this case VGA is emulating the Monochrome Display Adapter. In enhanced mode 7 the VGA displays its highest horizontal resolution (720 pixels) and uses a 9-by-16 dots text font. However, in this mode the VGA has no graphics capabilities. Buffer address A000H is active while VGA is in a graphics mode. Also note that video modes 17 and 18, with 480 pixel rows, were introduced with the VGA and MCGA standards. Therefore they are not available in CGA and EGA systems.

These modes produce a symmetrical pixel density of 640-by-480 screen dots. Mode 19 has 256 simultaneous colors, the most extensive one in the VGA standard, however, its horizontal resolution is half of the one in mode number 18. In addition, VGA mode 19 has a resolution of 320-by-200 pixels. This creates a nonsymmetrical pixel grid; in other words, the screen aspect ratio is not 1:1, as it is in mode number 18. In this environment the program code must generate a rectangle in order to display a square and an ellipse in order to display a circle.

VGA video memory

[video systems] All VGA systems contain the 256K of video memory that is part of the hardware. This memory is logically arranged in four 64K blocks. In some modes these blocks form the video maps. The four maps are sometimes referred to as bit planes 0 to 3.

VGA Video Modes

MODE	TYPE	COLORS	PALETTE	BUFFER SIZE	ADDRESS	CHAR. BOX	MAX. PAGES	VERT. FREQ.	RESOLUTION IN PIXELS
0,1	text	16	256K	40 x 25	B8000H	9 x 16	8	70 Hz	360 x 400
2,3	text	16	256K	80 x 25	B8000H	9 x 16	8	70 Hz	720 x 400
4,5	graphics	4	256K	40 x 25	B8000H	8 x 8	1	70 Hz	320 x 200
6	graphics	2	256K	80 x 25	B8000H	8 x 8	1	70 Hz	640 x 200
7	text			80 x 25	B0000H	9 x 16	8	70 Hz	720 x 400
13	graphics	16	256K	40 x 25	A0000H	8 x 8	8	70 Hz	320 x 200
14	graphics	16	256K	80 x 25	A0000H	8 x 8	4	70 Hz	640 x 200
15	graphics			80 x 25	A0000H	8 x 14	2	70 Hz	640 x 350
16	graphics	16	256K	80 x 25	A0000H	8 x 14	2	70 Hz	640 x 350
17	graphics	2	256K	80 x 30	A0000H	8 x 16	1	60 Hz	640 x 480
18	graphics	16	256K	80 x 30	A0000H	8 x 16	1	60 Hz	640 x 480
19	graphics	256	256K	40 x 25	A0000H	8 x 8	1	70 Hz	320 x 200

Video Electronics Standards Associations

(See SuperVGA).

Video graphics array (VGA)

[video systems] [historical] Video Graphics Array (VGA) was introduced in 1987 with the IBM PS/2 line. *Multi-Color Graphics Array* (MCGA), an under-featured version of VGA, was furnished with the lower-end PS/2 machines Models 25 and 30. Since then VGA has been the standard PC video system.

The main technological innovation introduced by VGA is a change from digital to analog video display driver technology. The basis for this change is that analog monitors can produce a much larger color selection than digital ones. VGA graphics hardware includes a digital-to-analog converter, usually called the DAC, and 256K of video memory. The DAC outputs the red, green, and blue signals to the analog display. Video memory is divided into four 64K video maps, called the *bit planes*. VGA supports all the display modes available in its predecessors, MDA, CGA, and EGA. In addition, it creates several new alpha-numeric and graphics modes. The most interesting of the new standard graphics modes are mode 18, with 640-by-480 pixel resolution in 16 colors, and mode 19, with 320-by-200 pixel resolution in 256 colors. The effective resolution of the VGA text modes is 720-by-400 pixels. These text modes can execute in 16 colors or in monochrome. Three different fonts can be selected in the alphanumeric modes.

In the VGA access to the video system registers and to video memory is through the system microprocessor. The microprocessor read and write operations to the video buffer are automatically synchronized by the VGA hardware with the CRT controller so as to eliminate interference. For this reason VGA programs, unlike those for the CGA, can access video memory at any time without fear of introducing screen snow or other unsightly effects.

VGA resolution is of 640 pixels per screen row and 480 vertical pixels per screen column.

The major limitations of the VGA system are resolution, color range, and performance. VGA density of 80 pixels per inch is a substantial improvement in relation to its predecessors, the CGA and the EGA, but still not very high when compared to the 600 dots per inch of a state-of-the-art laser printer or the 1200 and 2400 dots per inch of a quality color plate.

Video Graphics Array (VGA)

[historical] [video systems] The original set of IBM PS/2 computers with Microchannel architecture, namely the Model 30, 50, 60, 70, and 80, came equipped with a video system named the Video Graphics Array or VGA. The VGA is furnished with 256K of video memory divided into four 64K video maps, or bit planes. The system supports all the display modes of the MDA, the CGA, and the EGA. The VGA also provides graphics mode 18, with 640 by 480 pixels resolution in 16 colors, which is exclusive of this standard.

The effective resolution of the text modes is 720-by-400. Three text fonts with different box sizes can be selected in order to display text in the graphics modes. The VGA circuitry operates in conjunction with a digital-to-analog converter.

Video hardware

[video systems] [historical] Many computers of the PC line, namely the PC, PC XT, and PC AT, and some compatible machines, require plug-in adapters for the video functions. The following are among the better known video adapter cards used in the PC line:

1. *The Monochrome Display Adapter by IBM (MDA)*. The MDA is a black-and-white card that can be installed in all computers of the PC line, except the PCjr.

2. *The Color Graphics Adapter by IBM (CGA)*. This was the first color and graphics card offered for the PC line.

3. *The Enhanced Graphics Adapter by IBM (EGA)*. This is a color graphics card designed to improve the graphics quality and overcome the problems of its predecessor, the Color Graphics Adapter.

4. *The Professional Graphics Controller by IBM*. This is a high-quality graphics card intended mainly for technical applications that require graphics with higher definition than those that can be obtained with the CGA and the EGA.

5. *The Hercules Graphics Card by Hercules Computer Technology*. This card makes possible high-resolution graphics on the IBM monochrome display.

6. *The VGA cards*. These cards, made by IBM and by other manufacturers, allow certain models of the PC line to be upgraded to the VGA graphics standard of the PS/2 line.

A few models of the PC line have video systems that are furnished as standard hardware. These are the PCjr, the PC Convertible, and the Portable PC. On the other hand, all IBM models of the PS/2 line come equipped with integrated display support that includes color and graphics capabilities. On both lines, PC and PS/2, there is some flexibility in the selection of display monitors.

The following video systems are used in various models of PS/2 and later machines:

7. *The 8514/A Display Adapter by IBM*. This adapter can be considered the PS/2 version of the Professional Graphics Controller. When equipped with the optional memory expansion, the 8514/A can address 1024-by-768 pixels in 256 colors.

8. *The XGA Video System by IBM*. XGA was introduced by IBM in 1991 as a replacement for the VGA standard. The system, which is equipped with a graphics coprocessor, can display 1024-by-768 pixels in 256 colors.

9. The SuperVGA systems. This is a host of improvements on the VGA standard used in the PC. SuperVGA systems are furnished as adapter cards and in motherboard implementations (See SuperVGA).

Video modes

[video systems] The BIOS classifies the possible settings of the video hardware into display modes, which are numbered consecutively starting with mode 0. The modes are grouped into alphanumeric or graphics. The alphanumeric modes, also called text or alpha modes, are capable of displaying the individual, predesigned characters of the IBM character set (See character set -- PC). The graphics modes, also known as all-points addressable or APA modes, allow control of the individual screen dots that constitute the display surface.

The text modes are usually defined in terms of the number of characters per screen row and the total number of rows displayed. In the APA modes, the definition is the number of screen dots (called pixels) in each row by the number of pixel rows on each screen. Some video modes are in color, while others can display only monochrome images. Monochrome modes are also called black-and-white.

Video systems

[video systems] The video display hardware in the PC has undergone many changes in its 16-year history.

Most PC video display systems are memory-mapped. The one exception is the 8514/A display adapter operating in the advanced function mode. In memory-mapped video displays, a part of the system's memory space is dedicated to video functions (See memory -- video). This area can be reached both by the microprocessor and by the electronic components that handle the actual screen display operations. For this reason it has been called a dual-ported system. Because of their relatively slow response, memory-mapped displays are not well suited for animated graphics applications.

VIEW (statement)

[BASIC] [QuickBASIC] Defines a rectangle that serves as a viewport for all subsequent images. There are three variations of the VIEW statement. In medium-resolution graphics mode, the pair of statements:

```
WINDOW SCREEN (0,0)-(319,199): VIEW (x1,y1)-(x2,y2),c,b
```

establish a viewport with upper left-hand corner at physical coordinates $(x1,y1)$ and lower right-hand corner at physical coordinates $(x2,y2)$. The rectangle will have background color c and a boundary of color b. Subsequent graphics statements will scale their displays and place them into the viewport as if it were the entire screen. For the other graphics modes the coordinates should be replaced by the physical x- and y-coordinates of the point in the lower right-hand corner of the screen.

If no WINDOW statement is active, the statement:

Video Modes

MODE	TYPE	DEFINITION	MONO OR COLOR	BUFFER ADDRESS	BUFFER SIZE	CHARACTER BOX SIZE	MDA	CGA	EGA	PCjr	VGA	MCGA
								PC /AT			PS2 /COMPATIBLES	
0	Text	40 x 25	B & W	B8000H	2K	8 x 8		X	X	X	X	X
1	Text	40 x 25	Color	B8000H	2K	8 x 8		X	X	X	X	X
2	Text	80 x 25	B & W	B8000H	2K	8 x 8		X	X	X	X	X
3	Text	80 x 25	Color	B8000H	4K	8 x 8		X	X	X	X	X
4	APA	320 x 200	Color	B8000H	8K	8 x 8		X	X	X	X	X
5	APA	320 x 200	B & W	B8000H	8K	8 x 8		X	X	X	X	X
6	APA	640 x 200	B & W	B8000H	16K	8 x 8		X	X	X	X	X
7	Text	80 x 25	B & W	B0000H	4K	9 x 14	X		X		X	
8	APA	160 x 200	Color	B8000H	16K	8 x 8				X		
9	APA	320 x 200	Color	B8000H	32K	8 x 8				X		
10	APA	640 x 200	Color	B8000H	32K	8 x 8				X		
13	APA	320 x 200	Color	A0000H	8K	8 x 8			X		X	
14	APA	640 x 200	Color	A0000H	16K	8 x 8			X		X	
15	APA	640 x 350	B & W	A0000H	28K	8 x 14			X		X	
16	APA	640 x 350	Color	A0000H	28K	8 x 14			X		X	
17	APA	640 x 480	Color	A0000H	38K	8 x 16					X	X
18	APA	640 x 480	Color	A0000H	38K	8 x 16					X	
19	APA	640 x 480	Color	A0000H	38K	8 x 8					X	X

Abbreviations: MDA = Monochrome Display Adapter　CGA = Color Graphics Adapter　MCGA = PS/2 Multicolor Graphics Array
EGA = Enhanced Graphics Adapter　VGA = Video Graphics Array

```
VIEW (x1,y1)(x2,y2),c,b
```

establishes a viewport at the same location and with the same colors. However, instead of forcing a future drawing to fit inside the viewport, subsequent graphics statements do no scaling, but simply translate the drawing $x1$ points to the right and $y1$ points down, and clip the drawing at the edge of the view port.

The statement:

```
VIEW SCREEN (x1,y1)-(x2,y2),c,b
```

establishes a viewport at the same location and with the same colors as in the first discussion. However, instead of scaling down or translating a future drawing, subsequent graphics statements clip the drawing at the edge of the viewport.

VIEW PRINT (statement)

[QuickBASIC] Established a viewport for text operations. The statement format is:

```
VIEW PTRIN linea TO lineb
```

In the default state the screen holds 25 lines of text numbered 1 through 25. However, only lines 1 through 24 scroll. After its execution, all text displayed with PRINT statements will appear in the viewport and only the lines in the viewport will scroll. The LOCATE statement is only valid if the line number specified is within the current text viewport, and the CLS statement affects only the viewport. Text lying outside of the text viewport stays fixed. The statement VIEW PRINT by itself causes the entire screen to scroll. It has the same effect as VIEW PRINT 1 TO h, where h is the number of text lines on the screen.

W

WAIT

[Assembler] 8086 machine instruction. Mnemonic for coprocessor WAIT. Causes the CPU to enter into a wait state until the BUSY pin, which is driven by the 8087 mathematical coprocessor, is inactive. The original purpose of the instruction was to synchronize processor and coprocessor interaction. The FWAIT opcode performs identical action as WAIT.

In 8087 systems the 8086 must not present a new instruction to the coprocessor while it is still executing the previous one. This is ensured by inserting a WAIT before or after every coprocessor ESC opcode. In this case the 8086 does nothing while the 8087 is executing. In order to allow concurrent processing by the CPU and the NDP, most assembler programs insert the WAIT instruction before the coprocessor ESC. In this case, the CPU can continue executing its own code until it finds the next ESC in the instruction stream.

On the other hand, if the WAIT precedes the ESC it is possible that the CPU will access a memory operand before the coprocessor has finished acting on it. In this case the program must insert an additional WAIT. The alternative mnemonic FWAIT is usually preferred in this case. The following code fragment shows a typical circumstance that requires the insertion of an FWAIT instruction:

```
; Code to store and recover the 8087 control word
FSTCW   CTRL_WORD           ; Store control word
FWAIT                       ; Force CPU to wait
MOV     AX,CTRL_WORD        ; Recover the control word
                            ; into AX
```

Programs intended for 8087 systems must follow 8087 synchronization requirements. However, some 80287 assemblers (such as Intel's ASM286) omit the FWAIT opcode. Other assemblers (such as Microsoft MASM version 5.0 and later) have options that allow the FWAIT instructions to be automatically inserted or not. In either case, code in which the ESC instructions are not accompanied by a CPU WAIT or FWAIT do not execute correctly in 8087 systems.

WAIT (statement)

[BASIC] [QuickBASIC] Suspends program execution while monitoring a port status. The statement format is:

```
WAIT port, n[,m]
```

where port is a port number, and *n,m* are integers in the range 0 to 255.

WBINVD

[Assembler] 486 machine instruction. Mnemonic for Write-Back and INVali-Date cache. The internal cache is flushed, and a special-function bus cycle is issued which indicates that the external cache should write-back its contents to main memory. Another special-function bus cycle follows, directing the external cache to flush itself.

Intel documentation states that INVD should be used with care since the instruction does not write back modified cache lines; therefore, it can cause the data cache to become inconsistent with other memories in the system. Unless there is a specific requirement or benefit to invalidate a cache without writing back the modified lines (i.e., testing or fault recovery where cache coherency with main memory is not a concern), software should use the WBINVD instruction.

See also INVD.

while loop

[C] Makes possible an alternative construct to the for loop. As the keyword implies, this loop repeats execution of a statement or statement block while a certain condition evaluates to true. Like the for loop, the *while* loop requires initialization, processing, and testing steps. However, the *while* loop is sometimes simpler to code than the *for* loop because the initialization and testing steps are performed outside the statement body. For example, the following program uses a *while* loop to display the ASCII characters in the range 0x10 to 0x20:

```
#include <stdio.h>
main()
{
    unsigned char ascii_val;
    ascii_val = 0x10;                /* initialization step    */
    while (ascii_val < 0x20)  {       /* while loop expression */
        printf("%c", ascii_val);      /* processing step       */
        ascii_val ++;                 /* updating variable     */
    }
}
```

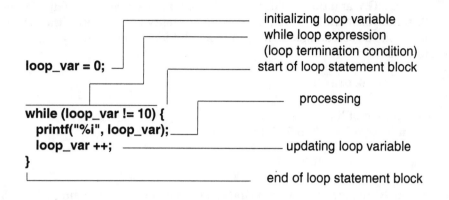

Structure of the C while Loop

Observe that initialization of the loop variable is performed outside the loop construct. Also that the loop variable is updated in a separate statement. Therefore, the only element contained in the loop expression is the test element, which states the condition for the termination of the loop.

In operation, the *while* loop evaluates the test expression before the loop statement block executes. For this reason the loop illustrated in this figure displays all the integers between 0 and 9, but not the integer 10. Note that this mode of operation is consistent with the meaning of the word *while*.

WHILE/WEND (statements)

[BASIC] [QuickBASIC] Execute a series of statements in a loop as long as a given condition is true. The statement format is:

```
WHILE expression
    .
    .
    .
WEND
```

where expression is a numeric expression. The statements located between the WHILE and the WEND keywords continue to execute while expression evaluates to true.

WIDTH (statement)

[BASIC] [QuickBASIC] Sets the screen width. The statement format is:

```
WIDTH n
```

where *n* is 40 for double-wide characters and 80 for normal display.

The EGA, VGA, and the MCGA video adapter cards are capable of displaying 25, 30, 43, 50, or 60 lines of text depending on the type of adapter, the type of monitor, and the screen mode. When *t* is a valid length for the video adapter, the statement:

```
WIDTH ,t
```

sets the number of lines of text to *t*.

If *s* is an integer less than 255, the statement:

```
WIDTH "LPT1:",s
```

causes BASIC to permit at most *s* characters to be printed on a single line by LPRINT statements. In this case BASIC sends a carriage return/line feed to the printer after *s* characters have been printed on a line, even if LPRINT would not otherwise start a new line at that point.

WINDOW (statement)

[BASIC] [QuickBASIC] Redefines the viewport coordinates while in a graphics mode. The statement format is:

```
WINDOW [[SCREEN] (x1,y1)-(x2,y2)]
```

where (x1,y1)(x2,y2) are programmer defined world coordinates, in single-precision format. Subsequent graphics statements place figures on the screen scaled in accordance with this coordinate system. If the statement WINDOW is replaced by WINDOW SCREEN, then a left-hand coordinate system is imposed. That is, the *y*-coordinates of points are lower in the higher areas on the screen.

Word

(See memory organization).

WRD

[MS-Pascal] Heading: (X :VALUE): WORD;
Data conversion procedure. Converts to WORD any of three types, as follows:

Type	Return Value
WORD	X
INTEGER >= 0	X
INTEGER < 0	X + MAXWORD + 1
CHAR	ASCII code for X
Enumerated	Position of X in the type definition,

```
                                 starting with 0
            INTEGER4             Lower 16 bits
            Pointer             Word value of pointer
```

WRITE

[MS-Pascal] Heading: (VAR F; P1, P2,...PN);
File system level intrinsic procedure to write data to files. WRITE is defined in terms of the more primitive operation PUT.

WRITE (statement)

[BASIC] [QuickBASIC] Outputs data to the screen. The statement format is:

```
WRITE [expression list]
```

Strings appear surrounded by quotation marks and numbers do not have leading or trailing spaces. All commas are displayed and do not induce jumps to successive print zones. After all the values are displayed, the cursor moves to the beginning of the next line.

WRITE# (statement)

[BASIC] [QuickBASIC] Writes data to a sequential file. The statement format is:

```
WRITE #filenum, expression .list
```

where filenum is the number assigned to the file with the OPEN statement, and expression list is a list of string or numeric expressions. The statement:

```
WRITE #n, expl,exp2,...
```

records the values of the expressions one after the other into the file. Strings appear surrounded by quotation marks, numbers do not have leading or trailing spaces, all commas in the expressions are recorded, and the characters for carriage return and linefeed are placed following the data.

WRITELN

[MS-Pascal] Heading: (VAR F;P1, P2,...PN);
WRITELN is the same as WRITE, except it also writes an end-of-line.

WRMSR

[Assembler] Pentium machine instruction. Mnemonic for WRite to Model Specific Register. The value in ECX specifies one of the 64-bit Model Specific Registers of the Pentium processor. The contents of EDX:EAX are copied into the Model-Specific Register. The high-order 32 bits are copied from EDX and the low-order 32 bits are copied from EAX. The following values are used to select model specific registers on the Pentium processor:

```
VALUE (IN HEX)   REGISTER NAME            DESCRIPTION
    00H          Machine Check Address     Stores address of cycle
                                           causing exception
    01H          Machine Check Type        Stores cycle type of
                                           cycle causing exception
```

An exception #GP(0) is generated if the current privilege level is not 0 or the value in ECX does not specify a Model-Specific Register of the Pentium processor.

X

XADD

[Assembler] 486 machine instruction. Mnemonic for eXchange and ADD. Load the destination into the source, then loads the sum of the destination and the original source into the destination. The instruction can be used with the LOCK prefix. XADD requires a source operand in a machine register and a destination operand, which can be a register or a memory variable. Either operand can be a byte, word, or doubleword. The main purpose of this instruction is to provide a multiprocessor mechanism whereby several CPUs can execute the same loop.

XCHG

[Assembler] 8086 machine instruction. Mnemonic for eXCHanGe. Switches the contents of the source and destination operands, which can be bytes, words, or doublewords.

```
; Sample encodings:
      XCHG    AX,BX         ; Exchange registers AX and BX
      XCHG    EBX,ECX       ; Exchange 32-bit registers
      XCHG    WORD_VAR,DX   ; Exchange word variable and
                            ; register
```

XGA

[historical] [video systems] In September 1990 IBM disclosed preliminary information on a new graphics standard designated as the Extended Graphics Array, or XGA. Two configurations of the XGA standard were implemented: as an adapter card and as part of the motherboard. The XGA adapter is compatible with PS/2 Micro Channel machines equipped with the 80386 or higher CPU. The XGA system is integrated in the motherboard of several high-end models of the PS/2 lines. Several independent vendors, including Radius Corporation, have developed XGA cards for non-IBM machines.

XGA Adapter Interface

[video systems] The Adapter Interface (AI) is a software package furnished with 8514/A and XGA systems that provides a series of low-level services to the graphics programmer. The AI was originally documented by IBM in the *IBM Personal System / 2 Display Adapter 8514 / A Technical Reference* (document number S68X-2248-0) published in April, 1987. IBM has also published a document named the *IBM Personal System / 2 Display Adapter 8514 / A Adapter Interface Programmer's Guide* (document number 00F8952). The AI driver software must be installed in the machine before its services become available to the system. In the case of the 8514/A the AI driver is in the form of a TSR program, while in the XGA it is furnished as a .SYS file. Installation instructions for the AI software are part of the adapter package. In the case of the XGA AI several versions are furnished by IBM: one for MS-DOS, another one for Windows, and a third one for the OS/2 operating system.

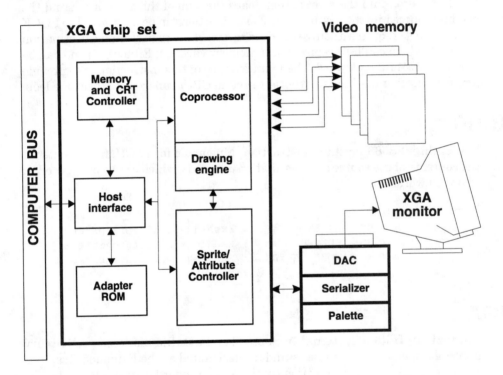

XGA Component Diagram

XGA AI Programming

[**video systems**] The Adapter Interface software was conceived as a layer of software services for initializing, configuring, and programming the 8514/A graphics system. XGA is furnished with a compatible set of services, which are a superset of those furnished for 8514/A. In both cases, 8514/A and XGA, the programming interface documentation assumes that programming is in C. Access methods from other languages have not been described to this date.

XGA Adapter Interface Services

NAME	ENTRY POINT NUMBER	DESCRIPTION
HLINE	0	Draw line
HCLINE	1	Draw line at current point
HRLINE	2	Draw line from start point
HCRLINE	3	Draw line from start point
HSCP	4	Set current point
HBAR	5	Begin area for fill operation
HEAR	6	End area for fill operation
HSCOL	7	Set current color
HOPEN	8	Open adapter for AI operations
HSMX	9	Set mix
HSBCOL	10	Set background color
HSLT	11	Set line type
HSLW	12	Set line width
HEGS	13	Erase graphics screen
HSGQ	14	Set graphics quality
HSCMP	15	Set color compare register
HINT	16	Synchronize with vertical retrace
HSPATTO	17	Set pattern reference
HSPATT	18	Set pattern shape
HLDPAL	19	Load palette
HSHS	20	Set scissors
HBBW	21	Write bit block image data
HCBBW	22	Write bit block at current point
HBBR	23	Read bit block
HBBCHN	24	Chain bit block data
HBBC	25	Copy bit block
HSCOORD	26	Set coordinate type
HQCOORD	27	Query coordinate type
HSMODE	28	Set adapter mode
HQMODE	29	Query adapter mode
HQMODES	30	Query adapter modes
HQDPS	31	Query drawing process state
HRECT	32	Fill rectangle
HSBP	33	Set bit plane controls
HCLOSE	34	Close adapter
HESC	35	Escape (terminate processing)
HXLATE	36	Assign multiplane color tables
HSCS	37	Select character set
HCHST	38	Display character string
HCCHSET	39	Display string at current point
ABLOCKMFI	40	Display character block (MFI mode)
ABLOCKCGA	41	Display character block (CGA mode)
AERASE	42	Erase character rectangle
ASCROLL	43	Scroll character rectangle
ACURSOR	44	Set current cursor position
ASCUR	45	Set cursor shape
ASFONT	46	Select character set
AXLATE	47	Assign color index
HINIT	48	Initialize adapter state
HSYNC	49	Synchronize adapter with task
HMRK	50	Display marker
HCMRK	51	Display marker at current point
HSMARK	52	Set marker shape
HSLPC	53	Save line-pattern count
HRLPC	54	Restore saved line-pattern count
HQCP	55	Query current point
HQDFPAL	56	Query default palette
HSPAL	57	Save palette
HRPAL	58	Restore palette
HSAFP	59	Set area fill plane
ASCELL	60	Set cell size

XGA Adapter Interface Services (continued)

NAME	ENTRY POINT NUMBER	DESCRIPTION
ASGO	61	Set alpha grid origin
HDLINE	62	Disjoint line at point
————	63	
HPEL	64	Write pixel string
HRPEL	65	Read pixel string
HPSTEP	66	Plot and step
HCPSTEP	67	Plot and step at current position
HRSTEP	68	Read and step
HSBMAP	69	Set bit map attributes
HQBMAP	70	Query bit map attributes
HBMC	71	Bit map copy
HSDW	72	Set display window
HSPRITE	73	Sprite at given position
HSSPRITE	74	Set sprite shape
HRWVEC	75	Read/write vector
————	76	
————	77	
HSFPAL	78	Save full palette
HRFPAL	79	Restore full palette
HQDEVICE	80	Query device specific (no action)

The AI installation selects one of two versions of the software according to the amount of memory in the graphics system. Once installed, the address of the AI handler is stored at interrupt vector 7FH. The AI services are accessed by means of an INT 7FH instruction or by a far call to the address of the service routine.

Before an application can start using the AI services it must first certify that the software is correctly installed and obtain the address of the service routine. Since interrupt 7FH has been documented as a reserved vector in IBM literature, the application can assume that the value stored at this vector is zero if no AI has been installed. However, this assumption risks that a nonconforming program has improperly used the vector for its own purposes; in this case the vector can store a nonzero value, while no AI is present.

XGA architecture

The following are the most important features of the XGA standard:

1. The maximum resolution is of 1024-by-768 pixels in 256 colors.

2. The XGA system is compatible with the 8514/A Adapter Interface software.

3. In the original XGA the display driver is interlaced at 1024-by-768 pixel resolution. In the new version of the standard, designated XGA-2, the display function is noninterlaced.

4. The original adapter version of XGA is furnished with either 512K or 1204K of on-board video RAM. The 512K RAM option is not available in XGA-2.

5. The XGA is compatible with the VGA standard at the register level. This makes possible the use of XGA in the motherboard while still maintaining VGA compatibility. This is the way in which it is implemented in the IBM Model 95 XP 486 microcomputer.

XGA Advanced Function Modes

	LOW-RESOLUTION MODE	HIGH-RESOLUTION MODE
RAM installed	512K	1024K
Interlaced	No	Yes
Pixel columns	640	1024
Pixel rows	480	768
Number of colors	16	256
Palette	256K	256K

6. XGA requires a machine equipped with a 80386 or higher CPU.

7. XGA implements a three-dimensional, user-definable drawing space, called a bitmap. XGA bitmaps can reside anywhere in the system's memory space. The application can define a bitmap in the program's data space and the XGA uses this area directly for drawing, reading, and writing operations.

8. XGA is equipped with a hardware controlled cursor, called the sprite. It maximum size is of 64-by-64 pixels and it can be positioned anywhere on the screen without affecting the image stored in video memory.

9. The XGA was designed taking into consideration the problems of managing the video image in a multitasking environment. Therefore it contains facilities for saving and restoring the state of the video hardware at any time.

10. The XGA hardware can act as a bus master and access system memory directly. This bus-mastering capability frees the CPU for other tasks while the XGA processor is manipulating memory.

11. IBM has provided register-level documentation for the XGA system. This facilitates cloning and development of high-performance software.

XGA graphics coprocessor

[video systems] One characteristic of XGA hardware that differentiates it from VGA and SuperVGA systems is the presence of a graphics coprocessor chip. Much of the enhanced performance of the XGA system is due to this device. The following are the most important features of the graphics coprocessor:

1. The coprocessor can obtain control of the system bus in order to access video and system memory independently of the central processor. This bus-mastering feature allows the coprocessor to perform graphics operations while the main processor is executing other functions.

2. The graphics coprocessor can directly perform drawing operations. These include straight lines, filled rectangles, and bit-block transfers.

3. The coprocessor provides support for saving its own register contents. This feature is useful in a multitasking environment.

4. The coprocessor supports several logical and arithmetic mixes including OR, AND, XOR, NOT, source, destination, add, subtract, average, maximum, and minimum operands.

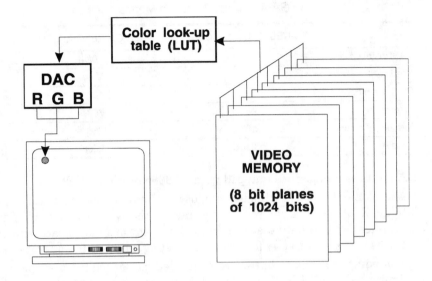

Bit-Plane Mapping in XGA High Resolution Modes

Default Setting of LUT Registers in XGA Systems

REGISTER NUMBER	6-BIT COLOR (HEX VALUE) R G B	COLOR
0	00 00 00	Black
1	00 00 2A	Dark blue
2	00 2A 00	Dark green
3	00 2A 2A	Dark cyan
4	2A 00 00	Dark red
5	2A 00 2A	Dark magenta
6	2A 15 00	Brown
7	2A 2A 2A	Gray
8	15 15 15	Dark gray
9	15 15 3F	Light blue
10	15 3F 15	Light green
11	15 3F 3F	Light cyan
12	3F 15 15	Light red
13	3F 15 3F	Light magenta
14	3F 3F 15	Yellow
15	3F 3F 3F	Bright white
16 to 31	00 00 2A	Dark blue
32 to 47	00 2A 00	Dark green
48 to 63	00 2A 2A	Dark cyan
64 to 79	2A 00 00	Dark red
80 to 95	2A 00 2A	Dark magenta
96 to 111	2A 15 00	Brown
112 to 127	2A 2A 2A	Gray
128 to 143	15 15 15	Dark gray
144 to 159	15 15 3F	Light blue
160 to 175	15 3F 15	Light green
176 to 191	15 3F 3F	Light cyan
192 to 207	3F 15 15	Light red
208 to 223	3F 15 3F	Light magenta
224 to 239	3F 3F 15	Yellow
240 to 255	3F 3F 3F	Bright white

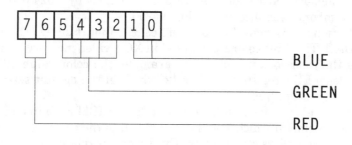

8-bit Color Bitmap

5. The coprocessor can manipulate images encoded in 1, 2, 4, or 8 bits per pixel formats. Pixel maps can be defined as coded in Intel or Motorola data storage formats.

6. The coprocessor can be programmed to generate system interrupts. These interrupts can occur when the coprocessor operation has completed, an access to the coprocessor was rejected, a sprite operation completed, or at the end or start of the screen blanking cycle.

The coprocessor registers are memory-mapped. To an application, programming the coprocessor consists of reading and storing data into these reserved memory addresses. In contrast, the XGA main registers are port-mapped and programming consists of reading and writing to these dedicated ports.

XGA operating modes

[video systems] XGA systems can operate in one of two modes: the VGA mode or the advanced functions mode. The operating mode is selected by the software. In the VGA mode the graphics system is a full-featured VGA. The advanced function mode refers to the Adapter Interface software.

XGA palette

[video systems] XGA video memory is organized in bit planes. Each bit plane encodes the color for a rectangular array of 1024-by-1024 pixels. In practice, since the highest available resolution is of 1024-by-768 pixels, there are 256 unused bits in each plane. This unassigned area is used by AI software as a scratchpad during area fills and in marker manipulations, as well as for storing bitmaps for the character sets. When the graphics system is in the low-resolution mode video memory consist of eight 1,024 by 512 bit planes. However, the eight bit planes are divided into two separate groups of four bit planes each. These two bit planes can be simultaneously addressed. In low-resolution mode the color range is limited to sixteen simultaneous colors. In the high-resolution mode video memory consists of eight bit planes of 1,024 by 1,024 pixels. In this mode the number of simultaneous colors is 256.

Color selection is performed by means of a color look-up table (LUT) associated with the DAC. The 8-bit color code stored in XGA video memory serves as an index into the color look-up table. For example, the color value 12 in video memory selects LUT register number 12, which in the default setting stores the encoding for bright red.

In the documentation for Display Adapter 8514/A IBM recommends an 8-bit color coding scheme in which 4 bits are assigned to the green color and 2 bits to the red and blue colors respectively. This scheme is related to the physiology of the human eye, which is more sensitive to the green area of the spectrum than to the red or blue areas. One possible mapping, which conforms with the XGA direct color mode, is to devote bits 0 and 1 to the blue range, bits 2 to 5 to the green range, and bits 6 and 7 to the red range.

XGA programming levels

[video systems] The XGA graphics programmer can operate at four different levels. The first and highest level are the graphics functions offered by operating systems and graphics environments. Such is the case in applications that execute under the Windows and OS/2 operating systems and use the graphics services provided by the system software. The second level of XGA programming is by means of the XGA Adapter Interface services (See XGA adapter interface). The third level is by programming the XGA registers and the graphics coprocessor. The fourth and lowest level of XGA graphics programming is by accessing video memory directly.

XGA VRAM memory

[video systems] Since the XGA is a memory-mapped system the color code for each screen pixel is encoded in video RAM. How many units of memory are used to encode the pixel's color depends on the adopted format. Possible values are of 1, 2, 4, 8, and 16 bits per pixel. Note that the 256 and 65536 color modes are available only in XGA systems with maximum on-board RAM (1Mb). The total amount of VRAM required depends on the number of screen pixels and the number of encoded colors. For example, to store the contents of the entire XGA screen at 1024-by-768 pixel resolution requires a total of 786,432 memory units.

In the 8-bits-per-pixel format the number of memory units is of 786,432 bytes (8 bits per byte). However, this same screen can be stored in 98,304 bytes if each screen pixel is represented in a single memory bit (786,432 / 8 = 98,304).

Therefore the video memory space of an XGA system in 1024-by-768 pixel mode, with each pixel encoded in 256 colors, exceeds by far the limit of an 80x86 segment register (65,536). Therefore an application accessing video memory directly while executing in 80x86 real mode requires some sort of memory banking mechanism by which to access a total of 768,432 bytes of VRAM memory. In fact, a minimum of 12 memory banks of 65,536 bytes are required to encode the 768,432 XGA pixels in 1024-by-768 pixel mode in 256 colors.

XLAT

[Assembler] 8086 machine instruction. Mnemonic for Translate table. Replaces a byte in the AL register with a byte from a 256-byte, user-coded translation table. Register BX is assumed to point to the beginning of the table. The byte in AL is used as an index into the table and is replaced by the byte at the offset in the table corresponding to AL's value. The first byte in the table has an offset of 0. For example, if AL = 5, and the sixth element of the translation table contains 44H, then AL will contain 44H following the instruction. XLAT is useful for translating characters from one encoding scheme into another one.

The alternate mnemonic XLATB, introduced with the 80386, requires no operand. Some assembler programs, including MASM version 5.1 and later, supply an operand if none is present in the encoding, thus making XLAT behave like XLATB.

```
; Code fragment to show the use of XLAT (or XLATB)
DATA     SEGMENT
HEX_TABLE        DB        'ABCDEF'
   .
   .
   .
CODE    SEGMENT
   .
; Code assume that AL holds a value in the range 10 to 15
      MOV      BX,OFFSET HEX_TABLE
      SUB      AL,10                  ; Subtract 10 to obtain table
                                      ; offset
      XLATB                           ; Obtain ASCII code from table
; At this point AL holds the corresponding ASCII code from
; HEX_TABLE
```

XMODEM

(See serial communications — programming character and file transfers).

XON/XOFF

(See serial communications — software handshake).

XOR

[Assembler] 8086 machine instruction. Mnemonic for logical Exclusive Or. Performs the logical exclusive OR of the two operands and returns the result to the destination operand. A bit in the result is set if the corresponding bite of the original operands contain opposite values. Otherwise the result bit is cleared. Flags Affected:

```
CF, OF, PF, SF, ZF. AF is undefined.
```

XOR bitwise operator

[C] The XOR bitwise operator (^) performs the Boolean exclusive OR (XOR) of the operands. This means that a bit in the result is set if the corresponding bits in the operands have opposite values. If the bits have the same value (1 or 0), the result bit is cleared. Note that XORing a value with itself always generates a zero result because all bits necessarily have the same value. On the other hand, XORing with a 1-bit inverts the value of the other operand because 0 XOR 1 = 1 and 1 XOR 1 = 0. By properly selecting an XOR mask the programmer can control which bits of the operand are inverted and which are preserved. For example, to invert the two high-order bits of an operand you can XOR with a mask in which these bits are set. If the remaining bits are clear in the mask, the original value of these bits is preserved in the result, as in the following example:

```
                        0101 0101B
BITWISE XOR             1100 0000B
                        ----------
                        1001 0101B
```